World Englishes in their Local Multilingual Ecologies

Hamburg Studies on Linguistic Diversity (HSLD)
ISSN 2211-3703

The HSLD series publishes research on issues of linguistic diversity, multilingualism, and multilingual development.

For an overview of all books published in this series, please see
benjamins.com/catalog/hsld

Editors

Peter Siemund
English and General Linguistics
University of Hamburg

Ingrid Gogolin
Comparative and Intercultural Education Research
University of Hamburg

Volume 9

World Englishes in their Local Multilingual Ecologies
Edited by Peter Siemund, Gardy Stein and Manuela Vida-Mannl

World Englishes in their Local Multilingual Ecologies

Edited by

Peter Siemund
University of Hamburg

Gardy Stein
University of Hamburg

Manuela Vida-Mannl
TU University Dortmund

John Benjamins Publishing Company
Amsterdam / Philadelphia

The paper used in this publication meets the minimum requirements of the American National Standard for Information Sciences – Permanence of Paper for Printed Library Materials, ANSI Z39.48-1984.

DOI 10.1075/hsld.9

Cataloging-in-Publication Data available from Library of Congress:
LCCN 2024055615 (PRINT) / 2024055616 (E-BOOK)

ISBN 978 90 272 1936 7 (HB)
ISBN 978 90 272 4500 7 (E-BOOK)

© 2025 – John Benjamins B.V.
This e-book is Open Access under a CC BY-NC-ND 4.0 license.
https://creativecommons.org/licenses/by-nc-nd/4.0

This license permits reuse, distribution and reproduction in any medium for non-commercial purposes, provided that the original author(s) and source are credited. Derivative works may not be distributed without prior permission.

This work may contain content reproduced under license from third parties. Permission to reproduce this third-party content must be obtained from these third parties directly.

Permission for any reuse beyond the scope of this license must be obtained from John Benjamins Publishing Company, rights@benjamins.nl

John Benjamins Publishing Company · https://benjamins.com

The production of this series has been made possible through financial support to the Landesexzellenzcluster (State of Hamburg Excellence Initiative) *Linguistic Diversity Management in Urban Areas – LiMA* by the Forschungs- und Wissenschaftsstiftung Hamburg.

Table of contents

List of contributors	IX
Investigating World Englishes in their local multilingual ecologies: An introduction *Manuela Vida-Mannl, Gardy Stein & Peter Siemund*	1

PART I. Theory

CHAPTER 1. Prologue *Edgar W. Schneider*	12
CHAPTER 2. World Englishes and the third space: Insights from multilingual practices in Xhosa and English *Rajend Mesthrie*	20

PART II. Language policies and attitudes

CHAPTER 3. Hierarchies in the language ecology of Botswana *Sheena Shah*	40
CHAPTER 4. English in the multilingual ecology of anglophone and francophone Cameroon *Gardy Stein*	64
CHAPTER 5. Global English in multilingual Philippines: Language practices in government communications *Loy Lising*	91
CHAPTER 6. Top-down policies and the language profiles of Malaysians in a multilingual language ecology *Stefanie Pillai & Siti Zaidah Zainuddin*	116
CHAPTER 7. Multilingualism in Shanghai: A comparative perspective on university students' linguistic profiles and attitudes *Yongyan Zheng & Peter Siemund*	143
CHAPTER 8. The linguistic ecology of Cyprus *Manuela Vida-Mannl, Sarah Buschfeld & Kleanthes K. Grohmann*	166

CHAPTER 9. English in the Kurdistan region of Iraq: Historical background, new status, and future implications   190
Ludwig Paul & Zana Ibrahim

PART III. Case studies

CHAPTER 10. English in the linguistic landscape(s) of rural Tanzania   208
Amani Lusekelo & Roland Kießling

CHAPTER 11. The Zanzibari tourist space as a multilingual language ecology   231
Susanne Mohr

CHAPTER 12. The sociolinguistics of English in the plurilingual ecology of Lagos (Nigeria): A pilot study on class, ethnicity and entrepreneurship   258
Henning Schreiber & Mirjam Möller Nwadigo

CHAPTER 13. The role of English in the linguistic ecology of Northeast India   291
Robert Fuchs, Caroline Wiltshire & Priyankoo Sarmah

CHAPTER 14. Discourse-pragmatic *like* in East Asian Englishes: Focus on Taiwan   317
Jakob R. E. Leimgruber & Sofia Rüdiger

CHAPTER 15. Translanguaging the hero online: A case study on language ecology in praising Qatar's Emir during the 2017–2021 blockade   335
Irene Theodoropoulou

CHAPTER 16. English as a lingua franca in Croatia's multilingual ecology   364
Manuela Vida-Mannl

CHAPTER 17. Envoi   384
Simone E. Pfenninger

Language index   397

Subject index   401

List of contributors

Sarah Buschfeld is a Professor and Chair of English Linguistics (Multilingualism) at TU Dortmund University. She is the author of the *Extra- and Intra-territorial Forces (EIF) Model* (with A. Kautzsch) and has worked on a number of postcolonial and non-postcolonial varieties of English and in the fields of language acquisition and multilingualism. She has written and edited several articles and books on these topics and explores the boundaries between such disciplines and their concepts.

Robert Fuchs is Professor in Applied English Linguistics at the University of Bonn. His research interests include the study of varieties of English around the world on all levels of linguistic description, including their sociolinguistics, structure, and relevance for teaching. His current work focusses on the use of Artificial Intelligence in linguistics research, the modelling of varieties of English in micro – and macro – contexts, and big data approaches to public discourse on controversial issues in society.

Kleanthes K. Grohmann is a Professor of Biolinguistics at the University of Cyprus. His research interests lie in syntactic theorizing, (a)typical language development, and all issues of multilingualism, including dialects, heritage languages, and pathologies. He is editor-in-chief of the platinum journal *Biolinguistics* and most recently edited *Multifaceted Multilingualism* (John Benjamins Publishing Company 2024).

Zana Ibrahim is the Dean of the School of Social Sciences at the University of Kurdistan Hewlêr. His research interests are second language motivation, second language learning and pedagogy, second language affect, and English as a lingua franca. Dr. Ibrahim has contributed to the theorization of the concept of directed motivational current and has published on the motivational phenomenon.

Roland Kießling is a Professor of African Linguistics at the University of Hamburg. He specializes in descriptive and historical (socio)linguistics, with a focus on the languages of the Tanzanian Rift Valley, particularly Southern Cushitic and Southern Nilotic, as well as the Bantoid languages of the Grassfields in Cameroon.

Jakob R. E. Leimgruber is a Professor and Chair of English Linguistics at the University of Regensburg. He is interested in World Englishes (especially Asian Englishes), language planning and policy, and sociolinguistics. His most recent monograph is *Language Planning and Policy in Quebec* (Narr 2019).

Loy Lising is a Senior Lecturer in the Department of Linguistics at Macquarie University, Sydney. She is also a Senior Fellow of the Higher Education Academy. The main focus of her research is on multilingualism and social participation. She recently published a co-authored book entitled *Life in a New Language* (Oxford University Press 2024).

Amani Lusekelo is an Associate Professor of African Languages at the University of Dar es Salaam in Tanzania. He is interested in language contact in Africa, as well as the morphosyntax and ethnolinguistics of African languages. His recent publications are: *Multilingualism in the Linguistic Landscape of Karonga District in Northern Malawi* (with Agnes Hara, Routledge 2024) and *Portrayal of COVID-19 Pandemic in Political Cartoons in Tanzania* (Taylor & Francis 2023).

Rajend Mesthrie is an Emeritus Professor and Senior Research Scholar at the University of Cape Town. He is interested in general linguistics, sociolinguistics, contact linguistics including World Englishes and multilingualism, and has conducted research on Indian, African, and Germanic languages. He served as a co-editor of *English Today* (2008–2012). His most recent book is *Language in the Indian Diaspora* (co-edited with Sonal Kulkarni-Joshi, Edinburgh University Press 2024).

Mirjam Möller Nwadigo is currently studying speech therapy at Lund University. She builds on her previous research in linguistics, which focused on the description and documentation of minority languages in Nigeria and Cameroon.

Susanne Mohr is a Professor of English Sociolinguistics at the Norwegian University of Science and Technology in Trondheim. She is interested in variation in English, multimodality, discursive place-making, and postcolonial linguistics. Her most recent publication is the edited volume *Learning Languages, Being Social* (co-edited with Lindsay Ferrara, De Gruyter 2024).

Ludwig Paul is Professor of Iranian Studies at the Middle Eastern Department of the Asia-Africa-Institute at the University of Hamburg. His main research interests are Historical Linguistics, focusing mainly on Persian and West Iranian, and the cultural history and current development of Iranian languages. His most recent monograph is a co-authored edition of Persian documents of the 10th to 12th centuries that were written in Hebrew script (in print, Vienna 2024/25).

Stefanie Pillai is a Professor at the Faculty of Languages and Linguistics, Universiti Malaya. Her research interests include the Malaysian variety of English and language use in multilingual contexts. Additionally, she has been working on the documentation, research and revitalization of an endangered language in Malaysia, Melaka Portuguese. She recently co-edited the book *Contemporary Malaysian English Pronunciation*.

Simone E. Pfenninger is a Professor of English Linguistics at the University of Zurich. Her principal research areas are multilingualism, psycholinguistics, and variationist SLA, especially in regard to quantitative approaches and statistical methods for language application in education. She is co-editor of the *Second Language Acquisition* book series for Multilingual Matters.

Sofia Rüdiger is a Postdoctoral Researcher in English Linguistics at the University of Bayreuth. Her research interests include World Englishes, pragmatics, and discourse analysis. She is the author of *Morpho-Syntactic Patterns in Spoken Korean English* (John Benjamins Publishing Company 2019) and the editor of *Global and Local Perspectives on Language Contact* (Language Science Press 2024).

Priyankoo Sarmah is a Professor of Linguistics at the Indian Institute of Technology Guwahati, India. He specializes in the phonetics and phonology of Northeast Indian languages. He is also interested in the acoustic phonetic properties of English spoken by speakers speaking languages of various language families in Northeast India.

Edgar W. Schneider is an Emeritus Professor of English Linguistics at the University of Regensburg, Germany. He is a globally renowned sociolinguist and World Englishes scholar, best known for his *Dynamic Model* (*Postcolonial English*, Cambridge University Press 2007). He has published numerous books and articles and has lectured on all continents, including giving many keynote lectures.

Henning Schreiber is a Professor of African Linguistics at the University of Hamburg. He is interested in language contact, african sociolinguistics, and historical linguistics. He is the editor-in-chief of the *Journal of Language Contact* (Brill).

Sheena Shah is a Postdoctoral Researcher in English Linguistics at the University of Hamburg and a Research Fellow in African Languages at the University of the Free State. Her work centers on language documentation, maintenance, and revitalization, focusing on multilingual communities in Southern Africa, particularly among those speaking heritage, minority, and endangered languages.

Peter Siemund is a Professor and Chair of English Linguistics at the University of Hamburg. He is interested in World Englishes, the use of English as an additional language, and multilingual development. His most recent monograph is *Multilingual Development: English in a Global Context* (Cambridge University Press 2023).

Gardy Stein is a Postdoctoral Researcher in African Languages and Linguistics and is currently employed as a principal investigator in a DFG-funded project about *The Linguistic Landscapes of Guinea* at the University of Hamburg. Her main interests include sociolinguistics, African youth language practices, and language policies in West Africa.

Irene Theodoropoulou is a Professor of Linguistics at Qatar University. She is interested in sociolinguistics, political discourse analysis, and intercultural communication. Her most recent major publication is the co-edited *Research Companion to Language and Country Branding* (Routledge 2021).

Manuela Vida-Mannl is a Postdoctoral Researcher in English Linguistics at TU Dortmund University. Her research interests include multilingualism and the sociolinguistics of English around the globe. She is the author of *The Value of the English Language in Global Mobility and Higher Education: An Investigation of Higher Education in Cyprus* (Bloomsbury 2022) and co-author of *Multilingualism: A Sociolinguistic and Acquisitional Approach* (with Sarah Buschfeld and Patricia Ronan; Springer 2023).

Caroline Wiltshire is Associate Professor of Linguistics at the University of Florida, Gainesville, US, specializing in Indian English phonetics and phonology. She authored the monograph *Uniformity and Variability in the Indian English Accent* (Cambridge University Press 2020), and currently works with Priyankoo Sarmah on describing varieties of Indian English spoken in Assam.

Siti Zaidah Zainuddin is a Senior Lecturer in the Department of English Language, Faculty of Languages and Linguistics at Universiti Malaya. Her primary research interests include genre analysis in both written and spoken academic discourse and the incorporation of corpus linguistics methods in academic and professional discourse. In the field of language learning, she works on second language writing using several perspectives and frameworks, as well as teacher-learner interactions.

Yongyan Zheng is a Professor of Applied Linguistics and Vice Dean of College of Foreign Languages and Literature at Fudan University, China. Her research interests are bilingual and multilingual development, and language-in-education policy.

Investigating World Englishes in their local multilingual ecologies
An introduction

Manuela Vida-Mannl[1], Gardy Stein[2] & Peter Siemund[2]
[1] TU Dortmund University | [2] University of Hamburg

This volume is the result of a research endeavor, shared by scholars in English studies and regional studies, to understand and describe the current reality of English used in various parts of the world. Describing who uses English, when, why, where, in which forms, and with whom – and in which situations and contexts English does not play a role – the contributions to this volume take a novel approach to World Englishes: they incorporate English into their local multilingual ecologies in which it functions as one besides multiple other languages. In addition, rather than focusing on acrolects and the language use of social elites – to name just two commonly mentioned points of criticism towards World Englishes research – the volume at hand and the associated scholars pursue linguistic research on the ground and share their insight into the use and role of English by speakers and speaker groups that have often not been targeted yet. While this approach of investigating multilingual ecologies and speakers across various social groups carries forward current trends towards more inclusive research practices within the field of World Englishes, it also introduces new perspectives and insights into local speech communities all around the world.

The unprecedented spread, use, and prestige of the English language has emerged as a pivotal subject of scholarly inquiry and has resulted in the development of a wide range of models and frameworks (e.g., Buschfeld & Kautzsch 2020; Kachru 1985; Mair 2013; Mesthrie & Bhatt 2008; Nelson, Proshina & Davis 2020; Schneider 2003, 2007; Siemund 2013, 2023; see also Schneider (this volume), for an overview). In applying and testing these models, the World Englishes paradigm has often centered around the identification, description, and distinction of individual national varieties of English. Post-colonial varieties, for example, tend to be classified and ranked based on the five groups within Schneider's (2003, 2007) popular *Dynamic Model* to facilitate comparability and show similarities and differences in their development and their speakers' identification with it. Scholars have found that, despite the diversity of settings, especially in

https://doi.org/10.1075/hsld.9.int
Available under the CC BY-NC-ND 4.0 license.
© 2025 John Benjamins Publishing Company

terms of their political and socio-economic development, the English language has often developed similarly across these settings (Schneider 2020). Research in World Englishes, although contributing to detailed inventories of the grammatical and lexical characteristics of many varieties of English (e.g., Bolton, Botha & Kirkpatrick 2020 on Asian Englishes; Borlongan 2022 on Philippine English), has so far focused on English only. Studies have rarely considered other languages relevant to the contexts investigated, let alone considered them to be equally important to the investigation. Last but not least, the dynamic and fluid nature of multilingual interactions has largely been overlooked.

As mentioned above, another aspect the field has variously been criticized for is a bias towards elite speakers who typically received formal instruction in English (see Meierkord & Schneider 2021 for criticism). While adhering to national boundaries and including speakers with comparably high proficiencies have been fruitful starting points, these beginnings have somewhat developed into biases, resulting in a disregard of borderline areas and speakers that belong to groups of lower social status (see Leimgruber 2013 for criticism). There is the suspicion that current generalizations are skewed. Equally, research used to adhere to national boundaries and almost disregard countries, such as Cyprus, that do not fit smoothly into the developed paradigm. Based on these concerns, current research within the area of World Englishes has made an effort to be more inclusive when advancing prevailing theorizations by, for example, defocusing from post-colonial contexts (Seargeant & Tagg 2010), target non-elite speaker groups (Meierkord & Schneider 2021), or including other languages besides English (Van Rooy 2019).

To further this development, refocusing from identifying national acrolectal Englishes towards investigating Englishes within their local speech communities and multilingual ecologies is a promising next step. As a reaction to the current unparalleled global interconnectedness and ease of mobility, where national and social boundaries have become increasingly fuzzy and potentially irrelevant to the spread and use of English, research within the area of World Englishes must start local and aim at structurally investigating language practices within individual speech communities. In doing so, there are at least two aspects that must be considered when advancing and furthering World Englishes research: (1) English must be seen and researched as one relevant language in any linguistic environment rather than the only relevant language; (2) Despite the collection, annotation, and interpretation of linguistic data becoming more complex, all speaker groups must be considered to create a comprehensive and accurate representation of the respective linguistic reality. Following this line of thought, research can shed light on multi-language use and its diversity across and within speaker groups more accurately than it used to do. Especially regarding the latter point,

World Englishes research has already made significant progress in including speakers outside the local social elite. The growing interest in *grassroots Englishes* might serve as an example here, as it also successfully counteracts the prominence of data provided by WEIRD speaker groups (Western, Educated, Industrialized, Rich, Democratic; see Henrich, Heine & Norenzayan 2013; see also Pfenninger, this volume).

Interest in grassroots Englishes emerged for the first time around the turn of the century. Key characteristics of this first conceptualization have been, for example, spontaneous acquisition, basic language skills, and a multilingual context or setting (Khubchandani & Hosali 1999). Later, Schneider (2016:3) defined 'grassroots Englishes' as Englishes acquired by users of poor and uneducated backgrounds in direct interactions. While some scholars follow this narrow definition, others use the concept in a broader sense (Blommaert 2010; Han 2013). However, they all share the use of 'the grassroots' "as a social or socio-economic category vis-à-vis the elite." (Meierkord & Schneider 2021:4). Mainly due to the lack of formal instruction, Englishes at the grassroots level takes many forms and shapes that still show a few common denominators. Englishes at the grassroots are non-standard uses of English and one or more other languages. Hence, they are characterized by translanguaging practices and, due to the lack of education, a discrepancy between the written and oral proficiency of the speakers (see Han 2013 on grassroots multilingualism; Trimbur 2020 on grassroots literacy). Currently, the grassroots Englishes approach has been primarily applied to speakers in the Global South as well as refugees from the Global South who found refuge in the Global North (Han 2013 on China; Isingoma 2021 on Uganda; Wilson 2021 on Syrian refugees in Germany). By refocusing on the grassroots only, researchers are at risk to reproduce the field's bias towards certain speaker groups. Hence, to further its tendency towards inclusivity and comprehensiveness, English at the grassroots and at the higher end of society — as well as the large area in between — has to be investigated simultaneously. In addition, insights into diverse speech communities and individual speakers around the globe have to be combined to unveil the social, cultural, and linguistic trajectories of their linguistic developments.

To adequately consider other locally spoken and relevant languages — the second aspect we deem essential to more inclusive World Englishes research — and understand the speakers' behavior within the various social groups they belong to, we propose to expand Haugen's concept of language ecology (1972) and investigate Englishes within their multilingual ecologies. In utilizing Haugen's understanding of language as being context and speaker dependent (two factors that always influence the actual usage of language), research is able to work against the overgeneralization of findings and the assumption of homogeneous language use within speaker groups. Ideally, this refocusing of research and the resulting findings will result in an epistemic and ideological shift within the field that can, subsequently, be transferred into society.

We propose to assess the nine dimensions of language ecology introduced by Haugen (1972: 336–337) and to extend them by an acquisitional, mobility, and language proficiency dimension, for each relevant language. The first of Haugen's dimensions is language classification, i.e. categorizing the languages present in a multilingual ecology and relating them to one another. Assessing this dimension provides a first blueprint of a linguistic environment as it might include a historical, linguistic, and social perspective. The second dimension is concerned with the identification of user groups for each language. Considering factors such as ethnicity, social class, age, and education offers a fine-grained understanding of who uses which language. Thirdly, the domains of use are determined, unveiling potential restrictions of use. Potential overlaps of language use are the focus of Haugen's fourth dimension, as it is concerned with identifying concurrent languages used by various user groups. Shifting the focus from the users towards the languages themselves, Haugen's fifth dimension assesses each language's internal, i.e. regional, social, or other, variation to understand internal diversity. In addition to the nature and functions of their written traditions (the sixth dimension) which might unveil, amongst other aspects, the significance of their literary and non-literary writing and their divergence from speaking, the extent of their standardization of writing systems, i.e. of their unified codification, is explored. The considerations of formal uses and roles of a language are complemented by looking at whether and, if so, how the languages are supported by governmental, private, religious, and/or educational institutions. Finally, Haugen includes speaker attitudes towards their languages as the ninth dimension. Understanding which of a speaker's languages reflect intimacy (i.e. values and personal connections, especially in private domains), or status (i.e. power and influence, especially in public domains), is crucial to comprehend any linguistic environment. Assessing these dimensions, and consequently depicting the "interactions between any given language and its environment" (Haugen 1972: 325), provides a detailed understanding of the linguistic repertoires of individual speakers as well as speaker groups and the use and functions of relevant languages within larger societies. Subsequently, this approach creates greater explanatory power than conventional linguistic methodologies (Ludwig, Mühlhäusler & Pagel 2018; Mufwene 2001). Although Haugen's dimensions could be considered extensive enough, three further aspects of language use influence almost all of these dimensions. These are the acquisitional process, a speaker's (perceived) language proficiency, and their mobility trajectories.

Extending Haugen's framework by including an acquisitional dimension, and considering (perceived) language proficiencies and speaker mobility, assists further in disentangling the linguistic realities of speech communities and their members. How and when a language was acquired often has a significant influence on a speaker's identity, attitudes, and use (see Block 2007 on identity; De Houwer 2021 on language acquisition). A formally learned language, for example, might reflect status rather than intimacy and may or may not reflect a part of the speaker's identity. Considering the acquisitional process further contextualizes the organization and hierarchization of languages within multilingual environments and adds another level of relations between the dimensions. Type of acquisition is one of the most influential factors regarding language proficiency. We argue, however, that language proficiency cannot be fully subsumed under the acquisitional dimension, especially when looking at perceived proficiency. In contrast to categorizing speakers on a scale between *no knowledge* and *full proficiency* based on an objective analysis of their language use, the speakers' subjective assessment of their own language skills, for example, by using *can-do* statements such as those used in the Common European Framework of Reference (CEFR 2020), adds information about language preference and choice while also increasing comparability between speakers, domains, and cultural norms. Finally, to understand similarities and differences within and across speech communities, investigating the mobility trajectories of speakers is crucial. Facilitated by globalization and increasing ease of travel, chosen or forced mobility has become an increasingly relevant factor within various linguistic environments. Answering questions such as 'Where has the language been learned?' or 'Where was it used for the first time?' offer insight into the reasons for diversity within speech communities, for example, in case speakers bring their languages to their new places of residence. Hence, speaker mobility considerably impacts adding or subtracting languages to or from a speaker's linguistic repertoire and ultimately a multilingual ecology. Adding these three dimensions to Haugen's (1972) framework of language ecology creates an approach suitable to elicit the complexity of multilingual ecologies around the globe — as many of the contributions to this volume show.

Analyzing and interpreting such extensive and potentially heterogeneous data without losing the many details and nuances included calls for a flexible and adaptable model, such as Aronin & Singleton's (2012) *Dominant Language Constellations* (DLCs). While a linguistic repertoire denotes "the sum or the storage of available language varieties and/or skills, registers and styles and language assets accumulated in one's life", DLCs are considered "a group of one's most expedient languages, functioning as an entire unit, and enabling an individual to meet all needs in a multilingual environment" (Aronin 2016: 4; see Lüpke & Storch 2013 on linguistic repertoires). Hence, the languages in one's DLC can be considered an aggregate, used to fulfill all the functions needed in a speaker's daily linguistic routines and located in the center of various orbits determined by the contexts of use.

Similarly to linguistic repertoires, DLCs are indexical, for example, with respect to the users' cultural or geographical heritage or current position. In contrast to linguistic repertoires, however, they are flexible enough to instantly reflect sociolinguistic changes in the speaker's life (Aronin & Singleton 2012: 65–66). While languages that increase in importance in a speaker's daily linguistic needs enter the DLC, i.e. become part of a "translanguaged unit" (Banda 2020: 78), linguistic resources that decrease in importance remain part of their linguistic repertoire but leave the DLC. As a corollary, this means that a speaker's DLC can change in the course of their lifetime — even multiple times — and one further expects codeswitching and mixing across the languages in the DLC. Aronin (2016: 150) further points out that "[t]he concept of Dominant Language Constellation is relevant not only for individuals, but also for communities. Groups characterized by a common DLC may share territorial, social, ethnic and/or business characteristics." As DLCs reflect a combination of dominant skills and languages that are most valuable for the individual speaker in a particular space and time, they are a promising concept to visualize and disentangle the complex reality within multilingual ecologies around the globe.

As elaborated above, the volume at hand challenges traditional practices within the field of World Englishes and postulates refocusing linguistic research to explore the role(s) and position(s) of English as a global language within various local multilingual settings and across speaker groups. In taking this alternative perspective, the contributions to this volume continue recent developments in the field, such as incorporating language practices at the grassroots (Han 2013; Meierkord & Schneider 2021), defocusing from post-colonial contexts (Seargeant & Tagg 2010), and including other languages besides English (Van Rooy 2019). They add to our understanding of World Englishes in analyzing English as a by now autochtonized language that needs to be discussed on a par with the other languages present in the respective local context, thus avoiding the continuing silencing of the local languages.

This inclusive perspective on multilingualism includes speakers with various socio-economic backgrounds, language repertoires, and language attitudes. Some having been developed as part of a Hamburg-based research unit on *World Englishes and their local multilingual ecologies*, the contributions to this volume have set out to reshape the traditional approach to investigating and describing Englishes around the globe. By presenting socially and linguistically inclusive approaches to multilingual ecologies, for example by revisiting and expanding Haugen's (1972) concept of language ecologies, this volume and its contributions critically examine the functional, institutional, and attitudinal roles of languages within various local multilingual settings, contributing to a deeper understanding of the intricate interplay between English and local languages. It probes into the reasons and conditions that motivate individuals across social groups to alter their language repertoires, often consciously or unconsciously prioritizing English and prominent regional languages over less powerful home languages. In so doing, the volume further tries to paint a representative picture of the presented societies at large, avoiding a foregrounding of specific social groups such as the local, often English-speaking elites.

This volume offers a comprehensive and nuanced exploration of the roles, status, and use of English and other local languages within a variety of multilingual regions. By painting a more fine-grained picture of the presented societies and conceptualizing multilingual world regions as language ecologies, the volume provides the next step toward understanding the dynamics and interrelations of all local languages used in multilingual settings. Hence, it contributes to and advocates for a more inclusive and equitable approach to linguistic research.

Last but not least, we would like to acknowledge everyone who supported us during the editing process of this volume. First, we would like to thank Edgar W. Schneider and Simone E. Pfenninger for their special introductory and closing chapters. These add new perspectives to the volume, establishing links and connections that significantly enrich the book and its contributions. We are very grateful to have their contributions. We are further indebted to Aikaterina Koufopoulou and Yuting Wang for their invaluable support in editing, proofreading, and indexing the volume. Their attention to detail has been absolutely outstanding. Finally, we would like to thank Kees Vaes of John Benjamins for his constant support over the years. It is due to John Benjamins that the volume can appear in an open access format. The University of Hamburg needs to be credited for extensive financial support.

References

Aronin, Larissa. 2016. Dominant language constellations as a method of research. Paper presented at the 10th International Conference on Multilingualism and Third Language Acquisition. University of Vienna, Austria, 1–3 September.

Aronin, Larissa & David Singleton. 2012. The dominant language constellation (DLC). In Larissa Aronin & David Singleton (eds.), *Multilingualism*, pp. 59–75. Amsterdam: John Benjamins.

Banda, Felix. 2020. Shifting and multi-layered dominant language constellations in dynamic multilingual contexts: African perspectives. In Joe Lo Bianco & Larissa Aronin (eds.), *Dominant Language Constellations: A New Perspective on Multilingualism*, pp. 75–95. Cham: Springer.

Block, David. 2007. *Second Language Identities*. London: Bloomsbury.

Blommaert, Jan. 2010. *The Sociolinguistics of Globalization*. Cambridge: Cambridge University Press.

Bolton, Kingsley, Werner Botha & Andy Kirkpatrick (eds.). 2020. *The Handbook of Asian Englishes*. Hoboken, NJ: John Wiley & Sons.

Borlongan, Ariane (ed.). 2022. *Philippine English: Development, Structure, and Sociology of English in the Philippines*. London: Routledge.

Buschfeld, Sarah & Alexander Kautzsch (eds.). 2020. *Modelling World Englishes: A Joint Approach to Postcolonial and Non-Postcolonial Varieties*. Edinburgh: Edinburgh University Press.

CEFR Council of Europe. 2020. *Common European Framework of Reference for Languages*. Council of Europe. https://www.coe.int/en/web/common-european-framework-reference-languages/home (14 September 2024).

De Houwer, Annick. 2021. *Bilingual Development in Childhood*. Cambridge: Cambridge University Press.

Han, Huamei. 2013. Individual grassroots multilingualism in Africa Town in Guangzhou: The role of states in globalization. *International Multilingual Research Journal* 7: 83–97.

Haugen, Einar. 1972. The ecology of language. In Anwar Dil (ed.), *The Ecology of Language*, pp. 325–339. Stanford, CA: Standford University Press.

Henrich, Joseph, Steven J. Heine & Ara Norenzayan. 2013. The weirdest people in the world? In Stephen M. Downes & Edouard Machery (eds.), *Arguing about Human Nature: Contemporary Debates*, pp. 198–216. London: Routledge.

Isingoma, Bebwa. 2021. The sociolinguistic profile of English at the grassroots level: A comparison of Northern and Western Uganda. In Christiane Meierkord & Edgar W. Schneider (eds.), *World Englishes at the Grassroots*, pp. 49–69. Edinburgh: Edinburgh University Press.

Kachru, Braj Bihari. 1985. Standards, codification, and sociolinguistic realism: The English language in the outer circle. In Randolph Quirk & Henry Widdowson (eds.), *English in the World: Teaching and Learning the Language and the Literature*, pp. 11–30. Cambridge: Cambridge University Press.

Khubchandani, Lachman M. & Hosali Priya. 1999. Grassroots English in a communication paradigm. *Language Problems and Language Planning* 23(3): 251–272.

Leimgruber, Jakob R. E. 2013. The trouble with World Englishes. *English Today* 29(3): 3–7.

Ludwig, Ralf, Peter Mühlhäusler & Steve Pagel. 2018. Linguistic ecology and language contact: Conceptual evolution, interrelatedness, and parameters. In Ralf Ludwig, Peter Mühlhäusler & Steve Pagel (eds.), *Linguistic Ecology and Language Contact*, pp. 3–42. Cambridge: Cambridge University Press.

Lüpke, Friederike & Anne Storch. 2013. *Repertoires and Choices in African Languages*. Berlin: De Gruyter Mouton.

Mair, Christian. 2013. The world system of Englishes. Accounting for the transnational importance of mobile and mediated vernaculars. *English World-Wide* 34(3): 253–278.

Meierkord, Christiane & Edgar W. Schneider. 2021. Introduction: English spreading at the grassroots. In Christiane Meierkord & Edgar W. Schneider (eds.), *World Englishes at the Grassroots*, pp. 1–22. Edinburgh: Edinburgh University Press.

Mesthrie, Rajend & Rakesh Bhatt. 2008. *World Englishes*. Cambridge: Cambridge University Press.

Mufwene, Salikoko S. 2001. *The Ecology of Language Evolution*. Cambridge: Cambridge University Press.

Nelson, Cecil, Zoya Proshina & Daniel Davis (eds.). 2020. *The Handbook of World Englishes*, 2nd edn. Malden, MA: Wiley-Blackwell.

Schneider, Edgar W. 2003. The dynamics of New Englishes: From identity construction to dialect birth. *Language*, 79(2): 233–281.

Schneider, Edgar W. 2007. *Postcolonial English: Varieties around the World*. Cambridge: Cambridge University Press.

Schneider, Edgar W. 2016. Grassroots Englishes in tourism interactions. *English Today* 32(3): 2–10.

Schneider, Edgar W. 2020. Developmental patterns of English: Similar or different? In Andy Kirkpatrick (ed.), *The Routledge Handbook of World Englishes*, pp. 408–421. London: Routledge.

Seargeant, Philip & Caroline Tagg. 2010. English on the internet and a 'post-varieties' approach to language. *World Englishes* 30(4): 496–514.

Siemund, Peter. 2013. *Varieties of English. A Typological Approach*. Cambridge: Cambridge University Press.

Siemund, Peter. 2023. *Multilingual Development: English in a Global Context*. Cambridge: Cambridge University Press.

Trimbur, John. 2020. *Grassroots Literacy and the Written Record: A Textual History of Asbestos Activism in South Africa*. Bristol: Multilingual Matters.

Van Rooy, Bertus. 2019. Reconsidering Kachru's work on Englishes in their multilingual ecologies. *World Englishes* 38(1–2): 280–293.

Wilson, Guyanne. 2021. Language use among Syrian Refugees in Germany. In Christiane Meierkord & Edgar W. Schneider (eds.), *World Englishes at the Grassroots*, pp. 211–232. Edinburgh: Edinburgh University Press.

PART I

Theory

CHAPTER 1

Prologue

Edgar W. Schneider
University of Regensburg

Another new volume on World Englishes, even if there are plenty by now, with this term in their titles (Melchers & Shaw 2003; Mesthrie & Bhatt 2008; Klemola, Filppula & Sharma 2017; Nelson, Proshina & Davis 2020; Schreier, Hundt & Schneider 2020; Buschfeld & Kautzsch 2020; Meierkord & Schneider 2020), or without (Platt, Weber & Ho 1984; Kachru 1992; Kortmann, Schneider et al. 2004; Kortmann & Lunkenheimer 2012; Schneider 2007, 2020; Siemund 2013)? Yes, absolutely! Apart from the fact that the field is huge, somehow still young (40 years or so — not really hoary for a scholarly discipline), constantly evolving, and its object domain is rapidly changing it is some specific traits of this volume which make it special and promise many fresh insights and a timely, innovative, and comprehensive perspective. Setting the scene, this prologue is meant as an appetizer; its job is to highlight distinctive topics that the book's contributions share and that differentiate it from other volumes on World Englishes.

Above all, there has been a strong tendency in World Englishes research, if only implicitly, to focus on English (almost) only, to present the global spread of English as a somewhat "romanticized" (as Pillai & Zainuddin in this volume call it), triumphalist success story of conquest, dominance and adoption, downplaying the agency of indigenous populations (who, after all, were the core creators of new varieties of English!). Instead, the contributions here explicitly widen the perspective to encompass the role, character, and usage contexts of all languages spoken in a given territory on equal terms. Both English and indigenous tongues are assessed in their respective multilingual settings; almost all papers start out with detailed accounts of the languages interacting in their respective territories, looking into aspects of historical evolution, speaker proportions, functional roles, status associations, and the like.

This novel view of linguistic settings in a wide range of contexts is supported and unified by a coherent theoretical perspective which is explicitly revitalized and adjusted: Central to the overall assessment of language constellations is Haugen's (1972) notion of linguistic ecology. The term as such has come to be fairly widely employed in linguistics over the last few decades mainly through the influence of Mufwene (2001), though often it is used in a rather loose fashion

https://doi.org/10.1075/hsld.9.01sch
Available under the CC BY-NC-ND 4.0 license.
© 2025 John Benjamins Publishing Company

implying little more than "conditions of sociolinguistic context". It is important that in this volume the concept as used in linguistics is traced back and applied more rigorously through the explicit reference to Haugen (1972), where it is determined by nine constitutive dimensions which are applicable independently of regions or cultures. Haugen calls for the identification and collection of pertinent information on these dimensions, including users and usage domains, relationship to other concurrent languages, internal variability, written tradition, codification and institutional support, and speakers' attitudes. And the papers in this volume react to this call, addressing all or some of these issues in some way or another. This shared theoretical baseline engenders a strongly homogenizing force to the present volume. The notion of ecology is referred to throughout the book, more or less explicitly (it is strongly embraced in the papers on the Philippines, on Malaysia, and on Cyprus, for instance). Importantly, helpful as it is it is not taken at face value and uncritically: Some authors clearly state that social and technological changes in the intervening fifty years have necessitated some critical re-thinking and some adjustments to the original framework as proposed by Haugen. A case in point, for example, is the paper on Northeast India, where the notion of ecology is specifically enhanced by its application to a hugely diverse setting and developed further by the definition of relevant sub-types relating it to different measured degrees of diversity.

Most importantly, perhaps: Multilingualism reigns everywhere, and this is highlighted very strongly in all papers and with reference to all the ecologies considered. While the status of English is strong (and often increasing) in many localities discussed, the importance of local indigenous languages and often the growing impact of regional dominant languages, too often disregarded or downplayed, are emphasized throughout the contributions of this book, thus gaining a more realistic perspective than a plain focus on 'World Englishes'. The volume contributes substantially towards the removal of a conservative, perhaps western-derived mindset which views monolingualism as the norm and as natural — on a global scale it clearly is not. Language repertoires are documented in great detail, both as found in a community or country in question and relative to individual speakers. Mutual influences, relationships, and competition between co-existing languages are worked out. We see Xhosa and English influencing each other mutually in South Africa and English influencing Swahili in Tanzania. In some countries trilingualism is shown to be the norm, often involving an indigenous national language (or strong regional language), English, and a local language. This is documented convincingly for Tanzania (involving Swahili) and for Botswana (with Setswana as the main national language), but it also shown to apply similarly to the Philippines (with Filipino), Malaysia (with Malay), or also Kurdistan (where Kurdish competes with Arabic and English). Especially in modern megacities Vertovec's (2007) notion of "superdiversity" has been found to be widely applicably (here in the paper on Qatar), but in the paper on Shanghai it is also explicitly supplemented by a look into a metropolis without a British colonial background and without the impact of a huge amount of transnational migration, i.e., the presence of a large proportion of expatriates. Importantly, multilingualism is also no longer understood as the largely independent co-existence of discrete languages (typically tied to nation states) in speakers' minds but rather as a dynamic mutual exchange and influence of available linguistic resources, closely associated with the notion of translanguaging (applied in the Qatar paper).

The volume has a truly global outreach: it covers as many as fifteen thematically focused contributions relating to fourteen countries: South Africa, Botswana, Cameroon, Nigeria (Lagos), Tanzania (with two papers), Iraq (specifically Kurdistan), India (looking into the Northeast), the Philippines, Malaysia, China (focusing on Shanghai), Taiwan, Qatar, Cyprus, and Croatia, on three continents (Africa, Asia, and Europe). In fact, it covers some regions, countries, and linguistic settings which have not or hardly at all been looked into in this context before, such as Shanghai, the Kurdistan region of Iraq, Taiwan, Qatar, or Croatia. Of these, perhaps the most interesting and innovative one from a World Englishes perspective is Kurdistan, where, as the contribution convincingly details, English has grown from a language of little presence to a major competitor (and a requirement for white-collar jobs, for instance) in just one or two decades — a remarkable process, and certainly one worth tracing in some detail; the present paper represents a major first step in that direction. In some cases, rather slim earlier documentation of the local language situation and the role of English in it is expanded substantially (as in Botswana or in India, concentrating on the Northeast region which is often not strongly considered). In addition, some chapters add important pieces of new information on countries which have been described in the World Englishes context before (such as South Africa, Cameroon, the Philippines, or Cyprus).

A multitude of methods are employed. Earlier writings on a region with a focus on extant languages and multilingual settings mostly provide baseline information, often enhanced by demographic and statistical data (see the papers on Kurdistan or Northeast India). Some papers analyze sociolinguistic interview data (e.g., the ones on South Africa, Zanzibar, and Croatia). Others focus on the analysis of different types of written documents (statistical data and government Facebook posts in the case of the Philippines). Questionnaires and (in some cases) semi-structured interviews provide pertinent information on Botswana, Shanghai, Malaysia, Zanzibar, and Lagos. Different kinds of informants have been addressed and recruited; in Malaysia and Shanghai university students are the explicit targets of investigation. Further approaches include ethnographic research (e.g., on Zanzibar and Lagos, or qualitative interview data from Kurdistan), linguistic landscape studies (in rural Tanzania), and corpus compilation and analyses (see Lange & Leuckert 2020), including self-compiled, customized corpora (see the contribution on Taiwan). Descriptive statistics on overall frequency distributions of speaker proportions and language choices as determined by different situations are provided in some papers; the one on Lagos also applies advanced models of correlation and variation analysis. The study of Northeast India builds upon a detailed analysis of Census data and introduces a novel quantitative tool borrowed and adapted from research in biological ecology, a diversity index.

Thematic versatility is another obvious quality of this collection — a wide range of topics, approaches, and contexts are addressed. Language attitudes play a role wherever English claims a spot in local ecologies, and possibly gets rooted. A really interesting and complex, seemingly contradictory set of language attitudes is reported for Cameroon, where English is both a minority language lacking prestige locally and a respected and desirable language when it comes to its international aura. In the paper on Qatar it is shown how attitudes are associated with emotions and expressed by multimodal means, e.g., in photos, songs, and tweets. Very often we find English used as a lingua franca, mediating between speakers as their predominant shared linguistic resource (as documented, for example, in the papers on Northeast India, Croatia, or Zanzibar). Individuals who embrace English often view it as a tool towards prosperity, offering better job opportunities, typically in tourism (illustrated for Tanzania, notably also Zanzibar, and Croatia; Schneider 2016, 2024) or in small-scale entrepreneurship (see the paper on Lagos). In general, components of multilingual repertoires tend to be distributed functionally, as is shown in some detail for Shanghai, where English stands for modernity and internationalization, Putonghua for national purposes and unity, Chinese dialects for the private domain, and other languages for individual interests and orientations and leisure activities. Given the association of English with modernity, technology, business, and a western cultural orientation, the language obviously cascades most strongly into and within urban centers, so in assessing and understanding its ecologies an urban-versus-rural divide is often noticeable. Thus, it is valuable that for Botswana not only data from Gabarone but also from villages and towns in other regions are reported. In Tanzania, it is equally welcome that evidence is provided from fairly remote rural regions. This is typically also visible in varying kinds of signage: the role of English components in linguistic landscapes varies greatly, as documented in the papers on Tanzania and, less intensely, Cyprus, Kurdistan, and Zanzibar. More broadly, of course, both usage and visual representation of languages co-vary strongly with degrees and measures of linguistic diversity. Other, partly new and more specialized approaches look into multimodal appraisal (relating to the Emir of Qatar), the special character of government communication (in the Philippines), and Homi Bhabha's notion of an interactive "third space", applied to postcolonial identities expressed by linguistic means in South Africa. In the latter paper, it is shown that speakers maintain fluency in two or more languages and use situationally appropriate choices between these and also intermediate forms and code-switching as sources of "innovation and complexity" and for the projection of their individual identities.

While many contributions focus on general sociolinguistic settings and usage conditions (as is implied in the core notion of ecology), some also offer detailed structural analyses. In South African English, for example, established forms gain new functions in bilingual usage, so prefixation (involving problematic issues of segmentation and semantic classification of linguistic items), borrowings, and logical connectors are investigated. We learn about uses of the form *like* (widely studied and found to be spreading vehemently around the globe) in the English of Taiwan, and about morphosyntactic forms characteristic of lingua franca usage in Croatia. The paper on Tanzania identifies more abstract processes of the adoption and transformation of linguistic material, which the authors call localization, translocation, and creative appropriation. Pragmatics, less commonly focused on in World Englishes studies, is investigated in the Zanzibar paper, with a focus on specific speech act types, such as greetings (interestingly enough, in a pidginized "Hakuna Matata Swahili") and other interactions (often also involving some reduced Swahili — which is thus also commodified somehow).

Diversity is an immensely important topic in our modern, globalized societies, and an important reflection of this is found in appraising the origin of contributors to scholarly works and in promoting cross-cultural collaboration. It is noteworthy and praiseworthy that many of the papers in this volume are authored and co-authored by scholars from diverse cultural contexts, including an impressive range of local experts from the countries under discussion.

Intentions and plans are one thing, implementation and reality are another — and this, obviously, applies to language policies and educational practice as well. Often a tension is recorded between official language policies and real-life local practices. In Cameroon, for example, the quasi-official division of the country into anglophone and francophone regions is shown to be undermined by both informal alternatives (like Pidgin English and Camfranglais) spreading and by francophones increasingly seeking access to English. The paper on the Philippines shows that not even the government adheres to their stipulated language policy, employing English much more strongly than called for, and certainly more than the local official language Filipino, in regional governments' Facebook posts. Malaysia's language policy has changed its course, especially implementation strategies in education, repeatedly over the last few decades, and it is shown to have influenced (though not fully determined) undergraduate students' language choices. Cyprus is portrayed as a very special and interesting case where the linguistic ecology has been shaped not by some abstract language policy but by the explicit political division of the country, with consequences for the roles of and interaction between Turkish and Greek (and their respective local variants), for different degrees of implementation of English, and also for the roles of additional languages and heritage languages (spoken by smaller groups, partly immigrants).

In all of this, the core agents are simply individuals with their own life settings, intentions, and language acquisition backgrounds. Several papers highlight the role of speakers in the evolution of linguistic ecologies. They inquire into the motivations of indigenous speakers to change their linguistic repertoires by modifying the balance between local languages and by integrating English for specific functions. Individual language repertoires are related to speakers' acquisition paths and contexts and to their attitudes to linguistic options in their environments. A strong case in point is the study of students' linguistic choices and motivations in Malaysia. The paper on South Africa explicitly addresses a distinctive "bilingual mode" which bi- or multilingual speakers can activate. Similar to what has been found in other global megacities, it is documented that for students in Shanghai bilingualism involving English has become the norm, and this study usefully introduces and employs the notion of "dominant language constellations".

All of these processes are of course embedded in social worlds, with their distinctive hierarchies, interactions, power relationships, and bonding patterns. Languages are assigned sociopolitical and economic market values (as is shown in the papers on Shanghai, Zanzibar, the Philippines, the Kurdistan region of Iraq, Tanzania, or Lagos), with social consequences for individuals' inclusion or exclusion in certain activity domains. The contribution on Botswana explicitly identifies a local "language power scale", with English (and partly Setswana) on top and local languages, notably those of the former hunter-gatherers, at the bottom (and endangered, more by Setswana and other regional Bantu languages than by English), and it outlines a few instances of ongoing language shift. Social mobility and migration are repeatedly recognized as important forces, both within a nation (see the South African paper or the account of immigration to Botswana) and transcending national boundaries (see some contributions in Meierkord & Schneider 2020). Such moves increase or cause a strong role of multilingual repertoires and translanguaging.

World Englishes are often associated with higher education, a certain elitist stance and certainly background of speakers (as argued in this volume for Botswana, Kurdistan, Tanzania, and, recapitulated in a separate paper, Zanzibar). It is not a coincidence that informants recruited for the *International Corpus of English* project are defined as educated speakers. In line with the point discussed in the previous paragraph, however, this is certainly not the whole story. Consequently, an attempt is made consistently by the authors in this book to avoid the conventional, conservative bias of scholarship towards educated, elitist speakers of English and to integrate the grassroots perspective, experiences and linguistic aspirations of less fortunate strata in society. For Cameroon, for instance, it is shown that in daily interactions informal variants of both English / Pidgin and French / Camfranglais and also African indigenous languages prevail, and the standard forms of the two European languages are perceived as elitist, so the relationships between overt and covert prestige associated with all languages spoken are really intricate.

In sum, overall a much more realistic, down-to-earth perspective on many local linguistic ecologies is provided successfully in this volume. It substantially challenges the "western" mindset privileging monolingualism as a putative norm and constitutes a breakthrough towards the recognition of the importance of multilingual settings and ecologies.

References

Buschfeld, Sarah & Alexander Kautzsch (eds.). 2020. *Modelling World Englishes: A Joint Approach towards Postcolonial and Non-Postcolonial Englishes.* Edinburgh: Edinburgh University Press.

Haugen, Einar I. 1972. The ecology of language. In Anwar S. Dil (ed.), *The Ecology of Language*, pp. 325–339. Stanford, CA: Stanford University Press.

Kachru, Braj B. (ed.). 1992. *The Other Tongue: English across Cultures*, 2nd edn. Urbana, IL: University of Illinois Press.

Klemola, Juhani, Markku Filppula & Devyani Sharma (eds.). 2017. *The Oxford Handbook of World Englishes.* Oxford: Oxford University Press.

Kortmann, Bernd & Kerstin Lunkenheimer (eds.). 2012. *The Mouton World Atlas of Variation in English.* Berlin: Mouton de Gruyter.

Kortmann, Bernd, Edgar W. Schneider, Kate Burridge, Rajend Mesthrie & Clive Upton (eds.). 2004. *A Handbook of Varieties of English. Volume 1: Phonology, Volume 2: Morphology and Syntax.* Berlin: Mouton de Gruyter.

Lange, Claudia & Sven Leuckert. 2020. *Corpus Linguistics for World Englishes: A Guide for Research.* London: Routledge.

Meierkord, Christiane & Edgar W. Schneider (eds.). 2020. *World Englishes at the Grassroots.* Edinburgh: Edinburgh University Press.

Melchers, Gunnel & Philip Shaw. 2003. *World Englishes. An Introduction.* London: Arnold.

Mesthrie, Rajend & Rakesh Bhatt. 2008. *World Englishes.* Cambridge: Cambridge University Press.

Mufwene, Salikoko S. 2001. *The Ecology of Language Evolution.* Cambridge: Cambridge University Press.

Nelson, Cecil, Zoya Proshina & Daniel Davis (eds.). 2020. *The Handbook of World Englishes*, 2nd edn. Malden, MA: Wiley-Blackwell.

Platt, John, Heidi Weber & Mian Lian Ho. 1984. *The New Englishes*. London: Routledge & Kegan Paul.

Schneider, Edgar W. 2007. *Postcolonial English. Varieties around the World*. Cambridge: Cambridge University Press.

Schneider, Edgar W. 2016. Grassroots Englishes in tourism interactions. *English Today* 32(3): 2–10.

Schneider, Edgar W. 2020. *English around the World. An Introduction*, 2nd edn. Cambridge: Cambridge University Press.

Schneider, Edgar W. 2024. English in Southeast Asian tourism. In Andrew J. Moody (ed.), *The Oxford Handbook of Southeast Asian Englishes*, pp. 706–728. Oxford: Oxford University Press.

Schreier, Daniel, Marianne Hundt, & Edgar W. Schneider (eds.). 2020. *The Cambridge Handbook of World Englishes*. Cambridge: Cambridge University Press.

Siemund, Peter. 2013. *Varieties of English. A Typological Approach*. Cambridge: Cambridge University Press.

Vertovec, Steven. 2007. Super-diversity and its implications. *Ethnic and Racial Studies* 30(6): 1024–1054.

CHAPTER 2

World Englishes and the third space
Insights from multilingual practices in Xhosa and English

Rajend Mesthrie
University of Cape Town

> This chapter takes as its starting point the further spread of English since the new millennium in terms of both breadth and depth. The language continues to be favored in international education, media, and cross-cultural communication, even as other languages continue at more local levels, and a few others at international levels. The chapter examines the influence of English on local languages among fluent bilinguals of this era. Data comes mainly from young speakers in Soweto, South Africa, fluent in Xhosa and English (and still other languages like Zulu). The chapter argues for the existence of a third space in which the rules of Xhosa and English show mutual influences not found in monolingual varieties of either code. Focus falls on (a) the extension of prefixes under switches or nonce-borrowings of nominal elements from English, (b) the rise of a new prefix for verb switches or nonce-borrowings, and (c) the interchangeable use of logical connectors. In all of these, the third space is a source of innovation and complexity, while also implicated in sociolinguistic issues of identity projection.

Keywords: bilingualism, code-switching, loanword adaptation, logical connectors, third space, Xhosa

1. Introduction

This paper argues that World Englishes research can be strengthened by considering the space between new (or relatively new) local varieties of English studied within the paradigm and the local languages with which they co-exist. Code mixing and switching have in fact not been neglected within World Englishes studies — witness early accounts by Kachru (1978) and Sridhar & Sridhar (1980) among many others. Outside this sub-field deep insights into the dynamism of code-switching practices can be found in especially Poplack (1980), Myers-Scotton (e.g., 1993a, 1993b), and Muysken (e.g., 2011). This paper examines the third space when fluent bilinguals in English and Xhosa keep both languages active in their speech. The data from Xhosa is based on the work of Mesthrie & Mfazwe-Mojapelo (forthc.), while the L2 English of Xhosa speakers comes from published sources including De Klerk (2009) and Makalela (2015). The focus falls on new elements or new functions for old elements that surface in bilingual speech.[1] In all of these, the third space is a source of innovation and complexity, while also implicated in sociolinguistic issues of identity creation and projection.

As globalization and the consequences of colonial and post-colonial contact increase in a changing world, so has World Englishes as a field necessarily had to update its approaches, assumptions, and descriptions. There is now closer attention to changing power dynamics in the recent past and present day. Thus, Buschfeld, Kautzsch & Schneider (2018) identify power dynamics beyond British colonialism in countries like Cyprus and Namibia. Mair (2013) factors in new bases of power and prestige within the World Systems account of De Swaan (2001). Mesthrie (2020) focuses on indigenous challenges to the power and authority of standard varieties of English in post-apartheid South Africa. Inevitably the influence of new social media in an era of semiotic saturation has also led to revisions of older models. Thus, Schneider (2014) built in a notion of "transnational attraction" (of the forces of globalizing media) to his earlier Dynamic Model (2003) — see also Buschfeld, Kautzsch & Schneider (2018). Mair (2013) has noted the increased role for varieties like African American Vernacular English, Jamaican Creole, and Nigerian Creole (known as Pidgin) on social media as counter forces to standard varieties.

Two other emphases within a now globalizing sociolinguistics have been labelled a mobility turn as well as a multilingual turn. Blommaert (2008) and others have focused on the movement of people as well as the mobile resources they develop and call upon in enabling communication. This scholarship lays stress on multilingual repertoires, amidst which speakers need not have full command of all components of specific languages therein. Thus, translanguaging among migrants and their descendants is a salient theme (Canagarajah 2013). These approaches have inevitably influenced researchers working within World Englishes as a field. At the more linguistic and structural-generative levels are scholars drawing on adjacent fields like corpus linguistics and language typology. These have been less responsive to new forces of globalization, and remain rooted in

---

1. In this chapter bilingual and multilingual are more or less synonymously used; the differences between using two or more than two languages not being in focus. I use African language names without prefixes (hence Xhosa rather than isiXhosa, acknowledging that many local scholars prefer otherwise).

the nation-based characterization of World Englishes. They have been able to add a robust comparative dimension not noticeable in other approaches. Corpus findings have greatly enhanced our understandings of now classic World English forms, like the progressive in extended uses (Paulasto 2014; Sharma 2009; Van Rooy 2008). Peter Siemund's work (e.g., 2018) pays close attention to linguistic typology within a multilingual ecology. Siemund has made, *inter alia*, the testable claim that typological hierarchies and universals (e.g., those concerning animacy or accessibility for relative clause structures) might sometimes be more evident in dialects and World Englishes than in the standard varieties which remain prescriptively resistant to certain natural changes. Here the class of language-shift Englishes (or shifted varieties) bear closer scrutiny — see, e.g., Hickey (2006) on Irish English structures, Mesthrie (1992) on relative clauses and topicalization in South African Indian English, and Lim (2009) on Singapore English as a tone language.

2. Multilingualism, bilingual modes, and third space effects

In this chapter, I wish to emphasize a particular aspect of globalization and language, consequent upon not just the spread of English but its impact upon young peoples' multilingualism, especially those who have English as their main educational language. I will be focusing mainly on the influence of English on the other languages of a speaker's repertoire that goes beyond borrowing and switching. I will consider the term 'switching' broadly to encompass concepts or terms like mixing, meshing, translanguaging, etc., but not necessarily borrowing. Borrowing — as is well known — prototypically adapts an individual item from the "donor" language to suit the phonological and syntactic structures of the "recipient" language, making it in time essentially a part of the latter. The origins of a borrowed term are not always known — or relevant — to speakers (Appel & Muysken 1987; Haugen 1950). The structures of the donor language itself need not be well known to the "borrowers". Code-switching, on the other hand, presumes a degree of familiarity with the codes being switched, and in many cases is a result of both codes being active pragmatically and psycholinguistically as speakers engage in bilingual talk (Myers-Scotton 1993b). Between these prototypical extremes are some complexities that are entirely expectable when dealing with entities as sophisticated as human beings and their language systems or sub-systems. In particular, elementary switching while one is only partially acquainted, or becoming acquainted, with one of the codes appears to me to be the main point of the concept of translanguaging.

2.1 The bilingual mode

Grosjean (1998) speaks specifically of a "bilingual mode" which differs from the modes of not only monolingual speakers but also of a bilingual person speaking in one of their monolingual modes. Grosjean (1998: 136) emphasizes that this is a language mode continuum, rather than three discrete states. Grosjean's language mode continuum is given in Figure 1. As Grosjean notes, the bilingual may take up different positions on the continuum depending largely on the bilingual proficiency of the interlocutor, though other issues like setting and topic also count. These positions are schematically represented by the three broken vertical lines. The least bilingual mode (or essentially monolingual mode) is on the left, as when speaking to a monolingual. The most bilingual mode is on the right when speaking to a fellow bilingual in informal conversation. In this mode code-switching is not uncommon. The squares at the top and bottom represent different levels of language activation of the base language (at the top) and the other language (designated Language B – at the bottom). A black shade represents complete activation, while a white background indicates an inactive state. Striped lines thus indicate a degree of bilingual activation (increasing from left to right according to the thickness of the stripes).

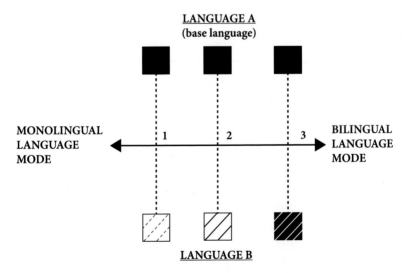

Figure 1. The language mode continuum – based on Grosjean (1998: 136)

Looking more closely at code-switching, in the first instance speakers keep two (and sometimes more) languages psycholinguistically active and use them appropriately via lexical insertion or in alternation (Muyskens' 2000 term "code alternation" and Mesthrie & Hurst's 2013 "syntactic switching"). The new multilinguals of this study appear at the same time to be analyzing and adjusting elements of the one code in relation to the other in an even more dynamic fashion. Sebba (2009:52) notes that speakers not only exploit similarities between languages, but also maximize and even build up similarities. They do so by adapting each language in ways that lead to convergence: bilingual code-switchers "create convergence between two existing languages, if necessary, by making adjustments to the monolingual norms" (Sebba 2009:55).

2.2   The third space

It is the contention of this paper that certain kinds of code-switching qualify as a third space activity. The term originates in the work of Homi Bhabha (1994) who conceived of first-generation migrants living in a physical, social, and mental space that existed not just between two worlds, but as an amalgam that transcended those worlds. The characterization need not apply to migrants alone. In World Englishes studies we are familiar with hybrid forms that go by various (but not always elegant) names like Singlish, Hinglish, Konglish, Namlish, Tamlish etc. (for Singapore English, Hindi English, Hong Kong English, Namibian English, Tamil English, respectively). The hybridity is particularly common among young people and in informal contexts, reaching its zenith in social media. Speaking of Hinglish, the *Lonely Planet* booklet (2008) entitled *Indian English – Language and Culture*, makes the point that utterances in the variety can only be understood by those familiar with both languages (see Mesthrie 2019). However, it seems to me that speakers of these new hybrids are more commonly able to shift in formal contexts to English (a form of "unmixing"), while finding it increasingly difficult to do so for the other code (see McCormick 2002; Shivachi 1999).

Bhabha's sociological concept has been applied to code-switching by, *inter alia*, Bhatt (2008), who describes the increasing juxtaposition of Hindi and English in what were once English-medium Indian newspapers. He gives as an example the phrase *Kotwal Uncle*, which draws on Hindi for the archaic term *kotwal*, denoting a relatively high-ranking police officer as part of the colonial presence in his district (Bhatt 2008:194). *Uncle* on the other hand is the term for an older male community member, showing a mixture of community solidarity and respect. The term is not usually used with relatives, for whom a Hindi term would be applicable. Bhatt (2008:185) argues that such juxtapositions blur the specific indexicalities of the languages involved and create a compositional semantics involving both colonial social formations and local-indigenous culture. Bhatt cites Hall's (1997:48) insistence that "the notion [...] of two histories, one over here, one over there, never having spoken to one another, never having anything to do with one another

[...] is simply not tenable any longer in an increasingly globalized world" (Bhatt 2008: 184–185).

The notion of a third space is not, however, endorsed within syntactic theory, which prefers a more parsimonious account of language generation. Thus, Pfaff (1979) declared a requirement of 'no third grammar' for code-switching. This position is endorsed by MacSwann (2009) in his account of generative approaches to the phenomenon, and in particular for current minimalist approaches: "... all of the facts of code-switching may be explained just in terms of principles and requirements of the specific grammars used in each case" (MacSwann 2009: 325). Thus, there are no statements, rules, or principles of grammar within minimalism that refer to code-switching. This might apply in a very abstract account of language, but does not appear convincing in a processual approach that takes into account ongoing changes in "real" languages at a surface level. A much less abstract sociolinguistic approach to the contrary stresses ways in which the two languages in the bilingual mode are not only kept together "online" but show an interplay between their rules.

In analyzing the third space morphological and syntactic effects of "new multilingualism", I will draw on data from South Africa showing a post-colonial African multilingualism, in which English and one or more Bantu languages are prominent (see Makalela 2015 for South Africa, Myers-Scotton 1993a more generally for Africa). The data comes from interviews undertaken by Lulu Mfazwe-Mojapelo with speakers of Xhosa from a part of Soweto. De facto, the speakers were fluent in English, Zulu, and had some knowledge of Sotho and Afrikaans. In terms of Grosjean's model the base language was Xhosa, and the relevant "language B" for this paper – English (with roles for languages C and D, which need not concern us here). The bilingual mode was most certainly active in the interviews, arguably at the level of the rightmost vertical line, as will be clear from the data cited. How best to position the data from the interviews within the model provided by Figure 1 will be discussed in the conclusion to this study.

Xhosa (known as isiXhosa in the language itself) is a Southern Bantu Language (a subgroup of the larger group of Southeast Bantu languages that cover the range of structurally similar languages from South Africa to East Africa). It is closely related to Zulu, the majority language of South Africa, with which it shares a past history and commonalities, as well as present innovations arising from influences of Afrikaans and English in colonial and current times. In earlier phases both languages show the influence of the unrelated Khoe-San languages, leading to – among other things – the large-scale incorporation of clicks (Bourquin 1935). Present-day Xhosa is involved in extensive code-switching, showing the educational and commercial influence of English mainly, though in some cities Zulu is also an influence on speakers of migrant Xhosa background. I will discuss the following cases: (a) choice of noun-class prefixes sometimes being bilingually determined, rather than by one code alone, (b) influence of English adjectives on noun-class prefixation in "multilingual Xhosa", (c) re-analysis of English verbs in relation to causatives in multilingual Xhosa, and (d) interchangeability of logical connectors in multilingual speech.

2.2.1 *Noun class prefixes*

Noun class prefixes are a central and entrenched feature of most Bantu languages, in which every noun is assigned to a class with a particular prefix. This prefix is believed to have had greater consistency in the past, traceable to Proto Bantu which is reconstructed to have up to 23 classes along fairly clearly demarcated lines (see e.g., Schadeberg 2014). Since these classes feature widely in the examples in this chapter, they are worth elucidating (the discussion is based on, *inter alia*, Doke 1956, Jordan 1966, and Pinnock 1994). In Xhosa (and related Nguni languages) today we have the following basic system:

Table 1. Xhosa noun class prefixes — a skeletal guide

Class	Prefix	Meaning	Plural prefix
1	-um	human	2 -aba
3	-um	non-human living things	4 -imi
5	-i(li)	miscellaneous, including some loanwords[*]	6 -ama
7	-isi	things used for a particular purpose (e.g., dish, snare, anvil), though again much generalized today	8 -izi
9	iN	animals, miscellaneous inanimates not found in other classes, many loanwords[**]	10 -i(z)iN
11	-ulu	prototypically long objects (e.g stick, row, rib)	
14	-ubu	abstract nouns, quality, essence	
15	-uku	actions and occasions derived from verbs	

[*] Pinnock (1994: 201) suggests that hard objects (e.g., stone, fruit, clod) form a notable sub-class here. *Ili-* and *i-* are allomorphs.
[**] N in the prefix denotes a nasal.

Classes 2, 4, 6, 8, 10 are the plurals of Classes 1, 3, 5, 7, 9 respectively with the prefixes given above. Missing classes in the sequence are a result of gradual changes from Proto Bantu to languages like Xhosa, and may be found in one or more other contemporary Bantu languages (see e.g., Doke 1956). The noun class prefixes are important since they determine — by an elaborate system of concords — the related prefixes for verbs, adjectives, pronouns, demonstratives, and so forth. Example sentences (1)–(2) show this elaborate system of concord, with *b*-prefixes showing concord with the class 2 human prefix *aba-* in Example (1) and class 10 animal prefix *-iin* in Example (2) (or *izin* underlyingly).[2]

(1) Aba-fana ba-mi   aba-khulu ba-ya-sebenza   b-onke
    2-son   2.POSS-me 2.ADJ-big 2.they-PROG-work 2-all
    'All my big sons are working.'

(2) Ii-nkomo za-m   ezi-nkulu zi-ya-dla   z-onke
    10-cattle 10.POSS-me 10.ADJ-big 10.they-PROG-graze 10-all
    'All my big cattle are grazing.'

Cole (1953: 262) remarks upon the alliterative effect of this system of concords which "puts music and poetry into every Bantu sentence" as witnessed by the two examples above (adopted here for Xhosa).

2.2.2 Variation in loanword morphology

Loanwords are assigned a class on the basis of their semantics (with the insertion of the appropriate suffix — hence a noun denoting a language might be placed in class 7 and given a prefix *-isi*). There is also a default class into which loanwords may generally be placed, less determined by semantics alone (class 9, though in keeping with Zulu, some loans fall into class 5). Sometimes a loanword is assigned a class on phonological grounds, when the first syllable of the English form resembles a class prefix of Xhosa (thus *um-atshini* 'machine' is in class 3 because the initial [m] of the English root resembles the prefix *um-* of this class).

A relatively new pattern of variation introduced by younger bilinguals well versed with English concerns the assignment of prefixes to certain loanwords beginning with [s]. Originally noted by Ngcobo (2013) for Zulu, the variable pattern also applies to Xhosa. Traditionally, early historical borrowings like *spoon*, *stairs*, and *school* in Zulu and Xhosa were put into class 7, the *-isi* class on the basis of the initial /s/ of the English originals. Hence *isi-kolo* 'school' is the form accepted by all speakers, showing a re-segmentation of the English word (and hence with plural equivalent in class 8, *izi-kolo*). This re-segmentation is sometimes contested by younger bilingual speakers well versed in English. Ngcobo's example of 'cellphone' will suffice here: in Zulu, most speakers accept the segmentation *is-elulafoni*, with plural *iz-elulafoni*. However, some younger speakers conscious of English norms insist that the [s] be treated as part of the root of the word and not a prefix, and so put the loan in class 5 as *i-selulafoni* with plural

---

[2]. In these example sentences a numeral denotes the class affiliation of a noun and its agreement markers in other parts of speech. An element of interest is illustrated is given in bold, while words from English are in italics.

ama-selulafoni. Ngcobo cites this as a kind of hypercorrection. For Xhosa speakers, similar dilemmas exist, and plural forms like *ii-selfowuni* treat [s] as part of the root in Xhosa. This suggests that the English segmentation is indeed now dominant.[3] From the perspective of the multilingual repertoire the example shows how some forms of one language can influence morphological choices in the other. This applies more to the influence of English as prestige language of education, which sets up competing borrowing ideologies and hence variation. Other instances of influence are less contestable, prescriptive or ideological, and show younger bilinguals thriving in new (or seemingly new) forms of bilingual innovation.

2.2.3 *English adjectives and the extension of class 14 nouns*

This section provides an entrée to a longer account by Mesthrie & Mfazwe-Mojapelo (forthc.) of a multilingual extension to the noun class 14 prefix *ubu-*. This class — as noted above — contains abstract nouns, described by Pinnock (1994: 202) as "the quality or essence of a thing" — e.g., *ubuhle* 'beauty', *ubuntu* 'humanity', etc., derived from concrete forms like *-hle* 'beautiful' (adj.) and *-ntu* 'person' (noun). Whereas adjectives — like verbs — were not frequently borrowed in earlier phases of contact, multilingual Xhosa gives a new lease to *ubu-* by using it as the prefix to introduce adjectives from English. However, as in traditional Xhosa, the combination of adjective plus *ubu-* results in the formation of an abstract noun. Furthermore, the effect of *ubu-* seems to open up a slightly new semantics, not only of abstractness without reference to time ('quality or essence' as noted above) but of a slightly more concrete participial (or perhaps gerundial) quality. Thus, our *ubu-* examples convey the sense of 'being selfish', or 'being casual', rather than 'selfishness', or 'casualness' alone, as suggested by Examples (3) and (4) below:

(3) Ma-ka-yeke **ubu-*selfish*** a-sherishe i-gumbi no-mzala wa-khe.
let-her-stop 14-selfish and-share 5-room with-cousin 14.POSS-her
'She must stop being selfish and share a room with her cousin.'

(4) **Ubu-*casual*** ba-khe bu-m-enze aka-hlonitsh-wa tu nga-bantu
14-casual 14POSS-his 14.it-him-made NEG-respect.PASS at-all by-people
aba-sebenz-elayo.
REL-work-REL
'His being casual made him not to be respected at all by his employees.'

This opens up a channel within multilingual Xhosa for drifting towards English in respect of allowing in a vast number of (mostly) Latinate adjectives (ubu-*sophis-*

---

3. The form is often reduced to *ii-fowuni*.

ticated, ubu-*critical*), compound adjectives (ubu-*short-tempered*), complex adjectives with affixes (*ubu-antisocial, ubu-unfair, ubu-forgetful*) and phrasal adjectives (*hands-on*). *Ubu-* almost never combines with monosyllabic "Germanic" adjectives like *big, deep*, etc.

2.2.4 *The use of -isha as a suffix to enhance verb borrowings*

Traditionally verbs borrowed from English into Xhosa were uncommon compared to nouns. Verb borrowings from Afrikaans were slightly more numerous (Owen-Lloyd 1900). These usually added the final vowel -*a* of Bantu languages, as in -*ayina* 'to iron' and -*danisa* 'to dance western style' (Pinnock 1994: 143).[4] A popular usage that has evolved among younger people sees a large number of verbs from English (and Afrikaans in former times) with their special status marked by a suffix -*isha* (Madubela 2017). Hence *fry-isha* 'to fry', *bother-isha,* 'to bother', *struggle-isha* 'to struggle', *continue-isha* 'to continue', etc. Two examples are provided below, sentence (5) with -*isha* and (6) with its negative form -*ishi*.

(5) Kodwa ke si-ya *continue*-**isha** uku le nza cli siku
    but   DM we-FUT continue-ISHA INF-5-do 5.this custom
    'But we will **continue** to do this ritual.'

(6) A-ndi-*study*-**ish**-i   apha e-Soweto, ndi-ya e-*Sammy   Marks Library*
    NEG-I-study-ISHA-NEG here in-Soweto, I-go   LOC-Sammy Marks Library
    'I **don't study** here in Soweto, I go to Sammy Marks Library.'

The origins of this suffix are unclear. It is reminiscent of the causative form -*isa,* which is an established morpheme in Bantu languages, and routinely turns a verb root into a causative form: hence Xhosa *bona* 'to see' versus *bon-isa* 'cause to see, show'. However, -*isha* dos not generally have causative meaning. Simango (2011) considers it to be a transitivising suffix that occurs with loanwords only, while Mesthrie & Mfazwe-Mojapelo (forthc.) argue for a more general 'predicative' function in connection with loanwords. Among the explanations for the etymological origins of the suffix are (a) an innovation based on the causative (or at least parallel to it), without having any causative meaning, (b) a 'spontaneous' verb-forming suffix, or (c) related to the English suffix -*ish*. Option (c) seems unlikely to me, despite being upheld by Mfenyana (1977) who proposes the -*ish* of adjectives like *English* and *British* to be the models and by Koopman (1999: 50–52) who cites instead the verb endings in *finish, polish,* and *punish*. So, we are left with options (a) and (b), of which (a) seems the most likely — i.e., -*isha* is an inno-

---

4. The example of -*danisa* is perhaps complicated by what superficially resembles the causative -*isa* at the end. The word, though, is non-causative in meaning and comes from the English form [daːns] 'dance' with vowel insertion.

vation that surfaces in the third space which is probably modelled on analogy of causative -*isa* without any causative meaning. Once considered non-standard, a few forms might well be accepted in formal and classroom language — e.g., *tadisha* 'to study' (Isaac Mndawe, p.c.). Madubela (2017) studied a range of such forms, concluding that they do not show clear correlations with syllable structure, semantic groupings etc., but are part of a young peoples' informal, modern style. My analysis suggests that -*isha* is a crucial structural element in bilingual discourse, subject to several constraints. These constraints are part of the matrix language (Xhosa) since they determine the presence or absence of -*isha*. But as the discussion will show, the embedded language English is also crucially involved, in having its lexemes analyzed "online" as speakers decide which English verbs are open to selection.

A number of perspectives are needed to characterize the use of -*isha*: phonological, syntactic, lexical, morphological, sociolinguistic, and even historical. All of them relate to a third space analysis, that would not be relevant in monolingual English or monolingual Xhosa. In asking under what conditions in multilingual Xhosa does -*isha* appear, it is easier to analyze conditions under which it is disallowed. The most important phonological constraint is that it is disallowed with English verbs that already end in -*ish*: hence forms like *publish-isha, *flourish-isha, and *perish-isha are disallowed and would have to be expressed as *publish-a, flourish-a*, and *perish-a*, all of which take the Xhosa -*a* ending for verbs. The phonological structure of Xhosa suggests that the -*ish* is part of the base of the word (as base forms like *publ-, flour-*, and *per-* are unintuitive). There is a related morphological constraint on English verbs ending in -*ise* (phonetically [aɪz]. Hence *diarise, finalise*, and *memorise* turn up in multilingual Xhosa as *diaris-a, finalis-a*, and *memoris-a* and not *diaris-isha, *finalis-isha, and *memoris-isha. These are fairly natural, phonetically-based constraints, but — crucially — are applied cross-linguistically. The suffix is from Xhosa, but the base forms that it is affixed to are English verbs (with a few from Afrikaans in the past).

More purely syntactic considerations also come into play. Compound verbs of English do not appear to take -*isha*: Hence *up-date-a, e-mail-a*, and *s-m-s-a* occur in the data base (Mesthrie & Mfazwe-Mojapelo forthc.) rather than *up-date-isha, *e-mail-isha, and *s-m-s-isha. Most importantly, the English verb that takes -*isha* is a content word and not a purely grammatical one. It is prototypically polysyllabic, but monosyllabic verbs are not entirely ruled out. While Jespersen's (1965) original distinction between a "light" verb and other verbs comes to mind, it is not an entirely accurate characterization here. Light verbs in his sense pertain to verbs that are devoid of their full meaning when used in conjunction with a noun (as in to *take a trip, give a reply, make a blunder* etc.) For the multilingual Xhosa case we need a term that includes light verbs but also includes auxiliaries, copulae, semi-auxiliaries (*want, gonna*), causatives (*make, cause, force*), raising verbs (*seem, appear*), and so forth. For want of a better term I call these "small verbs". The constraint is that small verbs do not enter into construction with *-isha*. In other words, English forms like *want, know, come, go, become* etc. do not occur in multilingual Xhosa, whose own small verbs prevail. Since these are in fact key elements that initiate and anchor any predication, they ensure that the Xhosa template of multilingual Xhosa is maintained, despite the eye-catching neologisms from English. For parallels in other contact situations and the use of what he terms "integration auxiliaries", see Matras (2009: 134–135).

Clearly, speakers are thus heeding morphosyntactic rules of Xhosa when speaking multilingually within a Xhosa matrix (or base language), as evident in Examples (3)–(8). But they also pay heed to aspects of English syntax and morphology and come up with rules (or constraints) that are not part of the monolingual English speaker's concerns. In speaking multilingual Xhosa, one cannot simply embed any English verb, without attention to its structure. As part of their multilingual competence, speakers unconsciously ask: is it small?, phrasal?, monosyllabic?, ending in a suffix that clashes phonologically with *-ish*?, etc.). And since some of these constraints overlap, this is a fairly complex variable and hierarchical subsystem being integrated in multilingual speech.

2.2.5 Logical and discourse connectors

English logical connectors, discourse operators, or utterance modifiers like *and, so, however, because*, and *already* have proved influential in many languages implicated in code-switching with English (e.g., Poplack 1980; Matras 2009: 136; Myers-Scotton 1993a; Schiffrin 1987). At the same time, it has been noted that World Englishes have strengthened conjunctions by internal doubling (e.g., *supposing if, because why*) or doubling across clauses, e.g., in Example (7) from Indian English (Nihalani, Tongue & Hosali 1977: 177):

(7) Though the farmer works hard, but he cannot produce enough.

Similar examples have been reported for English in Singapore, Southern Africa, East and West Africa (Mesthrie & Bhatt 2008: 175). The attractiveness of these connectors may well have something to do with English as medium of instruction.[5]

Turning to multilingual Xhosa we see a predilection for English connectors. The following are fairly widespread in the data base of Mesthrie & Mfazwe-Mojapelo: *and, but, because, 'coz, whether, since, then, whenever, although*, and *so*. Two examples in context are given below:

---

5. The author knows of two persons, whose official first names are logical connectors taken from English.

(8) **Whenever** e-ku-*Facebook,* u-hlala njalo e-*updater* i-*status* sa-khe.
whenever REL-on-Facebook she-remains as REL-updater 5-status 5-her
'Whenever on Facebook, she remains one who updates her status.'

The form '*coz* exemplified in Example (9) shows the influence of colloquial English beyond that of the classroom:

(9) A-ndi-zuku-*jog*-a namhlanje *coz* ndi-diniwe.
NEG-I-will-jog-FV today 'cos I-am.tired
'I am not going to jog today because I am tired.'

The incorporation of these connectors is motivated by both sociolinguistic and structural factors. In most instances there is an equivalence between the connectors in English and Xhosa, leading to relatively straightforward substitution. In Example (9) the standard Xhosa equivalent *ngenxa yokuba* (literally 'because of') is more complex in its phrase structure than *coz*. However, a colloquial contraction of this standard form *kuba,* which is much more like *coz* is also possible. Substitution is aided by the structural fact of both English and Xhosa connectors occurring in clause initial position. Matras (2009:140) noted more generally that connectors are 'pragmatically detachable' and also relatively easy to produce in peripheral position. The main motivation for the high number of English connectors relates to sociolinguistic factors pertaining to identity. In their bilingual mode speakers signal their educational and work status as modern individuals comfortable with a language of community (Xhosa) and one of wider opportunities and contacts (English). Poplack (1980) gives further support for this claim in her pioneering work on Spanish in the US, arguing that the detachability of connectors makes them attractive elements for speakers wishing to highlight their bilingual repertoire, even if their proficiency in English is still developing.

Further support for the sociolinguistic identity position can be seen from the somewhat surprising reversal in multilingual speech when English is the matrix language in in-group conversations. De Klerk (2006:606) notes a "fairly high level of usage" of logical connectors and discourse markers in her corpus of English among Xhosa speakers (see De Klerk 2009). These include *ukuthi* 'that', *uyabona* 'you see' (also truncated to *uyabo* 'you know'), and *ukuba* 'if'. The conversations in her corpus were intended to be in English, but since interviewers and interviewees shared a Xhosa background, they used these markers of in-groupness. The practice may well be on the increase as noted in other studies from South Africa. Makalela (2015) studied radio conversations among students in Limpopo province, with English as the main language interspersed with some Tswana. He also remarks on connectors like *ukuthi* and discourse markers like *uyabo* signaling a multilingualism that highlights or subtly indicates an African identity. Muysken (2013:714) used the term 'back-flagging' when the L2 is "marked with flagging elements from the original community language". Back-flagging serves to signal the shared traditional ethnic or cultural identity of interlocutors (see also Heine et al. 2021: 219), and is in fact a kind of social indexing. More recent work by Unuabonah & Mtembu (2023) has uncovered further examples and practices in the large GloWbE corpus of online newspapers, blogs, and forums (see Davies 2013). The authors focus on five elements of Xhosa and Zulu serving pragmatic and sociolinguistic uses: *nje* 'indeed', *mara* 'but', *kanti* 'but', *vele* 'really', and *kaloku* 'by the way, you know' (primary meanings indicated).

3. The bilingual mode and the third space

To return to Grosjean's (1998, 2001) model of the bilingual mode, we believe that the data in this paper show a special kind of psycholinguistic activity that needs to be factored into Figure 1 above. While using Xhosa as base language and English as "language B", speakers show signs of analyzing language B in ways that differ from monolingual versions of B. The third space of this paper can be conceptualized as occurring at the rightmost mode of Grosjean's model, with both languages active. Grosjean's model though requires acknowledgement that advanced proficiency in both base language (Xhosa) and language B (English) is a requirement before speakers can engage in third-space convergence activities. In their least bilingual mode this third space is inactive. Instead, only established and some nonce-borrowings occur, the latter showing the activation of only the lexicon of language B. Third space rules facilitate the relatively seamless use of the two languages. Canagarajah's (2011) term 'code-meshing' in an educational context comes to mind here, though contact linguists have long talked of convergence between codes in multilingual speech.

Sebba (2009) provides a valuable overview of convergence in code-switching that is entirely consistent with the arguments of this paper. He uses the analogy of bilingual speech with code-switching being analogous to teams playing two sports at once — football (soccer to some) and basketball, which I here adapt and advance, capitalizing on the applicability of the term 'code' for both sport and language. Of course, the new game does not physically employ the two sports entirely simultaneously, but in alternation. There is, however, simultaneity at a deeper level since code A picks up where code B ends off (and so forth) rather than going back to an earlier stage of play (or conversation). So, in a way, players are playing two games at the same time, linguistically speaking.[6] What this

---

6. Further sub-types of "sport-mixing" parallel to switching, mixing, and perhaps translanguaging may also be possible. For the record, the author has indulged in sport-mixing, once irritating his American friends by playing "head tennis" in a semi-competitive volleyball game — i.e. refus-

paper has shown is that each *code* of sport has the potential of influencing the other as the dual game is played. In terms of Sebba's example, we would have to say that certain stretches of the game may show rules that integrate the two codes but strictly speaking belong to neither historically. One can think of scoring bonus points for carrying the ball and then kicking it into the basketball net when inside a specially demarcated zone. Third space users get maximum bonus points.

Sebba (2009: 51) also notes the role of educated speakers with some explicit (albeit sometimes prescriptive) grammatical knowledge in making the language systems in contact function harmoniously. We have pointed to a kind of multilingual prescriptivism when such educated speakers try to apply the rules of English segmentation to the playing of the Xhosa segment of the game. Back-flagging (of the use of connectors), however, appears to be the opposite. Not only is it free of any prescriptive motivation or intent, but it may well be an attempt to reign in the more powerful and prestigious language (English) when it is the matrix language in bilingual conversation. Both of these processes (prescriptivism and back-flagging) within multilingual speech are of enormous interest to World Englishes studies going forward. Above all, we should be alert to third space creativities in a global context in which English grows as a language of education, information, and aspiration.

Acknowledgements

Special tribute is due to Lulu Mfazwe-Mojapelo† who passed away in 2021 while working on her doctoral dissertation, and without whom this paper would not have been possible.

Abbreviations

ADJ	adjective	LOC	locative
DM	Discourse marker	NEG	negative
FUT	future	PASS	passive
FV	final vowel (denoting verb ending)	POSS	possessive
INF	infinitive	PROG	progressive
ISHA	predicative marker -isha		

---

ing to use his hands and still gaining points with his unexpected football-style headers. He was not invited back. On reflection, this game was parallel to code-switching with volleyball as the matrix code and football as the embedded code, but only with headers as a kind of embedded lexis.

References

Appel, Rene & Pieter Muysken. 1987. *Language Contact and Bilingualism*. London: Edward Arnold.
Bhabha, Homi. 1994. *The Location of Culture*. London: Routledge.
Bhatt, Rakesh. 2008. In other words: Language mixing, identity representations, and third space. *Journal of Sociolinguistics* 12(2): 177–200.
Blommaert, Jan. 2008. *The Sociolinguistics of Globalization*. Cambridge: Cambridge University Press.
Bourquin, Walter. 1935. Click words that Xhosa, Zulu and Sotho have in common. *Bantu Studies* 10: 59–81.
Buschfeld, Sarah, Alexander Kautzsch & Edgar Schneider. 2018. From colonial dynamism to current transnationalism: A unified view on postcolonial and non-postcolonial Englishes. In Sandra Deshors (ed.), *Modelling World Englishes: Assessing the Interplay of Emancipation and Globalization of ESL Varieties*, pp. 15–44. Amsterdam: John Benjamins.
Canagarajah, Suresh. 2011. Code-meshing in academic writing: Identifying teachable strategies of translanguaging. *The Modern Language Journal* 95(3): 401–417.
Canagarajah, Suresh. 2013. *Translingual Practice: Global Englishes and Cosmopolitan Relations*. London: Routledge.
Cole, Desmond. 1953. Fanagalo and the Bantu languages of South Africa. *African Studies* 12: 1–9.
Davies, Mark. 2013. *Corpus of Global Web-Based English*. https:english-corpora.org/gloWbE/ (11 October 2024).
De Klerk, Vivian. 2006. Codeswitching, borrowing and mixing in a corpus of Xhosa English. *International Journal of Bilingual Education and Bilingualism* 9(5): 597–614.
De Klerk, Vivian. 2009. *Corpus Linguistics and World Englishes: An analysis of Xhosa English*. London: Continuum.
De Swaan, Abram. 2001. *Words of the World: The Global Language System*. Cambridge: Polity.
Doke, Clement. 1956. Language. In Isaac Schapera (ed.), *The Bantu-speaking Tribes of South Africa*. Cape Town: Maskew Miller.
Grosjean, Francois. 1998. Studying bilinguals: Methodological and conceptual issues. *Bilingualism: Language and Cognition* 1: 131–149.
Grosjean, Francois. 2001. The bilingual's language modes. In Janet Nichol (ed.), *One Mind Two Languages: Bilingual Language Processing*, pp. 1–25. Oxford: Blackwell.
Hall, Stuart. 1997. Old and new ethnicities. In Antony D. King (ed.), *Culture, Globalization and the World System*, pp. 41–68. Minneapolis, MN: University of Minnesota Press.
Haugen, Einar. 1950. The analysis of linguistic borrowing. *Language* 26(2): 210–231.
Heine, Bernd, Gunther Kaltenböck, Tania Kuteva & Haiping Long. 2021. *The Rise of Discourse Markers*. Cambridge: Cambridge University Press.
Hickey, Raymond. 2006. Contact, shift and language change: Irish English and South African Indian English. In Hildegard Tristram (ed.), *The Celtic Englishes*, pp. 234–258. Potsdam: Potsdam University Press.
Indian English — Language and Culture. 2008. Victoria: Lonely Planet.
Jespersen, Otto. 1965. *A Modern English Grammar on Historical Principles, Part VI, Morphology*. London: George Allen and Unwin.

Jordan, Archibald C. 1966. *A Practical Course in Xhosa*. Cape Town: Longmans.

Kachru, Braj. 1978. Toward structuring code-mixing: An Indian perspective. *International Journal of the Sociology of Language* 16: 27–46.

Koopman, Adrian. 1999. *Zulu Language Change*. Howick: Brevitas.

Lim, Lisa. 2009. Revisiting English prosody: (Some) New Englishes as tone languages. *English World-Wide* 30(2): 218–239.

MacSwann, Jeff. 2009. Generative approaches to code-switching. In Barbara E. Bulock & Almeida Jacqueline Toribio (eds.), *The Cambridge handbook of linguistic code-switching*, pp. 309–335. Cambridge: Cambridge University Press.

Madubela, Ndumiso. 2017. Eish — when to use -ish-: A study in the verbalization of English lexical items in spoken Xhosa. M.A. thesis. University of Cape Town.

Mair, Christian. 2013. The world system of Englishes: Accounting for the transnational importance of mobile and mediated vernaculars. *English World-Wide* 34: 253–278.

Makalela, Leketi. 2015. Translanguaging practices in complex multilingual spaces: A discontinuous continuity in post-independent South Africa. *International Journal of the Sociology of Language* 234: 115–132.

Matras, Yaron. 2009. *Language Contact*. Cambridge: Cambridge University Press.

McCormick, Kathleen. 2002. *Language in Cape Town's District Six*. Oxford: Oxford University Press.

Mesthrie, Rajend. 1992. *English in Language Shift: The History, Structure and Sociolinguistics of South African Indian English*. Cambridge: Cambridge University Press.

Mesthrie, Rajend. 2019. Indian English in theory and action: A tribute to Braj B. Kachru. *World Englishes* 38(1–2): 155–161.

Mesthrie, Rajend. 2020. Colony, post-colony and world Englishes in the South African context. *World Englishes* 40(1): 12–23.

Mesthrie, Rajend & Rakesh Bhatt. 2008. *World Englishes*. Cambridge: Cambridge University Press.

Mesthrie, Rajend & Ellen Hurst. 2013. Slang registers, code-switching and restructured urban varieties in South Africa: An analytic overview of Tsotsitaals with special reference to the Cape Town variety. *Journal of Pidgin and Creole Languages* 28(1): 103–30.

Mesthrie, Rajend & Lulu Mfazwe-Mojapelo. Forthcoming. Speaking Xhosa multilingually: A study of contact innovations among Xhosa speakers in Soweto. *Language Dynamics and Change*.

Mfenyana, Buntu. 1977. Isikhumsha Nesitsotsi: The Sociolinguistics of School and Town Sintu in South Africa (1945–5975). M.A. thesis, Boston University.

Muysken, Pieter. 2000. *Bilingual Speech: A Typology of Code-mixing*. Cambridge: Cambridge University Press.

Muysken, Pieter. 2011. Code-switching. In Rajend Mesthrie (ed.), *The Cambridge Handbook of Sociolinguistics*, pp. 301–314. Cambridge: Cambridge University Press.

Muysken, Pieter. 2013. Language contact outcomes as the result of bilingual optimization strategies. *Bilingualism: Language and Cognition* 16(4): 709–730.

Myers-Scotton, Carol. 1993a. *Social Motivations for Code-Switching: Evidence from Africa*. Oxford: Clarendon.

Myers-Scotton, Carol. 1993b. *Duelling Languages: Grammatical Structure in Codeswitching.* Oxford: Clarendon.

Ngcobo, Mtholeni. 2013. Loan words classification in isiZulu: The need for a sociolinguistic approach. *Language Matters* 44(1): 21–38.

Nihalani, Paroo, Ray K. Tongue & Priya Hosali. 1977. *Indian and British English: A Handbook of Usage and Pronunciation.* New Delhi: Oxford University Press.

Owen-Lloyd, George. 1900. *A Study of Some Xhosa Words of Afrikaans Origin.* Edikeni: Lovedale Press.

Paulasto, Heli. 2014. Extended uses of the progressive form in L1 and L2 Englishes. *English World Wide* 35(3): 247–276.

Pfaff, Carol W. 1979. Constraints on language mixing: Intrasentential code-switching and borrowing in Spanish/English. *Language* 55(2): 291–318.

Pinnock, Patricia. 1994. *Xhosa — A Cultural Grammar for Beginners.* Cape Town: African Sun Press.

Poplack, Shana. 1980. Sometimes I'll start a sentence in Spanish, y termino en espanyol: Toward a typology of code-switching. *Linguistics* 18: 581–618.

Schadeberg, Thilo. 2014. Historical linguistics. In Derek Nurse & Gérard Phillipson (eds.), *The Bantu Languages*, 2nd edn, pp. 143–163. London: Routledge.

Schiffrin, Deborah (ed.). 1987. *Discourse Markers.* Cambridge: Cambridge University Press.

Schneider, Edgar W. 2003. The dynamics of new Englishes: From identity construction to dialect birth. *Language* 79: 233–281.

Schneider, Edgar W. 2014. New reflections on the evolutionary dynamics of world Englishes. *World Englishes* 33(1): 9–32.

Sebba, Mark. 2009. On the notions of congruence and convergence in code-switching. In Barbara E. Bullock & Almeida Jacqueline Toribio (eds.), *The Cambridge Handbook of Linguistic Code-switching*, pp. 40–57. Cambridge: Cambridge University Press.

Sharma, Devyani. 2009. Typological diversity in New Englishes. *English World-Wide* 30(2): 170–195.

Shivachi, Caleb. 1999. A Case Study in Language Contact: English, Kiswahili and Luhyia among the Luhyia People of Kenya. PhD dissertation, University of Cape Town.

Siemund, Peter. 2018. Modelling World Englishes from a cross-linguistic perspective. In Sandra Deshors (ed.), *Modelling World Englishes: Assessing the Interplay of Emancipation and Globalization of ESL Varieties*, pp. 133–162. Amsterdam: John Benjamins.

Simango, Ron. 2011. When English meets isiXhosa in the clause: An exploration into the grammar of code-switching. *Southern African Linguistics & Applied Linguistics Studies* 19(2):127–134.

Sridhar, Shikaripur N. & Kamal Sridhar. 1980. The syntax and psycholinguistics of bilingual code-mixing. *Canadian Journal of Psychology* 34(4): 407–416.

Unuabonah, Foluke & Noloyiso Mtembu. 2023. Multilingual pragmatic markers in South African English. *Southern African Linguistics and Applied Language Studies* 41(3): 264–279.

Van Rooy, Bertus. 2008. An alternative interpretation of tense and aspect in Black South African English. *World Englishes* 27(3): 335–358.

PART II

Language policies and attitudes

CHAPTER 3

Hierarchies in the language ecology of Botswana

Sheena Shah
University of the Free State | University of Hamburg

This chapter provides insights into Botswana's rich language ecology and prevailing language hierarchies. English holds a prominent position as the *de facto* official language, although its everyday use is limited to a small population, namely the educated urban elite. Setswana, as the *de facto* national language, is the most widely spoken L1, with substantial numbers of the population also acquiring this Bantu language as their L2; it is used extensively across most domains of everyday life. English and Setswana compete at the top of the language hierarchy of Botswana, with English being key to upward social and economic mobility, while Setswana symbolizes national unity and expresses solidarity and close social ties. Other Bantu languages, such as Shekgalagadi, Shiyeyi, Sebirwa, and even Ikalanga, the largest of the minority languages, play only minor roles in the public domains. At the bottom of the language power scale are the languages of the former hunter-gatherers, the first people of southern Africa, namely the Tuu and Kx'a languages, followed by the languages of the Khoe language family. These languages are gradually replaced by Setswana and regionally dominant Bantu languages, and some are on the verge of extinction. While the smaller languages are not in competition with English, Setswana is, and this power struggle might have a significant impact on the language ecology of the country.

Keywords: Botswana, English, language hierarchy, language replacement, Setswana

1. Introduction

Botswana is landlocked in the center of southern Africa, bordering Namibia to the west and north, Zimbabwe to the northeast, South Africa to the southeast and south, and touching with only 150 meters Zambia in the northeast. The almost 2.4 million citizens (Statistics Botswana 2022: iii) are unevenly distributed in this country of the size of France. While only 353 people (Bird et al. 2023, Table S1) live in the Central Kalahari Game Reserve (52,800 sq. km, about 10% of Botswana's total land area), more than 80 percent of the country's population resides in southeastern and eastern Botswana. Located in this part of the country are the two major urban centers, the capital, Gaborone, with a population of ca. 246,000, and the historic mining town, Francistown, with a population of ca. 103,000 (Statistics Botswana 2022:2, 5). These cities are the main destinations for migrants from within Botswana, neighboring countries, and abroad. Since its independence from the United Kingdom in 1966, it has been the longest uninterrupted democracy in Africa. In the late 1960s, Botswana was one of the world's poorest countries, but today it is among the wealthiest countries in Africa with a fast-growing economy. Botswana has about 28 languages (Andersson & Janson 1997) from five language families. Setswana is the national language spoken by more than 80 percent of the population. Most people in the country are multilingual and speak, besides Setswana, one or several of a plethora of indigenous languages. English is the official language and was introduced in Botswana during the British Protectorate era (1885–1966). This chapter provides insights into the language ecology of Botswana and specifically discusses the roles and relationships among the different languages.

2. A bird's eye view of Botswana's language ecology

Language ecology as a research approach in sociolinguistics was introduced by Einar Haugen in 1972 as "the study of interactions between any given language and its environment" (Haugen 1972:325). As summarized by Creese & Martin (2008:XIII), language ecology is "the study of diversity within specific sociopolitical settings where the processes of language use create, reflect, and challenge particular hierarchies and hegemonies, however transient these might be." Rather than "merely listing languages, varieties, variants, and identifying their rank order and interaction within a country, region or institution", we are concerned here "with understanding processes of domination and resistance" (Deumert 2014:210).

In Botswana, the national language, Setswana, competes with the official language, English, in several domains, such as government administration and education, where English, as the official language, is expected to function as the primary language but faces competition from Setswana, resulting in a "double overlapping diglossia" (Bagwasi 2004:118). Still, both are on the upper part of the power scale in the language hierarchy of the country. On the lower end are the marginalized languages of the so-called 'Basarwa', a cover term imposed by Bantu speakers for the diverse ethnic groups of the former hunter-gatherers. Many of their languages are threatened by extinction due to a lack of recognition and support by the government; they survive through bottom-up initiatives by language communities, who are being assisted by NGOs or Christian missions. However, even the Bantu languages — with the notable exceptions of Setswana and, to a much lesser extent, Ikalanga — receive little attention from the government (Chebanne 2016). Some of these Bantu languages, such as Shiyeyi, are affected by language shift and are losing speakers among the younger generation (Sommer 1995).

In 1966, with the independence of Botswana after 80 years of being a British Protectorate, English became the *de facto* official language of the country[1] and has been the dominant language in the parliament, the administration, and the courts since then. Setswana, the *de facto* national language of the country, is the most widely used language in public domains and is also the medium of instruction when entering public schools in Standard 1 (age 6). According to the Revised National Policy on Education, English then becomes the medium of instruction "from Standard 2 [age 7] or as soon as practical" (Botswana Government 1994: 59). While Setswana is spoken by most citizens, full competence in English is still limited to the educated elite.

"With English [being] established as the official language, and Setswana as the national language, the exclusion of the other indigenous languages continues" (Kamwendo, Mooko & Moumakwa 2009: 221). Languages other than English and Setswana are officially labeled 'minority languages', and among them are Bantu languages, such as Ikalanga, Shekgalagadi, Shiyeyi, and Thimbukushu, the Khoe languages Khwe (Buga), ǁAni, Naro, Ts'ixa, Shua, Tshwa, etc., the Kx'a languages !Xun and ǂAmkoe, the Tuu language Taa, as well as diaspora languages such as Afrikaans, Gujarati, and Kiswahili (Hasselbring, Segatlhe & Munch 2000), and Botswana Sign Language. Minority languages generally do not have a presence in official domains, although there appears to be a gradual shift occurring in at least two areas: the media[2] and education[3]. With the prevailing language hegemony of English and Setswana, speakers of the smaller language communities such as Khwe (Buga), ǁAni, Shiyeyi, and ǂAmkoe are generally at least trilingual in that they acquire the languages of the dominant neighbors as their first additional lan-

---

1. The Constitution of Botswana is written in English, but neither English nor Setswana are assigned *de jure* statuses, as they are not mentioned in the constitution.
2. During the COVID-19 pandemic, some radio stations began tailoring their content to non-Setswana-speaking audiences. This practice has remained in certain stations like the private radio station Duma FM, which continues to broadcast in several Botswanan languages, such as Ikalanga and Shekgalagadi (p.c., Naledi Kgolo-Lotshwao, 2023).
3. A policy change in early 2023 resulted in the introduction of several minority languages as media of instruction in pre-primary and early primary education (Mogara & Chebanne 2023).

guages, followed by Setswana, and only then, if at all, by English. English is the L1 of foreigners from diaspora communities but also of some members of the urban elite; this elite predominantly consists of members of the Tswana and Kalanga communities, who opt to send their children to private English-medium schools. English is the L2 for most other Batswana[4] and Bakalanga[5]. However, for the latter group, Setswana, rather than English, may serve as their L2. For all others, English is acquired as their L3, L4, L5, etc.

With 94 percent of the population of Botswana speaking Bantu languages, these languages dominate the country's language ecology. More than 50 years ago, Guthrie (1967–1971) introduced a coding system for Bantu languages with geographical zones as their primary reference. These zones receive the Roman letters A–S and are numbered starting from the northwestern and proceeding to the southeastern part of Bantu-speaking Africa. While Guthrie's reference system is still in use, it has been revised and updated by Jouni Maho (2003: 639–651; 2009) and more recently by Harald Hammarström (2019). Within the zones, language clusters receive decimal numbers, such as S30 for the Sotho-Tswana group. Within these groupings, individual languages are assigned numbers of two or three digits, such as S31 for Setswana or S311 for Shekgalagadi. Additional Roman letters indicate dialects of languages (e.g., S32E Sebirwa, S32F Setswapong). The Botswanan Bantu languages fall under the Guthrie zones S, R, and K (see Table 1 below).

In Botswana, the omnipresent and exclusive name for the languages spoken by former hunter-gatherers is 'Sesarwa'. This term resembles 'Khoisan', by which colonialists — out of ignorance and disrespect — merged 'Bushman/San' and 'Hottentots/Khoekhoe', as well as their languages. This practice lives on in Botswana in that the terms 'Basarwa' and 'Sesarwa' lump the former hunter-gatherers and their languages, respectively, despite their diverse ethnic identities and distinct languages. The languages of the former hunter-gatherers in Botswana belong to three separate language families, namely Kx'a, Tuu, and Khoe-Kwadi[6] (Güldemann 2014).

---

4. Noun class prefixes are prominent features of Bantu languages. Mo-Tswana and Ba-Tswana mean Tswana person and people, respectively, as the noun class prefixes *mo-* and *ba-* refer mainly to human beings. The prefix *bo-* in Bo-Tswana refers to the land of the Tswana, while the prefix *se-* in Se-Tswana refers to the Tswana language. Noun class prefixes are not identical among the approximately 500 Bantu languages — for example, in Otjiherero, the prefix equivalents for people are Omu-Herero and Ova-Herero, and Mu-Shona and Va-Shona in Chi-Shona.

5. The Bakalanga are an educated elite in the country, with many having completed higher education and being visible in large numbers in the civil service, in the army, in politics, and in higher education (Andersson & Janson 1997: 60). Most Bakalanga are bilingual in Ikalanga and Setswana, with English also being spoken among the educated elite.

6. Kwadi is an extinct language, which was classified as a higher-order relative of the Khoe family. It therefore appears in the label 'Khoe-Kwadi family' at a higher level of classification

The Khoe language family is well-established and consists of Khoekhoegowab (Nama), Naro, Khwe, ǁAni, Gǀui, Gǁana, Ts'ixa, Shua, and Tshwa (Vossen 1997). All of these languages are spoken to various extents in Botswana. Despite Proto-Khoe being associated with pastoralists, all Khoe languages today — except for Khoekhoegowab — are exclusively spoken by people who identify themselves as former hunter-gatherers and who often accept the ethnonyms 'San', 'Bushman', or 'Basarwa'. Language shift of hunter-gatherer communities from their own click-using languages to Khoe languages is one possible explanation for this fact. A shift from pastoralism to a hunter-gatherer mode of life due to the loss of cattle might be another reason for the former hunter-gatherer ('San/Bushman') communities speaking Khoe languages today (Güldemann 2008b).

The few surviving languages associated with the autochthonous foraging societies of southern Africa belong to the Kx'a[7] and Tuu families. The Kx'a and Tuu languages might have a common origin, as they "are structurally surprisingly homogeneous and some of the shared features are rare if not unique on a global level" which might "be due to linguistic inheritance from a common ancestor" (Güldemann 2014: 36). However, this common ancestry cannot be verified partly due to the depth of time, when a possible splitting might have occurred and partly due to the lack of language data, since most of these languages have disappeared undocumented. Today, only four 'Non-Khoe languages', a cover term used for the Tuu and Kx'a languages (Güldemann 2008a), are still spoken: !Xun and ǂAmkoe, which form the Kx'a language family (Heine & Honken 2010), and Taa and Nǀuu, which form the Tuu language family (Güldemann 2014). Three of these languages are found in Botswana: ǂAmkoe (consisting of the ǂHoan, N!aqriaxe, and Sasi varieties) is exclusively spoken in Botswana, while !Xun and Taa are cross-border languages (see Table 2).

Table 1 includes the languages that appear in the intercensal Botswana Demographic Survey conducted in 2017 (Statistics Botswana 2018). The individual languages are presented within their phylum/family, branch, and group. The glossonyms in official use (also in the census) are the Setswana names for the languages. These are followed by the endonyms or autonyms, the language names the speakers themselves use to refer to their languages. (=) indicates that the official Setswana name and the endonym are identical. The revised Guthrie references are provided in the two columns 'code'.

(Güldemann 2014; Güldemann & Fehn 2017). In this chapter, the term 'Khoe family' is used instead, as we are dealing here with languages which are still spoken.

7. Heine & Honken (2010) established the Kx'a language family by reconstructing Proto-Kx'a.

Table 1. Languages of Botswana in the Botswana Demographic Survey of 2017 (Statistics Botswana 2018)

Phylum, family	Branch	Group	Code*	Official glossonym	Endonym	Code	Number of speakers	% of speakers of total	% of group of total
Niger-Congo	Bantu	Shona	S10	Kalanga	Ikalanga	S16	127,596	6.22%	7.27%
				Shona	Chishona	S12	21,466	1.05%	
		Sotho-Tswana	S30	Setswana	(=)	S31	1,571,039	76.63%	83.33%
				Sekgalagari	Shekgalagadi	S311	75,428	3.68%	
				Setswapong	Chegwapong	S32F	33,651	1.64%	
				Sebirwa	(=)	S32E	28,446	1.39%	
		Nguni	S40	Ndebele	Sindebele	S44	14,629	0.71%	0.71%
		Yeyi	R40	Yeyi	Shiyeyi	R41	5,381	0.26%	0.26%
		Herero	R30	Herero	Otjiherero	R31	15,271	0.74%	0.74%
		Subiya-Totela	K40	Subiya	Chiikuhane Chisubiya	K42	6,126	0.30%	0.30%
		Luyana	K30	Mbukushu	Thimbukushu	K333	28,888	1.41%	1.41%
Khoe				Sesarwa	Glui	N/A	29,203	1.42%	1.42%
					G‖ana	N/A			
					‖Ani	N/A			
					Ts'ixa	N/A			
					Shua	N/A			
					Tshwa	N/A			
					Naro	N/A			
					Khwe (Buga)	N/A			
					Nama	N/A			
Kx'a					ǂ'Amkoe	N/A			
					!Xun	N/A			
Tuu					Taa	N/A			
Indo-European	Germanic			English		N/A	63,999	3.12%	3.51%
				Afrikaans		N/A	7,880	0.38%	
N/A	N/A			Sign language		N/A	1,431	0.07%	0.07%
N/A	N/A			Others		N/A	18,779	0.92%	0.92%
N/A	N/A			Unknown**		N/A	1,053	0.05%	0.05%

* Code: Guthrie's code. ** No information provided.

Figure 1 shows the approximate location of speakers of the languages of Botswana listed in Table 1. The grey areas indicate mostly uninhabited territories of national parks.

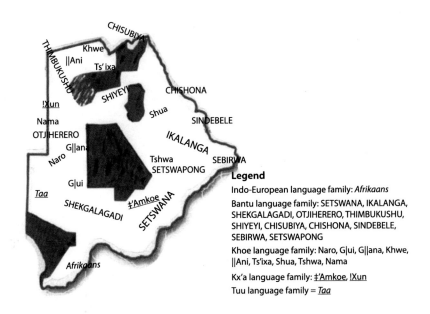

Figure 1. Location of languages in Botswana

At the Berlin Conference of 1884–1885, the colonial powers divided the African continent among themselves on a drawing board by ignoring existing political, language, ethnic, and cultural boundaries and relationships between the different African communities. One effect of this is that many languages in Botswana — like in most other African countries — are spoken across the national borders. Table 2 lists the 25 Botswanan languages from the 2017 Botswana Demographic Survey (Statistics Botswana 2018), of which only eight are exclusively spoken in Botswana. Towards the bottom of the table are those languages which are predominantly spoken in neighboring countries. Even Botswana's national language, Setswana, has more than triple the number of L1 speakers in South Africa, i.e., approximately 5.15 million, which corresponds to 8.3 percent of the total South African population (Statistics South Africa 2023) in contrast to 1.57 million, which is 76.6 percent of the total population of Botswana (Statistics Botswana 2018).

The political stability and economic growth of post-independence Botswana has attracted and still attracts large numbers of migrant workers from other

Table 2. Languages of Botswana and neighboring countries

Language	Family / Branch	Spoken in countries other than Botswana
Shekgalagadi	Bantu	no
Gǀui	Khoe	no
Gǁana	Khoe	no
ǁAni	Khoe	no
Ts'ixa	Khoe	no
Shua	Khoe	no
ǂAmkoe	Kx'a	no
Setswapong	Bantu	no
Ikalanga	Bantu	known as TjiKalanga in Zimbabwe
Tshwa	Khoe	last 9 speakers of the Tjwao in Zimbabwe
Sebirwa	Bantu	few in Zimbabwe and South Africa
Naro	Khoe	less than 10% in Namibia
Taa	Tuu	about 20% in Namibia
Thimbukushu	Bantu	majority in Namibia, very few in Angola and Zambia
Khwe (Buga)	Khoe	mainly in Namibia, some in South Africa, and very few in Angola and Zambia
Shiyeyi	Bantu	fewer in Namibia
Nama	Khoe	more than 95% in Namibia, few in South Africa
Chisubiya	Bantu	mainly in Namibia, very few in Zambia
!Xun	Kx'a	mainly in Namibia
Otjiherero	Bantu	mainly in Namibia
Afrikaans	Germanic	mainly in South Africa, much less in Namibia, very few in Zambia and Zimbabwe
Chishona	Bantu	major language of Zimbabwe, few in Mozambique
Sindebele	Bantu	second largest language in Zimbabwe
Setswana	Bantu	main language in Botswana, but spoken by three times more citizens of South Africa; it is also found in Zimbabwe and Namibia
English	Germanic	global language

African countries, especially from neighboring Zimbabwe (50.5% of all immigrants, Statistics Botswana 2018: 36) and South Africa (21.6% of all immigrants, Statistics Botswana 2018: 36). Most of these foreigners have no command of Setswana (unless they come from the Northwest Province of South Africa, where

Setswana is the principal language, spoken by 72.8% of the province's population, Statistics South Africa 2023: 23), but have competence to various degrees in English.[8] They generally look for work in Gaborone, Francistown, and other urban areas, and the rise in the number of English L1 speakers between the 2001 and the 2017 censuses (see Table 3) derives partly from the growth of immigration into Botswana during these years.[9]

The significant rise in the Otjiherero, Sindebele, and Chishona speaker numbers between 2001 and 2011 (see Table 3) is also the result of immigration. Large numbers of Ovaherero migrated within Namibia, from Hereroland into the Juǀ'hoan area, in search of pasture. From there, many crossed into Botswana with their cattle and stayed in rural areas of Botswana. The Chishona and Sindebele speakers in contrast left their homes in Zimbabwe because of the country's political and economic instability. While many went to South Africa, quite a number came to urban areas of Botswana. The reverse trend in the figures of all three language groups between 2011 and 2017 seems to indicate that many of these immigrants have returned to their home countries or moved on to other countries, such as South Africa.

Table 3. Number of speakers of Sindebele, Chishona, Otjiherero, and English in Botswana in 2001, 2011, and 2017

Language	2001	2011	2017
Sindebele	8,174	18,959	14,629
Chishona	11,308	38,489	21,466
Otjiherero	10,998	18,710	15,271
English	34,433	52,921	63,999

---

8. In cross-border language contact settings, 'non-standard' English varieties are used as lingua franca and are in competition with Afrikaans in the west (Namibia) and south (Northern Cape Province, South Africa), with Chishona and Sindebele in the northeast (Zimbabwe), and with Setswana in the southwest (Northwest Province, South Africa).

9. These towns are also the destination of many jobless people from rural Botswana; however, these internal migrant workers are generally competent in Setswana and much less so in English.

3. English, still a foreign language after 200 years

In the 1820s, the first European missionaries and traders arrived in present day Botswana (formerly Bechuanaland), speaking English and other European languages. The most prominent among the various missionary societies was the London Missionary Society. Because Setswana was used in mission work, it developed in the following decades into the lingua franca of the country, with English playing a minor role in the language ecology. According to Andersson & Janson (1997: 170), "it can safely be said that the use of English in the country before 1885 must have been insignificant." During the more than 80 years in which Bechuanaland was a British Protectorate (1885–1966), the situation hardly changed, and command of English remained restricted to administrators and a small number of Botswanan intellectuals.

With Botswana's independence in 1966, English became the *de facto* official language of the country and was, from then on, used in the parliament, in administration, in courts, and in education. English holds a *de facto* rather than a *de jure* official language status, as the Constitution of Botswana neither designates English as the official language nor addresses language status and use within the country. Bagwasi & Costley (2022: 126) note in this respect that "the country [Botswana] does not have a formally stated national language policy. English and Setswana have acquired their *de facto* roles as official and national languages respectively mostly out of practice rather than legislation." Botswana resembles in this sense Australia, the United Kingdom, and several other countries, which also have no *de jure* official languages. The liberal language policies of neighboring South Africa, which has 12[10] *de jure* official languages, and that of Zimbabwe with 16 *de jure* official languages are in sharp contrast to Botswana's two other neighbors, Namibia and Zambia, which designated English as their sole official language at their independence in 1990 and 1964, respectively. Despite English being either the sole or one of several *de jure* official languages in these four countries, competence in this language seems to remain limited; L1 English speakers amount to 8.7 percent in South Africa (Statistics South Africa 2023), 3.4 percent in Namibia (Namibia Statistics Agency 2011), and 1.7 percent in Zambia (Central Statistical Office Zambia 2012).[11] Since the available census figures for the two latter countries are

---

10. In July 2023, President Cyril Ramaphosa signed a Constitutional Amendment to make Sign Language the 12th official language of South Africa, https://www.gov.za/speeches/president-cyril-ramaphosa-signing-ceremony-south-african-sign-language-bill-19-jul-2023; 01 March 2024.

11. Zimbabwe is not included here, as a census that enumerates people by language has never been conducted in the country.

more than a decade old, one may expect that the number of L1 English speakers might be much higher in these countries today.

With an estimated 35–40 percent of the citizens having at least some knowledge of English, full proficiency is still limited to a small — mainly urban, often educated — minority (Bagwasi 2004: 116), which has led some researchers to argue that English has the status of a foreign language rather than a second language in the country (see, for example, Schmied 1991; Bagwasi 2004). The level of competence in English correlates mainly with the level of formal education (Nkosana 2011) and the type of school attended (private vs. public) (Bagwasi 2004). Given that English is (at least on paper)[12] the primary medium of instruction and that most of the Botswanan population has had some level of education,[13] it is somewhat surprising that English has not made more ground as an L1 yet. Even among university students in Gaborone, only 1 percent named English as their first language in surveys conducted in 1990 and 2008 (Andersson 2014: 306). While English is used extensively in lecture halls and on campus more generally, most students name other Botswanan languages as their L1. In the more recent censuses, a slight trend becomes visible, with English gradually gaining a stronger position over the years: 2.2 percent of the total Botswanan population claimed to use English as their home language in 2001 (Chebanne & Nyati-Ramahobo 2003: 96), which increased to 2.8 percent in 2011 (Statistics Botswana 2014: 42) and to 3.1 percent in 2017 (Statistics Botswana 2018: 64–65). Most of these English-speaking homes are families who can afford the expensive school fees of private English-medium schools. Even in public schools, English is the recommended medium of instruction from Standard 2 onwards and is taught as a school subject from Standard 1. This language policy in the educational sector might contribute to English spreading as an L1 in the wider population. There is also increasing exposure to English in Botswana in other domains. English is the dominant language in the electronic and print media (Friedrich-Ebert-Stiftung 2019)[14] and in

---

12. While the language-in-education policy (LIEP) recommends that Setswana is the medium of instruction in Standard 1 (age 6) and English from Standard 2 (age 7) onwards, Bagwasi & Costley (2022: 136) found that language use in the classroom "is much more fluid and dynamic than that imagined in, or mandated by, the LIEP", with code-switching between English and Setswana being the norm in public schools (Arthur 1996; Chimbganda & Mokgwathi 2012; Mafela 2009; Mokibelo 2016).

13. The 2017 intercensal Botswana Demographic Survey shows that only 15.1 percent of the Botswanan population never attended school (Statistics Botswana 2018: 22–23). In 2017, 90.2 percent of the primary-school-age children were attending school compared to 51.2 percent of the secondary-school-age children (Statistics Botswana 2018: 22).

14. The state radio and television stations broadcast in both English and Setswana (Friedrich-Ebert-Stiftung 2015).

the main tourist destinations, such as the national parks, game farms, and the Okavango Delta.

English generally enjoys superior prestige in the country. While English spreads among the younger generation through formal education and mass media, particularly the internet, television, and radio, older generations primarily acquire English informally, with competence often being limited to oral communication. Historically, full competence in English was confined to a select portion of the population, namely the urban elite who received their education in private schools. However, it is likely that the growing accessibility of electronic media, which allows informal language acquisition regardless of income or educational level, will accelerate the spread of English across various strata of society. Studies focused on the urban-based elite in Botswana emphasize the importance of English for upward social mobility, participation in the national economic and political discourse, and secondary and tertiary education (Bagwasi 2004; Smieja & Mathangwane 2010). According to Schmied (1991: 170), "the English language is seen as a personal asset, as an instrument to promote one's personal career, as a stepping stone to getting a better job and as a social status marker."

Due to Botswana's history of being a British Protectorate, the English spoken in Botswana is modeled on Standard British English (StBrE). While the English varieties of South Africa and Namibia have received considerable scholarly attention, 'Botswana English' (BE) is, by contrast, weakly documented, with only a few descriptive studies and no publicly available language corpus. BE has been subsumed under the umbrella label 'South African Englishes' (Trudgill & Hannah 2017: 127) by suggesting shared features due to geographical proximity, intertwined with cross-border intelligibility, and a joint colonial past. While it is reasonable to expect areal linguistic features extending beyond Botswana's borders,[15] there is nowadays agreement and awareness among Botswanans that a local variety of English, i.e., BE, exists.

Arthur (1994: 65) was one of the first scholars to highlight that the English spoken in Botswana is an "identifiable variety". In most earlier works, BE has been treated as a homogeneous variety (see, i.a., Merkestein 1998; Arua & Magocha 2000; Bagwasi 2002; 2006; Arua 2004), which seems to be the English variety used by the educated elite of the country. In most cases, specific characteristics of BE that are at variance with StBrE have been examined in terms of the structure of Setswana (see, for example, Alimi 2007; 2008; Arua 2004; Arua & Magocha 2000). English varieties that have evolved from contact with other Botswanan languages

---

15. Pronoun doubling (*me I...; us we...*) and the modal *can be able* have been documented not only in Botswana English (Arua 2004), but also in Namibian English (Schneider & Schröder 2021: 286).

or the diaspora languages spoken in Botswana have not yet entered the academic discourse.

BE has been described and characterized from a synchronic perspective (e.g., by Arthur 1994; Arua 2004; Arua & Magocha 2000) and a diachronic perspective (e.g., by Merkestein 1998; Bagwasi 2002; 2006). Arthur (1994: 65) exemplifies the "distinctive formal features on multiple linguistic levels" of BE by providing examples in the areas of phonology (e.g., *live* and *leave* are homophones in BE, with the vowel in both words being pronounced as /iː/), lexicon (e.g., BE *foot it* vs. StBrE *walk*), and syntax (e.g., state verbs in BE are often in the progressive aspect, e.g., BE *I am having a cold* vs. StBrE *I have a cold*). Arua (2004) claims that BE is syntactically closely related to other dialects of English in southern Africa, but is lexically distinct, which is further reiterated by Alimi & Bagwasi (2009). The latter authors illustrate this point by providing examples of borrowed lexical items depicting traditional practices which cannot be translated into English (e.g., the Setswana terms *kgosi* 'chief' and *mophato* 'initiation school') and those which reflect recent socio-political experiences in the country (e.g., Setswana *omang* 'identity card').

StBrE has traditionally been taught in schools in Botswana. Arthur (1994: 65, 67) observed in the 1990s that Botswanan citizens, including teachers, "still defer to standard British English" because BE is considered "deviant and unacceptable". According to her, this negative attitude towards BE stems from the fact that the government imposed StBrE as the prescribed English variety for instruction and was fostered by the "prescriptive influence of expatriate British teachers and teacher trainers". However, a shift in attitude towards BE emerged in the early 2000s. Arua & Magocha (2000: 279) reported a more positive outlook among Botswanans, attributing it to increased exposure to the variety over the previous decade. The participants in their study considered BE to be an internationally acceptable variety, which might even be taught in schools. No recent empirical research on this topic has been undertaken, and further investigation of the present situation is needed. Preliminarily, however, it can be observed that there seems to be a growing acceptance of different English varieties. This is, for example, evidenced by the presence of both local accents and native-like British accents in national broadcasting and public speeches.

4. Setswana, the language of national identity

Setswana emerged as the undeniable choice to become the *de facto* national language and the symbol of national unity and identity. This is not surprising, given

> its long standing lingua franca role serving as an inter-ethnic medium, its history of superiority over the other languages, the demographic and socio-economic predominance of its speakers, and its long association with semi-official functions, particularly in the traditional administration and customary settings as well as during the British indirect rule system. (Batibo 2004: 53)

In addition to the overall presence of Setswana in the country, it seems impossible to be a Botswanan citizen without speaking Setswana fluently and "the Department of Immigration requires immigrants applying for Botswana citizenship to undergo a Setswana test and therefore to be competent in Setswana" (Bagwasi 2021: 47). Batswana who lack proficiency in their ancestral language, Setswana, and are proficient only in English are viewed unfavorably by some, with derogatory terms such as 'Coconuts' and 'Oreos' used to label them (Mibenge 2016).

Botswana differs from many other African countries in that it has a nationwide established autochthonous lingua franca spoken by most of the population as a home language. Setswana is the L1 of 77 percent of the total population (Statistics Botswana 2018: 64–65) and is spoken regularly by another 10 percent of the citizens (Bagwasi 2004: 117). Setswana dominates the multilingual settings in Botswana as a lingua franca, being used in most contexts of daily life, even in the cities. It is the language of everyday communication "in government offices, local business, transport, shops, marketplace, traditional courts and gatherings, political rallies and at home" (Bagwasi 2004: 117).

Table 4 shows that Setswana is a dominant L1 in almost all areas of the country, except for Ghanzi and Kgalagadi, where Shekgalagadi dominates (Statistics Botswana 2018). By contrast, L1 English speakers are not notably present in any region of the country. The highest percentage of L1 English speakers is concentrated in the urban areas of the only two cities of Botswana, Gaborone and Francistown, in the Southeast District which encircles Gaborone, in mining towns with a high proportion of immigrants (Jwaneng, Orapa, Sowa Town, Selebi Phikwe), and in areas which are major tourist destinations (Kasane with the Chobe River).

Robert Moffat (1795–1883), a Scottish missionary, was important in the early promotion of Setswana. He played a crucial role in the production of printed materials in Setswana. Moffat was sent to South Africa by the London Missionary Society in 1816 and spent almost 50 years in Kuruman in the Northern Cape Province of South Africa. During this time, he acquired Setswana and translated and published religious materials in this language from 1830 onwards. Today, he is best known for the first bible translation in Setswana, which he completed in 1857.

Table 4. Number of L1 English and Setswana speakers in Botswana (Statistics Botswana 2018)

District (d) / City (c) / Town (t)	English L1	English L1 %	Setswana L1	Setswana L1 %	Total population
Gaborone (c)	28,473	12.65%	168,684	74.92%	225,146
Francistown (c)	3,774	3.67%	73,012	71.07%	102,739
Lobatse (t)	427	1.56%	26,554	96.96%	27,387
Selebi Phikwe (t)	1,531	3.28%	39,196	83.88%	46,729
Orapa (t)	520	5.39%	8,622	89.39%	9,645
Jwaneng (t)	1,070	7.02%	12,863	84.45%	15,232
Sowa Town (t)	131	3.53%	2,705	72.91%	3,710
Southern (d)	1,613	0.82%	183,422	92.69%	197,891
Southeast (d)	6,539	6.83%	84,097	87.81%	95,774
Kweneng (d)	6,825	2.13%	265,536	82.98%	320,002
Kgatleng (d)	2,588	2.72%	88,832	93.24%	95,273
Central (d)	5,960	1.03%	434,862	74.86%	580,878
Northeast (d)	451	0.75%	32,754	54.29%	60,332
Ngamiland (d)	1,893	1.30%	96,955	66.45%	145,904
Chobe (d)	1,224	4.64%	16,413	62.16%	26,405
Ghanzi (d)	269	0.64%	9,294	22.05%	42,155
Kgalagadi (d)	712	1.29%	27,239	49.46%	55,072

Missionaries like Moffat, and later linguists, developed orthographies for Setswana, often without consulting the speakers of the language and their aspirations. The contributions by Solomon Tshekisho Plaatje (1876–1932)[16] were crucial for the evolution of Setswana. Commonly referred to as Sol Plaatje, he was one of the leading African intellectuals of his time. In one of his last articles before his death in 1932, he criticizes decisions made by foreigners on the orthography of his language. He complains about the white missionaries and scholars who met at a conference entitled 'Standardising a Bantu Language: Conference on Chuana, 50 years' controversy ended' in 1932 (Willan 2016: 456, fn 89). Plaatje strongly

---

[16]. Plaatje was a South African political activist, linguist, translator, as well as writer, who fought for the emancipation of Setswana during the British colonial rule. Plaatje was not only the first General Secretary of the South African Native National Congress, which a decade later became the African National Congress (ANC), but also composed 'Nkosi Sikelel' iAfrika', the current national anthem of South Africa.

objected to the decisions on a standard orthography for Setswana,[17] which were made at this conference without the involvement and consultation of mother-tongue speakers of this language.

While Plaatje is best known for *Mhudi* (written in 1919, published in 1930; Plaatje 1930), the first novel in English by a black South African, the primary focus of his work was on his L1, Setswana. As a journalist, editor, and translator, he published extensively in Setswana and produced — among others — translations of some of William Shakespeare's plays. Plaatje's work had a lasting impact on the evolution of Setswana (Makhudu 2012).

Batswana generally have a positive attitude towards their national language, Setswana. While they learn English "because they benefit from using it, now and in future, in terms of earning respect, getting a job, and communicating internationally", they favor Setswana for integrative reasons, as "it is their national language, part of their culture, and a language the majority of them learned from childhood" (Magogwe 2007: 320). This goes hand in hand with the language preference choices of parents for their children and further shows that the domains in which Setswana and English are used in the country are demarcated. Arua & Magocha (2002) found that despite speaking two, three, or more languages, children in Botswana generally prefer Setswana in most contexts. Still, parents commonly encourage their children to speak English rather than Setswana in school because of the numerous advantages associated with competence in English. Nevertheless, Setswana remains the most commonly used language in the home environment. Given the positive attitudes towards Setswana, it is not surprising that shift, both linguistically and culturally, to Setswana has been documented for several communities in the country (e.g., from Shekgalagadi to Setswana, see Monaka 2013, and from the Shua dialects 'ǀXaise' and 'Shuakwe' to Setswana, see Batibo 1998), see Section 5 for more details.

5. Language hierarchies and hegemonies

Many of Botswana's smaller languages are threatened by being replaced by bigger languages. The dominance of a colonial language is often the cause of language endangerment, especially when English is part of the language repertoire. However, in many parts of Africa, the threat tends to come from the regionally dominant or nationally dominant languages, i.e., other African languages (Batibo 2005;

---

[17]. Unlike with Sesotho, where different official orthographies exist in Lesotho and South Africa, the same orthography is used for Setswana in Botswana and South Africa (Sebolela 2009).

Brenzinger, Heine & Sommer 1991; Connell 2015). In the case of Botswana, languages like Shekgalagadi, spoken across much of the interior of Botswana, Naro, a lingua franca in the Ghanzi area, and Setswana, the country's national language, are replacing some of the smaller languages. As mentioned in Section 3, English generally does not seem to have much of an impact on the day-to-day life of the average person in Botswana, especially in the countryside (see Mogara et al. 2017 for a case study in parts of rural northeastern Botswana).

An example where a local language is replaced by the regionally dominant languages rather than English has been provided by Nakagawa (Tanaka & Sugawara 2010: 85–86) for the G|ui and G||ana communities. Language repertoires and use patterns among G|ui and G||ana speakers vary depending on the language contact settings. While there are 'healthy' areas (such as inside the Central Kalahari Game Reserve) in which also the younger generation speaks G|ui and G||ana as their first and main language, Nakagawa noticed a shift to Naro[18] in one settlement (East Hanahai) and to Shekgalagadi in various other settlements (in the Khute District) (Tanaka & Sugawara 2010: 85–86). These language shifts are mainly due to intermarriage, which is common among the G|ui and G||ana, but also due to work opportunities, as many community members migrate between farms, cattle posts, and towns, often in response to seasonal shifts, employment opportunities, or social relationships (p.c., Junko Maruyama, 2014).

Another example of language shift to a regionally dominant language has been reported by Gerlach & Berthold (2011) for the ǂAmkoe. ǂAmkoe is a highly endangered language spoken in the Kweneng District of Botswana. Children no longer acquire the ancestral language, ǂAmkoe, but instead grow up with Shekgalagadi, the local lingua franca. Even those elders who still speak ǂAmkoe are also fluent in Shekgalagadi. In addition, most ǂAmkoe speakers are in contact with G|ui (Khoe) and some with Taa (Tuu) (see Gerlach & Berthold 2014: 211). Competence in Setswana varies and is higher among the younger members of the community, as they are educated in Setswana (Gerlach & Berthold 2011: 7). Knowledge of English remains low or non-existent, even among the younger generation.

Setswana has become the most prominent replacing language among speakers of Bantu languages. For example, language shift from Shekgalagadi to Setswana has

---

[18]. Naro enjoys significant prestige and appreciation not only among its L1 speakers, but also among the numerous L2 speakers, who are mainly G|ui, G||ana, and Taa (Gabanamotse-Mogara & Batibo 2016: 107). Among them, Naro is the lingua franca in many contexts. The positive attitude towards Naro is in large part due to the highly commendable work done by the Naro Language Project based in D'Kar conducted by Hessel and Coby Visser over a period of several decades (Batibo 2009). The project has played a key role in describing, codifying, and producing teaching and learning materials for Naro, and has increased literacy among the Naro people by teaching children to read and write in their language.

been reported by Vossen (1988), Lukusa (2000), and Monaka (2013), with some of the regional varieties of Shekgalagadi such as SheBolaongwe and SheShaga having almost disappeared (Chebanne 2016: 161). Even among the non-Bantu languages, cases of language shift to Setswana have been observed. Examples from the Khoe language family are provided below.

Ts'ixa is spoken in the village of Mababe in northern Botswana. Although it is used in daily communication by most adult community members, it is nonetheless threatened due to its small community size (less than 200 speakers) and the lack of intergenerational language transmission. Children are generally addressed in Setswana by their parents, and many young Ts'ixa are educated in boarding schools, in which Setswana and English are used as media of instruction. In these boarding schools, they are alienated, not only from their environment and culture but also from their language. They often feel more at ease speaking Setswana, the language they predominantly use in the boarding schools, rather than Ts'ixa, their heritage language; with the latter, they often retain only a passive competence (Fehn 2016: 13).

In the case of ǁAni and the Buga variety of Khwe, even though both are still spoken by hundreds of people in northern Botswana, many of the younger community members have shifted to Setswana as their L1 due to formal education but also due to an improvement of the infrastructure (Brenzinger 2013: 22–23). While they used to live remotely in rural areas of Ngamiland with poor infrastructure, they have moved over the last decades and now live near roads, and with that are connected to more urban settings, in which the use of Setswana prevails.

One way of conceptualizing language endangerment in complex language repertoires found in rural settings on the African continent is the "language repertoire onion model" (Brenzinger & Shah 2024: 4). It states that within the language repertoires, the closest languages in the language hierarchies are the most likely replacing languages. Brenzinger (2001) introduced this model and applied it to various language shift situations in Ethiopia. For example, 'Ongota has now been completely replaced by Ts'amay, which itself is also a highly endangered language that faces a high risk of being replaced by Gawwada. The languages in the outermost layers of the onion, which are at the top of the hierarchy, namely Amharic and English, are not playing any role in the language replacement as they are highly unlikely to become the L1 of the speakers of these small languages. Language shift in Botswana among the former hunter-gatherer communities is far less complex than in the Ethiopian example above, but generally still seems to follow the same principle, i.e., Naro, Shekgalagadi, and Setswana are replacing languages, while English at the top of the hierarchy does not replace Botswanan minority languages.

6. Summary and outlook

English and Setswana are at the top of the language hierarchy of Botswana, with English serving as a conduit for social mobility and job market success, while Setswana retains its role in fostering unity and social cohesion. Other Bantu languages, such as Ikalanga and Shekgalagadi, are primarily home languages, being used rarely in public domains. At the bottom of the language power scale are the languages of the former hunter-gatherer communities, namely the Khoe, Tuu, and Kx'a languages, often subsumed under the misnomer 'Sesarwa'.

The home languages of most Botswanan citizens are Bantu languages of the southeastern and southwestern branches. The Bantu language, Setswana, which serves as the national language, is spoken by the vast majority of the citizens of Botswana and is the language used most widely in almost all domains. Some of the smaller linguistic communities struggle to preserve their languages amid cultural assimilation and economic pressures and face extinction as Setswana and regionally dominant languages replace them. This is especially the case with the numerically small former hunter-gatherer communities, as in the case of some G|ui and G||ana who are shifting to Naro and Shekgalagadi, but also among Bantu languages such as Shiyeyi, which is currently being replaced by Setswana.

English, historically confined to the educated elite, seems to now be penetrating various societal strata through electronic media, which increasingly facilitates informal language acquisition, irrespective of one's income or educational background. The existing studies of BE have focused on the English varieties of the educated elite of the country and have treated BE as a homogeneous variety. To the best of my knowledge, no descriptive studies of BE have been carried out which consider regional, generational, and social varieties of English in the country. Moreover, no studies exist which consider the impact on English from L1s other than Setswana. With English no longer being limited to the educated elite, there is a need for further investigation into these linguistic dynamics.

Acknowledgements

I wish to extend my gratitude to Matthias Brenzinger and Naledi Kgolo-Lotshwao for valuable suggestions and constructive feedback on an earlier draft. Additionally, my thanks go to Matthias Brenzinger for creating the map in Figure 1.

References

Alimi, Modupe M. 2007. English articles and modals in the writing of some Batswana students. *Language, Culture and Curriculum* 20(3): 209–222.

Alimi, Modupe M. 2008. English pronouns in the writing of some Batswana students. *Marang: Journal of Language and Literature* 18(1): 85–101.

Alimi, Modupe M. & Mompoloki Mmangaka Bagwasi. 2009. Aspects of culture and meaning in Botswana English. *Journal of Asian and African Studies* 44: 199–214.

Andersson, Lars-Gunnar. 2014. Language ecology in Africa. The case of Botswana. In Wim Vandenbussche, Ernst Håkon Jahr & Peter Trudgill (eds.), *Language Ecology for the 21st Century: Linguistic Conflicts and Social Environments*, pp. 293–315. Oslo: Novus Press.

Andersson, Lars-Gunnar & Tore Janson. 1997. *Languages in Botswana: Language Ecology in Southern Africa*. Gaborone: Longman Botswana.

Arthur, Jo. 1994. English in Botswana primary classrooms: Functions and constraints. In Casmir M. Rubagumya (ed.), *Teaching and Researching Language in African Classrooms*, pp. 63–78. Clevedon: Multilingual Matters.

Arthur, Jo. 1996. Code switching and collusion: Classroom interaction in Botswana primary schools. *Linguistics and Education* 8(1): 17–33.

Arua, Arua E. 2004. Botswana English: Some syntactic and lexical features. *English World-Wide* 25(2): 255–272.

Arua, Arua E. & Keoneng Magocha. 2000. Attitudes of parents to their children's use of English in Botswana. *Language, Culture and Curriculum* 13(3): 279–290.

Arua, Arua E. & Keoneng Magocha. 2002. Patterns of language use and language preference of some children and their parents in Botswana. *Journal of Multilingual and Multicultural Development* 23(6): 449–461.

Bagwasi, Mompoloki Mmangaka. 2002. A Historical Development of a Botswana Variety of English. Ph.D. dissertation, Indiana University.

Bagwasi, Mompoloki Mmangaka. 2004. The functional distribution of Setswana and English in Botswana. In Margaret Jepkirui Muthwii & Angelina Nduku Kioko (eds.), *New Language Bearings in Africa*, pp. 116–121. Clevedon: Multilingual Matters.

Bagwasi, Mompoloki Mmangaka. 2006. A developing model of Botswana English. In Arua E. Arua, Mompoloki Mmangaka Bagwasi, Tiro Sebina & Barolong Seboni (eds.), *The Study and Use of English in Africa*, pp. 115–132. Newcastle upon Tyne: Cambridge Scholars Press.

Bagwasi, Mompoloki Mmangaka. 2021. Education, multilingualism and bilingualism in Botswana. *International Journal of the Sociology of Language* 2021(267-268): 43–54.

Bagwasi, Mompoloki Mmangaka & Tracey Costley. 2022. A defiance of language policy: Seamless boundaries between languages in Botswana classrooms. *Journal of the British Academy* 10(s4): 125–140.

Batibo, Herman Michael. 1998. The fate of the Khoesan languages of Botswana. In Matthias Brenzinger (ed.), *Endangered Languages in Africa*, pp. 267–284. Cologne: Rüdiger Köppe.

Batibo, Herman Michael. 2004. Setswana: An under-exploited national resource? In Katrin Bromber & Birgit Smieja (eds.), *Globalisation and African Languages*, pp. 53–63. Berlin: De Gruyter Mouton.

Batibo, Herman Michael. 2005. *Language Decline and Death in Africa: Causes, Consequences and Challenges*. Clevedon: Multilingual Matters.

Batibo, Herman Michael. 2009. Language documentation as a strategy for the empowerment of the minority languages of Africa. In Masangu Matondo, Fiona McLaughlin & Eric Potsdam (eds.), *Selected Proceedings of the 38th Annual Conference on African Linguistics: Linguistic Theory and African Language Documentation*, pp. 193–203. Somerville, MA: Cascadilla Proceedings Project.

Bird, Tharina L., Smith Moeti, Robert K. Hitchcock, Melinda C. Kelly, Lefang L. Chobolo, Nonofo Gotcha, Kgosi K. Moatlhodi, Leungo D. Mukoka, Emmanuel K. Sekopo & Caroline S. Chaboo. 2023. Orb-web spider Argiope (Araneidae) as indigenous arrow poison of G/ui and G//ana San hunters in the Kalahari. *PLOS ONE* 18(1): e0276557.

Botswana Government. 1994. *The Revised National Policy on Education*. Gaborone: Government Printer.

Brenzinger, Matthias. 2001. Language endangerment through marginalization and globalization. *Lectures on Endangered Languages* 2: 91–116.

Brenzinger, Matthias. 2013. The twelve modern Khoisan languages. In Alena Witzlack-Makarevich & Martina Ernszt (eds.), *Khoisan Languages and Linguistics. Proceedings of the 3rd International Symposium* (Research in Khoisan Studies 29), pp. 1–31. Cologne: Rüdiger Köppe.

Brenzinger, Matthias & Sheena Shah. 2024. Endangered languages. In Hilary Nesi & Petar Milin (eds.), *International Encyclopedia of Language and Linguistics*, 3rd edn, pp. 1–7. Amsterdam: Elsevier.

Brenzinger, Matthias, Bernd Heine & Gabriele Sommer. 1991. Language death in Africa. *Diogenes* 39(153): 19–44.

Central Statistical Office Zambia. 2012. *Zambia 2010 Census of Population and Housing: National Analytical Report*. Lusaka: Central Statistical Office.

Chebanne, Anderson Monthusi. 2016. Found and lost languages: A survey of the past and current situation of Botswana ethic and linguistic communities. *Botswana Notes and Records* 48: 160–175.

Chebanne, Anderson Monthusi & Lydia Nyati-Ramahobo. 2003. Language use and language knowledge in Botswana. *Proceedings of the CSO: 2001 Population and Housing Census Dissemination Seminar, 8–11 September 2003*, pp. 392–404. Gaborone: Government Printer.

Chimbganda, Ambrose B. & Tsaona S. Mokgwathi. 2012. Code-switching in Botswana's ESL Classrooms: A paradox of linguistic policy in education. *International Journal of English Linguistics* 2(2): 21–32.

Connell, Bruce. 2015. The role of colonial languages in language endangerment in Africa. In James Essegbey, Brent Henderson & Fiona Mc Laughlin (eds.), *Language Documentation and Endangerment in Africa*, pp. 107–130. Amsterdam: John Benjamins.

Creese, Angela & Peter Martin. 2008. Preface. In Angela Creese, Peter Martin & Nancy Hornberger (eds.), *Encyclopedia of Language and Education, Vol. 9: Ecology of Language*, pp. i–vi. New York, NY: Springer.

Deumert, Ana. 2014. South Africa's language ecology — Hierarchies, hegemonies and resistances. In Wim Vandenbussche, Ernst Håkon Jahr & Peter Trudgill (eds.), *Language Ecology for the 21st Century: Linguistic Conflicts and Social Environments*, pp. 209–240. Oslo: Novus Press.

Fehn, Anne-Maria. 2016. A Grammar of Ts'ixa (Kalahari Khoe). Ph.D. dissertation, University of Cologne.

Friedrich-Ebert-Stiftung. 2015. *African Media Barometer: The First Home Grown Analysis of the Media Landscape in Africa*. Windhoek: Friedrich-Ebert-Stiftung.

Friedrich-Ebert-Stiftung. 2019. *African Media Barometer: The First Home Grown Analysis of the Media Landscape in Africa*. Windhoek: Friedrich-Ebert-Stiftung.

Gabanamotse-Mogara, Budzani & Herman Michael Batibo. 2016. Ambivalence regarding linguistic and cultural choices among minority language speakers: A case study of the Khoesan youth of Botswana. *African Study Monographs* 37(3): 103–115.

Gerlach, Linda & Falko Berthold. 2011. The sociolinguistic situation of ǂHoan, a moribund "Khoisan" language of Botswana. *Afrikanistik Online* 2011(8). http://www.afrikanistik-online.de/archiv/2011/3164 (11 October 2024).

Gerlach, Linda & Falko Berthold. 2014. N!aqriaxe (ǂ'Amkoe) spatial terms from a genealogical and areal perspective. In Tom Güldemann & Anne-Maria Fehn (eds.), *Beyond 'Khoisan': Historical Relations in the Kalahari Basin*, pp. 209–232. Amsterdam: John Benjamins.

Güldemann, Tom. 2008a. Greenberg's "case" for Khoisan: The morphological evidence. In Dymitr Ibriszimow (ed.), *Problems of Linguistic Historical Reconstruction in Africa*, pp. 123–153. Cologne: Rüdiger Köppe.

Güldemann, Tom. 2008b. A linguist's view: Khoe-Kwadi speakers as the earliest food-producers of southern Africa. *South African Humanities* 20: 93–132.

Güldemann, Tom. 2014. 'Khoisan' language classification today. In Tom Güldemann & Anne-Maria Fehn (eds.), *Beyond 'Khoisan': Historical Relations in the Kalahari Basin*, pp. 1–41. Amsterdam: John Benjamins.

Güldemann, Tom & Anne-Maria Fehn. 2017. The Kalahari Basin Area as a 'Sprachbund' before the Bantu Expansion. In Raymond Hickey (ed.), *The Cambridge Handbook of Areal Linguistics* (Cambridge Handbooks in Language and Linguistics), pp. 500–526. Cambridge: Cambridge University Press.

Guthrie, Malcolm. 1967–1971. *Comparative Bantu: An Introduction to the Comparative Linguistics and Prehistory of the Bantu Languages*, 4 Vols. Farnborough: Gregg International Publishers.

Hammarström, Harald. 2019. An inventory of Bantu languages. In Mark Van de Velde, Koen Bostoen, Derek Nurse & Gérard Philippson (eds.), *The Bantu Languages*, 2nd edn, pp. 17–78. London: Routledge.

Hasselbring, Sue, Thabiso Segatlhe & Julie Munch. 2000. *A Sociolinguistic Survey of the Languages of Botswana*. Mogoditshane: Tasalls.

Haugen, Einar Ingvald. 1972. *The Ecology of Language: Essays by Einar Haugen*. Stanford, CA: Stanford University Press.

Heine, Bernd & Henry Honken. 2010. The Kx'a family: A new Khoisan genealogy. *Journal of Asian and African Studies* 79: 5–36.

Kamwendo, Gregory, Theophilus Mooko & Tshiamiso Moumakwa. 2009. International languages and education in Botswana and Malawi: A comparative study. *Language Problems and Language Planning* 33(3): 218–233.

Lukusa, Stephen Tchidiessa M. 2000. The Shekgalagadi struggle for survival: Aspects of language maintenance and shift. In Herman Michael Batibo & Birgit Smieja (eds.), *Botswana: The Future of the Minority Languages*, pp. 55–77. Frankfurt: Peter Lang.

Mafela, Lily. 2009. Code-switching in Botswana history classrooms in the decade of education for sustainable development. *Language Matters* 40(1): 56–79.

Magogwe, Joel M. 2007. An investigation into attitudes and motivation of Botswana secondary school students towards English, Setswana and indigenous languages. *English World-Wide* 28(3): 311–328.

Maho, Jouni Filip. 2003. A classification of the Bantu languages: An update of Guthrie's referential system. In Derek Nurse & Gérard Philippson (eds.), *The Bantu Languages*, pp. 639–651. London: Routledge.

Maho, Jouni Filip. 2009. *NUGL Online: The online version of the New Updated Guthrie List, a referential classification of the Bantu languages.* Version dated 4th June 2009. https://brill.com/fileasset/downloads_products/35125_Bantu-New-updated-Guthrie-List.pdf (11 October 2024).

Makhudu, Papi Dennis Khekhethi. 2012. Sol T. Plaatje and Setswana: Contributions Towards Language Development. Ph.D. dissertation, University of Limpopo.

Merkestein, Aria. 1998. Deculturizing Englishes: The Botswana context. *World Englishes* 17(2): 171–185.

Mibenge, Catherine. 2016. English language: A 'tool' for social connectedness: A study of native teens in Botswana. *Power and Education* 8(2): 196–202.

Mogara, Budzani & Anderson Monthusi Chebanne. 2023. Local language as a resource for sustainable development: Way forward for implementing local language teaching in Botswana. *Mosenodi: International Journal of the Educational Studies* 26(1): 1–12.

Mogara, Budzani, Ethelbert Kari, Maxwell Kadenge & Dipogiso Molefhi. 2017. Investigating language vitality in some parts of North Eastern Botswana. *Marang: Journal of Language and Literature* 29: 9–30.

Mokibelo, Eureka. 2016. Code-switching: A strategy for teaching and learning or a problem in Botswana? *Research & Reviews: Journal of Educational Studies* 2(4): 30–38.

Monaka, Kemmonye C. 2013. A sociolinguistic study of Shekgalagari: Issues of survival in the shadow of Setswana. *Nawa Journal and Language and Communication* 7(2): 42–53.

Namibia Statistics Agency. 2011. *Namibia 2011: Population and Housing Census Main Report.* Windhoek: Namibia Statistics Agency.

Nkosana, Leonard B. M. 2011. Language policy and planning in Botswana. *The African Symposium: An Online Journal of the African Educational Research Network* 11(1): 129–137.

Plaatje, Solomon Tshekisho. 1930. *Mhudi: An Epic of South African Native Life a Hundred Years Ago.* Alice, South Africa: Lovedale Press.

Schmied, Josef J. 1991. *English in Africa. An Introduction.* New York, NY: Longman.

Schneider, Edgar W. & Anne Schröder. 2021. The dynamics of English in Namibia: A World Englishes perspective. In Anne Schröder (ed.), *The Dynamics of English in Namibia: Perspectives on an Emerging Variety*, pp. 275–297. Amsterdam: John Benjamins.

Sebolela, Fannie. 2009. *The Compilation of Corpus-Based Setswana Dictionaries.* Ph.D. dissertation, University of Pretoria.

Smieja, Birgit & Joyce T. Mathangwane. 2010. The development of English in Botswana: Language policy and education. In Andy Kirkpatrick (ed.), *The Routledge Handbook of World Englishes*, pp. 212–228. London: Routledge.

Sommer, Gabriele. 1995. *Ethnographie des Sprachwechsels: Sozialer Wandel und Sprachverhalten bei den Yeyi (Botswana)* (Sprachkontakt in Afrika 2). Cologne: Rüdiger Köppe.

Statistics Botswana. 2014. *Population and Housing Census 2011.* Gaborone: Statistics Botswana.

Statistics Botswana. 2018. *Botswana Demographic Survey Report 2017.* Gaborone: Statistics Botswana.

Statistics Botswana. 2022. *Population & Housing Census 2022: Population of Cities, Towns, Villages & Associated Localities.* Gaborone: Statistics Botswana.

Statistics South Africa. 2023. *P0301.4 – Census 2022: Statistical Release.* Pretoria: Statistics South Africa.

Tanaka, Jiro & Kazuyoshi Sugawara (eds.). 2010. *An Encyclopedia of ǀGui and ǁGana Culture and Society.* Kyoto: Laboratory of Cultural Anthropology, Graduate School of Human and Environmental Studies, Kyoto University.

Trudgill, Peter & Jean Hannah. 2017. *International English: A Guide to Varieties of English Around the World*, 6th edn. London: Routledge.

Vossen, Rainer. 1988. *Patterns of Language Knowledge and Language Use in Ngamiland, Botswana* (African Studies Series 13). Bayreuth: Eckhard Breitinger.

Vossen, Rainer. 1997. *Die Khoe-Sprachen: Ein Beitrag zur Erforschung der Sprachgeschichte Afrikas* (Quellen zur Khoisan – Forschung 12). Cologne: Rüdiger Köppe.

Willan, Brian (ed.). 2016. *Sol Plaatje: Selected Writings.* Johannesburg: Wits University Press.

CHAPTER 4

English in the multilingual ecology of anglophone and francophone Cameroon

Gardy Stein
University of Hamburg

Even in comparison to the extensive multilingualism on the African continent, the linguistic ecology of Cameroon is special. In addition to a vast diversity of indigenous languages, it has two official languages, English and French, the lingua franca Cameroon Pidgin English (CPE), and the emerging urban code Camfranglais, all of which compete for domains and usage. To better understand the dynamics at work in Cameroon, this chapter presents a summary of existing literature on the unique linguistic situation of this Central African state, combining the findings of recent studies to form a tentative overview of its multilingual ecology. A special focus lies on the varieties of English used and their relationship with local languages, CPE, and French, thus presenting a holistic view of what position English takes in Cameroon today. While being a minority language in terms of speaker numbers, English becomes more important as the language of globalization, as even francophone parents seek English-medium instruction for their children. Reflecting the ongoing, in many cases hostile debate on the use of the two official languages as well as the promotion of national languages, results from empirical studies about language attitudes of francophone and anglophone Cameroonians are discussed. The author adds findings from her research on francophone adolescents in Yaoundé, which seem to herald a more conciliatory point of view.

Keywords: bilingualism, Cameroon, Cameroonian English, Camfranglais, language attitudes, multilingual ecology of Cameroon

1. Introduction

In the pantheon of multilingual ecologies in Africa, Cameroon occupies a special position because of its unique historical and sociolinguistic situation. It is one of those African countries in which a multitude of languages is spoken: the estimated number ranges from 248 (Tadadjeu & Mba 1996, as cited in Anchimbe 2006a: 100) to 279 (Eberhard, Simons & Fennig 2023). In the aftermath of the First World War, the then Kamerun, a German protectorate since 1884, was divided unevenly by the League of Nations in March 1916. The western part bordering on Nigeria was put under British, the rest of the territory under French administration (Echu 2004). After the independence of French Cameroon and Nigeria in 1960, a referendum was held in the British-dominated Cameroonian region in 1961. As a result, its smaller northern part was integrated into Nigeria, while the bigger southern part united with French Cameroon, thus yielding the republic's borders that are existent until today (Wolf 2001).

1.1 The development of official French-English bilingualism in Cameroon

After the unification of the Cameroonian anglophone and francophone[1] parts, both French and English were chosen as official languages. Today's constitution, first drafted in 1960, states concerning national language use:

> The official languages of the Republic of Cameroon shall be English and French, both languages having the same status. The State shall guarantee the promotion of bilingualism throughout the country. It shall endeavour to protect and promote national languages.[2]

Cameroon has attempted to pursue a bilingual language policy, the challenge of which lies in the discrepancies in number, size, and power between the two linguistic areas: the smaller anglophone part covers around 1/5th of the country's territory in which around 20 percent of Cameroon's inhabitants live and have English as their official language, while most of the remaining 80 percent live in the bigger francophone part (Dassé 2014: 118; other sources put the numbers at 25% vs. 75%, e.g., Takam 2007: 26). It is in the latter that the capital and the presidential residence are located, making French the language of government and most official affairs.

A comprehensive overview of the first 40 years of bilingualism is given in Kouega, who describes in detail the state's efforts to promote official bilingualism in Cameroon, including educational policies (see Section 1.2) and the establishment of so-called "Pilot Centers", where civil servants and interested citizens can learn the second official language (1999: 40). When describing the reality in the public service sector, though, he states that English and French did not achieve "the same status", since most state affairs are handled in French, and concludes

---

1. Following Biloa & Echu (2008: 200), the terms Anglophone and Francophone will be capitalized whenever they denote a person; in adjectival use, they will not be capitalized.
2. Art. 1.3 of the Constitution of Cameroon (https://www.ilo.org/dyn/natlex/docs /ELECTRONIC/43107/97788/F-2103476279/CMR43107Eng.pdf; 03 December 2024.)

that the declaration in the constitution did not result in widespread bilingualism among the population (Kouega 1999: 42).

Several studies have assessed the linguistic competence of different segments of the inhabitants of Cameroon over the past decades (Kouega 1999; Tchoungui 1977, 1983), and most of them conclude that citizens fluent in both official languages are a minority. Thus, "only 28% of the children in the francophone towns speak CamE [Cameroon English, see Section 2.3], and only 22% of the children in the anglophone towns speak French" (Tchoungui 1983: 93). In 2005, the official bilingualism rates for English and French are given as 11.5 percent for men and 8.9 percent for women aged 15 and older (Ayafor & Green 2017: 15).

1.2 English and French in education

Especially in education, a rigorous definition and application of language policies[3] for Cameroon have long been lacking. Although important objectives for the teaching of the two official languages throughout the country do exist on paper, there are no strict regulations in place to make sure they are implemented (Pütz 2020: 320). As "most kids leave primary school with a limited knowledge of the other official language" (Kouega 1999: 41), in 1998, a new *Education Orientation Law* was supposed to intensify the teaching of English for Francophones and French for Anglophones, but the fact that qualified teachers were lacking hindered success (Takam & Fassé 2020: 72). In fact, it was only in 2001 that a new law was issued which made both official languages obligatory in primary school (Takam 2007: 33).

In a more recent study, Takam & Fassé analyze the current state of affairs and come to the conclusion that the language policy in education is "mostly based on indifference and laissez-faire [...]" and that there are few or no governmental controls if and how the educational goals are met (Takam & Fassé 2020: 69). This is one of the reasons for the failure of the program known as *opération bilinguisme*, which had as its goal the "progressive acquisition of bilingualism" as stated by former president Ahidjo (quoted by Ayafor 2005: 5).[4] Most schools continued to focus on English in West Cameroon and French in East Cameroon (Wolf 2001: 136), and even in secondary education, "very little linguistic competence is acquired during the seven years of schooling" (Kouega 2010: 204). Studying the language use of 170 students of the University Youndé II (Soa), Kouega finds that French-English bilingualism hardly exists, claiming that Francophones use French and Anglophones use Pidgin or English for communication on and off campus (2010: 203).

---

3. The official bilingualism policy of Cameroon in education is well documented in studies such as Ayafor (2005), Kouega (1999, 2005), Tchoungui (1977), and Takam (2007).

4. For a further discussion of the reasons for this failure, see Fassé (2012).

This situation might be about to change, however. There are many local experiments to promote bilingualism, such as the "dual-curriculum bilingual education programme" (not officially acknowledged; Takam & Fassé 2020: 76–77) or the "Content and Language Integrated Learning", a state-run project in selected secondary schools (Takam & Fassé 2020: 80–81), both successful models for children attaining bilingual fluency. As mentioned above, English in francophone schools and French in anglophone schools is compulsory by now, and the teaching of both languages seems to be effective, at least in urban areas (personal conversation with Christiane A. Nsom, March 5th 2023). It might, thus, be a mere matter of time until Cameroon's citizens become truly bilingual in the official languages — as long as ideologies do not stand in their way, a problem that will be discussed in the next section.

1.3 The 'Anglophone Crisis'

In a setting where the imbalance in using the official languages is mirrored in an imbalance in the distribution of political power, nation-building proves rather difficile. The division into East and West Cameroon is largely a cultural division that originates in the French and British colonial administrations and is still reflected in the different official languages used in the respective regions.[5] Cameroonians identify with either French or English as "their" language, leading to alienation and feelings of contempt for the "other" (Biloa & Echu 2008: 212).

In November 2016, the latent tensions between anglophone and francophone Cameroon erupted into a grim, civil-war-like situation that has been termed *Anglophone Crisis* (French: 'crise anglophone'). Konings & Nyamnjoh, who state that the linguistic division of the two parts of the country and the minority status of the anglophone citizens hinder the forging of national unity, discuss the political roots of the so-called *anglophone problem* that led to the crisis in Cameroon (1997: 207). In their opinion, grievances such as the Anglophones' under-representation in political decision-making processes, the drain of the region's resources, and attempts at their "frenchification" (Konings & Nyamnjoh 1997: 211) were the most important reasons for the growing dissatisfaction of the English-speaking minority in Cameroon; and the authors even foresaw the escalation of the situation (Konings & Nyamnjoh 1997: 229). A timeline of the conflict is found in Kamé (2018), Okereke (2018), and in a report by the International Crisis Group (2017), the latter including valuable suggestions for ending it.

---

5. As Eko explains, "The country effectively has a de facto "one country, two systems" situation in education, law, and the press" (Eko 2003: 89).

The influence of the crisis on the Cameroonian English in use in the anglophone region as well as the subsequent influence of certain novel linguistic forms on attitudes and identity of the Anglophones is analyzed by Nkwain, who suggests that a form of "Ambazonian English"[6] might develop as a result of these sociopolitical circumstances (2021: 26). Discussing the 'anglophone problem' from a sociolinguistic point of view, Eko focuses on the role of the English-language press in raising awareness and forging an anglophone sentiment (2003: 101). He adds that "the Internet [...] has greatly contributed to the forming and maintenance of an Anglophone identity" (Eko 2003: 100).

The discussion above explains in part why, today, English and French do not act as neutral languages in Cameroon (Wolf 2001). On the one hand, French-speaking Cameroonians despise English because it is seen as the identity marker of the Anglophones (Ayafor 2007: 58) while, on the other hand, francophone parents try to secure English-based education for their children because of the international value of the language (Fonyuy 2010).

Slowly, however, the voices bemoaning the marginal position of English are heard and measures are taken to accommodate their demands. Since 2006, the *National Week of Bilingualism* has been celebrated annually nationwide. In 2017, the *National Commission on the Promotion of Bilingualism and Multiculturalism* was created to promote bilingualism and the peaceful coexistence of Cameroonian cultures (NCPBM 2017). More importantly, on December 24th 2019, a new law was promulgated which states that "[t]he official languages of Cameroon [English and French] shall have equal value" (Republic of Cameroon 2019: Chapter I, Section 2.2) and that "[u]sers shall have the right to ask to be rendered service in any of the official languages" (Republic of Cameroon 2019: Chapter III, Section 13.3). In its wake, all ministerial departments of Cameroon were visited by mission teams to "evaluate the practice of bilingualism in the issuance of official documents" (Amabo 2020).

After the most important historical developments in language policy and education as well as the political movements that have shaped the actual sociolinguistic situation in the country have been presented, Section 2 will discuss Cameroon's multilingual ecology. Section 3 then turns to the field of language attitudes, before Section 4 summarizes the findings and discusses possible future research questions.

---

6. "Ambazonia" is the name that those striving for independence of the anglophone regions from Cameroon have given to their homeland, inspired by the Portuguese name of the region: Ambas Bay. On October 1st 2017, different secessionist groups even joined forces in an official "declaration of the independence of Ambazonia" (Okereke 2018: 11).

2. The multilingual ecology of Cameroon today

The historical developments described in Section 1 have led to a heterogeneous linguistic situation which will be briefly summarized in this section.[7] There are three zones in Cameroon, each with their respective lingua franca: Fulfulde in the North, Pidgin English in the West, and French in the remaining areas of the country (Wolf 2001: 155). Next to these, Ewondo, Basaa, Duala, Hausa, Wandala, Kanuri, and Arab Choa function as languages of wider communication in several regions (Echu 2004: 21). Kießling (2022: 11) adds Bulu, Fang, Mungaka, and Bamileke to this list. Official figures of the 2005 *Cameroonian Census of Population and Housing* claim that 56 percent of Cameroon's population speak French, 23 percent speak English, and 3 percent each Bulu, Ewondo, and Bassa, while Duala, Arab Choa, and Fulfulde have 1 percent, respectively. "Other indigenous languages" are listed as being spoken by 8 percent of the population (as cited in Translators Without Borders 2021).

Especially in the big cities, extensive and long-lasting language contact has led to a great diversity of language varieties, and these forms are used by the majority of urban Cameroonians. A recent estimation puts the urban population at 52 percent in 2015 (Ayafor & Green 2017: 14), with Douala and Yaoundé being the most highly populated cities (3 million inhabitants in total).

It becomes clear from this wealth of languages that rarely any Cameroonian citizen is monolingual. Having a command of at least two, most often three and more, languages is the norm. Simo Bobda & Mbouya even list six "typical cases" of informants who speak between four and twelve languages (2005: 2128–2130). In their sample, the first languages learned were always autochthonous languages, with French and/or English – depending on where the family lives – being added to the speakers' repertoire once they enter school. While this pattern might still hold for rural areas and most smaller towns, the situation has changed dramatically in the urban centers, where French (in francophone zones; Wamba & Noumssi 2003: 3) and CPE (in anglophone zones; Chiatoh & Nkwain 2020: 88) have become the first languages of a growing number of children.

Exploring the linguistic landscape of Cameroon, Pütz comes to the conclusion that English and French have a vital presence in all aspects of public life, while "both the indigenous languages and the lingua franca Cameroon Pidgin English (CPE; likewise Camfranglais) are relegated to the background" (2020: 304). We will look at each of these language varieties in more detail in the following.

---

7. Several scholars have contributed to a good understanding of the general multilingual ecology in Cameroon, e.g., Anchimbe (2006b), Echu (2003), Mforteh (2006), and Wolf (2001).

2.1 Indigenous languages

Cameroon's indigenous languages belong to three of the four major African language families, namely Afro-Asiatic, Nilo-Saharan, and Niger-Kordofanian. As many of these languages are spoken by less than 10,000 people, they are under severe threat of extinction (Chiatoh 2014: 378).

As mentioned above, the Cameroonian constitution states that the country "shall endeavor to protect and promote national languages" (see Section 1.1), an addition that found its way into the document as late as 1996. Until then, and for many years after this initial declaration, only the following private organizations worked on promoting indigenous languages: *PROPELCA* (Programme de Recherche Opérationnelle pour l'Enseignement des Langues au Cameroun), active since 1977 in mother tongue education; *SIL-Cameroon* (Summer Institute of Linguistics); *CABTAL* (Cameroon Association for Bible Translation and Literacy); and *NACALCO* (National Association of Cameroonian Language Committees, a successor of PROPELCA) (Echu 2004: 24). These bodies have made considerable efforts regarding the standardization of indigenous languages,[8] and created written materials that could be used to develop a school curriculum. According to Echu, "the absence of a clearly defined language policy in Cameroon constitutes a major handicap to the development of these languages" (2003: 32). Also, as described in Section 1.2, English and French are used as exclusive languages of education to the detriment of the indigenous languages.[9]

Unfortunately, even if Cameroonian languages are introduced into the education system in pilot projects (Takam & Fassé 2020: 70), "[e]xperience has shown that most parents in Cameroon seem to be generally hostile towards the introduction of early childhood education in the indigenous languages" (Echu 2004: 28).

This negative attitude certainly is a remnant from colonial times, during which the indigenous languages were stigmatized as inferior modes of expression (Ngefac 2010: 150), and were, as a result of this learned devaluation which Bokamba (2007) calls *Ukolonia*,[10] excluded from all official domains. Pütz confirmed that indigenous languages are almost non-existent in the linguistic landscape of Yaoundé and claims that they "play a very marginal role beyond the family, peer-group and informal

---

8. Mforteh (2007: 94) quotes a 2004 SIL report according to which 166 Cameroonian languages were or are in the process of being standardized, and the Bible (or parts thereof) is translated into 30 Cameroonian languages.
9. Due to their restricted use, Mforteh (2006) describes them as 'home languages'.
10. Ukolonia is understood as "a curable mental disorder that obfuscates rational thinking and causes the patient to evaluate itself in terms of values and standards set by people from other cultures" (Bokamba 2007: 41).

domains such as the market, streets and the home" (2020: 319). Likewise, none of them is used in administration, written media, advertisements, national television, formal education, or alphabetization campaigns (Bitja'a Kody 2001). The radio is an exception to this pattern, however. Several provincial radio stations air programs in national languages ranging from 4.17 percent of total airtime in Bamenda to 27.36 percent in Maroua (Echu 2004: 30).

Another domain that seems to play an important role in preserving indigenous languages is church. From personal observations in Yaoundé, I can confirm that many church services are held partly in the respective local languages, in addition to French and Latin. Also, church-based study or volunteer groups that meet once a week for bible discussions, cleaning, or event preparations use their dominant indigenous language for communication. A scientific treatment of this matter is contributed by Kouega, who, studying masses at Catholic Churches in Yaoundé, confirms that "Cameroon minority languages [...] are used in all the parishes observed, [...] mainly for singing and occasionally for epistle reading" (2008a: 149).

Worth investigating is also the very common practice of women's associations and micro-financial cooperatives, which frequently meet for discussions, fundraising, sewing, or other purposes, as these groups often use their respective indigenous languages (Mforteh 2007: 91).

While, in rural environments, the transmission of Cameroonian languages seems to be mostly intact,[11] it is often interrupted in urban areas, as parents tend to speak French or English with their offspring in order to give them an advantage in the educational system or because they do not share a common indigenous language. In a study conducted in 2004 in Yaoundé among francophone adolescents aged 12–24, I found that only 27.1 percent of the participants ($n = 225$) claim to speak their native language fluently, a fact many of them regret (Stein 2022: 114). Consequently, when asked which language is used most during the day, only 3.7 percent said it is an indigenous language, the rest answered French (75.6%) and Camfranglais (19.4%) (Stein 2022: 109).

The heavy and exclusive promotion of English and French as well as factors like urbanization and an economic orientation to global markets have contributed to the disuse of autochthonous languages in Cameroon, 10 percent of which are described as 'neglected' and 7 percent as severely threatened in their existence (Tomedes 2021). Recently, officials have become more active, supporting pilot programs that teach Cameroonian languages in schools (Kindzeka 2020), and the

---

11. Although even here, there seem to be changes, as a study by Spreda (1997) on the language use of rural women shows. Wolf cites the results of this study and claims that indigenous languages are on the decrease in favor of CPE, even in the 'home' domain. The L1 is used to talk to older people, while the younger ones are addressed in CPE (2001: 194).

Département de Langues et Cultures Nationales at the Higher Teachers' Training School (ENS) was opened in Yaoundé for the training of indigenous language instructors (Chiatoh 2014: 382). Given these new developments, and the growing interest in indigenous languages by a young generation seeking to express an African identity, the future of Cameroon's autochthonous linguistic heritage looks much brighter today than 30 years ago.

2.2   French in Cameroon and its varieties

French is the language that dominates all public aspects of life in the bigger francophone part of the country (Simo Bobda 2013: 290). Especially in the urban metropoles, it has succeeded in taking over many of the domains that were reserved for the indigenous languages before (Wolf 2001: 167). Biloa, who published the probably most comprehensive monograph about French in Cameroon to date, claims that the language is a prerequisite for successful participation in the administrative, political, economic, and social life in Cameroon (Biloa 2004: 1–2).

Due to the strict policy of assimilation and an insistence on using French by the norms set by "la Francophonie", the variety used in all state-governed institutions, in schools, and the media is very close to the standard set by France (Wolf 2001: 73). Still, the French spoken in Cameroon has undergone several processes of adaption and indigenization, processes that are most noticeable on the phonological level of the language. Thus, Wamba & Noumssi (2003: 6–9) describe four regional accents that show certain systematic changes:

- the Bamileke accent (Western region)
- the Nordish accent (Northern region)
- the Bassa accent (Center and Littoral region)
- the Beti/Bulu accent (Center and Southern region)

Since a nationwide lingua franca is absent, French is used in a variety of interethnic communications and has entered many private domains. As a result, a colloquial form has developed and is used in non-official contexts, as Echu confirms (2004: 22). The exact terminology for this variety is disputed: while authors like Dang (1986), Chia (1990), and Chia & Gerbault (1992) argue for the existence of a Cameroon Pidgin French, Wamba & Noumssi (2003: 13) chose the denomination Mesolectal French ('français mesolectal'), and Echu (2006) calls it Cameroon Popular French, claiming that, along with Camfranglais (see Section 2.5), it is a pidginized local variety of French. Since the start of the *IFACAM* (Inventaire des particularités lexicales du Français du Cameroun; Biloa & Echu 2008) which resulted in a monograph by Mendo Zé & Tabi-Manga (1979), a solid body of work about French in Cameroon has been published.[12]

French has definitely become the language used most in all public domains in Cameroon, but, except for a minority, it has mainly instrumental value and, especially in its standard form, does not serve to express a Cameroonian identity, as Wamba & Noumssi (2003: 16) remark. The following section will discuss the rather different position the English language has in Cameroon.

2.3 English in Cameroon and its varieties

In contrast to French, English has a much "broader range of types" (Wolf 2001: 73). The author claims that the linguistic tolerance of British indirect rule is responsible for the wide spectrum found in the anglophone regions and beyond, a spectrum that starts with Standard British English (SBE henceforth) at one end and, according to some scholars (e.g., Mbassi-Manga 1976: 62, as cited in Alobwede 1998: 55), has CPE at its other end.

English parallels the functions that French has in the francophone parts of Cameroon, i.e., it is used in "national daily life including education, politics, media, administration, employment, literary creativity, sociocultural communication" (Anchimbe 2006a: 38). Both British and American English can be found in Cameroon, as institutions such as the British Council or the American Cultural Center spread the respective standards (Wolf 2001: 185).[13]

While the value of the English language in relation to the global economy and international relations of the country is undisputed, some scholars criticize the dependency on it in education and national affairs. Nkwetisama, for example, blames the "English language terrorism" for the threatening "linguistic genocide" of Cameroonian languages, but does not suggest an alternative in his paper (2017: 106).

SBE is described as a rather elitist mode of expression in Cameroon, only to be found in university, journalism, jurisdiction, and international affairs (Biloa & Echu 2008: 199). This holds although English was introduced as a subject and medium of education right from the primary level in schools in West Cameroon (Anchimbe 2006a: 38). As teachers are rarely native speakers of SBE themselves, however, the variety used and passed on to the students is closer to the local variety of English, and so the following will focus on the development of what came to be called *Cameroon English* (CamE henceforth).

---

12. Biloa (2004), Mendo Zé (1992), Nzéssé (2008), Wamba & Noumssi (2003), and Zang Zang (1999), to name a few.
13. As Atechi remarks, "[i]n some cases Cameroonians are more used to American forms than to the British forms […] e.g., 'cheque' instead of 'bill', or 'term paper' instead of 'essay'" (2008: 192).

The systematic study of those so-called "New Englishes" or "indigenised varieties of English" started in the early 1950s according to Anchimbe (2006a: 7), but, as Ngefac (2008: 73) remarks, these first written accounts focused on showing how deviant those varieties were from SBE. With reference to Kachru (1986), Cameroon belongs to the countries of Outer Circle Englishes, while, in Schneider's Dynamic Model, CamE can be described as having attained the phase of nativization (Schneider 2007).

After initial descriptions by Simo Bobda (1994) and Bamgbose (1998), the most comprehensive overviews of CamE are presented by Wolf (2001) and Anchimbe (2006a). The latter's monograph not only investigates typical linguistic features of CamE (morphological, lexical, and semantic evidence) but also discusses the question of how "Cameroonianisms" develop into a norm or standard of common usage, presenting a theory of filtration to account for the way certain patterns of nonstandard English usage are gradually accepted in the Cameroonian speech community (Anchimbe 2006a: 7). Anchimbe, thus, explains that what used to be seen as "speech errors"[14] by authors such as Todd (1982: 25) are in fact "Cameroonianisms" and represent innovations that spur the indigenization of English. This development has resulted in a variety which serves as an identity marker for anglophone Cameroonians, a variety that became "linguistically identifiable, geographically delimitable, functionally indispensable, and now command[s] an emotional affiliation that cuts across sub-cultural, tribal, and linguistic contours" (Todd 1982: 25).

Applying Kachru's (1986) concept of nativization to the situation in Cameroon, Mbufong compares features of CamE and SBE at the levels of phonology, lexis, and grammar, including a detailed description of the influence of what he calls 'home languages' on CamE. He concludes that "the interference of local languages is most marked in less educated and more informal styles" (Mbufong 2013: 480). Thus, the features of CamE are well documented, and more results can be expected from ongoing research such as the *CamE Corpus Project* initiated in 1997 by Tiomajou at the University Yaoundé I (mentioned by Ayafor 2007: 33).

In another important contribution to the study of CamE, Ngefac (2008) analyzes the approximation of SBE pronunciation in different sectors of the anglophone population, considering speakers' level of education, gender differences, age group, as well as ethnic and regional differences. He concludes that SBE approximation does not so much depend on gender or age (although older speakers tend to use more SBE features) but on occupation (journalists and English teachers are closer to SBE than doctors and other teachers) and education (Ngefac 2008: 115–117).

---

14. "The characteristics discussed in this paper were once regarded as errors but are now increasingly accepted as distinctive contributions to the English language" (Mbufong 2013: 481).

When it comes to primary education, there are remarkable differences between anglophone and francophone students: "less than half of the first-grade children actually spoke CamE, as compared to 93% speakers of French among the francophone students. The low competence in CamE correlates with a high competence in PE [Pidgin English]" (Wolf 2001: 202). While children learn CPE at home or in the neighborhood in an informal manner, the exposure to SBE or CamE starts only once they enter school. Since CPE and CamE are closely related, children struggle with the acquisition of the standard form, and "PE interferes on all levels of language" (Wolf 2001: 203).

Presenting a case study in linguistic practices at a higher education institution, Chiatoh and Ntain interviewed 738 students at the University of Buea and found that 43.4 percent of the students reported using CPE, 39 percent English, 12.4 percent French, 2.1 percent Camfranglais (see Section 2.5), and only 1.8 percent their national languages for communications out of the classroom (2021:3). Another variety of English that developed among francophone speakers has been termed Cameroon Francophone English (henceforth CamFE). An overview of its features is found in Atechi (2015),[15] who attributes its emergence to the "transnational attraction" of English postulated by Schneider (2007).

The interrelation between CamE, CamFE, and CPE is not at all easy to analyze, as the borders between them are fluent. Ngefac & Sala (2006) have shown that the phonological gap between CamE and CPE is closing as a result of the efforts of educated people to avoid the stigma attached to CPE which, having a rather low prestige overall, is not the first choice for expressing an educated identity. On the other hand, the close approximation of SBE pronunciation is equally ridiculed and seen as snobbish[16] (Ngefac 2008: 71). In this situation, CamE (Wolf 2001: 243) seems to emerge as the prestige form, at least in urban anglophone Cameroon. Whether this variety will be officially recognized and developed remains to be seen; at least back in 2003, "[w]ork on lexical standardization of Cameroon English and Cameroon French is seriously lagging behind due to lack of institutional support" (Echu 2003: 40).

From a francophone point of view, it is not SBE that dominates the anglophone provinces, but CPE. In several interviews I conducted in 2004, the mastery of English by the anglophone population was heavily questioned. Views such as the following were expressed (my translation from French):

---

15. Other descriptions have been presented by Kouega (2008b), Safotso (2012), Simo Bobda & Mbangwana (1993), and Simo Bobda (2013).
16. "Cameroonians who insist on sounding like Britons are ridiculed rather than admired" (Mbangwana 1987: 423).

- "With the Anglophones, for instance… the Anglophones can't speak English well anymore, because they speak too much Pidgin!" (interview male informant, 20 years)
- "That's why the majority of girls, they are not interested [in speaking Camfranglais, author's note], they speak nothing but French. Well, if it is beyond them, they take the Pidgin, they don't speak English. English is not spoken anymore here in Cameroon, so we learn it [Pidgin] also." (interview female informant, 19 years)
- "In the anglophone part… ah, you don't need to go there to speak 'Grammar English', you know. When we were small, going to school, they imposed English on us, in elementary school. So, you speak English, English, English, then, when you finally arrive in an Anglophone environment, you speak the English that you have learned in school, and they don't understand it. There's no English in Cameroon!" (interview with rapper Krotal)

Whether this rather surprising estimation is true needs to be verified by further studies. One possible explanation for these statements is given by Anchimbe, who writes that "[t]he francophones […] now liken the Anglophone variety of English to Pidgin English — the low-class language generally identified with non-literates. The variety they claim they learn and purport to speak is the advanced, international variety […]" (2007: 72).

2.4 Cameroon Pidgin English

A presentation of the multilingual ecology of Cameroon would be incomplete without the inclusion of CPE (also called Kamtok),[17] an English-based creole that acts as a lingua franca for large parts of Cameroon,[18] even in the francophone zones. Ayafor & Green (2017: 2) classify it as "Atlantic Creole (West African Group)", the earliest descriptions of which were Ph.D. theses by Schneider (1966), Todd (1969), and Mbassi-Manga (1973).

Several varieties of these "Atlantic Creoles" were in use in the coastal regions of West Africa long before those became British colonies, and even after colonial conquest and independence, the local variant in Cameroon (i.e., CPE) spread quickly among the Anglophones, as Standard English was learned and spoken by a small elite only (Wolf 2001: 98). Given the duration of its existence in Cameroon and its deep roots among the country's inhabitants, Ngome (1982) sees "PE as

---

17. Ngefac (2010: 152) suggests that *Kamtok* should be the exclusive denomination, since CPE is not a mere Pidgin anymore, having sufficiently creolized and even acquiring native speakers.
18. Echu even calls it "the main lingua franca" of the country (2004: 19).

an African language operating in the same milieu as any other African language and being more akin to African languages in grammar, structure and lexis than to English" (as cited in Alobwede 1998: 56). Its value for the Cameroonian population is further elaborated by Alobwede, who claims that "it is the only language in Cameroon which expresses Cameroonian reality without provoking vertical or horizontal hostilities. Secondly, it is conveniently flexible and as such can be acquired at no cost" (Alobwede 1998: 59).

CPE is almost exclusively an oral mode of communication. Only a few written texts exist, which include a collection of folktales, a CPE Bible, and other religious texts. Currently, however, a pilot corpus of spoken CPE is being developed (Green, Ayafor & Ozón 2016). CPE is also increasingly used in performing arts and humor, and instances of written usage abound in online and social media exchanges.

CPE is also mostly an urban language, as Ayafor & Green argue (2017: 23), and has a covert prestige for the urban population, while Wolf mentions instances where CPE is the language of overt prestige among the rural population, where its usage often signals belonging to the anglophone community, even when SBE or CamE are not mastered (Wolf 2001: 230). Chiatoh and Ntain present the following figures for its usage:

> Todd [1979] suggests that CPE is spoken in some form by at least 50% of the population, while Mbufong [2013] argues that over 80% of Cameroonians speak CPE. A recent study by Lando & Ntain [2018] shows that, 81.8% of English-speaking teachers use CPE in class to ease understanding, and 78.9% of students prefer using it for peer tutoring to ease communication and understanding. (2021: 2)

Turning to the domains and functions of CPE, it is used to bridge the social gap between educated and non-educated speakers rather than bridging the Anglo-Franco-divide (Schröder 2003: 321). It is rarely used at home, but often among anglophone friends; Francophones tend to speak it more with Anglophones than vice versa (Ayafor & Green 2017: 24). Furthermore, while some schools have strict sanctions against its usage in the classrooms, it is frequently used among students to "ease understanding", as mentioned in the quote above. A topical class on pidgin and creole languages was introduced at the University Yaoundé I in 2008 (Chiatoh & Ntain 2021: 28), and its Department of English now offers "Pidgin Courses" (an immersion course in speaking, listening, reading, writing, and grammar) in its study program.[19]

CPE is absent in mass media and politics but is used in private radio broadcasts in the anglophone region[20] and in political campaigns targeting the rural

---

19. Information available at the University's homepage: https://uy1.uninet.cm/facultes-et-grandes-ecoles/departements-falsh/#anglais (04 December 2024).

population (Chiatoh & Ntain 2021:27). While educated Cameroonians use the official languages in administration, the less educated use CPE for these purposes. Likewise, its usage in religion, trade, education programs, crafts, and health is widespread in the anglophone regions (Chiatoh & Ntain 2021:27–28).

As far as its internal variation is concerned, several studies have established a distinction between an anglophone and a francophone variety (de Féral 1989) as well as rural and urban varieties. Biloa & Echu (2008:207) postulate four different varieties:

- the Grassland variety (spoken in the Northwest province)
- the Bororo variety (spoken by the Bororo people)
- the Coastal variety (spoken in the Southwest province)
- the Francophone variety

CPE is gaining mother-tongue status for a growing number of Cameroonians (Ngefac 2010:153) and slowly seems to be shedding its negative image of being just 'broken English'. Given its widespread, relative neutrality, and low cost of standardization, Echu (2003:43) even discusses the possible use of CPE as a national language for Cameroon.

2.5 Camfranglais

In the midst of the linguistic heterogeneity described so far, another variety developed that became part of Cameroon's multilingual ecology over the last few decades: Camfranglais (CFA henceforth). As its name suggests, it is a hybrid formation consisting of indigenous Cameroonian languages, French, English, and CPE. Its origins[21] seem to lie in a criminal argot developed by smugglers in Douala, but once it reached the secondary schools in the early 1990s, it rapidly spread to most other urban centers and became an identity language for adolescents (Stein 2022). For them, as Kießling argues, CFA has the potential to "index an alternative progressive and youthful urban identity" that sets them apart from their parents' generation as well as from rural peers and the elite, but also from other countries, as it "indexes a specific Cameroonian identity" (Kießling 2022:13). Kießling (2022:17–18) goes on to mention the existence of francophone and anglophone CFA varieties and describes it as a linguistic link "between a basilectal Cameroonian French, a francophone CPE variety and an anglophone CPE variety" (Kießling 2022:18).

---

20. The authors mention especially the existence of pidgin news, advertisements and educational programs in CPE (Ayafor & Green 2017:26).
21. Since space does not allow for a full discussion of this variety here, the reader is referred to works such as Essono (1997), de Féral (1997), Kießling (2005), and Stein (2022).

This link is not only established in combining different linguistic forms horizontally but also in forming a vertical continuum between different classes in society. Thus, CFA seems to have a colloquial variety that is spoken among peers, students, and secondary school children and a 'deep' form that is lexically elaborate, making it hardly understandable for outsiders. Furthermore, it is used as a secret code among sex workers, street children, and criminals (Stein 2022: 48).

While initially heavily opposed by parents and educators, CFA currently seems to find acceptance among a growing number of Cameroonians. Those who used it in their teenage days[22] carry certain words and expressions into their adulthood. It is used by singers such as Koppo, Krotal, and the new generation of Cameroonian Afro-Pop musicians in their lyrics, reaching a wide audience, and the explosion of internet users during the last decade has led to an active community online who uses CFA in their exchanges.

The often-cited merits of CFA include "its potential to mark urbanity, transcend ethnic identity and [...] feeling released from the pressure to constantly observe the norms of the not fully mastered European standard languages, French and, to a lesser extent, English" (Kießling 2022: 21–22). Thus, CFA is likely to continue to feature in the linguistic ecology of Cameroon in the years to come, and its development both within the country and within the Cameroonian diaspora is well worth studying.

3. Language attitudes in Cameroon

Having discussed the multilingual ecology of the country in the previous section, we will now turn to the field of language attitudes,[23] which are known to directly influence linguistic behavior (Giles et al. 1987: 592). The interesting case in Cameroon is that there exist marked differences in linguistic attitudes between Anglophones and Francophones. Thus, Ayafor remarks:

> In Francophones' perception, there is something invaluable about English but not about the Anglophones who speak it. In this sense, Cameroon provides an interesting sociolinguistic example where a language whose international aura is acknowledged world-wide [...] becomes a minority language [...]. (2007: 60)

---

22. In a study conducted in 2004 in Yaoundé, Stein found that 19.4 percent of the informants reported using CFA most, following French (75.6%), with native languages taking the last position with 3.7 percent (Stein 2022: 109).

23. Language attitudes are defined as "any affective, cognitive or behavioural index of evaluative reactions toward different language varieties or speakers" by Ryan & Giles (1982: 7).

In Section 3.1, several findings about language attitudes in Cameroon are summarized, while the subsequent Section 3.2 presents results from my own research that come to a slightly different conclusion.

3.1 Comparing Anglophones' and Francophones' language attitudes

Turning to the indigenous languages first, we have seen in Section 2.1 that the older generation of either anglophone or francophone background does not value them much and is even opposed to their usage in school, as both Echu (2003)[24] and Chiatoh (2014)[25] confirm. These negative attitudes have to be overcome by revaluation, stressing their importance as an expression of a unique culture and identity, as Chiatoh & Akumbu (2013) argue. They call for a decolonization of the educational system by "indigenisation, domestication and diversification [...], and this ideally takes place through the valorisation of indigenous languages" (Chiatoh & Akumbu 2013: 198), something that can be achieved by "awareness campaigns" (Chiatoh & Akumbu 2013: 212). A young generation eager to assert a Cameroonian identity as well as the global trend to value African cultural, creative, and linguistic heritage might contribute to the development of a positive attitude towards the indigenous languages, a field in which more research needs to be done.

Likewise suffering from negative attitudes, especially from the Francophones' point of view, is CPE. Until today, it is seen as "broken English" and not a "proper" language, as a communication medium for the uneducated (Ayafor & Green 2017: 24). Chiatoh & Nkwain (2020) studied the attitudes to CPE of 50 first-year francophone students at the University of Buea. Their study shows that English (54%), Indigenous Languages (20%), and even Camfranglais (16%) are reported to be chosen instead of CPE to communicate on campus, even though some of the respondents claim to speak CPE. The negative attitudes towards CPE are also seen in statements such as "It destroys the English we already know", "It is a rude and rough language" or "It is local and not international" (Chiatoh & Nkwain 2020: 92). They conclude that "a majority of Francophone students consider CPE as a substandard code [...] and so have negative attitudes towards it" (Chiatoh & Nkwain 2020: 93). CPE is thus not seen as a neutral language, as it "comes from Anglophones" (Schröder 2003: 321).

---

24. "Attitudes towards the official languages are positive, whereas they are negative towards the indigenous languages" (Echu 2003: 41).
25. "Cameroonians thus tend to view their languages as too inferior to serve as effective media of learning [...] and so should be completely excluded from the educational system. There is an equally dominant mentality within official circles even if publicly, authorities do acknowledge the importance of promoting indigenous languages" (Chiatoh 2014: 379).

From an anglophone point of view, however, CPE has at least covert prestige, as "everyone makes extensive use of it in everyday life" (Anchimbe 2006a: 33), and it fulfills functions as "language of the people" that Standard English cannot (Ayafor 2007: 55–56). Mforteh draws our attention to the fact that CPE is generally changing in status from "denigrated" to "normal" code (Mforteh 2007: 92) and Chiatoh and Nkwain state that CPE has been recognized by Anglophones as "one of the fundamental markers of their identity" (2020: 88).

Turning to the two official languages English and French, the attitudes are much more positive, although one has to differentiate between Anglophones' and Francophones' perspectives. While, for the former, English came to be seen as "associated with Christianity and modernity" (Wolf 2001: 69), the latter "use the word "Anglo" as an epithet to mean "uncouth", "backward", "uncivilized" […]" (Eko 2003: 81). In some cases, anglophone students at francophone universities were ridiculed and called "anglofou" if they are not able to speak French correctly, as Ayafor (2007: 17) has shown. Dassé adds to this that "Anglophones were confronted with a generalised supercilious attitude of francophones vis-à-vis their language, habits and manners" (2014: 119).

Concerning the language (not its speakers), these negative or rather indifferent attitudes towards English changed in the aftermath of an economic crisis that hit Cameroon in the early 1990s. Turning to the global market for economic opportunities, francophone Cameroonians were confronted with a necessity to learn English:

> They no longer saw it as a minority language spoken by Anglophones in Cameroon but as an indispensable tool for survival in a world that science and technology has reduced to a global village with English as the main lingua franca […].
> (Atechi 2015: 25)

Francophones' attitudes thus "changed drastically from very negative to very positive" (Atechi 2015: 29). However, Anchimbe (2007: 73) explains this change as "identity opportunism", as the motivations behind learning English for Francophones is instrumental rather than integrative (Ayafor 2007: 66) and the positive attitudes towards English do not (yet) extend to positive attitudes towards English-speaking Cameroonians.

While French, as the language of the administration, is seen as "argent linguistique […], as an investment and means to participate in modernity" by the francophone population (Dassé 2014: 98), Takam and Fassé claim that "Anglophones usually believe French will take them nowhere outside the country and content themselves with any functional mastery of it just for basic communication with Francophones" (2020: 77).

3.2 Changing attitudes of young francophone speakers towards English

A kind of middle course between these extreme positions seems to be taken by a new generation of truly bilingual Cameroonian children, who Anchimbe (2007) describes as "linguabrids".[26] These children, born either to anglophone-francophone couples ("perfect-linguabrids") or to francophone parents who enrolled them in English-medium schools ("semi-linguabrids"), "portray an identity that is a fusion of the two cultural and linguistic backgrounds inherited from their parents and the educational system" and thus fail to identify as strictly anglophone or francophone – they describe themselves as "bilingual Cameroonians" (Anchimbe 2007: 75).

Another shift in attitudes from negative to positive was noticeable among Cameroonian adolescents in 2004, when I did a field study about exposure to and usage of Camfranglais in Yaoundé. A part of the questionnaire used for that purpose focused on linguistic preferences, which was answered by the francophone informants[27] as follows:

Table 1. Language preference among students in Yaoundé (Stein 2022: 148; $n=325$)

	* Among these languages, which one is your favorite?								
	French	English	Native lang.	CFA	Spanish	German	Other AF	Other EU	Total
Male	46.7%	20.1%	13.6%	9.8%	6%	2.7%	1.1%	0%	100% (184)
Female	50.4%	17%	13.5%	5.0%	5.7%	4.3%	3.5%	0.7%	100% (141)
Total	48.3%	18.8%	13.5%	7.7%	5.8%	3.4%	2.2%	0.3%	100% (325)

* The question preceding this one was: "Which languages do you speak?".

As can be seen from Table 1, 48.3 percent of the informants stated that French is their favorite language, followed by 18.8 percent for English, 13.5 percent for

---

26. Coined from the words 'linguistics' and 'hybridity', linguabridity "is used here to refer to people (especially children) who grow up with two languages that belong to two, often competing or conflicting, cultures" (Anchimbe 2007: 66).

27. There were 325 informants in total (184 male and 141 female informants), aged 12–31 years. Most informants (250 or 77%) were still in school, while 51 of them (16%) were at university. The remaining 24 informants (7%) represent the older segment of the sample (>25 years) and were either at university or held various jobs as musicians, drivers or petty traders. In general, the sample consisted of people from the lower middle class.

their native language, and 7.7 percent for Camfranglais. Asked for their reasons for this preference, the informants who stated that English was their favorite language explained, among others (my translation from French):

1. "English, because I understand it quite easily and my artist stars all speak English." (male, 18 years)
2. "I love English because it's spoken in many countries and because, with French, it forms the two official languages of Cameroon." (female, 24 years)
3. "I like English most because for me English is a beautiful language and also it allows me to communicate with the Anglophones in my country." (male, 26 years)
4. "My country Cameroon is bilingual and I'm a Francophone, that's why I love English most, so I don't have difficulties in communication." (male, 16 years)
5. "I love English a lot because my dreamland is England. It is a language that I have dreamt of mastering since my childhood." (female, 15 years)

The answers show that this young generation recognizes English as both an expression of a global orientation and their own linguistic identity (of the 61 informants who chose English as their favorite language, 25 claimed to have done so because it is the language spoken most in the world, 10 praised its easy grammar, its beauty, or its wealth of expression, 9 said they needed it for their studies or future job opportunities, 7 stated that it was one of Cameroon's official languages, and 6 mentioned personal reasons like music or the wish to go to England; 4 did not give any reason). These positive attitudes might stem, in part, from the constant exposure to English via music, fashion, and the internet, which just started to take hold in Yaoundé in 2004.

Similar reasons were given in response to a study by Ngefac (2010), who asked 120 informants from both anglophone and francophone backgrounds about their linguistic choices. Among the Francophones' motivations for choosing English as a medium of communication were the following (Ngefac 2010: 159, $n = 41$):

1. "Because English guarantees communication with fellow Anglophone brothers and sisters." (17%)
2. "Because English is the language of the global village and a window to international opportunities." (54%)

To my knowledge, no recent studies exist about language attitudes towards English in Cameroon. It would be an invaluable contribution to the field to find out if the Anglophone Crisis, for instance, had an impact on the tender shoots of positive attitudes towards English and "the Anglophone brothers and sisters" mentioned above, an impact that is foreseeable to influence the attitudes of Anglophones towards French since the violent conflicts broke out.

4. Conclusion

As this chapter has shown, the multilingual ecology of Cameroon is characterized by a high diversity of languages and language varieties. French and English, as the official languages of the country, enjoy high prestige and are used in government, education, jurisdiction, science, media, and international relations, with the former clearly dominating the latter. The exonormative standard forms of the official languages, though aimed at in educational contexts, are in daily use only among a small elite; the vast majority uses more vernacular forms, termed Cameroon English and Cameroon Popular French, respectively.

CPE, or Kamtok, has installed itself firmly as the language of wider communication, not only in the anglophone region but throughout the country, even acquiring mother-tongue status in recent years. Additionally, there are several dominant regional languages, such as Fulfulde, Bamileke, Ewondo, Basaa, and Duala. Despite their widespread usage, indigenous languages have been neglected for a long time in the language policy of the country but have recently been introduced in education.

Given the shifting attitudes discussed in Section 3, a future linguistic policy in Cameroon might reconsider a suggestion made by Tadadjeu already back in 1975. He "advocates a trilingual language policy model whereby English, French and indigenous languages are encouraged not only in education but also in other domains." (as cited in Echu 2003: 43). Although the linguistic situation in Cameroon has been well documented since independence, the last few years have seen formative events such as the violent outbreaks of the Anglophone Crisis, the rush for English education, and new laws and linguistic policies that are bound to influence the status quo in the coming years. Thus, Cameroon represents an interesting field of constant linguistic evolution and dynamic developments that should be closely monitored and accompanied by longitudinal studies in the field of language attitudes, multilingual proficiency, and linguistic variation. Of special interest is, for instance, the development of *Ambazonian English* as foreseen by Nkwain (2021; see Section 1.3.) or the change in attitudes by Anglophones to French and Francophones to English in the aftermath of the economic crisis and the most recent armed conflicts.

English will continue to play an important role in the multilingual ecology of Cameroon, and its further nativization is strongly foreseeable, given the close interaction with CPE and the heavy influence of both French and Cameroonian languages.

References

Alobwede, Charles D. 1998. Banning Pidgin English in Cameroon? *English Today* 14(1): 54–60.
Amabo, Eulalia. 2020. Promotion of official languages. *Cameroon Tribune*, August 25th 2020. https://www.cameroon-tribune.cm/article.html/34507/en.html/promotion-of-official-languages-bilingualism-commission-evaluates (16 February 2023).
Anchimbe, Eric A. 2006a. *Cameroon English: Authenticity, Ecology and Evolution*. Frankfurt: Peter Lang.
Anchimbe, Eric A. 2006b. Hybrid linguistic identities in postcolonial Africa: The intricacy of identity opportunism in multilingual Cameroon. In Alfonso De Toro & Frank Heidemann (eds.), *New hybridities: Societies and cultures in transition*, pp. 237–261. Leipzig: Olms.
Anchimbe, Eric A. 2007. Linguabridity: Redefining linguistic identities among children in urban areas. In Eric A. Anchimbe (ed.), *Linguistic Identity in Postcolonial Multilingual Spaces*, pp. 66–86. Newcastle upon Tyne: Cambridge Scholars.
Atechi, Samuel. 2008. The dilemma of the teacher and learner of English in a non-native English classroom: The case of Cameroon. *Alizés: Revue angliciste de La Réunion, Faculté des Lettres et Sciences Humaines (Université de La Réunion) Dilemnas* 30: 181–191. hal-02343083
Atechi, Samuel. 2015. The emergence of Cameroon Francophone English and the future of English in Cameroon. *British Journal of English Linguistics* 3(3): 23–33.
Ayafor, Isaiah Munang. 2005. Official bilingualism in Cameroon: Instrumental or integrative policy? In James Cohen, Kara McAlister, Kellie Rolstad & Jeff MacSwan (eds.), *Proceedings of the 4th International Symposium on Bilingualism*, pp. 123–142. Somerville, MA: Cascadilla Press.
Ayafor, Isaiah Munang. 2007. Official Bilingualism in Cameroon: An Empirical Evaluation of the Status of English in Official Domains. P.h.D. dissertation, Universität Freiburg.
Ayafor, Miriam & Melanie Green. 2017. *Cameroon Pidgin English: A Comprehensive Grammar*. Amsterdam: John Benjamins.
Bamgbose, Ayo. 1998. Torn between the norms: Innovations in World Englishes. *World Englishes* 17(1): 1–14.
Biloa, Edmond. 2004. *La langue française au Cameroun: Analyse linguistique et didactique*. Berlin: Peter Lang.
Biloa, Edmond & George Echu. 2008. Cameroon: Official bilingualism in a multilingual state. In Andrew Simpson (ed.), *Language and National Identity in Africa*, pp. 199–213. Oxford: Oxford University Press.
Bitja'a Kody, Zachée Denis. 2001. Emergence et survie des langues nationales au Cameroun. *TRANS* 11. http://www.inst.at/trans/11Nr/kody11.htm (28 February 2023).
Bokamba, Eyamba G. 2007. Arguments for multilingual policies in public domains in Africa. In Eric. A. Anchimbe (ed.), *Linguistic Identity in Postcolonial Multilingual Spaces*, pp. 27–65. Newcastle upon Tyne: Cambridge Scholars.
Chia, Emmanuel. 1990. The new speech forms of rapidly growing city: Pidgin French and Camfranglais in Yaounde. *Annales de la Faculté des Lettres et Sciences Humaines* 6(1–2): 102–127.

Chia, Emmanuel & Jacqueline Gerbault. 1992. Les nouveaux parlers urbains: Le cas de Yaoundé. In *Actes du Colloque International sur des langues et des villes, Dakar 15–57 décembre 1990*, pp. 263–277. Paris: ACCT et Didier Erudition.

Chiatoh, Blasius A. 2014. The Cameroonian experience in mother tongue education planning: The community response framework. *Current Issues in Language Planning* 15(4): 376–392.

Chiatoh, Blasius A. & Pius W. Akumbu. 2013. Towards a national language policy for Cameroon. In Pius W. Akumbu & Blasius Chiatoh (eds.), *Language Policy in Africa: Perspectives for Cameroon*, pp. 194–215. Kansas City, MO: Miraclaire Academic Publications.

Chiatoh, Blasius A. & Clovis N. Nkwain. 2020. Attitudes of francophone students towards Pidgin at the University of Buea (UB). *International Journal of Linguistics, Literature and Translation* 3(11): 87–93.

Chiatoh, Blasius A. & Patience C. Ntain. 2021. Challenging the monolingual habitus: An investigation of the linguistic practices of students at the University of Buea. *Journal of Social Sciences and Humanity Studies* 7(1): 1–9.

Dang, Dominic. 1986. Pidgin French: A Case Study of the French Spoken in Yaounde. P.h.D. dissertation, University of Yaoundé.

Dassé, Théodore. 2014. Them versus us: Bridging the ideological gap between English and French-speaking communities in Cameroon. In Valentine N. Ubanako & Jemina Anderson (eds.), *Crossing Linguistic Borders in Postcolonial Anglophone Africa*, pp. 115–151. Newcastle upon Tyne: Cambridge Scholars.

de Féral, Carole. 1989. *Pidgin-English du Cameroun. Description linguistique et sociolinguistique*. Paris: Peeters.

de Féral, Carole. 1997. Français orale et camfranglais dans le Sud Cameroun. In Ambroise Queffélec (ed.), *Alternances codiques et français parlée en Afrique*, pp. 205–212. Aix-en-Provence: PUF.

Eberhard, David M., Gary F. Simons & Charles D. Fennig (eds). 2023. Cameroon. In *Ethnologue: Languages of the World*, 26th edn. Dallas, TX: SIL International. https://www.ethnologue.com/country/CM/ (28 February 2023).

Echu, George. 2003. Coping with multilingualism: Trends in the evolution of language policy in Cameroon. *PhiN* 25: 31–46. https://web.fu-berlin.de/phin/phin25/p25t2.htm (10 April 2023).

Echu, George. 2004. The language question in Cameroon. *Linguistik Online* 18(1): 19–34.

Echu, George. 2006. Pidginization of the French Language in Cameroon. *Internet-Zeitschrift für Kulturwissenschaften* 16. https://www.inst.at/trans/16Nr/01_5/echu16.htm (14 February 2023).

Eko, Lyombe. 2003. The English-Language Press and the "Anglophone problem" in Cameroon: Group identity, culture, and the politics of nostalgia. *Journal of Third World Studies* 20(1): 79–102.

Essono, Jean-J. Marie. 1997. « Le camfranglais »: Un code excentrique, une appropriation vernaculaire du français. In Claude Frey & Danièle Latin (eds.), *Le Latin corpus lexicographique*, pp. 381–396. Louvain-la-Neuve: Duculot.

Fassé, Innocent M. 2012. Revamping school bilingualism in Cameroon primary education: Some strategies to avoid another failure. *Sino-US English Teaching* 9(12): 1754–1759.

Fonyuy, Ernesta K. 2010. The rush for English education in urban Cameroon: Sociolinguistic implication and prospects. *English Today* 26(1): 34–42.

Giles, Howard, Miles Hewstone, Ellen B. Ryan & Patricia Johnson. 1987. Research on language attitudes. In Ulrich Ammon, Norbert Dittmar, Klaus J. Mattheier & Peter Trudgill (eds.), *Sociolinguistics*, Vol. 1, pp. 585–597. Berlin: De Gruyter Mouton.

Green, Melanie, Miriam Ayafor & Gabriel Ozón. 2016. *A Spoken Corpus of Cameroon Pidgin English: Pilot Study*. http://ota.ox.ac.uk/desc/2563 (11 October 2024).

International Crisis Group 2017. *Cameroon's Anglophone Crisis at the Crossroads* (Africa Report No. 250). Brussels. https://www.crisisgroup.org/africa/central-africa/cameroon/250-cameroons-anglophone-crisis-crossroads (12 December 2022).

Kachru, Braj B. 1986. *The Alchemy of English: The Spread, Functions, and Models of Non-native Englishes*. Urbana, IL: University of Illinois Press.

Kamé, Bouopda Pierre. 2018. *The Anglophone Crisis in Cameroon*. Paris: L'Harmattan.

Kießling, Roland. 2005. Bàk mwà mè dó – Camfranglais in Cameroon. *Lingua Posnaniensis* 47: 87–107.

Kießling, Roland. 2022. Cameroon. In Paul Kerswill & Heike Wiese (eds.), *Urban Contact Dialects and Language Change: Insights from the Global North and South*, pp. 11–28. London: Routledge.

Kindzeka, Moki Edwin. 2020. *How Cameroon Plans to Save Disappearing Languages*. https://www.voanews.com/a/africa_how-cameroon-plans-save-disappearing-languages/6184626.html (1 March 2023).

Konings, Piet & Francis B. Nyamnjoh. 1997. The anglophone problem in Cameroon. *The Journal of Modern African Studies* 35(2): 207–229.

Kouega, Jean Paul. 1999. Forty years of official bilingualism in Cameroon. *English Today* 15(4): 38–43.

Kouega, Jean Paul. 2005. Promoting French–English individual bilingualism through education in Cameroon. *Journal of Third World Studies* 22(1): 189–196.

Kouega, Jean Paul. 2008a. Language, religion and cosmopolitanism: Language use in the Catholic Church in Yaounde – Cameroon. *International Journal of Multilingualism* 5(2): 140–153.

Kouega, Jean Paul. 2008b. The English of Francophone users in Cameroon: A phonological appraisal. *Annals of the Faculty of Arts, letters and Social Sciences, University of Yaounde I. Special Edition. Festschrift in honour of Professor Paul N. Mbangwana*, pp. 109–120.

Kouega, Jean Paul. 2010. Official bilingualism at Tertiary Level Education in Cameroon: The case of the University of Yaounde II (Soa). *Kaliao: Revue Pluridisciplinaire de l'École Normale Supérieure de Maroua (Cameroun), Série Lettres et Sciences Humaines* 2(4): 193–209.

Lando, Rodrick & Patience C. Ntain. 2018. Cameroon Pidgin English: An overview and implications for instruction in Anglophone Cameroon education. In Lamar L. Johnson, Gloria Boutte, Gwenda Greene & Dywanna Smith (eds.), *African Diaspora Literacy: The Heart of Transformation in K-12 Schools and Teacher Education*, pp. 137–153. New York, NY: Lexington Books.

Mbangwana, Paul. 1987. Some characteristics of sound patterns of Cameroon Standard English. *Multilingua* 6(4): 411–424.

Mbassi-Manga, Francis. 1973. English in Cameroon: A Study of Historical Contacts, Patterns of Usage and Current Trends. P.h.D. dissertation, University of Leeds.

Mbassi-Manga, Francis. 1976. The state of contemporary English in Cameroon. In Francis Mbassi-Manga (ed.), *Cameroon Studies in English and French (CASEF)*, pp. 49–63. Victoria: Presbook.

Mbufong, Paul K. 2013. The Cameroonization of English. *US-China Foreign Language* 11(6): 476–482.

Mendo Zé, Gervais. 1992. *Une crise dans les crises: Le français en Afrique noire francophone, le cas du Cameroun*. Paris: ABC.

Mendo Zé, Gervais & Jean Tabi-Manga. 1979. *Inventaire des particularités lexicales du français du Cameroun*. Yaoundé: Université de Yaoundé.

Mforteh, Stephen A. 2006. Cultural innovations in Cameroon's Tower of Babel. *TRANS* 16. https://www.inst.at/trans/16Nr/03_2/mforteh16.htm (24 April 2023).

Mforteh, Stephen A. 2007. In search of new identities in multilingual Cameroon. In Eric A. Anchimbe (ed.), *Linguistic Identity in Postcolonial Multilingual Spaces*, pp. 87–101. Newcastle upon Tyne: Cambridge Scholars.

NCPBM. 2017. *The NCPBM in brief*. https://www.ncpbm.cm/en/commission/ncpbm-brief (16 February 2023).

Ngefac, Aloysius. 2008. *Social Differentiation in Cameroon English: Evidence from Sociolinguistic Fieldwork*. Bern: Peter Lang.

Ngefac, Aloysius. 2010. Linguistic choices in postcolonial multilingual Cameroon. *Nordic Journal of African Studies* 19(3): 149–164.

Ngefac, Aloysius & Bonaventure M. Sala. 2006. Cameroon Pidgin and Cameroon English at a confluence. *English World-Wide* 27(2): 217–227.

Nkwain, Joseph. 2021. Current insights into the Evolution of Cameroonian English. *Athens Journal of Humanities & Arts* 8: 1–28.

Nkwetisama, C. Muluh. 2017. Rethinking and reconfiguring English language education: Averting linguistic genocide in Cameroon. *International Journal of Applied Linguistics & English Literature* 6(6): 106–114.

Nzessé, Ladislas. 2008. Le français en contexte plurilingue, le cas du Cameroun: Appropriation, glottopolitique et perspectives didactiques. *Francofonía* 17: 303–323.

Okereke, C. Nna-Emeka. 2018. Analysing Cameroon's Anglophone crisis. *Counter Terrorist Trends and Analyses* 10(3): 8–12.

Pütz, Martin. 2020. Exploring the linguistic landscape of Cameroon: Reflections on language policy and ideology. *Russian Journal of Linguistics* 24(2): 294–324.

Republic of Cameroon. 2019. *Law N° 2019/019 of 24 December 2019 on the Promotion of Official Languages in Cameroon*. https://www.prc.cm/en/multimedia/documents/8025-law-2019-019-of-24-december-2019 (16 February 2023).

Ryan, Ellen B. & Howard Giles. 1982. *Attitudes towards Language Variation*. London: Edward Arnold.

Safotso, Gilbert T. 2012. Aspects of Cameroon Francophone (CamFE) phonology. *Theory and Practice in Language Studies* 2(12): 2471–2477.

Schneider, Edgar. W. 2007. *Postcolonial English Varieties around the World*. Cambridge: Cambridge University Press.

Schneider, Gilbert. 1966. *West African Pidgin-English: A Descriptive Linguistic Analysis with Texts and Glossary from the Cameroon Area.* Hartford, CT: Hartford Seminary Foundation.

Schröder, Anne. 2003. Cameroon Pidgin English: A means of bridging the anglophone-francophone division in Cameroon? *Arbeiten aus Anglistik und Amerikanistik* 28(2): 305–327.

Simo Bobda, Augustin. 1994. *Aspects of Cameroon English Phonology.* Bern: Peter Lang.

Simo Bobda, Augustin. 2013. The emergence of a standardizing Cameroon Francophone English pronounciation in Cameroon. In Nils-Lennart Johannesson, Gunnel Melchers & Beyza Björkman (eds.), *Of Butterflies and Birds, of Dialects and Genres. Essays in Honour of Philip Shaw*, pp. 329–343. Stockholm: Stockholm University.

Simo Bobda, Augustin & Paul Mbangwana. 1993. *An Introduction to Spoken English.* Lagos: University of Lagos Press.

Simo Bobda, Augustin & Innocent F. Mbouya. 2005. Revisiting some linguistic concepts and beliefs in the light of the sociolinguistic situation of Cameroon. In James Cohen, Kara McAlister, Kellie Rolstad & Jeff MacSwan (eds.), *Proceedings of the 4th International Symposium on Bilingualism*, pp. 2122–2132. Somerville, MA: Cascadilla Press.

Spreda, Janice. 1997. Towards a Transitional Model of Basic Education for Rural Women in the North West Province of Cameroon. M.A. thesis. Gesamthochschule Siegen. SIL: Yaoundé.

Stein, Gardy. 2022. *Gender-based Differences in Exposure to and Usage of Camfranglais in Yaoundé. The Power to Exclude?* Newcastle upon Tyne: Cambridge Scholars.

Tadadjeu, Maurice. 1975. Language planning in Cameroon: Towards a trilingual education system. Patterns in language, culture and society: Sub-Saharan Africa. *Working Papers in Linguistics 19*: 53–75.

Tadadjeu, Maurice & Gabriel Mba. 1996. L'utilisation des langues nationales dans l'éducation au Cameroun. Les leçons d'une expérience. *TRANEL* 26: 59–75.

Takam, Alain F. 2007. Bilinguisme officiel et promotion de la langue minoritaire en milieu scolaire: Le cas du Cameroun. *Revue Électronique Internationale de Sciences du Langage SudLangues 7*: 26–48. http://www.sudlangues.sn/IMG/pdf/doc-163.pdf (20 January 2023).

Takam, Alain F. & Innocent M. Fassé. 2020. English and French bilingual education and language policy in Cameroon: The bottom-up approach or the policy of no policy? *Language Policy* 19: 61–86.

Tchoungui, Gisele. 1977. *Bilingualism in Cameroon: Historical Perspective and ssessment (1960–1980).* Yaounde: National Institute of Education.

Tchoungui, Gisele. 1983. Focus on official bilingualism in Cameroon: Its relationship to education. In Edna L. König, Emmanuel Chia & John Povey (eds.), *A Sociolinguistic Profile of Urban Centers in Cameroon*, pp. 93–115. Los Angeles, CA: Crossroads, University of California.

Todd, Loreto. 1969. Pidgin English of West Cameroon. P.h.D. dissertation. Queen's University, Belfast.

Todd, Loreto. 1979. *Some Day Been Day: West African Pidgin Folktales.* London: Routledge & Kegan Paul.

Todd, Loreto. 1982. The English language in West Africa. In Richard Bailey & Manfred Görlach (eds.), *English as a World Language*, pp. 281–305. Ann Arbor, MI: University of Michigan Press.

Tomedes. 2021. *Cameroon Language Insights: Exploring the Languages of Cameroon*. https://www.tomedes.com/translator-hub/cameroon-languages (1 March 2023).

Translators Without Borders. 2021. *Language Data for Cameroon*. https://translatorswithoutborders.org/language-data-for-cameroon (1 March 2023).

Wamba, R. Sylvie & Gérard M. Noumssi. 2003. Le français au Cameroun contemporain: Statuts, pratiques et problèmes sociolinguistiques. *Sudlangues: Revue Electronique Internationale de Sciences du Langage* 2: 1–20.

Wolf, Hans-Georg. 2001. *English in Cameroon*. Berlin: Mouton de Gruyter.

Zang Zang, Paul. 1999. Le phonétisme du français camerounais. In Gervais Mendo Zé (ed.), *Le français langue africaine*, pp. 112–129. Paris: Publisud.

CHAPTER 5

Global English in multilingual Philippines
Language practices in government communications

Loy Lising
Macquarie University

English has been used in the Philippines since the American occupation in 1898. Since its transplantation from the US through the American teachers who came and established the University of Santo Tomas, it has consistently been given a privileged position by the Constitution and in the national language policies alongside Filipino, the national language. Over the years, research on English as part of the Philippine linguistic ecology has largely encompassed four streams: the role of English alongside local languages in specific domains; the features of English as a localized language; the role of and attitude towards English in education; and critical views towards the hegemonic position of English. Research in these areas indicates the variable positioning and valuing of English in the country's multilingual ecology. This study contributes to existing knowledge by answering a fundamental research question: what is the role of English alongside local languages in government communications? To answer this question, this paper analyses two data sets: the Philippine Statistics Authority (PSA) data which outline language use across the 17 regions in the country and the local government Facebook posts of 15 of these 17 administrative regions and their comments over a five-year period (2018–2022). Findings from the analysis reveal two things: the perception or social construction of language and the discursive construction of a status of a language. There is a clear disjunction between policy and practice. While policy mandates the use of Filipino in government communications, data show an overwhelming use of English and in some cases the employment of English and Filipino. This affirms the perception of English as a local language with which even the government identifies itself and shows that English continues to hold a privileged status despite an Executive Order that stipulates the use of Filipino in government communications.

Keywords: English in the Philippines, language ecology, language policy, language practices in government communications, multilingual ecology, official language

https://doi.org/10.1075/hsld.9.05lis
Available under the CC BY-NC-ND 4.0 license.
© 2025 John Benjamins Publishing Company

1. Introduction

As of 2023, English has been used in the Philippines for exactly a century and a quarter since the American occupation in 1898 (Bernardo 2004). These 125 years of shifting language uses and values are considered in this chapter as shifting *language ecologies,* following Haugen (1971). That is, the chapter seeks to study the interactions between English and its Philippine environment (following Haugen 1971: 19) as a way of investigating English within the society in which it functions. This approach offers a useful prism through which to build on the entirety of the otherwise rather siloed literature about English in the Philippines.

Philippine English is viewed by some as a now-local language and an integral part of language use in many domains, without ignoring its history as a language of colonial power (Lising & Bautista 2022; Martin 2018). To other Filipino scholars, English continues to be seen as a colonial bequest that will always be foreign and which has persistent hegemonic effects on the local languages in the country (Tupas 2015). Both views are compatible with a language ecology approach, as the approach does not judge whether English (or any other language) *should* be used or valued; rather, it highlights the interactions between languages and their environments to better understand a multilingual social system.

Over the years, research on English in the Philippines has largely encompassed four streams: the role of English alongside local languages in specific domains (see Asuncion & Madrunio 2017; Jazul & Bernardo 2017; Magno 2017; Osborne 2015; Rosario 2010); the features of English as a localized language (see Bautista 2000; Gonzalez 1996); the role of and attitude towards English (see Amarles 2016; Jamora 2014; Mahboob & Cruz 2013; Martin 2018); and critical views towards the hegemonic position of English (see Lorente 2017; Tupas 2015). While these studies are disparate, the language ecology framework again enables these streams to converge: each tells us something about how English interacts with its environment and the other languages within that environment and, moreover, about how these interactions are structured to allow for both systemic features and dynamism (the features the ecology metaphor foregrounds). Research across these areas indicates the variable positioning and valuing of English in the country's multilingual ecology. From a language ecology standpoint, these studies are adding to our knowledge of the *status* and *intimacy* (Haugen 1971: 21) which English derives from its roles and functions.

However, most of these research studies examine English as it interacts with other languages in the local multilingual ecology mostly in the domain of education, and so it is important to consider how English interacts with other local languages in other domains.

In this chapter, the focus is on the domain of government communications, a domain as important as education. The chapter will contribute to our understanding of the role of English in the country's local multilingual ecology in an area that has not been investigated previously. It does so by answering this question: what is the role of English alongside local languages in government communications? Understanding the language practices in government communications is important as these will provide insights into language practice as a type of language policy (Spolsky 2004). That is, the use of specific language(s) by regional governments indexes their choices of language.

To do so, this paper first reviews the language profile of the Philippines based on census data published by the PSA, then it sketches an outline of the language policies of the country, both in Section 2. This is then followed in Section 3 by a description of social media data collected, and how these were analyzed. Section 4 presents the main findings — that official government social media posts across the country's 15 regions are overwhelmingly made in English. Section 5 is a discussion of their significance. The chapter concludes in Section 6 with insights for future research directions.

2. Language profile and language policies in the Philippines

2.1 Language profile of local governments and their publics

The Philippine archipelago is composed of 7,100 islands grouped geographically into three major island groups: Luzon to the North, Mindanao to the South, and Visayas between the two. Administratively, it is organized into 17 regions. These are listed in Table 1 with their respective regional center, population, and population density based on the 2020 Census (Philippine Statistics Authority 2021a). Understanding the population density is crucial in appreciating the findings on language use in local governments and the subsequent discussion in the paper.

When the COVID-19 pandemic hit the country at the start of 2020 (Edrada et al. 2020), like in most other parts of the world, communication across different sectors of society increasingly transitioned until fully online. It needs to be noted, however, that regional government communications started online long before the pandemic happened as a way of efficiently communicating with their local constituents. Other than using radio broadcasts, the Philippine local governments also shifted their communication strategy by employing the social media platform, Facebook. Each of the 17 administrative regions listed above created a Facebook account as a tool to communicate with their local constituents. To contextualize the findings about the languages these regional governments used on

Table 1. The 17 administrative regions, their regional center, their population, and density

Rank	Region & regional center	Population	Population density (Persons per square kilometer of land)
	Philippines	109,033,245	363
1	National Capital Region (NCR), Manila	13,484,462	21,765
2	IV-A CALABARZON,* Calamba	16,195,042	977
3	III Central Luzon, San Fernando	12,422,172	567
4	VII Central Visayas, Cebu City	8,081,988	509
5	I Ilocos, San Fernando	5,301,139	409
6	VI Western Visayas, Iloilo City	7,954,723	383
7	V Bicol, Legazpi	6,082,165	336
8	XI Davao, Davao City	5,243,536	257
9	X Northern Mindanao, Cagayan de Oro	5,022,768	246
10	IX Zamboanga Peninsula, Pagadian	3,875,576	229
11	XII SOCCSKSARGEN,** Koronadal	4,901,486	215
12	II Cagayan Valley, Tuguegarao	3,685,744	124
13	VIII Eastern Visayas, Tacloban	4,547,150	196
14	XIII Caraga, Butuan	2,804,788	133
15	Bangsamoro Autonomous Region in Muslim Mindanao (BARMM), Cotabato City	4,404,288	120
16	MIMAROPA Region,*** Calapan	3,228,558	109
17	Cordillera Administrative Region (CAR), Baguio	1,797,660	91

* A portmanteau of its five provinces of Cavite, Laguna, Batangas, Rizal, and Quezon.
** An acronym of the four provinces and one of its cities: South Cotabato, Cotabato, Sultan Kudarat, Sarangani, and General Santos city.
*** A portmanteau of its four provinces of Mindoro, Marinduque, Romblon, and Palawan.

Facebook, Table 2 lists the 17 administrative regions and their top three local languages based on the Philippine Statistics Authority data (2022).

The languages listed in Table 2 are the top three in each region based on their number of speakers (Philippine Statistics Authority 2022) and are part of the 184 living languages in the country as reported in Ethnologue (2023). While the lists show that there is great linguistic diversity between each of these regional multilingual ecologies, it is worth noting that Tagalog, Cebuano, and Bisaya are languages which are shared across a few of the regions. This reflects their posi-

Chapter 5. Global English in multilingual Philippines

Table 2. Administrative regions and their top three languages

Rank	Region	Top three languages
1	National Capital Region (NCR)	Tagalog,* Ilocano, Bisaya
2	IV-A CALABARZON	Tagalog, Romblon, Cuyunon
3	III Central Luzon	Tagalog, Kapampangan, Ilocano
4	VII Central Visayas	Cebuano, Bisaya, Boholano
5	I Ilocos	Ilocano, Pangasinan, Tagalog
6	VI Western Visayas	Hiligaynon, Karay-a, Capizeno
7	V Bicol	Bicol, Masbate, Tagalog
8	XI Davao	Cebuano, Bisaya, Hiligaynon
9	X Northern Mindanao	Bisaya, Cebuano, Hiligaynon
10	IX Zamboanga Peninsula	Bisaya, Cebuano, Chavacano
11	XII SOCCSKSARGEN	Hiligaynon, Cebuano, Bisaya
12	II Cagayan Valley	Ilocano, Ibanag, Tagalog
13	VIII Eastern Visayas	Waray, Bisaya, Cebuano
14	XIII Caraga	Cebuano, Bisaya, Surigaonon
15	Bangsamoro Autonomous Region in Muslim Mindanao (BARMM)	Tausug, Maranao, Maguindanao
16	MIMAROPA Region	Tagalog, Iraya, Romblomanon, Cuyonon
17	Cordillera Administrative Region (CAR)	Ilocano, Kankanaey, Ibaloi

* While the rest of the paper refers to *Filipino*, the Tables reflects *Tagalog* as reported in the data. This is because Filipino is Tagalog-based, and both nomenclatures are often used interchangeably.

tion as dominant vernaculars. It is reasonable to expect, therefore, that these top three languages in each region, and especially the dominant vernaculars that span across regions, would feature in regional government communications to local constituents or at least in the local constituents' responses to the government communications. Moreover, language policies seem to guide the use of many of these listed languages in government communications.

2.2 Language policies in the country

As I write this chapter, the country is in a state of flux with regards to its language policy reforms. The two language education policies that are still enforced but are under threats of scrutiny and potential reforms are the *Bilingual Education Policy* (Gonzalez 1998) and the *Mother Tongue-Based Multilingual Education* (MTBMLE) (Madrunio, Martin & Plata 2016). The *Bilingual Education Policy* (BEP) which promoted the separate use of English and Filipino (previously called Pilipino) as media of instruction for specific subject areas was first introduced in 1974 and was reinforced in the 1987 Constitution with an added provision for the use of major vernaculars as languages for transition to school (Bautista 1996). The BEP can be argued to have reinforced the dominance of English as it has consistently been employed as a medium of instruction alongside Filipino. The MTBMLE was introduced alongside the government's *Enhanced Education Act* in 2013 designed to enable the use of specific mother tongues for transition into schooling and literacy (Martin 2018). While there have been various changes to the national language policy over the years, English has remained an official second language, which, as often argued, is at the detriment of other local languages (Lising & Bautista 2022). Even the newly elected President Ferdinand Marcos Jr. in his first State of the Nation address delivered in July 2022 highlighted how he wants to reexamine the medium of instruction in schools, particularly emphasizing the importance of the Filipinos' English advantage relative to their marketability in the globalized world (Galvez 2022).

This tension between being rooted in the local identity and, at the same time, being marketable in the global arena (Madrunio, Martin & Plata 2016) is not new, despite being current. It has constantly plagued the country's language policy discussions except perhaps during the colonial period under Spanish rule from 1565–1898 as the Spaniards were not particularly invested in teaching the locals Spanish (Bautista 1996). Once the Americans arrived in 1898 and officially established the public school system and introduced the formal monolingual instruction in English, the 1939 Census saw a dramatic rise in people speaking English, 26.6 percent of the total population, which was at that time 16 million (Bautista 1996). So, English became an integral part of the local multilingual ecology. The late President Ferdinand Marcos Sr.'s "New Society" reform in 1978, which saw the official installation of the national strategy to market Filipino workers overseas as part of his economic strategy for the country through the installation of the Philippine Overseas Employment Authority (POEA) (Lising 2019), can be said to have strengthened the view of English as having economic capital (applying the concept from Bourdieu 1991). Since then, language policy discussions have always been largely anchored on how and which language(s) can best enhance the Filipinos' economic standing in the world.

Because language training primarily happens in schools, much of what is researched and written in the literature about these national language policies has focused on how they impact education. The other equally important domain which can provide key information on the role and impact of English in the local multilingual ecology of the country is government communications. This chapter brings this overlooked domain to the foreground. Language practices in government communications across the country are governed by Executive Order No. 335, which was issued by the late President Corazon Aquino in 1988 and which states that all government offices must take steps necessary to "use the Filipino language in official transactions, communication, and correspondence" (Office of the President of the Philippines 1988). In addition, and making *regional* government communications particularly worth investigating, there is contemporary debate in Philippine politics about the use of languages other than Filipino in government communications. Specifically, a bill called the *Plain Language Bill* was introduced to the national congress initially by Senator Miriam Defensor Santiago in 2009, 2010, and 2013. It did not pass at that time but continued to prompt debate: it was taken up and re-tabled by Senator Grace Poe in 2013, and more recently by Senator Manuel Lapid in 2020 and 2022. The bill requires the use of "plain language in English, Filipino, and/or other regional languages or dialects in all government-issued public advisories, notices, announcements and similar documents intended for public dissemination and distribution" (Lapid 2022: 2). This bill awaits approval to become law.

So, to explain how the research question that this chapter seeks to address is answered, in the following section, the data used in this paper, their manner of collection, and how they were analyzed is described.

3. Data and method

To answer the research question of this paper, two data sets were collected: language reports from the Philippine Statistics Authority (PSA) (2022) and Facebook posts of the 17 regional governments and comments made by the regional constituents in response to the posts. The PSA data are used to document the population (as reflected in Table 1) and the key languages of the 17 regions (as shown in Table 2). Information from the PSA on key languages in the region is based on census data, which are gathered every five years. During data collection, it was discovered that two of the 17 regions (Ilocos and SOCCSKARGEN) only launched their Facebook accounts in late 2022 and were therefore excluded from the analysis. In addition, some regions have no posts at various times, and these are indicated in the tables below that report the findings. So, in the end, social media data were only collected from 15 regional governments.

The Facebook posts were collected systematically from across the 15 regional government agencies' official accounts. These 15 administrative regions created their respective Facebook accounts at varying periods with all accounts up and running by the start of 2018, hence the decision to begin data collection from this point. To ensure breadth and depth of data, Facebook posts and their corresponding comments from the administrative regions across a five-year period from 2018 to 2022 were collected at the start of every quarter for the first three quarters of each year (i.e., posts published at the start of January, April, and July). The collection of multiple posts ensured that there was a variety of topics covered. Ideally, there would have been 225 posts collected. However, some regions were not as consistent in their posts, and so the data collection yielded a total of 205 Facebook posts with only 103 comments from constituents across all the posts. The 205 Facebook posts collected from across the 15 regions over the five-year period were analyzed for both topic and language(s) used.

The posts were then documented and tabulated in table form and are presented in Section 4. It is important to note that the COVID-19 pandemic hit Philippine shores at the start of 2020, which significantly influenced the kinds of topics posted by regional governments. Subsequently, these findings are discussed relative to the top three languages in each region as offered in Table 2; the language policy that ought to govern government communication as stipulated in Executive Order 335 (above); other existing studies on English alongside local languages in the Philippines, and Haugen's (1971) *language ecology* framework to tease out their implications and significance.

4. Findings and discussion

This section presents the findings from the analysis of 205 Facebook posts from the administrative regions in the five-year period between 2018 to 2022. It first presents the topics covered in these posts, then the language practices as evidenced by the language used in the posts and in the comments section, and finally, these are discussed relative to key concepts mentioned above.

4.1 Topics of local government posts

The Facebook posts cover a plethora of topics posted simply as texts and a few with embedded video-recorded information either as a news bulletin or a special message from the head official of the local government. Some of these include job postings, natural disaster warnings, information about vaccinations, New Year greetings, announcement of school closure, promotion of a region, and a fire warning. It is interesting to note here, however, that two topics dominated the posts: the COVID-19 pandemic and the presidential election. The kinds of sub-topic covered under these two most popular topics are quite extensive and include the following:

- For the COVID-19 pandemic: (1) Omicron, (2) Quarantine requirements, (3) Vaccines, (4) Year in review/annual report, (5) Health protocols, (6) Travel, (7) Contact tracing, (8) Public hearing, (9) Financial assistance, (10) Impact on businesses, (11) Task force, (12) Government statement, and (13) Case numbers.
- For posts to do with election, they include information such as the following: (1) The Presidential speech, (2) Announcement of the newly elected government official, (3) Award given, (4) Document signing, (5) Local officials' submission, (6) Meeting, (7) Government meeting with media, (8) Secretary's Press Conference, (9) Report, (10) Government project, (11) Conference, (12) Voting information session, (13) Event, (14) Honoring the President, (15) Passing of a law, (16) Press release, (17) Staff recognition, (18) Vacancies, and (19) Youth program.

All the posts bear information that serves to provide guidance and direction to the local constituents on topics concerned. Some of these posts are directly from the regional government while others contain embedded announcements from the Department of Interior and Local Government, i.e., the national executive department that is the governing body of all local administrative regions.

The predominance of the COVID-19 posts can be accounted for by the fact that the pandemic hit the country at the start of 2020 and like in most parts of the world continues to this day. The heightened rate of election posts, on the other hand, covers local elections and can also be attributed to the May 2022 election, which meant that campaigns would have begun in earnest at the start of 2022, if not earlier.

4.2 Linguistic choices in Facebook posts of administrative region

Most of the regional governments chose English for some of their Facebook posts each year. Tables 3 to 5 present the specific topics and the respective languages of the posts across the five-year period. The first of these, Table 3, shows findings from the analysis of the posts in 2018.

Table 3. Administrative regions and their Facebook posts in 2018

Rank	Region	Topics and language(s) of post
1	National Capital Region (NCR)	Election$_{19}$ (English), $_{13}$ (English & Filipino), Job Posting (English)
2	IV-A CALABARZON	Election$_6$ (English), $_5$ (English), Weather Warning (English & Filipino)
3	III Central Luzon	Election$_{13}$ (English), $_{10}$ (English)
4	VII Central Visayas	Election$_{10}$ (English)
5	I Ilocos	Facebook Page was not created until December 2022
6	VI Western Visayas	Election$_{10}$ (English), $_{11}$ (English), $_6$ (English)
7	V Bicol	Could not find posts
8	XI Davao	No posts until August 2018
9	X Northern Mindanao	Election$_6$ (English)
10	IX Zamboanga Peninsula	Election$_{11}$ (English)
11	XII SOCCSKSARGEN	Facebook Page was not created until September 2022
12	II Cagayan Valley	News Broadcast (Filipino), Election$_{17}$ (English & Filipino), Weather Warning (English)
13	VIII Eastern Visayas	Weather Warning (English), Election$_{10}$ (English & Filipino)
14	XIII Caraga	Election$_{19}$ (English), $_{17}$ (English)
15	Bangsamoro Autonomous Region in Muslim Mindanao (BARMM)	Could not find posts
16	MIMAROPA Region	Election$_{10}$ (English), Serious Fire (English)
17	Cordillera Administrative Region (CAR)	Election$_2$ (English), Government Warning (English & Filipino), Government Notice (English & Filipino)

* The number that follows either the COVID-19 or election topic indicates the sub-topic it is about based on the description in Section 4.1.

Table 3 shows that in 2018, of the 29 Facebook information posts collected across 12 of the 15 administrative regions, there are two different kinds of posts relative to language used as indicated in column four: English only and English and Filipino. The *English and Filipino* type of posts are those that use both languages in a single post as shown in Figure 1.

Figure 1. A sample post categorized as using both English and Filipino

In summary, in 2018, the majority (23 of 29) of the posts are in English only, with five in both English and Filipino and one in Filipino only, which is a birthday greeting for one of the local government officials (Cagayan Valley region).

Table 4 shows the local administrative regions' selected Facebook posts in 2019. Of the 42 posts collected across the 15 administrative regions, the language practices are like those in 2018, but with two new language practice combinations employed: an English post with an embedded videorecording that is in English and Filipino and one English post with a hashtag in Cebuano — the only time in these collection of posts in 2019 where the local language is featured.

Of all the 42 posts in 2019, the majority are in English (33); seven are in English and Filipino; and one post in English with a Cebuano hashtag, and one in

Table 4. Administrative regions and their Facebook posts in 2019

Rank	Region	Topics and language(s) of post
1	National Capital Region (NCR)	Election$_{18}$ (English), $_2$ (English), School Closures (Filipino & English)
2	IV-A CALABARZON	Election$_3$ (English), $_{13}$ (English), $_6$ (English)
3	III Central Luzon	Election$_{13}$ (English), $_2$ (English), $_6$ (English & Filipino)
4	VII Central Visayas	Election$_9$ (English), $_{13}$ (English), Job Posting (Cebuano)
5	I Ilocos	Facebook Page was not created until December 2022
6	VI Western Visayas	Election$_6$ (English), $_{10}$ (Filipino)
7	V Bicol	Election$_6$ (English)
8	XI Davao	Election$_3$ (English), $_6$ (English), $_2$ (English)
9	X Northern Mindanao	Election$_{10}$ (English), $_6$ (Filipino), $_2$ (English & Filipino)
10	IX Zamboanga Peninsula	Election$_{10}$ (English), $_6$ (English), $_2$ (English)
11	XII SOCCSKSARGEN	Facebook Page was not created until September 2022
12	II Cagayan Valley	Election$_{17}$ (Filipino), Vaccinations (English), Weather Warning (English)
13	VIII Eastern Visayas	Election$_2$ (English), $_9$ (English), Job Posting (English)
14	XIII Caraga	Election$_6$ (English)
15	Bangsamoro Autonomous Region in Muslim Mindanao (BARMM)	Election$_{10}$ (English), $_4$ (Filipino)
16	MIMAROPA Region	Election$_{10}$ (English), $_3$ (English), $_6$ (English)
17	Cordillera Administrative Region (CAR)	Election$_3$ (English), $_2$ (English & Filipino), $_7$ (English & Filipino)

Filipino only. Like in 2018, the only post purely in Filipino is a birthday greeting for a local government official (Cagayan Valley).

In 2020, 44 Facebook posts were collected from 15 administrative regions; we can see that the regional governments have gradually increased their Facebook usage year after year but from 2020 the increase stops and the number of posts in the data collection period stays at 45. Like in 2018 and 2019, most of the posts are in English (29); ten use English and Filipino; three with an English caption combined with an embedded text in English and Filipino; one with a Filipino caption

Table 5. Administrative regions and their Facebook posts in 2020

Rank	Region	Topics and language(s) of post
1	National Capital Region (NCR)	New Years (English), COVID$_{10}$ (English & Filipino), Election$_{15}$ (English & Filipino)
2	IV-A CALABARZON	Volcano Warning (English), COVID$_2$ (English & Filipino)
3	III Central Luzon	Job Posting (English), COVID$_9$ (Filipino & English)
4	VII Central Visayas	Election$_{10}$ (English), $_{13}$ (English), COVID$_9$ (English & Filipino)
5	I Ilocos	Facebook Page was not created until December 2022
6	VI Western Visayas	Election$_{13}$ (English), COVID$_2$ (Filipino), $_9$ (Filipino), $_{11}$ (Filipino)
7	V Bicol	Election$_6$ (English), COVID$_9$ (English)
8	XI Davao	Election$_{16}$ (English), $_{13}$ (English), COVID$_9$ (Filipino)
9	X Northern Mindanao	Volcano Warning (English), COVID$_9$ (English), $_2$ (English)
10	IX Zamboanga Peninsula	Election$_{10}$ (English), $_{13}$ (English & Filipino), COVID$_8$ (Filipino)
11	XII SOCCSKSARGEN	Facebook Page was not created until September 2022
12	II Cagayan Valley	Election$_{10}$ (English), COVID$_{12}$ (Filipino & English), $_2$ (Filipino & English)
13	VIII Eastern Visayas	Election$_{17}$ (English), $_6$ (English), COVID$_2$ (English)
14	XIII Caraga	Election$_6$ (English), COVID$_6$ (English)
15	Bangsamoro Autonomous Region in Muslim Mindanao (BARMM)	Election$_6$ (English), $_{13}$ (English), COVID$_{11}$ (English & Filipino)
16	MIMAROPA Region	Job Posting (English), COVID$_{13}$ (English), $_{11}$ (English)
17	Cordillera Administrative Region (CAR)	Election$_{10}$ (English), $_{13}$ (English), COVID$_2$ (English)

with a text in English and Filipino; and, yet again, one purely in Filipino. This only post in Filipino is a new year's greeting as in Figure 2.

Table 6 reflects the 2021 data which is composed of 45 Facebook posts collected from 15 administrative regions. For only the second time in four years, in the data examined, a local language is used. Specifically, one English post has a

Figure 2. A sample post in Filipino: Happy New Year!

Cebuano hashtag, #WHATISIT?. Otherwise, much like in 2018, 2019, and 2020, most of the posts are in English (29); nine are in English and Filipino; and six have an English caption combined with an embedded text in Filipino and English.

Table 6. Administrative regions and their Facebook posts in 2021

Rank	Region	Topics and language(s) of post
1	National Capital Region (NCR)	COVID$_5$ (English), $_2$ (English), Election$_3$ (Filipino)
2	IV-A CALABARZON	Election$_{10}$ (English), COVID$_2$ (Filipino & English), Natural Disaster (Filipino & English)
3	III Central Luzon	Election$_{10}$ (English), $_6$ (English), COVID$_2$ (Filipino)
4	VII Central Visayas	COVID$_1$ (English), $_6$ (Filipino & English), Election$_6$ (Filipino)
5	I Ilocos	Facebook Page was not created until December 2022
6	VI Western Visayas	Election$_3$ (English), $_{13}$ (Filipino & English), $_6$ (Filipino)
7	V Bicol	Election$_6$ (English), $_{10}$ (English), COVID$_1$ (Bicolano)
8	XI Davao	Election$_6$ (English), COVID$_7$ (English)

Chapter 5. Global English in multilingual Philippines 105

Table 6. *(continued)*

Rank	Region	Topics and language(s) of post
9	X Northern Mindanao	Election$_6$ (English), $_{10}$ (English), Job Posting (English)
10	IX Zamboanga Peninsula	COVID$_6$ (Filipino), $_3$ (English & Filipino) Election$_{13}$ (English)
11	XII SOCCSKSARGEN	Facebook Page was not created until September 2022
12	II Cagayan Valley	Election$_{16}$ (English), Job Posting (English), COVID$_3$ (English)
13	VIII Eastern Visayas	Election$_{10}$ (English), $_6$ (English), COVID$_8$ (Filipino)
14	XIII Caraga	Election$_6$ (English), $_{10}$ (English), COVID$_4$ (English & Filipino)
15	Bangsamoro Autonomous Region in Muslim Mindanao (BARMM)	Election$_{10}$ (English), $_{13}$ (English), COVID$_9$ (English)
16	MIMAROPA Region	COVID$_2$ (English), Election$_2$ (English), $_6$ (English)
17	Cordillera Administrative Region (CAR)	Election$_2$ (English), COVID$_3$ (Filipino)

Finally, Table 7 reflects the 2022 data which is composed of 45 Facebook posts collected from 15 administrative regions. Like in the four other data sets from 2018 to 2021, many of the posts are in English (21); 17 include English and Filipino constructions; six with an English post combined with an embedded text in Filipino and English; and one post codeswitched in English and Bicolano. This is the third time in the data examined that a local language is used, and the first time that Bicolano is featured.

What the data collected for this chapter have shown thus far concerning the language practices in local government communications for the benefit of their local constituents is that English is predominantly used whereas Filipino only is rarely used. When Filipino is used, it is alongside English. Overall, of the 205 posts collected and analyzed, 135 (66%) are in English only, 64 (31%) are in English and Filipino, 3 (1.5%) are in Filipino only, and 3 (1.5%) employ a local language of the region in which the post appears.

Given this extremely limited use of languages other than English or Filipino, and the clear dominance of English over Filipino, it is appropriate to investigate whether the threads in these posts in which constituents could register their comments and reactions reflected the regional governments' language choices or used local languages.

Table 7. Administrative regions and their Facebook posts in 2022

Rank	Region	Topics and language(s) of post
1	National Capital Region (NCR)	COVID$_1$ (English & Filipino), Election$_1$ (English), $_2$ (English)
2	IV-A CALABARZON	COVID$_2$ (Filipino & English), Election$_3$ (English), $_4$ (English)
3	III Central Luzon	COVID$_1$ (English & Filipino), $_3$ (English & Filipino), Election$_5$ (English)
4	VII Central Visayas	COVID$_1$ (English), Election$_1$ (Filipino), $_2$ (Filipino)
5	I Ilocos	Facebook Page was not created until December 2022
6	VI Western Visayas	Election$_6$ (English), $_7$ (Filipino), $_8$ (English & Filipino)
7	V Bicol	COVID$_4$ (English & Bicolano), Election$_3$ (English), $_2$ (Filipino)
8	XI Davao	Election$_9$ (English), $_{10}$ (English), $_3$ (English)
9	X Northern Mindanao	Election$_{11}$ (English), $_6$ (English), COVID$_2$ (Filipino)
10	IX Zamboanga Peninsula	Election$_1$ (English), $_6$ (English & Filipino)
11	XII SOCCSKSARGEN	Facebook Page was not created until September 2022
12	II Cagayan Valley	COVID$_1$ (English), Election$_{12}$ (Filipino & English), $_2$ (Filipino)
13	VIII Eastern Visayas	Election$_3$ (English), $_{13}$ (English), $_2$ (English)
14	XIII Caraga	COVID$_3$ (English), Election$_1$ (English & Filipino), $_3$ (English & Filipino)
15	Bangsamoro Autonomous Region in Muslim Mindanao (BARMM)	COVID$_4$ (English), Election$_{10}$ (Filipino), $_{14}$ (Filipino)
16	MIMAROPA Region	COVID$_2$ (English & Filipino), $_5$ (English)
17	Cordillera Administrative Region (CAR)	Election$_{15}$ (English & Filipino), $_{10}$ (English), Job Post (Filipino)

4.3 Linguistic choices of local constituents

Table 8 reflects the number of comments in the 205 Facebook posts and indicates the kinds of language practices employed by the local constituents in response to the posts.

Comments on Facebook threads are generally challenging to tabulate if there is an overwhelming number of them. As shown in Table 8, the local government

Table 8. Summary of comments in the data and the language practices

Comment/year	2018	2019	2020	2021	2022	Total
No comment	19	18	21	21	24	103
Tagging	3	2	3	5	4	17
English + Filipino	5	4	10	5	1	25
English	1	13	4	12	8	38
Filipino	–	2	5	2	3	12
English & local language	–	1	–	–	5	6
Local language	1	2	1	–	–	4
Total	29	42	44	45	45	205

communications through Facebook posts have not really generated a lot of comments except for one topic in 2022, which I have not included in the table above, and which I will discuss separately later. Where there are comments made, these are done through tagging, commenting in either English or Filipino, in English only, in Filipino only, in English and a local language, or in a local language.

However, of the 205 posts, the majority generated no comments at all (103 posts). There were 17 posts which generated tagging, a way of commenting by simply typing a person's name in the comment box whose attention the commentator wants to draw with regards the post. I have not categorized these comments by language as proper nouns/personal names are not sensibly classed as one language or another.

I will break the remaining 85 comments down by their language choices. There were 38 comments purely in English, 25 comments utilizing English and Filipino, 12 comments in Filipino, only six using English with a local language, and only four comments in a local language without English or Filipino: these four used Cebuano, Bicolano, and Arabic.

Of these three local languages, only Cebuano was used in full sentence structure (e.g., "*Nus-a pud nga bulan maglingkod ang* new officials?"). This is a query as to when the newly elected officials will take their seat in office. Bicolano was employed for a singular concept *pagsalingoy* meaning to "look back" as a title for the regional government's "year in review" post. The Arabic was used for the religious expression *Alhamdulillah!* meaning "Praise be to God!" in response to posts about the successful drive against COVID-19 and a free Licensure Exam for Teachers (LET) review available to everyone interested. This Arabic expression is used by a local constituent in the BARMM region.

The anomalous post of the 205 posts collected that generated 477 comments was posted by the administrative region of Calabarzon in 2022 (see Figure 3). It calls for the attention of the local constituents with regards to the alert levels relative to COVID-19 cases in their respective towns within the region. The alert levels are from 1 to 5. The higher number is indicative of a higher number of cases, therefore, stricter guidelines (Baclig 2022).

Figure 3. The post by the calabarzon region that generated 477 comments

    The comments for this post ranged from expressions of disbelief regarding the true existence of COVID-19, complaints against the incompetence of government officials and the way they have not managed the pandemic well, offers of prayer and encouragement to keep one's faith, criticism of the various government strategies in managing the pandemic, and expression of resignation for having to continue to deal with the pandemic for such a long period of time. What is striking in all these comments is the predominant use of both English and Filipino with some comments purely in Filipino. No other linguistic strategy was employed, that is, no English only and no other local languages (other than Filipino) were used in any of these 477 comments.

5. Discussion

What this paper has shown is that the 17 different administrative regions in the Philippines constitute a rich local multilingual ecology. The languages in this ecology collectively comprise the nation's 182 languages that make up multilingual Philippines. Against this multilingual reality, is Executive Order 335 issued in 1988 which mandates the use of Filipino, the national language, in all government communications. Spolsky (2004) would refer to this ordinance as language management by a government official as part of enacting a language policy, that is the use of Filipino in government communications. What we have seen, however, in the above findings is the predominance of English in the regional governments' communications to their local constituents, which essentially run counter to Executive Order 335. In fact, there is only a limited number of government communication that is purely in either Filipino or one of the respective dominant local languages of the regions. Such language practice which runs counter to the explicit policy mandated by the central government can be seen as a competing language policy through the observable use (Spolsky 2004) of English mostly in the government communications. While the use of the dominant local language is not a stipulated language policy, it would be reasonable to expect that government communications that seek to have as wide a reach as possible would employ the dominant local languages most common and accessible to all their constituents. However, they do not. Therefore, what we see at the two levels of government are language policy (from central government) and language practice (from regional governments) that are disjointed. To an extent, using Spolsky's (2004) three interrelated components to language policy, which are practices, beliefs, and management, one sees a competing government language policy, where language practice (by regional governments) runs counter to language management (the Executive Order). In addition, even in the comments by the local constituents, there is rarely any use of the local languages of the region. So, what do all these findings mean relative to multilingual practices, to existing research on English in the Philippines, and Haugen's notion of language ecology?

Employing the use of the social media Facebook as a communication strategy to have the widest reach among the local constituents is laudable. Of the 110 million people comprising the total population of the country (Philippine Statistics Authority 2021b), 80.3 million use Facebook as their social media platform (Kemp 2023). Facebook is therefore the most accessible tool government agencies can use for effective information dissemination, even compared to the usual modality of radio program, television news program, newspaper, and local municipal notice board. While the administrative regions' posts are expected to adhere to the language policy, the local constituents' comments, one might expect, should at least reflect the regions' dominant local languages. Neither is the case as I have shown in this chapter. The dominant use of English only in most of the 205 Facebook posts suggests that government practices see English as one of the local languages that everyone is familiar with. And this observable language choice and practice (Spolsky 2004) that is at odds with language management from the top suggests a language policy that pushes back on management per the Executive Order. This reaffirms what Lising & Bautista (2022) found in their study of university students from Manila and Cebu who view English not as a foreign linguistic code but as one of the languages in their local multilingual repertoire. At the same time, insofar as government communications are concerned, particularly at the level of the local administrative regions, English seems to replace Filipino, the national language. This implies that in terms of government communications, English is deemed the *de facto* lingua franca despite Filipino being the *de jure* language for government communications. Concerning the local constituents' limited comments on the post, it is impossible to conclude what the reasons may be for the current language practices as we have seen in the findings without further interview and ethnographic data. It would be interesting to see whether posts in one of the dominant local languages would generate more comments.

Relative to other studies investigating language practices in the country in general, the use of both Filipino and English is observed as rather common (Bugayong 2011; Gonzales 2016; Osborne 2015). These studies indicate that the use of English and Filipino simultaneously is seen as a key linguistic tool in navigating multilingual realities. However, the presented data do not show a very frequent use of both English and Filipino across the 205 posts compared to the use of English only.

The post highlighted in Figure 3 generated 477 comments that mostly employ English and Filipino. Other studies investigating multilingual practices in schools yield different language practices. Jamora (2014), for instance, studied Maranao school children and found a highly productive use of English and Filipino in schools, Sorsoganon in the community, and Maranao in the home. Whereas Turano & Malimas (2013) examined private schools in Cebu and found that parents and students prefer English over the use of English and Filipino because of the perceived privilege status of English in the global market. While these studies did not investigate the preferred language in government communications, what the findings indicate is that there is an array of preferred language practices depending on the language users' language beliefs and social circumstances. I find that the predominant use of English across the 15 administrative regions' 205 Facebook posts indicates the use of English as a lingua franca for government communications given multiple possible language choices. This dominance of English can also be argued to be based on the fact that English has been used alongside Filipino as medium of instruction for a long time now since the introduction of the Bilingual Education Policy. In turn, the use of English can perhaps also delimit the generation of comments in the local languages. The exception, of course, are the 477 comments for the one post, which are predominantly in both English and Filipino. What is rather absent is the use of the dominant local languages of the respective regions. Whether this is a case of internal hegemony where the language of the post dictates the language of the response, or whether the local constituents also view English as the default lingua franca of government communications can only be made clear with further research employing ethnographic data.

6. Conclusion

This paper set out to investigate the role of English alongside regional languages in government communications. It has done so by employing and analyzing PSA data to show the population and the languages in the local multilingual ecologies and the Facebook posts of 15 of the 17 administrative regions in the country. As mentioned earlier in the chapter, while there are 17 administrative regions, only 15 had posts for analysis as two regions (Ilocos and SOCCSKARGEN) set up their Facebook accounts only in late 2022. The analysis has shown the following findings. Firstly, each of the 17 administrative regions has distinct local languages with Tagalog, Cebuano, and Bisaya recurring in several regions. Secondly, the overwhelming majority of the 205 Facebook posts collected are in English. Thirdly, less than half of the 205 posts generated comments, and when they did, these employ language practices that mostly use English and Filipino. Overall, what these findings show is that language practices do not align with language policy. The use of mostly English in the majority of the 205 posts runs counter to the Executive Order 335 which mandates the language use in government communications and requires the use of Filipino. The disjunction between policy and practice appears to reflect a top-down approach to language policy that does not match with multilingual reality.

While the Executive Order ought to dictate the language of the government communications, we see in this case that it does not. Given that English has been enshrined in the Philippine Constitution for some time now as the official second language, and at the same time, it has been mandated as of equal status to Filipino in terms of being both media of instruction per the Bilingual Education Policy, its use seemingly as a lingua franca for government communications does not come as a surprise. What is surprising is that Filipino is not as equally used by either regional governments or their constituents on Facebook despite having been enshrined in the same Constitution as the national language and in the Bilingual Education Policy as the other medium of instruction. Rather, in multiple regions that have multilingual local ecologies, English, given its predominant use in the regional government posts, seems to be viewed as the *de facto* lingua franca. It seems to be the default lingua franca in government communications in the presence of other languages in the local multilingual ecologies. It can also be argued that the use of English in government communications is motivated by the fact that English is the lingua franca in business. Whether the use of English in the information dissemination of local administrative regions creates internal hegemony to the local languages is difficult to determine without interview data, but it is clearly dominant, and the commentators appear to accept and follow the governments' language choices rather than 'push back'. Whether this language practice on the ground has a dialectic impact on language policy (per Spolsky 2004) remains to be seen.

It is therefore clear that much work needs to be done to capture the linguistic practices in different regional multilingual ecologies. Such work needs to be comprehensive in capturing linguistic diversity (see Piller 2016 specifically on linguistic diversity that is defined by power and ideology), domains of use, sociocultural factors that impact language choice, and regional language ideologies. A turn to an ethnographic approach (Heller 2009; see Grey 2021 specifically on the emergence of ethnographic language policy studies; Piller et al. (forthc.) on multiple ethnographic work that captures language practices in various sites within one country), and particularly a multi-sited ethnography (Falzon 2016) is essential to be able to capture linguistic practices on the ground and contextualize and evaluate language policies in local multilingual ecologies.

Acknowledgements

I would like to acknowledge the invaluable assistance of Emily Pacheco, my research assistant and my incoming Master of Research student in 2024, for helping with data management which has been invaluable for my analysis.

I would also like to acknowledge the thorough and insightful feedback by Manu Vida-Mannl and Alex Grey on an earlier draft of this chapter, which tremendously helped me in fine-tuning the ideas presented here.

References

Amarles, Arceli M. 2016. Multilingualism, multilingual education, and the English language: Voices of public-school teachers. *Philippine Journal of Linguistics* 47: 90–105.

Asuncion, Zayda S. & Marilu R. Madrunio. 2017. Domains of language use among Gaddang Speakers in Nueva Viscaya, Philippines. *Philippine Journal of Linguistics* 48: 1–29.

Baclig, Cristina Eloisa. 2022. EXPLAINER: The Philippines' COVID-19 alert level system. Inquirer.Net. https://newsinfo.inquirer.net/1535963/explainer-the-philippines-covid-19-alert-level-system (15 March 2023).

Bautista, Ma. Lourdes S. 1996. An outline: The national language and the language of instruction. In Ma. Lourdes S. Bautista (ed.), *Readings in Philippine Sociolinguistics*, pp. 223–227. Manila: De La Salle University Press.

Bautista, Ma. Lourdes S. 2000. Studies of Philippine English in the Philippines. *Philippine Journal of Linguistics* 31(1): 39–65.

Bernardo, Allan B. I. 2004. McKinley's questionable bequest: Over 100 years of English in Philippine education. *World Englishes* 23(1): 17–31.

Bourdieu, Pierre. 1991. *Language and Symbolic Power*. Cambridge, MA: Harvard University Press.

Bugayong, Lenny Kaye. 2011. Taglish and the social role of code switching in the Philippines. *Philippine Journal of Linguistic* 42: 1–19.

Edrada, Edna M., Edmundo B. Lopez, Jose B. Villarama, Eumelia P. Salva Villarama, Bren F. Dagoc, Chris Smith, Ana Ria Sayo, Jeffrey A. Verona, Jamie Trifalgar-Arches, Jezreel Lazaro, Ellen Grace M. Balinas, Elizabeth Freda O. Telan, Lynsil Roy, Myvie Galon, Carl Hill N. Florida, Tatsuya Ukawa, Annavi Marie G. Villaneuva, Nobuo Saito, Jean Raphael Nepomuceno, … Rontgene M. Solante. 2020. First COVID-19 infections in the Philippines: A case report. *Tropical Medicine and Health* 48(21). https://www.ncbi.nlm.nih.gov/pmc/articles/PMC7154063/ (11 October 2024).

Ethnologue: Languages of the World. 2023. Philippines. https://www.ethnologue.com/country/PH (11 October 2024).

Falzon, Mark-Anthony. 2016. *Multi-sited Ethnography: Theory, Praxis and Locality in Contemporary Research*. London: Routledge.

Galvez, Daphne. 2022. Marcos wants to reexamine medium of instruction in schools. Inquirer.Net. https://newsinfo.inquirer.net/1634255/english-speaking-people-marcos-wants-to-reexamine-medium-of-instruction-in-schools (15 March 2023).

Gonzalez, Andrew, FSC. 1996. Philippine English. In Ma. Lourdes S. Bautista (ed.), *Readings in Philippine Sociolinguistics*, pp. 88–92. Manila: De La Salle University Press.

Gonzalez, Andrew, FSC. 1998. The language planning situation in the Philippines. *Journal of Multilingual and Multicultural Development* 19(5): 487–525.

Gonzales, Wilkinson Daniel Wong. 2016. Trilingual code-switching using quantitative lenses: An exploratory study on Hokanglish. *Philippine Journal of Linguistics* 47: 106–128.

Grey, Alexandra. 2021. *Language Rights in a Changing China: A National Overview and Zhuang Case Study*. Berlin: De Gruyter.

Haugen, Einar. 1971. The ecology of language. *The Linguistic Reporter* 13(1): 19–26.

Heller, Monica. 2009. Doing ethnography. In Li Wei & Melissa G. Moyer (eds.), *The Blackwell Guide to Research Methods in Bilingualism and Multilingualism*, pp. 249–262. Oxford: Blackwell.

Jamora, Michael J.A. 2014. Multilingualism: An ethnographic study on Maranao school children in Sorsogon City, Philippines. *CNU Journal of Higher Education* 9: 1–14.

Jazul, Maria Eina Maxine A. & Alejandro S. Bernardo. 2017. A look into Manila Chinatown's linguistic landscape: The role of language and language ideologies. *Philippine Journal of Linguistics* 48: 75–98.

Kemp, Simon. 2023. Digital 2023: The Philippines. DataReportal. https://datareportal.com/reports/digital-2023-philippines (15 March 2023).

Lapid, Manuel. 2022. The plain language act. *Senate of the Philippines*. https://legacy.senate.gov.ph/lisdata/3801235340!.pdf (15 March 2023).

Lising, Loy. 2019. Philippine languages in multilingual Sydney. In Alice Chik, Phil Benson & Robyn Moloney (eds.), *Multilingual Sydney*, pp. 205–211. London: Routledge.

Lising, Loy & Ma. Lourdes S. Bautista. 2022. A tale of language ownership and identity in multilingual society. *Journal of English and Applied Linguistics* 1(1): 1–14. https://animorepository.dlsu.edu.ph/jeal/vol1/iss1/1 (11 October 2024).

Lorente, Beatriz. 2017. *Scripts of Servitude: Language, Labor Migration and Transnational Domestic Work*. Bristol: Multilingual Matters.

Madrunio, Marilu Ranosa, Isabel Pefianco Martin & Sterling Miranda Plata. 2016. English language education in the Philippines: Policies, problems, and prospects. In Robert Kirkpatrick (ed.), *English Language Education Policy in Asia. Language Policy*, Vol 11, pp. 245–264. Cham: Springer.

Magno, Joseleanor. M. 2017. Linguistic landscape in Cebu city higher education offering communication programs. *Asia Pacific Journal of Multidisciplinary Research* 5(1): 94–103.

Mahboob, Ahmar & Priscilla Cruz. 2013. English and mother-tongue-based multilingual education: Language attitudes in the Philippines. *Asian Journal of English Language Studies* 1.

Martin, Isabel Pefianco (ed.). 2018. *Reconceptualizing English Education in a Multilingual Society: English in the Philippines*. Singapore: Springer.

Office of the President. 1988. *Executive Order Nos.: 171–190*. Manila: Presidential Management Staff. https://www.officialgazette.gov.ph/1988/08/25/executive-order-no-335-s-1988/ (15 March 2023).

Osborne, Dana M. 2015. Negotiating the Hierarchy of Languages in Ilocandia: The Social and Cognitive Implications of Massive Multilingualism in the Philippines. P.h.D. dissertation. The University of Arizona. https://repository.arizona.edu/handle/10150/556859?show=full (11 October 2024).

Philippine Statistics Authority (PSA). 2021a. *Highlights of the Population Density of the Philippines 2020 Census of Population and Housing (2020 CPH)*. https://psa.gov.ph/population-and-housing/node/164857 (15 March 2023).

Philippine Statistics Authority (PSA). 2021b. *2020 Census of Population and Housing (2020 CPH) Population Counts Declared Official by the President*. https://psa.gov.ph/content/2020-census-population-and-housing-2020-cph-population-counts-declared-official-president (15 March 2023).

Philippine Statistics Authority (PSA). 2022. *Ethnicity, Language/Dialect Generally Spoken at Home*. https://psa.gov.ph/issip-stat-activity/classifications (15 March 2023).

Piller, Ingrid. 2016. *Linguistic Diversity and Social Justice: An Introduction to Applied Sociolinguistics*. Oxford: Oxford University Press.

Piller, Ingrid, Donna Butorac, Emily Farrell, Loy Lising, Shiva Motaghi-Tabari & Vera Williams Tetteh. forthc. *Life in a New Language*. Oxford: Oxford University Press.

Rosario Jr., F. C. 2010. Languages at home: The case of bi/multilingualism in Pangasinan. In *Conference Proceedings of the International Conference on Language, Culture and Society in Asian Contexts*, pp. 247–258. Mahasarakham Province: Faculty of Humanities and Social Sciences, Mahasarakham University.

Spolsky, Bernard. 2004. *Language Policy*. Cambridge: Cambridge University Press.

Tupas, Ruanni. 2015. Inequalities of multilingualism: Challenges to mother tongue-based multilingual education. *Language and Education* 29(2): 112–124.

Turano, Charity & Mary Malimas. 2013. Medium of Instruction for KI-Grade 3 in the private schools in Cebu city: Revelations of language preference, usage, exposure and views of students. *Philippine Journal of Linguistics* 44(2): 61–82.

CHAPTER 6

Top-down policies and the language profiles of Malaysians in a multilingual language ecology

Stefanie Pillai & Siti Zaidah Zainuddin
University of Malaya Kuala Lumpur

Malaysia is a multilingual country with more than 100 languages comprising, among others, Standard Malay and its mainly geographical varieties as well as indigenous, Chinese, and Indian languages. Over the years, language and education policies have put the national and official language, Malay, at the forefront of the language ecology in the country, while English continues to be given considerable attention in the education and employment sectors. The language ecology in Malaysia is dynamic in reflecting the dominant languages within a multicultural environment. This chapter examines two interrelated aspects within the Malaysian multilingual language ecology: language and education policies and the language profiles of a group of Malaysian undergraduates. The examination of these two aspects against the demographic backgrounds of the undergraduates indicates that their backgrounds influence the language profiles of Malaysians. In short, this chapter offers a glimpse into the effect of top-down policies, as an ecological factor, on the language profiles of students from different ethnic and economic groups, language backgrounds, and medium of instruction streams at a public university in Malaysia.

Keywords: language ecology, language education, language policy, Malaysia, multilingualism

1. Introduction

Malaysia prides itself on being a multilingual country with an estimated 131 languages (Eberhard, Simons & Fennig 2023). These languages include the national and official language of the country, Malay, and its many geographical varieties, as well as indigenous languages such as Iban (1,452,000), Kadazan (264,000), Semai

(45,000), and Temuan (32,000).[1] Migration from China and South Asia, especially during the British colonial period from the 18th to the 20th centuries[2] has also resulted in various Chinese and Indian languages being spoken in Malaysia. These include Tamil (1,890,000), Cantonese (1,460,000), Hokkien (3,500,000), and an increasingly Mandarin-speaking Malaysian Chinese population (1,230,000).[3] Over the years, language and education policies have foregrounded the national and official language, Malay. However, English language education continues to be given considerable emphasis. This emphasis can be linked to Malaysia's colonial legacy, but it is also an effect of changing national and global priorities and opportunities. In addition, these changing opportunities have caused an increasing interest in speaking Mandarin not just among the ethnic Chinese population in the country, but among other ethnic groups (Pillai, Kaur & Chau 2021). It is not uncommon, for example, to find Malay and Indian children attending Chinese-medium primary schools in which Mandarin is the main language of instruction (Mohsen 2020).

The use and status of languages in Malaysia are linked to the many layers in which they function. These layers include language and education policies, socio-economic status, national agendas, as well as local and global economic trends and point to the need to apply a more ecological approach to languages (Eliasson 2015; Haugen 1972; Skutnabb-Kangas 2011). Such an ecological approach will be used to examine two interrelated aspects of Malaysia's language ecology: language and education policies and the language profiles of a group of Malaysian undergraduate students. The questions we explore in this chapter are as follows:

1. What are the policies that have shaped language education and use in Malaysia?
2. What are the language profiles of Malaysian undergraduates?

These students' profiles will provide a snapshot of the multilingual language profiles of young Malaysian adults which will be discussed within the context of the policies and the students' backgrounds to obtain a better understanding of how the policies and backgrounds of students have shaped their language experiences within Malaysia's language ecology.

---

1. Estimated number of speakers from Eberhard, Simons & Fennig (2023).
2. See Andaya & Andaya (2017) for a historical account.
3. Estimated number of speakers from Eberhard, Simons & Fennig (2023).

2. Malaysia's language ecology

The British colonial educational legacy of the country, the multi-ethnic composition, as well as laws and policies regarding language and education are among the key elements that have shaped the current linguistic ecology of Malaysia. These elements are likely to have shaped the changing language profiles of Malaysians. Using an ecological approach enables a contextual understanding of these elements and their interactions with language use within the Malaysian multilingual context.

Stemming from Haugen (1972), who called for a new way to examine languages in multilingual contexts, the central aspect of an ecological approach to language is to examine the relationship between languages and their environment. Mirroring the concept of ecology from biology, the links between various elements in the environment in which languages exist, or are used, are considered to be important in the study of these languages. Like the natural world, these elements and their connections may affect the status of the language and its 'survival'. The introduction of new elements in a language environment, for example, due to colonization and migration patterns, changes the ecology of this environment. The changes include the following: new languages are introduced (e.g., English), contact languages develop (e.g., Baba Malay, Melaka Chitty, and Melaka Portuguese), dominant languages take hold (e.g., Malay as a national language), and the survival of languages is threatened (e.g., indigenous languages). Language and language education policies are also elements that can have the same effect on the ecological system of a linguistic context. At the same time, we are reminded that "the ecology of a language is determined primarily by the people who learn it, use it, and transmit it to others" (Haugen 1972: 57). As put forth by Creese & Martin (2003: 161):

> [A]n ecological approach to language in society, then, requires an exploration of the relationship of languages to each other and to the society in which these languages exist. This includes the geographical, socio-economic, and cultural conditions in which the speakers of a given language exist, as well as the wider linguistic environment.

Based on this understanding of an ecological approach to the study of language, studies examining the language ecology of a particular context tend to have both a macro and a micro perspective. This could be in the form of policies shaping or attempting to shape language use in addition to the effects of these policies on language users.

One example that shows these two levels of examination is a study by Siemund, Schulz & Schweinberger (2014) on Singapore's linguistic ecology. Similar to the paper at hand, they focused on the language profiles of Singaporean students from two educational backgrounds (polytechnics and universities) and discussed their findings in relation to the official stance on multilingualism and the use of the local variety of English, Singlish. They posit that rather than multilingualism, "individual bilingualism" (Siemund, Schulz & Schweinberger 2014: 360) will become more common among Singaporeans with English as one of their languages. They also conclude that despite the government's *Speak Good English Movement*, Singlish is viewed positively by young Singaporeans who see it as a part of their national identity.

The focus on one segment of the linguistic ecology of Singapore, i.e., young adults in educational settings, was expanded by Leimgruber, Siemund & Terassa (2018), this time with the addition of students in vocational training schools. This study yielded findings that were similar to Siemund, Schulz & Schweinberger (2014) about the notion of multilingualism in the context of Singapore and general attitudes towards Singlish. The three different educational backgrounds of the students in this study were related to social and ethnic differences based on the typical demographic profiles of these institutions. One salient difference among the cohorts of students was that Chinese students, especially those from polytechnics, were more likely to be trilingual. In contrast, students from the vocational institutions, who were mainly Malays and considered to be from a lower social stratum, displayed a bilingual profile that included Malay. The use of Malay or being trilingual was not common among the university students. In the following sections, we examine these two interrelated aspects in Malaysia's language ecology: language and education policies, and the language profiles of a group of Malaysian undergraduate students. Before we do that, it should be noted that even though Malay is the national language of Singapore, it does not have the same standing as it does in neighboring Malaysia.

2.1 Language and ethnicity

Malaysians are assigned to a 'race' ('bangsa' in Malay) from birth. This term tends to be used synonymously with the term 'ethnicity' which is used in the national census (Reddy & Selvanathan 2020). Malays comprise 70 percent of the Malaysian population categorized as 'Bumiputra', which literally means 'sons of the soil' (Department of Statistics Malaysia 2022). This category also includes the indigenous groups in Peninsular Malaysia, the Orang Asli (Endicott 2015), and the indigenous groups of Sabah and Sarawak (Salleh et al. 2021). As for what constitutes being Malay, Article 160(2) of the Federal Constitution of Malaysia (Federal Constitution Malaysia 1957/1963) considers this to be "a person who professes the religion of Islam, habitually speaks the Malay language, [and] conforms to Malay custom" (130). In addition to the Bumiputras, the Chinese make up 23.2 percent of the population in Malaysia, while those classified as Indians make up 6.7 percent of the population (Department of Statistics Malaysia 2022). There is also a category called 'Others,' which is a catch-all category for members of the population who do not fall into the previous categories comprising 0.7 percent of the population (Department of Statistics Malaysia 2022).

These 'race'-based categories of Malay, Chinese, and Indian reflect the three main local languages in Malaysia: Malay, Mandarin, and Tamil. The standard spoken and written variety of Malay language is the national and official language of Malaysia. The colloquial spoken variety of Malay acts as a lingua franca among Malaysians while geographical or state-based varieties of Malay tend to be the local language of communication in many states in the country (e.g., Kelantan, Sabah, and Sarawak Malay). Malaysians of Chinese heritage are likely to speak a Chinese language as a first language followed by Malay and English. However, although there are many Chinese languages spoken in Malaysia, Mandarin is increasingly replacing other Chinese languages as the first language of Chinese Malaysians. This shift and emphasis placed on Mandarin is not only because it is used in education but also because it is rooted in the global influence of China and because Mandarin is "seen as a symbol of a wider, ethnic identity" among Malaysian Chinese (Vollmann & Soon 2018: 53).

For Malaysians of South Asian heritage, Tamil is the language of the largest group of Malaysia Indians. Malaysian Tamil speakers are mainly of South Indian Tamil heritage with a smaller number of them being of Sri Lankan Tamil descent. They are generally trilingual Tamil, Malay, and English speakers (Nalliannan, Perumal & Pillai 2021). However, studies have reported a shift from Tamil to English as the first language especially among the more educated and professional Tamils (David & Naji 2000; Schiffman 2002). Such a shift towards English as a first language has also been observed among other groups of Malaysian Indians. These include the Punjabis (David, Naji & Kaur 2003) and Malayalees (David & Nambiar 2002).

The various indigenous languages comprise about 85 percent of the living languages in Malaysia (Eberhard, Simons & Fennig 2023). There are also at least three contact languages, i.e., Melaka Portuguese or Papiá Cristang, Baba Malay, and Chitty Malay, in Malaysia (Austin & Pillai 2020). Unfortunately, these contact languages and most of the indigenous languages are endangered due to declining numbers of speakers and a lack of inter-generational transmission (Coluzzi 2017; Eberhard, Simons & Fennig 2023; Pillai, Soh & Kajita 2014). The Federal Constitution explicitly states that "no person shall be prohibited or prevented from using (otherwise than for official purposes), or from teaching or learning, any other language" (Federal Constitution Malaysia 1957/1963.). At present, three indigenous languages are taught in selected schools (Iban, Kadazandusun, and Semai).

2.2 Language and education policies

Preschool education is not legally mandatory for Malaysian children, although there are government-run and private preschools in the country. At present, only six years of primary education in three mediums of instruction (Malay, Chinese, and Tamil) is compulsory for all Malaysian children from the age of six. Malaysian students then have the option of three years of lower secondary education followed by two years of upper secondary education in public schools although this is not mandatory. At the lower secondary level, vocational education is offered in selected schools (Sulaiman & Ambotang 2017), while at the upper secondary level, there is also the option of technical schools and vocational colleges (Kementerian Pendidikan Malaysia 2023). There are also Islamic secondary schools with a focus on the Arabic language (Modern Standard Arabic or MSA), Islamic studies, and other academic subjects (Kementerian Pendidikan Malaysia 2020). Those who wish to pursue higher education will need to do an additional two years of post-secondary education in form six in public schools or equivalent programs in the public or private education system (see UNESCO 2017). Public examinations were replaced by school-based assessments for primary year six in 2021 and secondary year three in 2022. Only the Malaysian Certificate of Education and Malaysian Vocational Certificate remain as national examinations at the end of secondary year five.

Laws and policies concerning language and education in newly independent Malaya in 1957, and subsequently Malaysia (as of 1963), were initially focused on the creation of a common national identity via the national language. However, the pressure of globalization and being competitive as well as the desire to become an education hub have given rise to new developments in the education sector which in turn inadvertently affect the use of the national language. To begin with, the status of Malay as a national language is enshrined in Article 152 of the Federal Constitution (1957/1963), which at the same time recognizes the right to use and teach other languages. As part of the gradual process of weaning out English, exceptions were made in post-independent Malaya for the continued use of English in, for example, parliament, state assemblies, legislative matters, and legal proceedings.

Whilst Article 152 of the Federal Constitution (1957/1963) instituted Malay as national language, subsequently, upon the formation of Malaysia in 1963, Malay was declared as the official language throughout Malaysia via the National Language Acts (National Language Acts 1963/1967).[4] This was, however, with the

---

4. Note that the formation of Malaysia in 1963 comprised a merger of Peninsular Malaya, Singapore, Sabah, and Sarawak. However, Singapore left to become an independent nation in 1965.

exception of the two new states of Sabah and Sarawak on the island of Borneo which were given more time to transition from English to the national language in terms of its use for official purposes. Thus, there were different points in time when the transition to Malay was taking place in the two different geographical locations in Malaysia. This difference affects the way in which English is currently used and viewed in these two locations.

The provisions in the Federal Constitution (1957/1963) have had a spill-over effect on education. Upon independence, the socio-political focus in Malaysia was on national identity and unity and, thus attention was also paid to education. During the pre-independent period, there were schools with different mediums of instruction and school curricula. In other words, young Malaysians were learning different things in different languages (e.g., Malay, Tamil, and Mandarin). Thus, as part of an attempt to begin inculcating a sense of national identity and national values, a common national curriculum was introduced in the public school system (Report of the Education Committee 1956, also known as the Razak Report).

From the point of independence in 1957, Tamil and Chinese (Mandarin) remained alternative mediums of instruction in primary education along with English and Malay. Schools that used Tamil and Chinese as their medium of instruction were maintained due to socio-political pressure in newly formed Malaya against a Malay/English bilingual education system (Rei Tiah 2021). By the late 1960s, however, there was an earnest effort to phase out English-medium instruction at the primary and secondary school levels and replace it with Malay. By 1983, this transition was completed (Puteh 2006). This meant that by the 1980s, there were at least two main groups of Malaysians with different education backgrounds which in turn influenced the use and perceptions of English and Malay. Early descriptions of the Malaysian variety of English even divided it into two categories based on the type of schools the speakers went to. They differentiated between Malaysian English Type I and Malaysian English Type II spoken by those who attended English-medium schools and Malay-medium schools respectively (Platt & Weber 1980). Type I was described to be the same as Singapore English and was considered the educated variety of English. Type II was considered a second language variety with perceivable linguistic differences, from the educated variety.

The change to Malay-medium education was provided for in the 1961 Education Act (Raman & Tan 2015), which also affected Chinese-medium secondary schools during that period (Tan & Teoh 2015). These schools were given the choice to either become private Chinese-medium secondary schools or change their status to national schools which use Malay as the medium of instruction (Tan & Teoh 2015). At present, those that opted to become national secondary schools tend to have mainly Malaysian Chinese students and offer more hours of Mandarin language classes compared to the national secondary schools (Lim

2017) – that may not offer Mandarin as a subject at all. These two types of secondary schools use Malay as the main medium of instruction and the same national curriculum. However, the mainly mono-ethnic composition of the 81 national-type secondary schools (Lim 2017) suggests that Mandarin is extensively used in these schools. Other mainly mono-ethnic national secondary schools include technical, and residential schools. In the religious schools, apart from the national curriculum, Arabic is a compulsory subject and Islamic-based subjects are taught in Arabic (Haji Ibrahim & Abd. Rahman 2018). The ethnic composition and the languages used in the different schools influence the language profiles of the students attending these schools. One example is the inclusion of Arabic for those in the national religious secondary schools.

The status of Malay as the main medium of instruction in all educational institutions, except for the Chinese- and Tamil-medium primary schools, was further emphasized in the National Education Act 1996 which replaced the 1961 Act (Raman & Tan 2015). The transition to Malay as the main language of instruction affected the universities in the 1980s. This shift affected the oldest university in Malaysia, Universiti Malaya, the most as it had been using English as its medium of instruction since its inception.

Public universities were permitted to teach science-based subjects in English in the early 1990s (Gill 2002) in line with the country's response to globalization and its aim to be a regional education hub (Economic Planning Unit 1993). This came with a policy to increase the number of international students in public universities which led to many courses being taught in English. The shift from Malay to English for science, technology, engineering, and mathematics (STEM) courses at the tertiary level signaled the beginning of a policy change.

In 2003, a new policy of 'Teaching and Learning of Science and Mathematics in English' (ETeMS) – or its Malay acronym, PPSMI – was implemented in stages at primary and secondary schools based on what was perceived to be the increasing importance of English as a language of science and technology. As might have been expected, this policy was met with resistance, especially from Malay and Chinese language and education groups. One of the compromises was that Chinese-medium schools could teach science and mathematics in both English and Mandarin which was a labor and time-intensive exercise given the extra hours needed to do this. Subsequent reports of poor performance in the two subject areas were among the key reasons for the reversal of this policy in 2012 (Hashim 2009, 2014; Rashid, Abdul Rahman & Yunus 2017). Apart from resulting in two main cohorts of Malaysian students (ETeMS and non-ETeMs), the reversal of the policy involved a considerable amount of time and money in terms of, for example, in-service language and professional development for teachers and the development of new materials.

Where private education is concerned, the medium of instruction is mainly English. Policy changes allowed more private and international schools to operate, and in addition the 40 percent quota for Malaysian students to be enrolled in international schools was abolished in 2012. Previously confined to children of expatriates, the number of Malaysians in international schools has increased with more than half of the students in these schools being Malaysians (Nasa & Pilay 2017). This liberalization of education is echoed in the *Malaysia Education Development Plan 2013–2025* (Kementerian Pendidikan Malaysia 2013) which aimed to provide more access to and choice in the type of education systems provided. The opening of the private education sector including higher education was also part of the country's economic agenda as education was among Malaysia's National Key Economic Areas (Performance Management and Delivery Unit 2010). Like ETeMS, this has produced two major streams of Malaysians who have different educational experiences and levels of exposure to an English-speaking environment. In principle, these differences contradict the spirit of wanting to foster national unity through a common curriculum and language. Official statements reported in the media appear to still emphasize the national language (Pillai, Kaur & Chau 2021), but policies and practices related to public and private education, such as ETeMS, the internationalization of higher education, and the expansion of private and international schools, have all inadvertently shifted the focus from Malay to English. In addition, since the Malaysian students enrolled in international schools tend to come from higher socio-economic groups, a language-related social gap has also been created between Malaysians from public and international schools.

With the reversal of ETeMS in 2012, a new initiative, 'Upholding the Malay Language and Strengthening the English Language' or its Malay acronym MBMMBI, was introduced. This initiative aimed to create proficient bilingual speakers and was seen as a way to address the decreasing levels of proficiency in English. At the same time, this focus on bilingual proficiency has caused this initiative to be perceived as not supporting the national language. A related initiative was the Dual Language Programme (DLP), which gave schools the option of using Malay and/or English for the teaching of subjects related to science, technology, engineering, and mathematics (Kaur & Shapii 2018). The state of Sarawak decided to adopt this policy throughout the state from January 2020, with science and mathematics taught in English in Year One at all national primary schools, except for Chinese-medium primary schools. This policy obtained approval from the Ministry of Education and the Council of Ministers as education comes under the purview of the federal government.

The Malaysia Education Blueprint 2013–2025 (Ministry of Education Malaysia 2013) also mentions the learning of a third language. As of 2020, the list of elective language subjects that upper-secondary school students can take includes three indigenous languages, i.e., Iban, Kadazandusun, and Semai (Ministry of Education Malaysia 2019), although, in practice, these would only be available in the areas where these languages are spoken and would depend on the availability of teaching and learning resources. In the past, other languages were mainly offered at residential schools, but due to the third language policy, several day-schools now offer languages such as Arabic, French, German, Japanese, Korean, and Mandarin (Ministry of Education Malaysia 2018).

2.3 English in Malaysia

The present-day use and status of English in the country can be traced to the increasing influence of English which grew with the expanding British presence throughout the country from the 18th century (Andaya & Andaya 2017). English was used in administration and business and English-medium schools began to be set up mainly in urban areas (Shanmugavelu et al. 2020). These schools were considered more prestigious than Malay-medium and other vernacular schools and, as Omar (2012) suggests, they contributed to the increased use and influence of English in the country. This is not entirely surprising, as proficiency in English would have provided access to secondary and higher education and job opportunities, particularly in the civil service. However, the official use of English began to gradually decrease once Peninsular Malaysia (then Malaya) achieved independence in 1957 and Malay was declared the national language.

Apart from the educated variety of English taught in schools, a local contact variety of English has developed over the years and is used today as one of the local lingua francas among Malaysians of different ethnic and language backgrounds (Gill 2002). There are common linguistic and pragmatic features (Pillai & Ong 2018) that make the Malaysian variety of English "a carrier of a distinctly Malaysian identity" (Schneider 2007: 150). Used by bi/multilingual speakers, English is often interspersed with other local languages. Thus, translanguaging, i.e., "the deployment of a speaker's full linguistic repertoire without regard for watchful adherence to the socially and politically defined boundaries of named (and usually national and state) languages" (Otheguy, García & Reid 2015: 283), is a common phenomenon among Malaysians. In addition to varieties of local languages, Malaysian speakers may have both the more colloquial and a standard spoken variety of English as part of their linguistic repertoire and use these varieties in separate contexts or intermittently (Pillai 2008). There continues, however, to be tensions between the use of the colloquial and standard variety of spoken English (Mohd. Don 2016; Ng & Diskin-Holdaway 2023; Zainuddin et al. 2019). Particularly in the context of education, the more colloquial variety of English in general and especially features of pronunciation that do not conform to a 'native speaker' model tend to be seen as deficient and not fit for international communication. Such "linguistic conservatism" (Wee 2018: 42) also underlies the latest English language policy.

In the next section, we zoom in on the language profiles of Malaysian students at a public university. We will then discuss the findings in relation to the context of the language and education policies that have shaped their language profiles and experiences.

3. Methodology

As mentioned in Section 1, we explore two questions in this chapter i.e., 'What are the policies that have shaped language education and use in Malaysia?' and 'What are the language profiles of Malaysian undergraduates?'. The findings presented in this section relate to the second question. They are based on a survey that was carried out to examine the language profiles of undergraduate students at a public university in Malaysia. The findings will be discussed in the context of the students' backgrounds and in relation to the language and education policies (see previous sections) that have shaped these profiles.

3.1 Respondents and context

In 2023, the authors sent a link to a survey to Malaysian students from undergraduate degree programs at a public university in Malaysia with the help of colleagues teaching English language courses to undergraduates. There was no compulsion for the students to respond to the online questionnaire. Thus, the study employed a randomized sampling method on the students in these English courses. In the initial part of the questionnaire, the respondents were asked for their consent to participate in the study.

The university is a multidisciplinary comprehensive university in Malaysia offering undergraduate and postgraduate academic programs spanning from medicine to creative arts. Most science and technology courses are taught in English. Furthermore, many of the courses in the field of Humanities and Social Sciences are taught in English. This is furthered by the presence of international students at the university. Arabic is used in core courses related to Islamic studies as well as in the Arabic language degree program. For other language-related degree programs, such as Italian, French, German, Japanese, Mandarin, Spanish, and Tamil, the core courses at the department level are taught in their respective languages.

3.2 The survey

To obtain the students profiles, the questions in the survey were divided into three main sections:

1. Section A: Demographic information comprising 18 multiple choice and dichotomous closed-ended questions, e.g., gender, ethnicity, age, family household income, educational background (medium of instruction of their education), and language grades for Malay and English language.
2. Section B: Multilingual profiles consisting of 13 multiple-choice and closed-ended rating scale questions, e.g., language most frequently used, language use at home, at university, and on social media, and their perceived level of proficiency in Malay and English.
3. Section C: Perceptions about language use using 20 closed-ended rating scale questions, e.g., ability to speak Malay, English, and Mandarin, language mixing, heritage languages, and the use of English.

4. Results

4.1 Demographic information

A total of 157 Malaysian undergraduates participated in the study. The respondents were mainly aged between 18 to 24 years old ($n=156$, 99.4%), with 65 percent ($n=102$) of them being females. In terms of gender, the percentage mirrors the national statistics of students' enrolment at public institutions of higher education (Kementerian Pendidikan Tinggi 2021a). In relation to ethnic identity, the majority of the respondents identified themselves as Malay 68.8 percent ($n=108$) and four identified as other Bumiputra (two Kadazandusun, one Banjar, and one Bugis). There were 25.5 percent ($n=40$) of Chinese and 3.2 percent ($n=5$) of Indian ethnicity. This is reflective of the overall ethnic breakdown of the Malaysian population (see Section 2.1). In terms of the respondents' place of residence, most of the students were from urban ($n=67$, 42.7%) and semi-urban ($n=61$, 38.9%) areas of Malaysia while 18.5 percent ($n=29$) were from rural areas. More than half of them were from families with a household income of below RM4,850 per month ($n=80$, 51%) which would place them in the lower income group or Bottom 40 per ent of the population (B40) (Department of Statistics Malaysia 2021). This percentage is about 23 percent less than the national percentage of 74.2 percent for public university students in the B40 category (Kementerian Pendidikan Tinggi 2021b). 36.9 percent of the respondents indicated household incomes between RM4,850 and RM10,959 per month ($n=58$)

placing them in the middle-income or M40 group. Only 12.1 percent ($n=19$) declared household incomes as being more than RM10,960 a month (Top 20 or T20 income group).

4.2 Language and education

Most of the respondents attended national schools with only two respondents saying that they attended private or international primary and secondary schools. This is to be expected as Malaysians from private and especially international school backgrounds do not typically attend public universities. The type of schools and the medium of instruction at the different levels of education are consistent with the demographic profile of the respondents and the education system and policies of the country.

As shown in Table 1, the majority of the respondents attended preschools with Malay as the main medium of instruction. Given the information about household income, the choice of medium of instruction at the preschool level is related to ethnicity. Most ($n=29$, 72.5%) of the Chinese respondents, attended Chinese-medium preschools with only one Chinese respondent indicating that he attended a Malay-medium preschool. All the Chinese respondents who attended Chinese-medium preschools went on to Chinese-medium primary schools. Only five non-Chinese attended Chinese-medium preschools of which three (2.8%) were Malay and two were indigenous respondents. Four of these non-Malay respondents also went on to Chinese-medium primary schools.

Table 1. Medium of instruction at different levels of education[*]

Language	Malay	English	Mandarin	Tamil	Arabic	French	Japanese	Mixed
Preschool	59.2	18.5	21.7	0.6	0	0	0	0
Primary	65.6	4.5	29.3	0.6	0	0	0	0
Secondary	65.6	17.2	5.7	0	11.5	0	0	0
Pre-University	42.7	32.5	0	0	22.9	0.6	0	1.2
University	12.7	52.2	0	0	33.1	0	0.6	1.2

* Numbers indicate percentages.

All 40 Chinese respondents went to Chinese-medium primary schools, while there was a total of six non-Malay respondents who attended Chinese-medium primary schools. These figures indicate the preference for Chinese-medium primary education among Malaysian Chinese and is consistent with the decline in the percentage of Chinese students enrolling in national Malay-medium schools

(Rahim, Tan & Carvalho 2020). As Chinese- (and Tamil-) medium schools are only allowed at the primary school level, Chinese students had to switch to Malay-medium schools at the secondary level. However, as previously mentioned, the legacy of what were previously Chinese-medium secondary schools remains in the form of national-type secondary schools. Although Malay is supposed to be the main medium of instruction in these schools, the predominantly Chinese students and teachers and the emphasis on Mandarin suggest an inclination to use Mandarin in the classroom. Thus, it is not surprising that the nine respondents who attended Chinese-medium primary schools and went on to this type of secondary school all indicated Mandarin as the medium of instruction in these schools. However, after this level, Mandarin no longer features in the national education system (see Figure 1).

Figure 1 illustrates the shift in language used as a medium of instruction from preschool to the undergraduate level. It can be observed that the use of Malay tapers off after secondary school, while the opposite trend can be observed for English. English-medium education is available at the preschool level but not at the national primary school level. The only options to continue with EMI education would be private or international schools. The drastic rise in English after primary education is replicated by Arabic. Arabic (MSA) is quite present in this study because 37.6 percent ($n=59$) of the respondents were pursuing a degree in Arabic language and linguistics and another seven were doing Islamic-related degrees (e.g., Bachelor of Shariah, Bachelor of Islamic Education, and Bachelor of Muamalat Management) at the time of data collection.

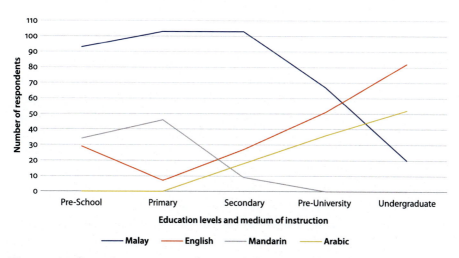

Figure 1. Medium of instruction trends across different levels of education of 159 undergraduate students in Malaysia

Malay and English are part of the compulsory entry requirements for public universities for Malaysians. For Malay, their grades in the examination at the end of their fifth form (Malaysian Certificate of Education or Sijil Pelajaran Malaysia) show that the vast majority of the students in this study obtained Grade A ($n=129$, 82.2%) and Grade B ($n=22$, 14%). Only six respondents obtained a Grade C (3.8%). The grades appeared to be linked to the respondents' ethnicity, given that most of the Chinese respondents scored Grade A ($n=31$), while all six respondents who obtained a C were Malay. As for English, the respondents' grades or bands were based on the Malaysian University English Test (MUET) (Majlis Peperiksaan Malaysia 2023) which aligns the bands with CEFR descriptors in line with the strategies outlined in the *English Language Roadmap* (Ministry of Education Malaysia 2015).

The highest MUET band of 5 (CEFR C1) was only obtained by 15 respondents (9.5%). It is interesting to note that 10 of them were from urban areas and five from semi-urban areas where there is likely to be more use of and exposure to English. In fact, only two of these respondents were from a Malay majority state on the east coast and another two were from B40 households. Nine of the 12 respondents who obtained a Band 2 (CEFR A2) were from Malay majority states as well. This suggests that there are geographical and socioeconomic differences in English language proficiency. There might also be an element of ethnicity as 37 of the Chinese students obtained a Band 4 and three of them had a Band 5. However, this could also be because there were mainly from urban and semi-urban areas in states which have a more mixed ethnic composition.

Most of the respondents obtained a Band 4 which is aligned to CEFR B2 ($n=95$, 60.5%). Based on the descriptors for this band, among the things that students can do at this level is "interact with a degree of fluency and spontaneity that makes regular interaction with native speakers quite possible without strain for either party" (Majlis Peperiksaan Malaysia 2023). The reference to "native speakers" is surprising given the debate surrounding the use of this term within the context of English as a global language. This reference to native speakers can be linked to what Savski (2021) finds to be a rigid interpretation of CEFR and the lack of localization of the CEFR-based curriculum. The latter, according to Savski (2021: 67), should consider "the question of how to accommodate the presence of different Englishes in the language ecology of Malaysia, and indeed the importance of these Englishes in the language repertoires of Malaysians." Obviously, Malaysians are more likely to use English to communicate with fellow Malaysians and non-Malaysians from different language backgrounds than with 'native' speakers.

4.3 Language profiles of graduates

Based on the languages the respondents use most frequently and the languages they use at home, they are mainly trilingual, except for some Chinese speakers who may also speak another Chinese language. Their language profiles seem to be structured as follows:

1. Malay respondents: Malay+Malay dialect+English
2. Chinese respondents: Malay+English+Mandarin[+Cantonese/Hokkien]
3. Indian: Malay+English+Tamil

Additional languages they use tend to be related to their educational backgrounds and/or the degrees they are currently pursuing, such as Arabic, German, Japanese, and Spanish. The other foreign languages mentioned, like French, Italian, Korean, and Russian, may be linked to the elective language courses the respondents had taken or are taking.

Although the respondents have learned Malay and English, as shown in Section 3.3.2, they have different levels of proficiency, especially for English. The frequency of use of these languages is also not the same for the respondents. As might be expected, 78.7 percent of the Malay respondents ($n=85$) indicated that they use Malay very frequently, whereas 75 percent of the Chinese respondents reported that they use it often ($n=17$) and occasionally ($n=13$). As for English, 87.5 percent of the Chinese respondents reported using it very frequently ($n=18$) and often ($n=17$), and all five of the Indian respondents said that they use English very frequently. However, only 54.6 percent ($n=59$) of the Malay respondents indicated that they frequently and often use English, and 38.9 percent of them stated that they occasionally used it.

When it comes to Chinese languages, Mandarin dominates over Cantonese and Hokkien as 92.5 percent ($n=37$) of the Chinese respondents indicated that they use Mandarin very frequently. In contrast, only four Chinese respondents reported that they frequently use Cantonese and another four, Hokkien. Furthermore, 16 of the Malay respondents indicated that they use Mandarin very frequently ($n=4$), often ($n=5$), or occasionally ($n=7$). The frequent use of a particular language by another ethnic group can also be seen with Tamil, where apart from the five Indian respondents, there were also 11 Malay respondents who indicated that their use of Tamil ranges from very frequently ($n=1$) and often ($n=4$) to occasionally ($n=6$).

Zooming into the languages most frequently used at home, about one-third of the Malay respondents ($n=36$) stated that they only use one variety of Malay (e.g., Malay, and its dialects such as Kedah, Kelantan, Terengganu, and Sarawak Malay) at home with 21 (58.3%) of them stating that this was not a geographical variety of Malay. The Malay variety being referred to here is an informal social variety. In fact, this social variety is frequently used at home by 81.4 percent ($n=88$) of the Malay respondents, whether it is used on its own or with other Malay varieties or languages. About half ($n=54$) of the Malay respondents use more than one Malay variety at home. English was indicated as one of the home languages by 33 respondents, of which 85 percent were from urban ($n=17$) and semi-urban ($n=16$) areas. Mandarin was also mentioned as one of the languages used at home but only by four respondents. This figure is too small to support any generalizations. However, the fact that all four of these Malay students went to Chinese-medium primary schools might suggest that they may have siblings who also went to the same type of school, or they may have a parent who speaks Mandarin which is why they use this language at home.

Of the four indigenous respondents from Sabah, all use Sabah Malay at home. However, none of them reported using their heritage languages like Banjar, Bugis, or Kadazandusun, at home, although the latter was mentioned in the section of languages frequently used by the two Kadazandusun respondents. They may have learned this language in school as this is one of the three indigenous languages offered as a subject. In general, however, there is a decline in the use of heritage languages at home (Coluzzi 2017; Smith & Smith 2017). A similar trend can be observed among the Chinese respondents as all but two of them reported using Mandarin at home and 12 of them indicated only Mandarin as the main home language. This suggests that Mandarin has considerable influence on the Chinese community in Malaysia. Only about half of the respondents ($n=22$) report using Mandarin along with Cantonese and Hokkien. The use of English and Malay at home was not common with only ten and three respondents respectively mentioning Malay as one of their home languages.

At university, the most frequently used languages were both Malay ($n=127$) and English ($n=129$). This echoes the bilingual context at their university (see Table 1). There was an observable pattern of Malay being the most frequently used language for respondents pursuing arts and humanities degree programs, such as Malay studies and early childhood education. In contrast, those who used English more frequently were mainly from science-based subjects like biotechnology, chemistry, computer science, and engineering.

Malay and English emerged as the 'most frequently' and 'often' used languages for social media (Malay $n=106$; English $n=129$). Only one respondent mentioned the use of 'Manglish' which refers to the colloquial variety of Malaysian English (Pillai & Ong 2018). A few of the respondents indicated that they frequently use Mandarin ($n=28$) and Arabic ($n=29$).

4.4 Perceptions about language use

The following sections present and discuss what the respondents thought about the ability to speak Malay, English, and Mandarin, language mixing, heritage languages, and the use of English. The responses were based on a five-point scale from *Strongly Agree* (1) to *Strongly Disagree* (5).

4.4.1 Fluency in Malay, English, and Mandarin

Most of the respondents ($n=112$, 71.3%) strongly agreed with the statement that Malaysians must be able to speak Malay fluently (see Table 2). There was no obvious link to ethnicity here as it was selected by 95.3% ($n=103$) of the Malay respondents and 80% of both the Chinese ($n=32$) and the Indian ($n=4$) respondents. In contrast, fewer respondents ($n=45$, 28.7%) strongly agreed that 'Malaysians must be able to speak English fluently'. For Mandarin, the majority of respondents selected 3 ($n=79$, 50.3%) which indicates a more neutral stance on whether Malaysians must be able to speak Mandarin fluently. Official statements in the media and the offering of Mandarin as one of the elective subjects in schools suggest an increasing interest in Mandarin as an important language given China's economic strength in the region (Pillai, Kaur & Chua 2021).

Table 2. Fluency in Malay, English, and Mandarin*

	Strongly agree	Agree	Neutral	Disagree	Strongly disagree
	1	2	3	4	5
Malaysians must be able to speak Malay fluently.	112 (71.3)	31 (19.5)	9 (5.7)	1 (0.6)	4 (2.5)
Malaysians must be able to speak English fluently.	45 (28.7)	69 (43.9)	33 (21)	8 (5.1)	2 (1.3)
Malaysians must be able to speak Mandarin fluently	9 (5.7)	26 (16.6)	79 (50.3)	37 (23.6)	6 (3.8)

* Numbers in parenthesis indicate percentages.

4.4.2 Language mixing

As shown in Table 3, most of the respondents ($n=78$, 49.7%) agree that it is natural for them to mix languages when they are speaking. In the Malaysian context, the same languages can be used in the same domains, such as family, social, and, in some cases, the work domain, as well as on social media. In such cases, it is not unusual for Malaysians to weave in and out of different languages, such as English and Malay, during meetings and on social media posts. However, at the same time, the majority of the respondents ($n=82$, 52.2%) strongly agree that they should not mix languages in formal situations. A point to reflect on here is what García and Otheguy (2019: 9) say about translanguaging:

> In bilingual communities and in situations that are unmonitored by governmental, educational or other type of authorities, bilinguals simply have access to their full linguistic repertoire. But in monitored situations, especially in schools, bilinguals (and monolinguals too, to a lesser extent) are forced to select and deploy only those particular linguistic or multimodal features that correspond to dominant practices.

Table 3. Language mixing*

	Strongly agree	Agree	Neutral	Disagree	Strongly disagree
	1	2	3	4	5
Mixing two languages (e.g., Malay and English, Mandarin, and English) when you are speaking is a natural thing to do.	78 (49.7)	45 (28.7)	22 (14)	8 (5.1)	4 (2.5)
You should not mix languages in a formal situation.	82 (52.2)	36 (22.9)	25 (15.9)	9 (5.7)	5 (3.2)

* Numbers in parenthesis indicate percentages.

4.4.3 *Heritage languages*

Table 4 shows the respondents' perceptions about heritage languages. Most of the Chinese respondents were mainly *neutral* ($n=17$, 42.5%) about the statement that their ethnic or cultural identity is affected if they are not able to speak their heritage language. A similar pattern emerged with the teaching of heritage languages ($n=15$, 37.5%). Based on their educational background and language profiles, the Chinese respondents have a strong affiliation with Mandarin. Speaking Mandarin might be perceived as a big part of their Chinese identity. This is supported by Vollmann & Soon (2018: 53) who found that "the Chinese identity (based on education, tradition, habits, culture, literature) is more important than smaller identities (e.g., being Hakka)" and, within this context, Mandarin represents a broader sense of ethnic identity. The Malay and indigenous respondents were mainly neutral about the teaching of heritage languages. The reason for such a sentiment could be attributed to the fact that geographical Malay varieties and Chinese languages (apart from Mandarin) as well as indigenous languages are generally learned at home and speakers are often not literate in these language varieties.

In general, it has been found that the language profiles of the respondents are indicative of the decline in the use of heritage languages, i.e., a home language that is different from the dominant language of a dominant ethnic, social, or geographical context in Malaysia. In this study, these include indigenous languages, like Banjar, Bajau, and Kadazandusun, and Chinese languages, like Cantonese and Hokkien. This finding is consistent with findings of other studies (e.g., David, Naji & Kaur 2003; David & Nambiar 2002; Pillai & Khan 2011; Pillai, Soh & Kajita 2014). The reactions of the respondents to the relationship between language and ethnic or cultural identity are somewhat mixed with as many of them being neutral ($n=55$, 35%) and strongly agreeing ($n=51$, 32.5%) that a person's ethnic or cultural identity is affected if they are not able to speak their heritage language. Almost equal numbers of respondents strongly agreed ($n=37$, 23.6%) and agreed ($n=34$, 21%) that heritage languages should be taught in schools, and, at the same time, 57 (36.3%) of them were neutral about this statement.

Table 4. Heritage language*

		Strongly agree	Agree	Neutral	Disagree	Strongly disagree
		1	2	3	4	5
Your ethnic or cultural identity is affected if you are not able to speak your heritage language	M	44	17	34	6	7
	C	5	9	15	5	6
	I	3	1	1	0	0
	Indig.	3	0	1	0	0
	Total	55 (35)	27 (17.2)	51 (32.5)	11 (7)	13 (8.3)
Heritage languages should be taught in schools	M	25	25	38	13	7
	C	6	9	17	6	2
	I	5	0	0	0	0
	Indig.	1	0	2	1	0
	Total	37 (23.6)	34 (21)	57 (36.3)	20 (12.7)	9 (5.7)

* Numbers in parenthesis indicate percentages. M: Malay, C: Chinese, I: Indian, Indig: Indigenous.

4.4.4 *Perceptions about English*

The respondents' perceptions about English reflect the tendency to veer towards a 'native' variety of English as the preferred spoken variety. Most of them agreed that they want to sound like a native speaker of English (77%) and that speaking with a native accent (e.g., British or American) makes a Malaysian sound more educated (63%) (see Table 5). Perhaps, this is why about half (55.4%) of the participants agreed that they changed the way they speak English to non-Malaysians. In other words, they feel that they need to sound different presumably from how they normally speak English. This reverence for a native variety could be why they seem to distance themselves from the local variety of English with less than half (47.7%) of the respondents agreeing that they could communicate in a local variety of English.

The majority of the respondents ($n = 118$, 75.2%) also agreed to mixing English with Malay and/or other local languages when speaking to other Malaysians. This is consistent with the responses shown in Table 3, which reflect both the way in which English is used by these respondents and their awareness of the existence of a more localized variety of English. These findings also mirror those in Ng & Diskin-Holdaway (2023) in that several of their respondents were conflicted about their own variety of English. Ng & Diskin-Holdaway (2023) point out that English is promoted as necessary for better employability and global competitiveness, with no official discourse on the use of the colloquial variety for intragroup or intranational communication. By not linking English to national identity, English is not perceived to undermine Malay despite the fact that it can also be a marker of Malaysian identity (see Section 2 in this chapter).

Table 5. Malaysian undergraduates' perceptions of English*

	Strongly agree	Agree	Neutral	Disagree	Strongly disagree
	1	2	3	4	5
I want to sound like a native speaker (e.g., British, American) of English.	66 (42.5)	56 (35.7)	22 (14)	9 (5.7%)	4 (2.5)
Malaysians who speak with a native English accent (e.g., British, American) sound more educated.	55 (35)	44 (28)	37 (23.6)	14 (8.9)	7 (4.5)
I change the way I speak English when I am speaking to non-Malaysians.	36 (22.9)	51 (32.5)	43 (27.4)	21 (13.4)	6 (3.8)
I can communicate in the local variety of English.	31 (35)	44 (28)	54 (34.4)	22 (14)	6 (3.8)
I mix English with Malay and/or other local languages when I speak to other Malaysians.	64 (40.8)	54 (34.4)	25 (15.9)	9 (5.7)	5 (3.2)

* Numbers in parenthesis indicate percentages.

5. Conclusion

The language ecology in Malaysia is dynamic, reflecting the changes in legal provisions and policies related to language and education which have influenced the status and use of Malay, English, Mandarin, Tamil, and other languages in Malaysia. These provisions and policies are among the many layers in the language ecology in Malaysia that have also influenced the language profiles of Malaysians over the years in tandem with changes in the medium of instruction and different levels of focus on Malay and English as well as the liberalization of school and higher education. For one, there is a decrease in the use of Malay as a medium of instruction from the pre-university level onwards. The opposite is true for English as its use increases from this level onwards. The increased emphasis on English language education is related to the national focus on increasing the global competitiveness of Malaysians as well as making Malaysia an international education hub as part of its economic growth area (Chan 2023). One of the implications of this is the push towards an exonormative variety of English in policy and mainstream discourse (Pillai, Kaur & Chau 2021). This is likely to influence more positive perceptions about 'proper' and 'good' English compared to a more localized colloquial spoken variety of English. The responses to the survey we conducted also show that geographical and socioeconomic differences influence the language profiles of the respondents. English language proficiency, for example, tends to be higher among the higher socio-economic groups and those from semi-urban and urban areas.

The choice of medium of instruction in preschool and primary school is mainly based on ethnicity, especially among the Chinese community. While in Chinese-medium schools, Mandarin is the main medium of instruction, based on the study at hand the dominance of Mandarin over other Chinese languages can also be seen in the home domain and in it being the most frequently used language among the Chinese respondents. This trend of not using one's heritage language at home was also observed among the indigenous respondents. In addition, there is a general indifference among the respondents about the relationship between ethnic identity and heritage language as well as about the teaching of heritage languages. It can be inferred that the lack of focus on other languages in the education system, coupled with home languages shifting to more dominant languages such as Mandarin for the Chinese respondents and a Malay variety for indigenous respondents does not bode well for the continued use of the many indigenous and minority languages in Malaysia. Already, about 72% of the 131 living languages in Malaysia are categorized as being under threat of disappearing (Eberhard, Simons & Fennig 2023), which is a challenge to the existing multilingual language ecology of the country.

In terms of the linguistic repertoires of Malaysians, Malay, which is the medium of instruction in public secondary schools, is most likely to be in their repertoires as is the case with the respondents. In addition, as English is a compulsory subject from primary school onwards, this is also likely to be another language in their repertoires. If they speak another language or variety, this is generally linked to whether they went to Chinese- or Tamil-medium schools, their ethnicities, and/or their current residence in Malaysia. These factors mean that there will be cases where, for example, a Malay person has Hokkien, Mandarin or Tamil apart from Malay in their repertoire.

In sum, the scope of this chapter, whilst limited in terms of the sample surveyed, provides a glimpse into the language profiles of students from different ethnic and socio-economic groups, and language and educational backgrounds at a public university in Malaysia. These are parts of the layers in the language ecology in Malaysia, along with language and education policies, national agendas, and the internationalization of education. However, the profiles of the respondents are likely to be quite different with students from the private education sector, who will generally be from a different socio-economic and ethnic demography. Future research should consider these privately schooled students and compare them with those from public schools to obtain a broader perspective of the interrelationship between the various layers such as policies and the background of students in relation to their language profiles within Malaysia's language ecology.

References

Andaya, Barbara Watson & Leonard Y. Andaya. 2017. *A History of Malaysia*, 3rd edn. London: Palgrave.

Austin, Peter K. & Stefanie Pillai. 2020. Language description, documentation and revitalisation of languages in Malaysia. *Journal of Modern Languages* 30(1): 1–5.

Chan, Mikha. 23 November, 2023. M'sian education to focus on English mastery next year onwards, says Anwar. *Free Malaysia Today*. https://www.freemalaysiatoday.com (11 October 2024).

Coluzzi, Paolo. 2017. Language planning for Malay in Malaysia: A case of failure or success? *International Journal of the Sociology of Language* 2017(244): 17–38.

Creese, Angela & Peter Martin. 2003. Multilingual classroom ecologies: Inter-relationships, interactions, and ideologies. *International Journal of Bilingual Education and Bilingualism* 6(3–4): 161–167.

David, Maya Khemlani & Ibtisam Naji. 2000. Do minorities have to abandon their languages? A case study of the Malaysian Tamils. *The International Scope Review* 2(3): 1–15.

David, Maya Khemlani & Mohana Nambiar. 2002. Exogamous marriages and out-migration: Language shift of the Malayalees in Malaysia. In Maya Khemlani David (ed.), *Methodological Issues in Language Maintenance and Language Shift Studies*, pp. 125–134. Bern: Peter Lang.

David, Maya Khemlani, Ibtisam Naji & Sheena Kaur. 2003. Language maintenance or language shift among the Punjabi Sikh community in Malaysia? *International Journal of the Sociology of Language* 161: 1–24.

Department of Statistics Malaysia. 2021. *Household Income Estimates and Incidence of Poverty Report, Malaysia, 2020*. https://www.dosm.gov.my/portal-main/release-content/household-income-estimates-and-incidence-of-poverty-report-malaysia-2020 (11 October 2024).

Department of Statistics Malaysia. 2022. *Key Findings Population and Housing Census of Malaysia 2020 (MyCensus 2020)*. https://www.dosm.gov.my/portal-main/release-content/launching-of-report-on-the-key-findings-population-and-housing-census-of-malaysia-2020- (11 October 2024).

Eberhard, David M., Gary F. Simons & Charles D. Fennig (eds.). 2023. *Ethnologue: Languages of the World*, 26th edn. Dallas, TX: SIL International. https://www.ethnologue.com/ (11 October 2024).

Economic Planning Unit. 1993. *Midterm review, The Sixth Malaysia Plan*. Kuala Lumpur: Government of Malaysia.

Eliasson, Stig. 2015. The birth of language ecology: Interdisciplinary influences in Einar Haugen's "The ecology of language". *Language Sciences* 50: 78–92.

Endicott, Kirk (ed.). 2015. *Malaysia's Original People: Past, Present and Future of the Orang Asli*. Singapore: NUS Press.

Federal Constitution Malaysia. 1957/1963. Federal legislation. Attorney General's Chambers of Malaysia. https://lom.agc.gov.my/federal-constitution.php (11 October 2024).

García, Ofelia & Ricardo Otheguy. 2019. Plurilingualism and translanguaging: Commonalities and divergences. *International Journal of Bilingual Education and Bilingualism* 23(1): 17–35.

Gill, Saran Kaur. 2002. *International Communication: English Language Challenges for Malaysia*. Serdang: UPM Press.

Haji Ibrahim, Majdi & Akmal Khuzairy Abd. Rahman. 2018. Teaching of Arabic in Malaysia. *Intellectual Discourse* 26(1): 189–206. https://journals.iium.edu.my/intdiscourse/index.php/id/article/view/1120 (11 October 2024).

Hashim, Azirah. 2009. Not plain sailing: Malaysia's language choice in policy and education. *AILA Review* 22(1): 36–51.

Hashim, Azirah. 2014. English and the linguistic ecology of Malaysia. *World Englishes* 33(4): 458–471.

Haugen, Einar. 1972. *The Ecology of Language*. Stanford, CA: Stanford University Press.

Kaur, Paramjit & Aspalila Shapii. 2018. Language and nationalism in Malaysia: A language policy perspective. *International Journal of Law, Government and Communication* 3(7): 1–10.

Kementerian Pendidikan Malaysia. 2013. *Pelan Pembangunan Pendidikan Malaysia 2013–3025 – Pendidikan Prasekolah hingga Lepas Menengah* [*Education Development Plan – Preschool to Post-Secondary Education*]. https://www.moe.gov.my/muat-turun/penerbitan-dan-jurnal/1818-pelan-pembangunan-pendidikan-2013-2025/file (11 October 2024).

Kementerian Pendidikan Malaysia. 2020. Sekolah Menengah Kebangsaan Agama (SMKA) National Religious Secondary Schools]. https://www.moe.gov.my (11 October 2024).

Kementerian Pendidikan Malaysia. 2023. Maklumat umum TVET [General information about TVET]. https://www.moe.gov.my (11 October 2024).

Kementerian Pendidikan Tinggi. 2021a. *Statistik Pendidikan Tinggi 2021: Universiti Awam* [*Higher Education Statistics 2021: Public Universities*]. https://www.mohe.gov.my/en/downloads/statistics/2021-1/850-statistik-pendidikan-tinggi-2021-04-bab-2-universiti-awam/file (11 October 2024).

Kementerian Pendidikan Tinggi. 2021b. *Quick Facts – Pendidikan Tinggi* [*Higher Education*] 2021. http://great.mohe.gov.my/img/quick_fact_2022.pdf (11 October 2024).

Leimgruber, Jakob. R. E., Peter Siemund & Laura Terassa. 2018. Singaporean students' language repertoires and attitudes revisited. *World Englishes* 37(2): 282–306.

Lim, Ida. 3 July 2017. What you should know about Chinese schools in Malaysia. *The Malay Mail*. https://www.malaymail.com/news/malaysia/2017/07/03/what-you-should-know-about-chinese-schools-in-malaysia/1412233 (11 October 2024).

Majlis Peperiksaan Malaysia. 2023. Keterangan BAND [Band Description]. https://www.mpm.edu.my/en/muet/band-description (11 October 2024).

Ministry of Education Malaysia. 2013. *Malaysia Education Blueprint 2013–2025*. Putrajaya, Ministry of Education Malaysia.

Ministry of Education Malaysia. 2015. *English Language Education Reform in Malaysia: The Roadmap 2015–2025*. Putrajaya: Ministry of Education Malaysia.

Ministry of Education Malaysia. 2018. *Annual Report Malaysia Education Blueprint 2013–2025*. Putrajaya: Ministry of Education Malaysia.

Ministry of Education Malaysia. 2019. *Surat Pekeliling Ikhtisas KPM Bil. 6 2019* [*General Circular MoE No 6. 2019*]. https://www.moe.gov.my/pekeliling/3054-spi-bil-6-tahun-2019-pelaksanaan-kssm-menengah-atas-dan-pakej-mata-pelajaran-tahun-2020/file (11 October 2024).

Mohd. Don, Zuraidah. 7 August, 2016. It's all in the pronunciation. In *Learning Curve. New Straits Times*, https://www.nst.com.my/news/2017/03/196764/its-all-pronunciation (11 October 2024).

Mohsen, Amar Shah. 11 Nov. 2020. Significant rise in Malay participation in Chinese schools in last decade. *The Vibes*. https://www.thevibes.com/articles/news/5695/significant-rise-in-malay-participation-in-chinese-schools-in-last-decade (11 October 2024).

Nalliannan, Pawathy, Thanalachime Perumal & Stefanie Pillai. 2021. Language use among Malaysian Tamil youth. *Sustainable Multilingualism* 19(1): 69–93.

Nasa, Aina & Pilay, Suzanna. 23 April 2017. International schools: Why their numbers are growing. *New Straits Times*. https://www.nst.com.my (11 October 2024).

National Language Acts 1963/1967. Federal legislation. Attorney General's Chambers of Malaysia. https://lom.agc.gov.my/ilims/upload/portal/akta/LOM/EN/Act%2032.pdf (11 October 2024).

National Education Act 1996. Federal legislation. Attorney General's Chambers of Malaysia. https://lom.agc.gov.my/act-detail.php?type=principal&lang=BI&act=550 (11 October 2024).

Ng, Jia Chi & Chloé Diskin-Holdaway. 2023. Attitudes to English in contemporary Malaysia. *World Englishes* 42(3): 562–578.

Omar, Asmah. 2012. Pragmatics of maintaining English in Malaysia's education system. In Ee-Ling Low & Azirah Hashim (eds.), *English in Southeast Asia: Features, Policy and Language in Use*, pp. 155–174. Amsterdam: John Benjamins.

Otheguy, Ricardo, Ofelia García & Wallis Reid. 2015. Clarifying translanguaging and deconstructing named languages: A perspective from linguistics. *Applied Linguistics Review* 6(3): 281–307.

Performance Management and Delivery Unit (PEMANDU). 2010. *Economic Transformation Programme: A Roadmap for Malaysia: Executive Summary*. Putrajaya: Prime Minister's Department.

Pillai, Stefanie. 2008. Politeness and power in family discourse. In Maya Khemlani David & Karen Kow (eds.), *Politeness in Malaysian Family Talk*, pp. 1–18. Serdang: Universiti Putra Press.

Pillai, Stefanie & Mahmud Hassan Khan. 2011. I am not English but my first language is English: English as a first language among Portuguese Eurasians in Malaysia. In Dipika Mukherjee & Maya Khemlani David (eds.), *National Language Planning and Language Shifts in Malaysian Minority Communities: Speaking in Many Tongues*, pp. 87–100. Amsterdam: Amsterdam University Press.

Pillai, Stefanie & Lok Tik Ong. 2018. English(es) in Malaysia. *Asian Englishes* 20(2): 147–157.

Pillai, Stefanie, Surinderpal Kaur & Meng Huat Chau. 2021. The ideological stance of multilingualism in education in Malaysia in the press 2000–0020. *Advances in Southeast Asian Studies* 14(2): 173–193.

Pillai, Stefanie, Wen-Yi Soh & Angela S. Kajita. 2014. Family language policy and heritage language maintenance of Malacca Portuguese Creole. *Language & Communication* 37: 75–85.

Platt, John & Heidi Weber. 1980. *English in Singapore and Malaysia: Status, Features, Functions*. Kuala Lumpur: Oxford University Press.

Puteh, Alis. 2006. *Language and National Building: A Study of the Language Medium Policy in Malaysia*. Petaling Jaya: SIRD.

Rahim, Rahimy, Tarrence Tan & Martin Carvalho. 11 November 2020. More non-Chinese enrol in Chinese schools now compared to a decade ago. *The Star*. https://www.thestar.com.my (11 October 2024).

Raman, Santhiram R. & Tan Yao Sua. 2015. The development of Chinese education in Malaysia: Problems and challenges. *The ISEAS Working Paper Series* 2. https://www.iseas.edu.sg (11 October 2024).

Rashid, Radzuwan A. B., Shireena Basree Abdul Rahman & Kamariah Yunus. 2017. Reforms in the policy of English language teaching in Malaysia. *Policy Futures in Education* 15(1): 100–112.

Reddy, Geetha & Selvanathan, Hema Preya. 2020. Multiracial in Malaysia: Categories, classification, and *campur* in contemporary everyday Life. In Zaina L. Rocha & Peter J. Aspinall (eds.), *The Palgrave International Handbook of Mixed Racial and Ethnic Classification*, pp. 649–668. Cham: Palgrave Macmillan.

Rei Tiah. 12 Oct. 2021. The constitutionality of vernacular schools in Malaysia. *Durham Asian Law Journal*. https://www.durhamasianlawjournal.com (11 October 2024).

Report of the Education Committee. 1956. Federation of Malaya. Kuala Lumpur: Government Press.

Salleh, Rafidah, Lenny James Matah, Ku Mohd Amir Aizat Ku Yusof. 2021. Who is a native of Sabah? A legal analysis. *Malaysian Journal of Social Sciences and Humanities* 6(10): 558–566.

Savski, Kristof. 2021. CEFR as language policy: Opportunities and challenges for local agency in a global era. *The English Teacher* 50(2): 60–70.

Schiffman, Harold. F. 2002. Malaysian Tamils and Tamil linguistic culture. *Language & Communication* 22(2): 159–169.

Schneider, Edgar W. 2007. *Postcolonial English*. Cambridge: Cambridge University Press.

Shanmugavelu, Ganesan, Khairi Ariffin, Nadarajan Thambu & Zulkufli Mahayudin. 2020. Development of British colonial education in Malaya, 1816 – 1957. *Shanlax International Journal of Education* 8(2): 10–15.

Siemund, Peter, Monika Edith Schulz & Martin Schweinberger. 2014. Studying the linguistic ecology of Singapore: A comparison of college and university students. *World Englishes* 33(3): 340–362.

Skutnabb-Kangas, Tove. 2011. Language ecology. In Jan-Ola Östman & Jef Verschueren (eds.) *Pragmatics in Practice*, pp. 177–198. Amsterdam: John Benjamins.

Smith, James A. & Karla J. Smith. 2017. Indigenous language development in East Malaysia. *International Journal of the Sociology of Language* 244: 119–135.

Sulaiman, Ghazali Hassan & Abdul Said Ambotang. 2017. Pengaruh pendidikan asas vokasional terhadap kebolehkerjaan murid sekolah menengah harian di Sabah [The Impact of basic vocational education on the employability of secondary school students in Sabah]. *Jurnal Pusat Penataran Ilmu dan Bahasa* 26: 211–236.

Tan, Yao Sua & Hooi See Teoh. 2015. The development of Chinese education in Malaysia, 1952–1975: Political collaboration between the Malaysian Chinese Association and the Chinese educationists. *History of Education* 44(1): 83–100.

UNESCO. 2017. *International Standard Classification of Education*. Country Diagrams – Malaysia. https://isced.uis.unesco.org (11 October 2024).

Vollmann, Ralf, & Tek Wooi Soon. 2018. Chinese identities in multilingual Malaysia. *Grazer Linguistische Studien* 89: 35–61. https://www.jstor.org/stable/24492399 (11 October 2024).

Wee, Lionel. 2018. *The Singlish Controversy: Language, Culture and Identity in a Globalizing World*. Cambridge: Cambridge University Press.

Zainuddin, Siti Zaidah, Stefanie Pillai, Francisco P. Dumanig & Adriana Phillip. 2019. English language and graduate employability. *Education and Training* 61(1): 79–93.

CHAPTER 7

Multilingualism in Shanghai
A comparative perspective on university students' language profiles and attitudes

Yongyan Zheng & Peter Siemund
Fudan University | University of Hamburg

Building on previous research on the multilingual global cities of Hong Kong, Singapore, and Dubai (Leimgruber, Siemund & Terassa 2018; Siemund & Leimgruber 2020), the present study looks into the multilingual/multidialectal texture of Shanghai, a recently emerged global city in China. To understand the societal multilingualism of Shanghai from the perspective of individuals' linguistic repertoires, this study implements a mixed-method approach, using questionnaire surveys and semi-structured interviews as the data collection instruments. The questionnaires were distributed to 398 students from one comprehensive university and one polytechnic university in Shanghai and follow-up interviews were conducted with 34 students from both universities. The analysis of the data indicates that Shanghai university students uniformly possess a Chinese-English bilingual profile, while a small number of individuals develop trilingual profiles of Chinese, English, and a language other than English. It also suggests that different language varieties are assigned hierarchical values and, in particular, regional dialects continue to be marginalized due to their limited pragmatic values. The findings reveal the far-reaching impacts of government-level foreign language education planning on individuals' multilingual profiles. Similar to other global cities such as Singapore and Dubai, students in Shanghai tend to develop English-centered bilingual language profiles, typically in combination with the national lingua franca. These bilingual profiles may be further enriched by heritage languages or world languages that are deemed economically useful.

Keywords: language attitudes, language profiles, multilingualism, Shanghai, university students

1. Introduction

This chapter is set in the context of language ecology in Shanghai and aims to understand societal multilingualism in this multilingual global city from the perspective of university students' language profiles. Researchers have called special attention to an ecological perspective in language planning, which situates language in the social environment and emphasizes the reciprocity between language and its environment (Haugen 1972; Kaplan & Baldauf 2008). Such a perspective includes dimensions like language repertoires, language use and proficiencies, attitudes, as well as language learning and acquisition. All languages are interconnected in a sociolinguistic system ranging from micro (individual) and meso (institution) to macro (society) levels, and languages are shaped by both the social environment at different levels and their relative position with other languages (Calvet 1999). In this regard, multilingualism is seen as a dynamic and multi-layered phenomenon that results from interactions between various languages and their social environments (Haugen 1972; Ludwig, Mühlhäusler & Pagel 2019). Research on multilingualism, thus, is concerned with how different languages co-exist with each other at these different levels and how languages within a linguistic ecology align with or negotiate with each other.

Universities serve as an ecological mesosystem, permeating language ideologies that are interlinked with individual language practices and sociocultural structures (Blackledge 2008; Creese & Martin 2008). With the increasing internationalization of higher education, a larger set of languages, varieties, and dialects are used for different purposes by students from different backgrounds. This has made universities an important kaleidoscope to examine societal multilingualism. A series of studies have been conducted to examine multilingual global cities' language ecology, particularly by investigating the multilingualism in universities in different contexts, such as Singapore (Leimgruber, Siemund & Terassa 2018; Siemund, Schulz & Schweinberger 2014), Hong Kong (Siemund & Leimgruber 2020), and Dubai (Siemund, Al-Issa & Leimgruber 2021). These studies have shown that individual bilingualism rather than extensive multilingualism seems to become the major pattern in multilingual global cities and that students indicate a set of language profiles with English almost always as the dominant language. Students' language use appears to converge on the same structure of Dominant Language Constellations (Aronin & Singleton 2012; Lo Bianco & Aronin 2018), which refer to a group of one's most important languages, functioning as an entire unit and enabling an individual to meet all their needs in a multilingual environment (Lo Bianco & Aronin 2018: 5). These developments are shared by many world regions. Nevertheless, the studies mentioned above have primarily focused on multilingual cities that were once British colonies featuring massive transnational migration and ethnic diversity, while the multilingual ecologies of newly recently emerged global cities without a British colonial history and less transnational migration remain under-researched. This chapter aims to address this gap by surveying the multilingual/multidialectal texture of Shanghai, the largest metropolitan city in mainland China. The following sections first review past research on language ecology and multilingual global cities, followed by a detailed introduction of methods, findings, and discussion.

2. Language ecology and multilingual global cities

2.1 Societal multilingualism vs. individual multilingualism

With increasing social mobility across the globe, the conceptualization of multilingualism has shifted from seeing it as being competent in multiple languages that have discrete boundaries to seeing it as a dynamic phenomenon where speakers have multiple linguistic resources to draw on (Aronin 2017; Ludwig, Mühlhäusler & Pagel 2019). Discreteness is being replaced by fluidity, which may be the more adequate concept to capture human linguistic history. The idea of discrete language boundaries can be viewed as a consequence of nation building projects and monolingual ideologies. In line with this, research on multilingualism has gradually shifted attention from context-free theorization to considering a wide range of contexts that shape multilingualism, such as language status, institutional environment, and social structures (Piller 2016). From an ecological perspective, a linguistic ecosystem is shaped by both socioeconomic structures, including language policy, and individual linguistic practices, such as language learning (Piller 2016). This means that in addition to language education policy, individuals' investment in foreign language learning can have an impact on the linguistic ecosystem, where investment is placed at the intersection of identity, ideology, and capital (Darvin & Norton 2015). As Mufwene (2001) states, "it is typically the small acts of individuals, or the effects of the ecology on them, which wind up having wide-ranging effects on the overall population" (p.14).

An additional factor that shapes the linguistic ecosystem is the interaction between different languages, i.e., the co-existence, contact, or conflicts between languages (Calvet 1999). The coexistence of languages can take place at the societal level or the individual level. In a community, many different languages can be spoken and used by different groups of individuals, while the individuals may not necessarily be multilingual. Similarly, individuals in a community may be multilingual but the community as a whole may only legislate one language for public use. This is often referred to as the distinction between societal multilingualism and individual multilingualism. While societal multilingualism concerns multilingualism outside the individual and their family and the status of languages in government, law, education, and other public domains (Sebba 2011), individual multilingualism relates to the use and level of proficiency of the individual in a particular language or variety (Bolton & Lee 2021). Universities can be seen as a focal area where we can see how students' motivations and efforts for language learning are mediated by university language policies and broader social environments, and how this, in turn, shapes the implementational space for different languages in the intuitions.

2.2 Previous studies on Singapore and Dubai

A series of studies have looked into multilingualism in Singapore (Leimgruber 2013; Leimgruber et al. 2018; Siemund et al. 2014). Findings have suggested the governmental multilingual policy of assigning the respective language of three major ethnic groups (Chinese, Malay, and Tamil) as the mother tongue and endorsing English as the working language has contributed to a gradual shift from multilingualism to a model of bilingualism of English plus another mother tongue, especially of English and Standard Mandarin due to their associated material benefits (Leimgruber 2013; Siemund & Li 2020). The most recent census of Singapore reports a home language use of English of nearly fifty percent (Singapore Department of Statistics 2021). This percentage may be even higher in the younger generations. An investigation into 300 Singaporean university and polytechnic students revealed that university students are primarily bilingual and held positive attitudes toward bilingualism. For example, in their research on language competence, language practices, and attitudes of 300 university students in Singapore, Siemund et al. (2014) found that students held positive attitudes towards English and their mother tongue. Students predominantly exhibited bilingual or trilingual identities and Singlish (i.e., Singaporean English) was perceived as a solidarity marker of Singaporean identity. Leimgruber et al. (2018) examined 450 students' language use and attitudes from a university and various polytechnics and vocational schools and found that university students have better bilingual competence than the polytechnic and vocational school students. Ethnic Malays and Indians are mostly bilingual in English and their mother tongues, while students from a Chinese background and with better socioeconomic conditions have shifted from their dialects to English and Standard Mandarin. These studies have provided comprehensive information about the language ecology of Singapore and have highlighted the far-reaching impact of macro-level language policy on societal and individual multilingualism.

In a similar vein, Siemund and colleagues continued their investigation of individual language profiles in Dubai, another multilingual global city (Siemund & Leimgruber 2020; Siemund et al. 2021). With the tremendous economic development and internationalization in Dubai, a large and highly transient international labor force has emerged there. This has immersed the city into a unique language ecology where English and Arabic constantly interact and compete with each other. Although Arabic is the official language of the United Arab Emirates, English represents the *de facto* working language. By investigating the individual language profiles of both Emiratis and non-Emiratis at the American University of Sharjah in the United Arab Emirates, Siemund et al. (2021) found that most Emiratis and non-Emiratis have high competence in both English and Arabic, and the English-Arabic bilingual model is used at a high frequency, which aligns with the development of societal bilingualism in Singapore. Citizenship (non-Emirati vs. Emirati) mediates individuals' linguistic repertoires in that non-Emiratis have more diverse language profiles. Besides other Arabic-speaking countries, students of non-Emirati citizenship often originate in countries formerly under British or American influence such as India, Pakistan, and the Philippines. The latter countries further represent important source countries of labor migration to the United Arab Emirates. In view of the great diversity of Englishes spoken in Dubai, it stands to reason that a new and unique variety of English is developing in the Gulf area (Gulf English) that can be distinguished from English as a lingua franca (Siemund et al. 2021). In sum, it is quite evident that massive international labor migration has to a large extent shaped the language ecology of the United Arab Emirates.

The findings from Singapore and Dubai collectively suggest that individual bilingualism, particularly in the form of English plus the dominant national language, has emerged as the major pattern in multilingual global cities instead of extensive societal multilingualism. We find it remarkable that students' language use appears to converge on a similar structure of Dominant Language Constellations despite different geographical contexts. There seems to be quite a restricted number of language profiles with regard to individual multilingualism with English dominating the profiles. However, it also needs to be noted that Singapore and Dubai were once governed by the British Empire and, thus, English represents a colonial legacy (see Leimgruber & Siemund 2021 for a review). It remains under-examined if such an English-dominating bilingual model would also be identified in a context with a different history, such as Shanghai, a newly emerged global city in Asia.

3. Foreign language education policy and multilingualism in Chinese universities

Foreign language education has long received administrative attention in the Chinese mainland, with the government closely involved in the university foreign language program development. In the early 1950s, the Russian language was promoted across the country due to the close diplomatic ties with the Soviet Union. Since the 1970s, English has taken the place of Russian and has become the most important foreign language in China, being associated with national modernization and globalization. English was designated as a compulsory subject in secondary and tertiary institutions in the 1980s. Since then, it has dominated the foreign language curriculum in universities, while languages other than English (LOTEs) were not given sufficient attention. This has led to a conspicuous imbalance between the learning of English and LOTEs in universities. As shown in Wei & Su (2012), 93.8% of the 416 million foreign language learners in China exclusively chose English as their major, while only a small proportion of the foreign language learners reported previously learning Russian (7.1%), Japanese (2.5%), and other foreign languages including Arabic, French, German, and Spanish (0.3%). However, the launch of the *One Belt and One Road Initiative* has become a turning point for foreign language education in Chinese universities. One of the objectives of the initiative is to enhance its business relationships with 64 non-Anglophone countries primarily situated in Central and Southeast Asia, the Chinese government has made more efforts to cultivate multilingual talents in LOTEs (Gao & Zheng 2019). For example, in 2016, the plan, *Developing Educational Cooperation along the Belt and Road* was issued by the Chinese Ministry of Education (MOE), which emphasizes the importance of developing multilingual education in secondary and tertiary institutions. In the following years, over 30 universities developed degree programs in more than 20 foreign languages, including Turkish, Swahili, and Slovak.

Shanghai is at the forefront of economic development in China and has attracted a large number of domestic migrants who speak various Chinese dialects. According to Shanghai Statistics Bureau (2021), among its total population of 24 million, there are 4,630,000 domestic migrants living, working, and studying in Shanghai. However, Shanghai is different from Singapore and Dubai in that it does not harbor a large population of transnational migrants, with only 172,000 foreigners residing in Shanghai (Shanghai Statistics Bureau 2021). This is quite a small proportion compared to the total population. Therefore, it is often assumed that Shanghai is a multidialectal but monolingual city. In addition, English has always been a foreign language, despite the far-reaching influences from the West in the city's history. These differences make Shanghai a unique context to examine the interplay between individual plurilingualism and societal multilingualism. In this regard, this study intends to investigate university students' language profiles and language use in Shanghai. To do so, we seek to answer the following research questions.

1. What are the individual multilingual profiles of university students in Shanghai?
2. How do the students use different languages/Sinitic dialects in their life?[1]
3. What language attitudes do they hold towards different languages/Sinitic dialects?

Answers to these questions will be compared and contrasted with findings from Singapore and Dubai, in order to shed some light on what factors may contribute to the language ecology of multilingual global cities.

4. The study

4.1 Research sites

Following previous studies on multilingual global cities (Leimgruber 2013; Leimgruber et al. 2018; Siemund et al. 2014; Siemund et al. 2021; Siemund & Li 2020), the present study was conducted in two institutions in Shanghai: one first-tier comprehensive university (University hereafter) and one second-tier polytechnic university (Polytechnic hereafter).

The University offers over 140 undergraduate and master's degree programs across the arts, humanities, medicine, and sciences. Its College of Foreign Languages and Literature offers seven modern foreign language degree programs, namely English, French, German, Russian, Japanese, Korean, and Spanish. In response to the plan for *Developing Educational Cooperation along the Belt and Road* proposed by the MOE, the College established a Multilingual Teaching Centre in 2016 and offers a wide range of modern language courses to both language and non-language majors, including Danish, Modern Hebrew, Portuguese, Arabic, and Swedish. All undergraduate students are supposed to complete eight credits in foreign language learning, with a minimum of six being spent on College English, a compulsory English language course for non-language major students.

---

1. It needs to be clarified that Chinese has many regional varieties, generally known as Sinitic dialects. The spoken forms of these varieties are mutually intelligible to different degrees, but nonetheless they share the same writing system. Modern Standard Chinese (MSC) is the national language of China and its spoken form is Putonghua, which is mainly based on the Northern Mandarin dialect of Beijing.

The Polytechnic has more strength in science and engineering subjects than in the humanities and arts. Its College of Foreign Languages consists, amongst others, of the degree programs of English, Japanese, Korean, and the Foreign Language Practical Training Centre. Three specialist majors are offered in this college: Applied English, Applied Japanese, and Applied Korean. With the aim to cultivate foreign language talents, language courses including English, Japanese, French, Korean, and Russian are also provided for non-language majors.

4.2 Research design and instrument

The present study adopts a mixed-method approach combining questionnaire surveys and follow-up semi-structured interviews. The questionnaires were distributed both online and offline. The online software was a well-known Chinese survey instrument called Wenjuanxing, which is available free of charge and can operate on various social media platforms. To make a cross-national comparison with previously researched multilingual global cities (Singapore and Dubai), we adapted the questionnaire used in Siemund & Leimgruber (2020). This questionnaire helps gain a fine-grained description of university students' language repertoire and language practices. It comprises five sections: (1) language profiles and self-reported language proficiencies; (2) language learning experiences; (3) language practices in different settings; (4) language attitudes towards English, LOTEs, Putonghua, and dialects; (5) demographic information.

In the first section, participants were asked to identify the language varieties they speak. They were given options including Putonghua, English, Korean, Japanese, French, German, Russian, Spanish, Shanghainese, and six empty slots to name others. Participants were then asked to rate their listening, speaking, reading, and writing competence in the foreign languages and dialects they speak using a Five-point Likert Scale, ranging from "most proficient" to "least proficient". In the second part, participants were asked to report their experiences of learning the language varieties they identified in the previous section and provide information including the onset of acquisition, years of language instruction, and frequency of language learning. In the third part, participants were asked to inform about the frequency of using these language varieties in various situations such as watching TV and reading newspapers via a Five-point Likert Scale ranging from "never" to "always". The frequency of using each variety with different interlocutors such as parents and friends was also elicited. The fourth section consists of nine statements to which participants were asked to respond using a Five-point Likert Scale coded from "Strongly disagree" to "Strongly agree" (see Table 1, for example). Their attitudes to accented English and Putonghua, attitudes towards code-switching between Chinese and English, and between

Putonghua and the local Sinitic dialects were also elicited in this section. Basic biographic information including gender, age, and educational level was consulted in the last section.

Table 1. Questions for language attitudes in the questionnaire

No.	Statement
S1	A good command of ____ (language type) can increase my chances of employment.
S2	To go further in life, ____ (language type) is important.
S3	____ (Language type) is a very suitable language for modern society.
S4	I feel confident and secure when using ____ (language type).
S5	____ (Language type) is great for expressing feelings and emotions.
S6	____ (Language type) is an important part of my family culture.
S7	____ (Language type) is an important part of my personal identity.
S8	I feel completely relaxed in a group speaking ____ (languge type).
S9	I tend to speak ____ (language type) whever I have a choice.

A further point to note is that considering the varied classification scheme of the Sinitic dialects, the present study adopts the classification released by China's Ministry of Education (2021) and categorizes the Sinitic dialects into 10 groups: Mandarin (spoken mainly in northern and southwestern parts of China), Jin (spoken in Shanxi, Henan, and Inner Mongolia Autonomous Region), Wu (spoken mainly in Shanghai and the provinces Jiangsu and Zhejiang), Min (spoken mainly in Fujian province), Hakka (spoken in the borders of Jiangxi, Fujian, and Guangdong as well as in Taiwan), Yue (or Cantonese, spoken mainly in the provinces of Guangdong and Guangxi), Xiang (spoken in Hunan province), and Gan (spoken in Jiangxi province). For the sake of clarity, the present paper uses Putonghua to refer to the spoken form of Modern Standard Chinese and the official national language and Mandarin when referring to the major dialect group.

4.3 Participants

In total, this research collected valid questionnaires from 398 participants, among which 216 were from the University and 182 were from the Polytechnic. All the participants were non-language majors. The 216 University students, aged from 17 to 26, were mostly in their second or third year. Among them, 20.4% are Shanghai locals while 79.6% are from other provinces in China. The 182 Polytechnic students, aged from 16 to 21, were mostly freshmen who only completed one semester's study. Among the respondents, 35% are Shanghai locals whereas 65% are from other provinces. 34 students participated in the follow-up interviews: 20 from the University and 14 from the Polytechnic.

4.4 Data analysis

The survey data were analyzed through descriptive statistics in MS Excel. Then, SPSS 26 was used for one-way ANOVA and Chi-square tests to conduct inferential statistics. The interview data were analyzed mainly to complement the survey results. An iterative process of inductive and deductive qualitative analysis (Merriam 1998) was adopted. The topics of the interview questions were used as the initial theme categories of the analysis and excerpts from the interview were mainly provided for additional support for the survey findings.

5. Findings

5.1 Multilingual profiles

5.1.1 *Language profiles and foreign language repertoires*

Findings showed that functional multilingualism seems to be the norm among the students, as none of them reported being monolingual (see Figure 1). 100% of the students reported having competence in Chinese and English. Among them, 110 (27.6%) students reported having competence in an additional foreign language and 26 (6.5%) reported speaking two or three additional languages. Among the multilingual profiles, Chinese + English + Japanese makes up 15.9%, Chinese + English + Korean reaches 7.8%, Chinese + English + French reaches 3.5%, and Chinese + English + Japanese + Korean reaches 2.5%. These figures do not elaborate on the label 'Chinese' but many students are of course bilinguals of Putonghua and a local Sinitic dialect or language.

Figure 2 indicates that English dominates the foreign language repertoires of students from both instituions. Among the second foreign languages acquired, Japanese, Korean, and French rank the top three. These findings corroborate the more frequent combinations of Chinese, English, and these three foreign languages as described in the previous paragraph. The number of Spanish learners is on the rise for the University students, but not for the Polytechnic students. Other less commonly taught languages, including Swedish, Sanskrit, and Arabic, were only learned by the University students but not the Polytechnic students. As confirmed by the interview data, this is because these languages were provided in the University's multilingual learning center but not in the Polytechnic.

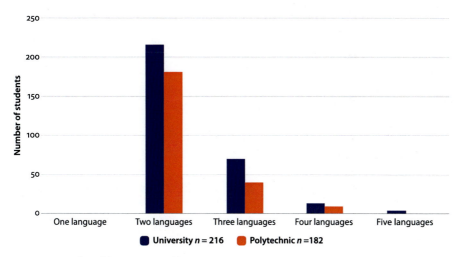

Figure 1. Students' language profiles

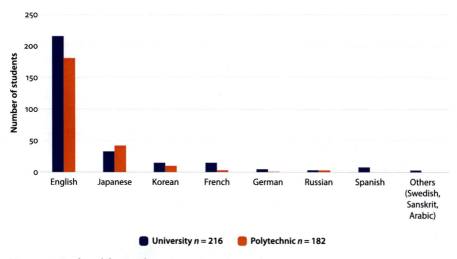

Figure 2. Students' foreign language repertoires

All students reported Putonghua as their most important language. They also reported having at least a local Sinitic dialect as their home language. As shown in Figure 3, the students' Sinitic dialects concentrate on Mandarin and Wu. Two possible explanations can account for this finding: First, Mandarin is the dialect group that covers all of the Chinese speech areas north of the Yangtze River and west of the Hunan and Guangdong provinces and thus has the largest population of speakers. Second, Shanghai is a regional hub of higher education which attracts many students from neighboring provinces, and these areas all belong to the Wu dialect area.

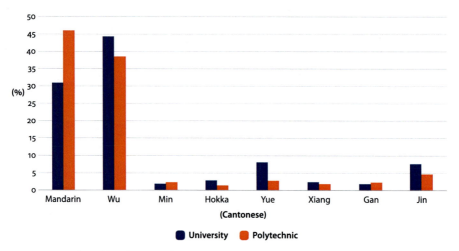

Figure 3. Students' local Sinitic dialects

5.1.2 *The mediating role of language proficiency*

Students from both institutions were more competent in their local Sinitic dialects as their self-reported proficiency in dialects (University: $M=4.61$; Polytechnic: $M=3.49$) was higher than that in foreign languages. Among foreign languages, all participants' self-reported English proficiency ($M=2.89$) was higher than their second ($M=2.01$) and third foreign language ($M=1.51$). But if we break down the figures into the student groups, it seems that the University students reported higher English proficiency ($M=3.53$) than the Polytechnic students ($M=2.25$), with the difference reaching statistical significance ($t=15.635$, $df=387$, $p=.000$).

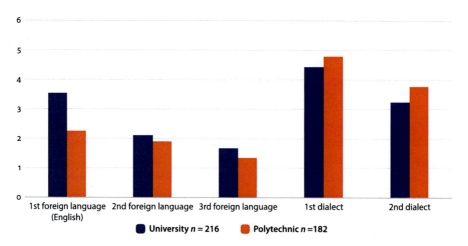

Figure 4. Students' self-reported proficiencies

It is noticeable that self-reported English proficiency was positively and significantly correlated with the number of foreign languages a student acquires ($r=0.193$, $p=.000$). In other words, students who reported having a lower proficiency level in English seem to be less inclined to choose a second foreign language. This tendency applies to both groups of students. This finding confirms the previous argument that English serves as a gatekeeper to students' investment in other foreign language learning (Zheng, Lu & Ren 2019, 2020).

5.2 Sociolinguistic use and attitudes towards different languages/dialects

5.2.1 Domains of use

We first investigated the use of foreign languages in different social domains. Figure 5 illustrates the frequency of use, with "1" indicating "never" and "5" indicating "always". It was found that the first foreign language, i.e., English, was used at a much higher frequency in all domains from entertainment activities to academic activities, while LOTEs were mainly used for entertainment purposes such as reading comics, playing games, and watching TV and movies.

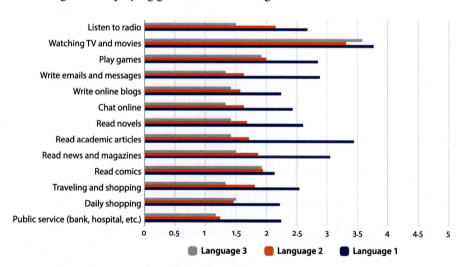

Figure 5. Use of foreign languages in different domains

Notably, it seems that English plays a predominant role in students' academic life, as it was extensively used in reading academic articles. This has been confirmed in the follow-up interview data (see Extracts 1 & 2).

Extract 1.
English has become an indispensable part of my academic study. I have to read a lot of academic papers in English, take English courses, and also attend English lectures. If I don't know English, it will bring a lot of trouble to my study.

Extract 2.
There are many English words in our major, which cannot be clearly explained in Chinese. If it is translated into Chinese, it may have ambiguity. Maybe also because the terminologies of some disciplines have not been translated into Chinese yet. For those technical terms, you have to use English.

As these accounts suggest, English has become integral to students' academic life. Competence in English controls their access to academic resources and understanding of key knowledge in their fields. The paramount role of English in Chinese higher education is similar to what has been found in other countries (e.g., Baker 2016; Bolton & Kuteeva 2012; Mauranen, Hynninen & Ranta 2010).

We also investigated the domains of use of the Sinitic dialects (Figure 6).[1] The Sinitic dialects are mainly used within the family domain, including visiting relatives and friends, hanging out with friends, and communicating with other family members. However, the Sinitic dialects are used less frequently in the public domain, such as in public services or daily shopping, and are used rarely when it comes to communication in the workplace or at school. It seems that in the linguistic ecology of Shanghai, therefore, different languages and Sinitic dialects occupy quite different niches.

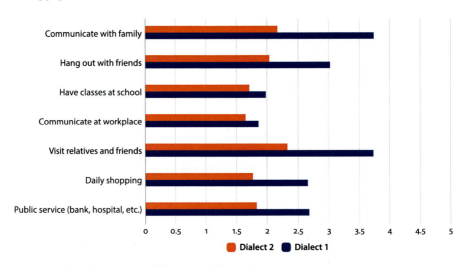

Figure 6. Use of the Sinitic dialects in different domains

---

1. It needs to be clarified that, due to the official language status and dominant position of Putonghua in the students' everyday life, our survey does not include Putonghua's domain of use.

5.2.2 Sociolinguistic attitudes

Overall, students attached primary importance to Putonghua, as it had the highest rating score in eight out of the nine statements (see Figure 7). Interview data are also presented to further illustrate the students' attitudes.

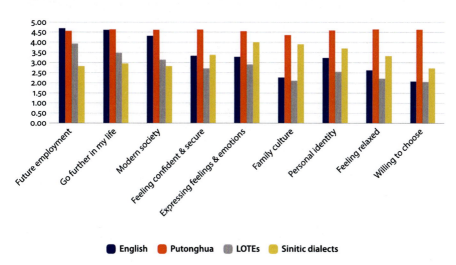

Figure 7. Language attitudes to English, Putonghua, LOTEs, and Sinitic dialects

5.2.2.1 Attitudes towards Putonghua

Overall and based on the interview data, Putonghua was seen as a language with both instrumental benefits and emotional values. The value of Putonghua as a national language was stressed by students. In their mind, Putonghua seems to be an efficient communicative tool across the country, which helps remove the intelligibility barriers between different dialects. No other language varieties could compete with it in daily life communication. In addition, Putonghua also has a pragmatic value that guarantees its speaker career prospects. Extracts 3 and 4 serve as examples.

Extract 3.
I am Chinese, and I have grown up and lived in China since I was born. In my daily life, I speak Putonghua most, otherwise, it is difficult to communicate and survive daily life.

Extract 4.
Putonghua is very important because you cannot speak a dialect now when you're looking for a job, which does not seem very good or formal, and you have to reach a certain standard of Putonghua to be a teacher now although I wouldn't want to go into teaching.

In addition to the pragmatic value, Putonghua was closely associated with students' personal identity and modernized image. As the quantitative data shows (Figure 7), nearly 90% of students agreed that Putonghua suits the modernized society and accounts for an important part of their identity. A further look at the interview data suggests that Putonghua was regarded as indexical to an urban identity in modern society (see Extract 5).

Extract 5.
I think Putonghua is more representative of my identity. Because, with no derogatory sense, the Dongbei dialect sounds more rural. Just by listening to the pronunciation, you can tell it's definitely a rural accent. And my perception of my own identity is not that rural. I think I am still a city boy.

As exemplified in Extract 5, students regarded Putonghua as the marker of their identity, particularly an urban identity. In their minds, unlike their regional dialects which may reveal their non-metropolitan backgrounds, Putonghua removes variations between speakers of different dialects and even adds another layer of urban identity, which ultimately agglomerates them into a unified Chinese national identity. Such identification was in line with the prevailing ideology in national language policies that associate Putonghua with national modernization and unity.

5.2.2.2 Attitudes to English

The students generally regarded English as a language of internationalization and recognized its values associated with future prospects and modernization, as shown by the high scores of the first three items in Figure 7. In particular, in the sentence "A good command _____ can increase my chances of employment", English received a slightly higher ranking than Chinese Putonghua. Typical examples are presented in Extracts 6 and 7.

Extract 6.
Now, against the background of internationalization, English is the lingua franca all over the world. If you learn English well, it will be very good for your future development. A good command of English will help you go well anywhere.

Extract 7.
English, the global language, you must learn it. Learning English is certainly useful and important. In future work or anything else, English is always useful.

As the above extracts demonstrate, students accorded high importance to English for its international status and influence. In their opinion, English is "always useful" and will benefit their "future development" and "future work".

Upon further scrutiny, it is found that such an ideology of English is more associated with its use as a benchmark to the job market than with its actual practical values. This has been evidenced by accounts such as Extract 8.

Extract 8.
I do not plan to go abroad at all. The reason I'm learning English is only to get a better job. I think it is (English) a necessity. Especially if you want to go to foreign companies or foreign-related financial or Internet industry, then you must take IELTS. It feels that IELTS 7.0 is the standard, and 7.5+ is a bonus.

As the extract demonstrates, even in the Chinese domestic job market, English competence is a *sine qua non* for their future career prospects and personal development. Thus, students exhibited a strong instrumental orientation, viewing competence in English as a "must-have" skill. In this case, English serves as a marketable commodity in workplaces (Heller 2010) and students have to keep investing in English learning with the hope to cash out its symbolic value in their future.

However, despite the high utilitarian values attached to English, the students felt rather unconfident and insecure in using the language. For example, in completing the sentences "I feel confident and secure when using _____" and "I tend to speak _____ whenever I have a choice", English ranks lower than both Chinese Putonghua and dialect, and only slightly higher than LOTE. The conflicting attitudes held by students suggest that English is to some extent a language externally imposed on the students.

5.2.2.3 *Attitudes towards Sinitic dialects*

As shown in Figure 5, dialects are closely associated with personal identity and emotional attachment, but are deemed as having limited practical utility. Dialects were seen as language varieties that emotionally tie students with their families, as Extracts 9, 10, and 11 demonstrate.

Extract 9.
Dialects have some colloquialism that cannot be found in other places. And when hearing or speaking these, it gives people a sense of intimacy.

Extract 10.
Shanghainese does not have much use for my studies, but it made me feel more connected to my family and the city.

Extract 11.
Even if I were to learn Shanghainese, I would learn it as a hobby. But I don't think there is much use for Shanghainese in my future. As I plan to go abroad afterwards, I will definitely use English more. So, I probably won't continue to learn Shanghainese.

As the above extracts show, students commonly regarded their Sinitic dialects as intimate language varieties that connect them with their families and hometowns. While they acknowledged the emotional functions of dialects, the limited instrumental value of dialects was frequently mentioned. Unlike Putonghua and English, the Sinitic dialects with limited intelligibility would hinder their speakers to approach broader speech communities. Accordingly, they were seen as of little use to the future development of the youth. In other words, in comparison with the utilitarian value of Putonghua as a lingua franca in China and English as a global language, the emotional functions of dialects pale into insignificance. Indeed, as keenly observed by Klöter (2020: 101), "[w]henever this position is challenged nowadays, the competitor is not a Sinitic alternative but English as the most important international language."

5.2.2.4   *Attitudes to LOTEs*

Many students held positive attitudes towards LOTEs, as they expressed their willingness to learn these languages. The main motivation for learning LOTEs is to gain an understanding of those foreign cultures and to approach the target language community. Extracts 12 and 13 serve as examples.

Extract 12.
I want to learn French because I like musicals. And I feel that French, well, it sounds somewhat romantic.

Extract 13.
I want to learn Japanese and Korean. Because I like Japanese anime. And some Japanese shows do not have Chinese subtitles. The reason for Korean is also similar, mainly to get some cultural information there.

As shown in Excerpts (12) and (13), students usually associated LOTEs with certain images, for example, French representing being melodic and romantic and Korean representing pop culture. In this sense, it seems that an investment in LOTEs was seen as a means to diversify their culture repertoire (Ushioda & Dörnyei 2017). Nevertheless, LOTEs were only valued as an additional tool when someone had already mastered English and the value students attached to LOTEs was mostly related to recreational use (see Extract 14).

Extract 14.
Korean is what I usually use when I watch TV, variety shows, movies, something like that. For me, Korean is just an additional option. But English, whether you're studying or working in the future, English is definitely something that you can't avoid. It's much more useful.

As shown above, students drew a contrast between LOTEs and English in terms of the language's instrumental value. English was deemed as having utilitarian values in almost all contexts including the academic field, while LOTEs were deemed as only useful for personal entertainment needs. The cultural and entertainment value associated with LOTEs was dwarfed by the materialistic value attached to

English. The contrasting perceived values further corroborate the role of English as a gatekeeper that mediates language learners' investment motivations in multilingual learning as mentioned in Section 5.1.2.

6. Discussion

The present study aims to continue the line of investigation of multilingual global cities (Leimgruber 2013; Leimgruber et al. 2018; Siemund et al. 2014; Siemund et al. 2021; Siemund & Li 2020). Shanghai as a recently emerged metropolitan city in China is not a former British colony and does not have massive transnational migration, but nonetheless, individual multilingualism is found among the university students with several identifiable patterns: (1) students from both institutions unanimously have a Chinese Putonghua-English bilingual profile and many of them also have multilingual profiles, albeit with a limited number of language combinations; (2) English is mainly used in the students' academic learning, LOTEs for entertainment and leisure, and Sinitic dialects are restricted to the private domain; (3) the students generally considered Chinese Putonghua the symbol of national unity and English the language of globalization. On the other hand, LOTEs were attached to values of cultural diversity and Sinitic dialects were regarded as emotional conduits and identity markers.

The present study highlights language-in-education planning as the major shaping force of individual multilingualism in Shanghai. Despite its different sociohistorical and sociopolitical conditions, Shanghai is similar to other multilingual global cities such as Singapore and Dubai in the structure of the students' Dominant Language Constellations (Aronin & Singleton 2012; Lo Bianco & Aronin 2018) with the English-centered bilingual language profiles in combination with the national language. Similar to Singaporean students (Leimgruber et al. 2018; Siemund et al. 2014), students from the University have better bilingual competence than the Polytechnic students. However, different from Singapore and Dubai where local English varieties could be identified (e.g., Singlish or Gulf English), the present study is not concerned with the emergence of a local English variety and finds that English is not often used in the students' daily lives, due to the lack of transnational migration in Shanghai. Considering this limited mobility, it seems that foreign language education planning is the most salient influential factor to the language ecology in Shanghai. Further evidence is that the University students have more diversified language profiles and even have learned some less commonly taught languages, simply because the University provides these languages. Therefore, we argue that the bilingual profiles can be further enriched by world languages as a function of language-in-education planning.

The findings confirm the pattern of English dominance in other multilingual global cities and its impact on other languages and regional dialects in the local linguistic ecology (Leimgruber et al. 2018; Siemund et al. 2014; Siemund & Leimgruber 2020; Siemund et al. 2021). The study has further shown that English functions as the gatekeeper to allow other world languages to filter in, illustrated by the finding that the self-reported English proficiency was positively correlated with the number of foreign languages a student acquires. In other words, a student needs to master English at least to some level and, hence, be in possession of the symbolic capital of English first, before they can start to consider the possibility of learning another foreign language (Zheng et al. 2019). It implies that languages are stratified in a pecking order in the local context, reflecting the macro-level linguistic hierarchy in the world language system (de Swaan 2001). By the same token, the local language ecology is to some extent a fractal replication of the global language ecology with English as the major force that marginalizes other foreign languages, heritage languages, and home languages/dialects.

While it is not new to say that English as a global language is attached with strong utilitarian values in non-Anglophone contexts, the present study provides a more nuanced understanding of English as a neoliberal tool for social inclusion or exclusion (Heller 2010; Park 2011). For example, Standard English proficiency test scores (such as IELTS) serve as a main mechanism that controls prospective employees' access to the job market as shown in the present study, regardless of the less frequent use of English in the students' actual life. This finding probably also explains why the students hold conflicting attitudes towards English: while recognizing its indispensable necessity, they also feel unconfident and insecure in using it, at least partially due to the testing pressure. Therefore, the resulting multilingual language profiles are functionally and attitudinally stratified such that issues of power, prestige, and solidarity come to be negotiated with different languages and Sinitic dialects.

7. Conclusion

Admittedly, the present study only sampled university/college students to investigate the multilingual texture of Shanghai and could not fully reveal the intricate complexity of the linguistic landscape of this multilingual global city. Nonetheless, our findings have defied the stereotypical assumption of Shanghai as a monolingual society. By revealing the kaleidoscopic linguistic profiles of the students in Shanghai, the study can extend our understanding of the tension between the national language, the dominant foreign language, other world languages, and home languages/dialects in the local linguistic ecology. By comparing and contrasting the findings from Shanghai with Singapore and Dubai, we can see that English extended from its historical role as the colonial language to its today's status as a global language in almost all official sectors of society and has also served as a neoliberal tool to control social access to future opportunities. From this point of view, critical awareness needs to be raised regarding how the mechanisms of the English-dominated bilingual and multilingual profiles come into being through the complex interplay between multiple languages/dialects and the social, cultural, and economic forces.

References

Aronin, Larissa. 2017. Conceptualizations of multilingualism: An affordances perspective. *Critical Multilingualism Studies* 5(1): 174–207.
Aronin, Larissa & David Singleton. 2012. *Multilingualism*. Amsterdam: John Benjamins.
Baker, Will. 2016. English as an academic lingua franca and intercultural awareness: Student mobility in the transcultural university. *Language and intercultural Communication* 16(3): 437–451.
Blackledge, Adrian. 2008. Language ecology and language ideology. In Nancy H. Hornberger (ed.), *Encyclopedia of Language and Education*, pp. 2923-2936. Boston, MA: Springer.
Bolton, Kingsley & Maria Kuteeva. 2012. English as an academic language at a Swedish university: Parallel language use and the 'threat' of English. *Journal of Multilingual and Multicultural Development* 33(5): 429–447.
Bolton, Kingsley & Siu-lun Lee. 2021. A socio-historical approach to multilingualism in Hong Kong. In Peter Siemund & Jacob R. E. Leimgruber (eds.), *Multilingual Global Cities: Singapore, Hong Kong, Dubai*, pp. 38–62. London: Routledge.
Calvet, Louis Jean. 1999. *Pour une écologie des langues du monde*. Paris: Plon.
Creese, Angela & Peter Martin. 2008. Classroom ecologies: A case study from a Gujarati complementary school in England. In Angela Creese, Peter Martin & Nancy H. Hornberger (eds.), *Encyclopedia of Language and Education* (Ecology of Language 9), 2nd edn, pp. 263–272. New York, NY: Springer.
Darvin, Ron & Bonnie Norton. 2015. Identity and a model of investment in applied linguistics. *Annual Review of Applied Linguistics* 35: 36–56.
de Swaan, Abram. 2001. *The World Language System: A Political Sociology and Political Economy of Language*. Cambridge: Polity.
Gao, Xuesong & Yongyan Zheng. 2019. Multilingualism and higher education in Greater China. *Journal of Multilingual and Multicultural Development* 40(7): 555–561.
Haugen, Einar. 1972. The ecology of language. In Anwar S. Dil (ed.), *The Ecology of Language: Essays by Einar Haugen*, pp. 325–339. Stanford, CA: Stanford University Press.
Heller, Monica. 2010. The commodification of language. *Annual Review of Anthropology* 39(1): 101–114.
Kaplan, Robert B. & Richard B. Baldauf (eds.). 2008. *Language Planning and Policy in Asia, Volume 1: Japan, Nepal and Taiwan and Chinese Characters*. Bristol: Multilingual Matters.

Klöter, Henning. 2020. One legacy, two legislations. Language policies on the two sides of the Taiwan Strait. In Henning Klöter & Mårten Söderblom Saarela (eds.), *Language Diversity in the Sinophone World*, pp. 101–121. London: Routledge.

Leimgruber, Jakob R. E. 2013. *Singapore English: Structure, Variation, and Usage*. Cambridge: Cambridge University Press.

Leimgruber, Jakob R. E. & Peter Siemund. 2021. The multilingual ecologies of Singapore, Hong Kong, and Dubai. In Peter Siemund & Jakob R. E. Leimgruber (eds.), *Multilingual Global Cities: Singapore, Hong Kong, Dubai*, pp. 1–15. London: Routledge.

Leimgruber, Jakob R. E., Peter Siemund & Laura Terassa. 2018. Singaporean students' language repertoires and attitudes revisited. *World Englishes* 37(2): 282–306.

Lo Bianco, Joe & Larissa Aronin. 2018. *Dominant Language Constellations: A New Perspective on Multilingualism*. Springer.

Ludwig, Ralph, Peter Mühlhäusler, & Steve Pagel. 2019. Linguistic ecology and language contact. In Ralph Ludwig, Peter Mühlhäusler & Steve Pagel (eds.), *Linguistic Ecology and Language Contact*, pp. 3–42. Cambridge: Cambridge University Press.

Mauranen, Anna, Niina Hynninen & Elina Ranta. 2010. English as an academic lingua franca: The ELFA project. *English for Specific Purposes* 29(3): 183–190.

Merriam, Sharan. 1998. *Qualitative Research and Case Study Applications in Education*, 2nd edn. San Francisco, CA: Jossey-Bass.

Ministry of Education of China. 2021. *Overview of Chinese Language and Characters* [Zhongguo Yuyan Wenzi Gaikuang]. Beijing: Ministry of Education of China.

Mufwene, Salikoko S. 2001. *The Ecology of Language Evolution*. Cambridge: Cambridge University Press.

Park, Joseph S. 2011. The promise of English: Linguistic capital and the neoliberal worker in the South Korean job market. *International Journal of Bilingual Education and Bilingualism* 14(4): 443–455.

Piller, Ingrid. 2016. Monolingual ways of seeing multilingualism. *Journal of Multicultural Discourses* 11(1): 25–33.

Sebba, Mark. 2011. Societal bilingualism. In Ruth Wodak, Barbara Johnstone & Paul Kerswill (eds.), *The Sage Handbook of Sociolinguistics*, pp. 445–459. London: Sage.

Shanghai Statistics Bureau. 2021. *Shanghai Statistics Yearbook*. Shanghai: China Statistics Press.

Siemund, Peter, & Jakob R. E. Leimgruber (eds.). 2020. *Multilingual Global Cities: Singapore, Hong Kong, Dubai*. Bristol: Multilingual Matters.

Siemund, Peter & Lijun Li. 2020. Multilingualism and language policy in Singapore. In Henning Klöter & Marten Söderblom Saarela (eds.), *Language Diversity in the Sinophone World*, pp. 205–228. London: Routledge.

Siemund, Peter, Ahmad Al-Issa & Jakob R. E. Leimgruber. 2021. Multilingualism and the role of English in the United Arab Emirates. *World Englishes* 40(2): 191–204.

Siemund, Peter, Monika E. Schulz & Martin Schweinberger. 2014. Studying the linguistic ecology of Singapore: A comparison of college and university students. *World Englishes* 33(3): 340–362.

Singapore Department of Statistics. 2021. https://www.singstat.gov.sg (24 August 2021).

Ushioda, Ema & Zoltán Dörnyei. 2017. Beyond global English: Motivation to learn languages in a multicultural world: Introduction to the special issue. *The Modern Language Journal* 101(3): 469–482.

Wei, Rining, & Jinzhi Su. 2012. The statistics of English in China: An analysis of the best available data from government sources. *English Today* 28(3): 10–14.

Zheng, Yongyan, Xiuchuan Lu & Wei Ren. 2019. Profiling Chinese university students' motivation to learn multiple languages. *Journal of Multilingual and Multicultural Development* 40(7): 590–604.

Zheng, Yongyan, Xiuchuan Lu & Wei Ren. 2020. Tracking the evolution of Chinese learners' multilingual motivation through a longitudinal Q methodology. *The Modern Language Journal* 104(4): 781–803.

CHAPTER 8

The linguistic ecology of Cyprus

Manuela Vida-Mannl[1], Sarah Buschfeld[1]
& Kleanthes K. Grohmann[2]
[1] TU Dortmund University | [2] University of Cyprus

This chapter brings together findings from different research activities investigating the (socio)linguistic situation in Cyprus. It offers an overview of the role of English, but also other languages and dialects, their historical origins, and their relevance for present-day multilingualism in Cyprus. The complex linguistic landscapes of Cyprus are approached from a linguistic ecology perspective according to which languages in Cyprus are assessed through language classification and prestige, their speech communities, domains of use, modes of use, and characteristics of variation. Throughout the chapter, the (multi)lingual situation in both the southern part and the northern part of the divided island will be addressed, with special mention of English and Cypriot dialects and their development. This approach allows researchers to depict and disentangle the complexity of the linguistic situation in Cyprus and, at the same time, shed light on it from different angles. The chapter may also serve as the beginning of a new line of research that investigates English in the context of the complex linguistic ecology of Cyprus as a whole, in particular in its relation to the two main local varieties spoken on the island, Cypriot Greek and Cypriot Turkish.

Keywords: bilectalism, Cypriot Greek, Cypriot Turkish, English in Cyprus, language ecology, multilingualism

1. Introduction

The island of Cyprus, officially referred to as the Republic of Cyprus (RoC), has always been "home to a complex mixture of different nationalities and ethnic groups" (Ker-Lindsay 2011: 11), which has caused the emergence of a unique, diverse, and bipartite linguistic ecology. This bipartite nature is reflected in the two major groups of inhabitants, Greek Cypriots and Turkish Cypriots, as well as in the two official languages spoken on the island, Greek and Turkish. In addition, the local varieties Cypriot Greek and Cypriot Turkish are widely used, so that

Greek Cypriots, for example, are "(discrete) bilectal" speakers of Standard Modern Greek and Cypriot Greek (Rowe & Grohmann 2013).

English was introduced to Cyprus under British rule (1878–1960). Unlike in some other post-colonial settings, for most inhabitants of Cyprus, English is not (one of) their first language(s). However, it is still the most important and most widely used additional language on the island. In some parts of Cyprus, however, the importance of English has recently been challenged by Russian, the most widely spoken migrant language (Kuznetsova-Eracleous 2015). In addition to Russian, other migrant languages such as Romanian, Spanish, Kurdish, Persian, and various varieties of Arabic are used on the island. There are also a number of other heritage languages, some going back centuries, such as Sanna (Cypriot (Maronite) Arabic), Kurbetcha (Gurbetcha), or (Western) Armenian (see, e.g., Hadjioannou, Tsimplakou & Kappler 2011 for discussion and references; and more recently, with relevance to heritage languages in Cyprus, Grohmann & Pavlou 2021).

While officially the whole island is considered the RoC, only the southern part is, *de facto*, under its governance. The northern part of Cyprus separated from it in 1974, but the then-founded Turkish Republic of Northern Cyprus (TRNC)[1] is internationally only recognized by Turkey. Although the two major ethnic groups, Greek Cypriots and Turkish Cypriots, have always socialized primarily within their own communities, until 1974, they have co-inhabited the whole island. The division of the island and the accompanied relocation of Turkish Cypriots from the south to the north and of Greek Cypriots from the north to the south of the island led to the geographical separation of Cypriots. Currently, only very few villages on the island are co-inhabited by members of both ethnic groups. As a result of the separation, English was no longer needed as a frequent link language between Greek and Turkish Cypriots but is mainly used in its function as a global lingua franca. Furthermore, the linguistic ecologies of the two parts have developed separately and today differ considerably from each other (see also Hadjioannou et al. 2011). The present-day political constellation is depicted in Figure 1, which also marks the buffer zone (UN Green Zone) between the two parts and the two Sovereign Base Areas, Akrotiri and Dhekelia, which belong to the UK.

The linguistic ecology of the southern part is dominated by Greek and its local dialect, a non-codified variety which linguists typically refer to as Cypriot Greek (at least since Newton 1972; e.g., Arvaniti 2010; Hadjioannou et al. 2011; Rowe & Grohmann 2013; though see Papapavlou & Pavlou 1998 for use of the term "Greek Cypriot dialect"). While those Greek-speaking Cypriots who iden-

---

[1]. The terms Northern Cyprus, Turkish Republic of Northern Cyprus, or TRNC are used to increase readability and not to make any kind of political statement.

Figure 1. Map of Cyprus (http://www.afp.gov.au/cyprus50; 04 December 2024)

tify as distinctly Cypriot gravitate towards using Cypriot Greek, those who feel a strong connection to the Greek mainland prefer to use the standard variety of Greek (Buschfeld 2013; Rowe 2024). Furthermore, the southern part has been influenced by a prominent Russian-speaking adstrate community, while Turkish is no longer widely used. English has gradually declined in usage domains, functions, and speaker fluencies since the end of British rule. In the Greek-speaking community in the southern part of the island, English has developed from an emerging second language variety prior to the island's separation in 1974 towards foreign language status nowadays (Buschfeld 2013). In the linguistic ecology of the TRNC, English serves primarily as a foreign language. Due to the political, social, and economic power of Turkey over the TRNC, Turkish is the most powerful and most important inter- and intranational language (Vida-Mannl 2022), while Greek has largely vanished from the North after the division of the island.

The present chapter brings together relevant literature as well as findings and considerations from different research projects conducted by the authors on the (socio)linguistic situation in Cyprus. These range from Rowe & Grohmann (2013) on the varietal classification of Cypriot Greek and the bilectal identification of its speakers and Fotiou & Grohmann (2022) on speakers' perception of and attitudes towards Cypriot Greek to Buschfeld (2013) on the variety status and use of English in the southern part and Vida-Mannl (2022) on the value and use of English in higher education settings in both parts, all the way to Buschfeld & Vida-Mannl (forthc.) on the role and status of English in both parts of Cyprus. As such, it provides readers with an overview of the languages of Cyprus, especially of the role of English and the local varieties of Greek and Turkish.

To reflect the complex linguistic landscapes of Cyprus, we employ a language ecology approach, which allows for the incorporation of a larger range of parameters that influence language structure and use than system-oriented approaches (Ludwig, Mühlhäusler & Pagel 2018). We start with a presentation of the history of multilingualism in Cyprus in Section 2 and describe how the various languages, dialects, and cultures emerged and were implemented in Cyprus. Section 3.1 focuses on the current linguistic landscape in Cyprus. After introducing Haugen's (1972) ecology of language, we assess languages in Cyprus based on levels such as (1) language classification and prestige, (2) speech communities, (3) domains of use, (4) modes of use, and (5) characteristics of variation. In separate sub-sections, we cover the southern part (Section 3.2) and the northern part (Section 3.3) and then zoom in on Cypriot dialects and their development (Section 3.4). This approach enables us to depict and disentangle the complexity of the linguistic situation in Cyprus and to shed light on it from a number of different angles. English in the context of the complex linguistic ecology of Cyprus as a whole has not yet been investigated, in particular not in its relation to the two local varieties spoken on the island (but see Buschfeld & Vida-Mannl forthc. for a first approach). Its role within the current linguistic ecology of Cyprus is discussed in detail in Section 4 before we draw our conclusions in Section 5.

With a diversity index of 0.44, Cyprus occupies place 118 of the 232 countries listed by SIL International (2017) and thus exhibits medium linguistic diversity when compared to some other countries around the world. Still, its exceptional sociolinguistic situation as a divided island makes it an interesting case in point for researching multilingual ecologies.

2. A brief history of multilingualism in Cyprus

2.1 The emergence of multilingualism on the island

The strategically valuable location of Cyprus at the intersection of Europe, Asia, and Africa has caused various nations and colonial powers to be interested in and rule the island in the course of its history (Hadjioannou et al. 2011; Ker-Lindsay 2011). The Achaean and Mycenaean Greeks settled in Cyprus during the middle Bronze Age (13th and 12th centuries BCE). This settlement resulted in the 'Hellenization' of Cyprus and is believed to be the origin of Greek culture and language on the island and, consequently, of its Greek Cypriot community (Kaikitis 1998;

Ker-Lindsay 2011). Over the following centuries, Cyprus was, among others, under Phoenician, Egyptian, Assyrian, Persian, Arab, Macedonian, Roman, Frankish, and Venetian rule (Browning 1980; Ker-Lindsay 2011; Tsiplakou 2006) and each of these settlements contributed to the cultural, linguistic, and social structures of Cyprus.

This long history of occupation has immediate ramifications for the languages and language use of present-day Cyprus, especially speakers' 'lingualities' (Grohmann & Kambanaros 2016; Grohmann et al. 2016; Leivada et al. 2017). Throughout its history, the island's inhabitants were bilingual, sometimes even multilingual, in different languages at different times. One constant in these multilingual dynamics has been the continued evolution of both local modern languages — Greek and Turkish. From a linguistic perspective, the former is arguably better studied than the latter in relation to Cyprus. For this, we can state that the diverging linguistic developments of the Greek variety that eventually became Standard Modern Greek and the Greek variety that we know today as Cypriot Greek reach back to Cyprus' isolation from the Greek-speaking world under continued Arab raids and occupations (7th to 10th centuries; Browning 1980). Cypriot Greek thus developed from Byzantine Medieval Greek and as such is part of the southeastern dialect group of Modern Greek: "As is the case with most other Modern Greek dialects, the modern form of [Cypriot Greek] probably evolved from Hellenistic (Koiné) Greek" (Hadjioannou et al. 2011: 509, referring to Browning 1983 and Horrocks 1997). This has led to today's diglossia in the Greek-speaking community of Cyprus and its concomitant individual bilectalism, which will be discussed in Section 3.4.

In 1571, the Ottoman Empire conquered Cyprus, which, at that time, was inhabited mostly by the Orthodox Christian community of Greek Cypriots. During Ottoman rule, Muslim settlers from Anatolia arrived in Cyprus and implemented the Turkish culture and language on the island. These settlers are believed to have been the first members of the Turkish Cypriot community (Ker-Lindsay 2011). For various social, religious, and political reasons, the Greek Cypriot and the Turkish Cypriot communities have always remained somewhat distinct from each other (Ker-Lindsay 2011; see also Kızılyürek 2005 as cited in Dietzel 2014). Although the two communities are currently opposing each other geographically, politically, socially, and linguistically — and had been even before the 1974 division of the island — this has not always been the case. For most of the Ottoman rule, i.e., up until 1878, Greek and Turkish Cypriots cohabitated Cyprus peacefully (Ekici 2019; Selvi & Silman-Karanfil 2023). They developed individual schooling systems and curricula that determined, for example, that Turkish Cypriots were educated in Ottoman Turkish, while the Greek Cypriots were schooled in Greek (Selvi & Silman-Karanfil 2023). Greek was the language of the majority of inhabitants and hence used for bicommunal communication. For this reason,

Turkish Cypriots were often bilingual speakers of (Cypriot) Greek and (Cypriot) Turkish (Annual Colonial Reports 1937, Kızılyürek & Gautier-Kızılyürek 2004). Therefore, the years under Ottoman rule did not only initiate bilingualism but also bilectalism on the island. Ottoman rule officially lasted until 1923, although the Ottomans *de facto* gave Cyprus to the British Empire in 1878; in exchange for their support against future Russian aggressions, the British Empire was allowed to occupy and administer Cyprus while it was still under Ottoman authority (Ker-Lindsay 2011; Poew 2007).

As we have seen, Cyprus looks back on a history full of political, social, and cultural changes as it had been ruled by various powers before its independence. While these recurring changes have hindered the growth of a traditional nation-state with a distinct and autonomous identity (Poew 2007), the cultural and linguistic properties of the various ruling nations have contributed to the emergence of multilingualism and diversity in Cyprus. The unique blend of cultural and political agendas has, furthermore, led to the division of the Cypriot people and their country into South and North. In fact, due to a troubled history, both major communities, Greek Cypriots and Turkish Cypriots, are divided in terms of how they identify and understand their ethnic orientation. Some see themselves as Cypriots who just happen to belong to either the Orthodox Christian or the Muslim community. Others identify very closely with the so-called 'motherlands', i.e., Greece and Turkey, and thus do not necessarily see a bond between the two Cypriot communities (Ekici 2019). While only little remains shared between the two communities, one of the assets both parties continue to use, however, is the English language.

2.2 The emergence of English in multilingual Cyprus

As repeatedly pointed out above, English is an important language in Cyprus, even if nowadays the extent of its use and its roles might differ in the two parts. As in many countries around the world, the origin of the emergence of English in multilingual Cyprus lies in rising British expansionism during which, after 300 years of Ottoman rule, the island fell under British protectorate in 1878. As briefly mentioned in Section 2.1, on June 4, 1878, the British Empire agreed on a treaty with the Ottoman Empire to protect the Ottoman possessions in Asia against Russian intervention (Georghiades 1963; Poew 2007; Schwenger 1964). An additional treaty was signed on August 14 of the same year which granted Great Britain absolute legislative authority over the island (Schwenger 1964). This treaty, however, did not bring about territorial sovereignty initially and led to *de facto*, but not *de jure*, sovereignty of Great Britain over Cyprus. Only in 1914 did the British declare the 1878 treaties invalid and announced the island's annexation (Kaikitis

1998; Poew 2007; Schwenger 1964). The British crown officially gained full territorial and *de jure* sovereignty of Cyprus under the treaty of Lausanne in 1923. English was finally implemented on the island in 1925, when Cyprus became a crown colony of Great Britain (Kaikitis 1998; Poew 2007; Terkourafi 2007).

All in all, the British pursued a rather moderate language policy and did not try to impose their culture and language on the local population (Tsiplakou 2009). However, under British rule, English was implemented as the language of the law and increasingly picked up by people of higher social status in Cyprus. While legal and official documents were drafted in English during this time, daily routines could be conducted without using English. Provided assistance, such as the translation of any communication with the colonial authorities into Greek and Turkish, made a nation-wide high level of proficiency in English redundant (Karoulla-Vrikki 2004). Consequently, speakers of both communities added the English language to their language repertoires only if necessary (Karoulla-Vrikki 2004; Tsiplakou 2009), but most did not become fully competent speakers of English. Cypriots' English language proficiency primarily increased due to school education.

With the change of the British language policy from tolerant to more controlling after the nationalist upheaval of the Greek Cypriot community in 1931, English became compulsory in the education system. As a control measure against this uprising and as a means of convergence of Cyprus with the British Empire, Governor Palmer (1933–1936) intensified the teaching of English in the education system of Cyprus (Tsiplakou 2009). It became a mandatory subject in the last two years of elementary school (Rappas 2008) but remained optional in secondary education. While some Cypriots became bilingual speakers of English and their native variety, the partly strong resistance against British rule (for details, see Richter 2006; Schwenger 1964) might have prevented widespread bilingualism. Furthermore, English became increasingly perceived as threatening both local languages and also as excluding Cypriots from understanding their administration (Karoulla-Vrikki 2004). Serious conflicts began to develop between Great Britain, Greek Cypriots (who were supported by Greece), and Turkish Cypriots (who were supported by Turkey) during this period of de-colonization and fighting for independence, as each group wished for a different outcome. Greek Cypriot supporters of the underground organization *EOKA* (*Ethniki Organosi Kyprion Agoniston*, 'National Organization of Cypriot Fighters') aimed at the independence of the island from the British and at *ENOSIS* (Greek: 'union'), i.e., unification with Greece. On the Turkish Cypriot side of the population, however, the organization KITEB aimed at *TAKSIM* (Arabic: 'divide'), i.e., the division of the island (for details, see Kaikitis 1998).

These conflicts over the future of Cyprus ended in September 1958 when Archbishop Makarios, the then ethnarch of the Greek Cypriot people, gave up the idea of unification with Greece and approved of the possibility to turn Cyprus into an autonomous state. His only condition was that the island was not going to be divided (Kaikitis 1998). This paved the way for the Zurich and London Agreements, which stipulated the island's independence, sovereignty, and territorial integrity (Kaikitis 1998) and ultimately led to the independence of Cyprus in 1960 (for further details on the agreements and the issue of independence, see Joseph 2006). Thus, after nearly 2,000 years of foreign domination, Cyprus was finally ruled by Cypriots — even though Great Britain, Greece, and Turkey retained political influence in the function of guarantor powers (Kaikitis 1998). In addition to their guarantor power function, Great Britain enforced the retention of two UK Sovereign Base Areas, namely Akrotiri/Episkopi/Paramali and Dhekelia/Pergamos/Ayios Nikolaos/Xylophagou (The Zurich and London Agreements 1959, D — Declaration by the Government of the United Kingdom, B).

However, since independence was based on a number of concessions and compromises, and in the long run did not bring about stability and peace for the newly founded state, conflicts between Greek Cypriots and Turkish Cypriots restarted with even greater intensity than before. After the pro-*enosis* Greek Cypriot underground organization EOKA-B executed a military coup against Makarios in 1974, Turkish Cypriots were convinced that the unification of Cyprus with Greece (*enosis*) was unavoidable (Ker-Lindsay 2011; Poew 2007). In an attempt to prevent this, Turkey tried to convince Britain of a collective intervention under the Treaty of Guarantee.[2] After these diplomatic efforts failed, the Turkish military invaded Cyprus on July 20, 1974. Within a few days, Cyprus was divided and the military junta was overthrown, allowing negotiations to resume. However, a second wave of Turkish militia arrived in Cyprus on August 14, 1974 and permanently captured more than one-third of the island (Ker-Lindsay 2011; Poew 2007). While the first invasion is argued to have been legal under the Treaty of Guarantee, the second is mostly assumed to have been illegal, transgressing international law as well as the Treaty of Guarantee (Ker-Lindsay 2011; Richter 1997; for an extensive legal discussion of the topic, see Poew 2007). This has resulted in the foundation of the self-declared TRNC which, however, is internationally recognized by only a single country — Turkey.

These developments, and in particular the power struggles between the three parties involved, have led to a unique language ecology in Cyprus (see Section 3.1). As portrayed in the current section, Cyprus has gone through two millennia of changing hands and power struggles. It has also been an island divided between two religious and cultural groups — if not two nations — for nearly 50 years (for

---

2. With signing the Treaty of Guarantee in 1960, Greece, Turkey, and the UK have guaranteed the independence and territorial integrity and security of Cyprus and both Cypriot groups.

a more detailed historical overview, see Buschfeld 2013). The linguistic consequences of such a development and rather unique power constellation are outlined in Sections 3.2 and 3.3, which zoom in on the current sociolinguistic conditions and the current role of English in the two parts; this overview will be rounded off with a note on the bilectal linguality of Cypriot speakers in Section 3.4.

3. English in multilingual Cyprus today

3.1 A preface on the ecology of language

As we described above, Cyprus has been home to different cultures and different languages for a long time. To adequately incorporate the resulting level of social, political, and linguistic complexity in our assessment of multilingual Cyprus, we will make use of an ecological approach. Since most commonly used methods to describe a linguistic context, such as the conceptualization of language as an instrument of communication or as a system, include only parameters that fit their respective focus, these approaches are somewhat limited in their assessment and the insights they can offer. Such descriptions might focus on only one language in a certain setting, thereby ignoring all other linguistic entities that do not belong to this language, or they might focus on spoken language only, excluding all written forms of language. The ecological approach to language description is less limited but aims at depicting the ecology of language, namely "interactions between any given language and its environment" (Haugen 1972: 325). To this end, investigating language ecologies can include a wide range of parameters, i.e., potentially all factors that influence the use of languages in a certain environment. Due to the fact that parameters or factors that may influence the use and role of a language in a certain context are not excluded *a priori*, such a more open approach potentially results in more explanatory power (Ludwig et al. 2018).

To implement an ecological approach in the present chapter, we assess the languages of Cyprus from various perspectives. We present the languages spoken in Cyprus, their respective speaker groups, and the contexts of their use to provide a general overview. Furthermore, we discuss their interrelation to capture where each language stands in comparison to other languages present. To apprehend the language ecology of Cyprus as a whole as well as for both parts individually, several ecological questions will be assessed. These include (1) the classification of the most important languages in relation to each other; (2) the respective user groups and (3) domains of use; (4) the degree of bilingualism amongst users and (5) of language-internal variation; (6) the respective written tradition and (7) the degree of the standardization of this tradition; (8) the influence of institutions on its (non-)use; and (9) the attitudes of language users towards the respective language (Haugen 1972). Assessing these factors will allow us to relate the languages of Cyprus to one another and describe their position within the language ecology of the island overall (see Section 4).

However, since "in linguistic ecology, one begins not with a particular language but with a particular area" (Voegelin & Voegelin 1964: 2), and due to the long-standing separation of the island, we assess the language ecologies of Cyprus individually for the southern and the northern parts of Cyprus (Sections 3.2 and 3.3, respectively). We start with the larger, southern part of the island that is *de jure* and *de facto* controlled by the RoC before turning towards the northern part which is only *de jure* part of the RoC but, *de facto*, not under its governance (see our elaborations in Section 1). Due to limited research and publications on certain parameters that should be assessed as part of language ecologies, we cannot discuss every parameter in detail for both parts of Cyprus (see Vida-Mannl 2022 for a current overview of languages in Cyprus).

3.2 English in the southern part

When looking into the sociolinguistic developments and current situations in the two parts of Cyprus, it is important to mention that the English language once played a much stronger role on the island than it does today. As pointed out in Section 2.2, for a long time, English had been the language of the law in the RoC; court hearings were conducted in Greek and English until the late 1980s. English further retained its function in other public domains for a while, for example in hospitals, the customhouse, and post offices (Karyolemou 2005; Pavlou & Davy 2001; Tsiplakou 2009). Still, during British times, "communication between the British and the native populations was generally limited" (Fotiou 2022: 3; see also Persianis 1996). And even though English was stipulated as the official language by the colonizer, most Cypriots had only limited proficiency in English; the native population mainly resorted to the Greek and Turkish varieties spoken on the island. Therefore, English never really gained ground as a language of intranational communication or *lingua franca* (Fotiou 2022), particularly not after the 1974 division of the island.

Even though English lost many of its former official functions, it is still used in Cyprus, especially in international contexts and the education sector. Here, English is taught or is the medium of instruction from as early as grade 1 in primary education but is especially used in higher education (see Fotiou 2022; Karyolemou 2005; Papapavlou 2001; Tsiplakou 2009; Vida-Mannl 2022 on English in the higher education landscape of Cyprus). Due to the different educational options available to Greek Cypriot students, contact intensity and amount of use of English vary and generally depend on whether they attend one of the many private educational institutes or a governmental educational institution. Contact intensity and amount of use of English after schooling, in turn, depend on the professional career pursued (McEntee-Atalianis 2001; McEntee-Atalianis & Pouloukas 2001).

Beyond the education sector, English is widely used in such domains as tourism and, to different extents, the media, diplomacy, industry, science and technology, and business and commerce (McEntee-Atalianis 2004; Tsiplakou 2009). As pointed out by Fotiou (2022), some media outlets in Cyprus, such as certain radio stations and newspapers, produce English-only content. The British station BFBS (British Forces Broadcasting Services), for example, has been available in Cyprus since 1948 (Buschfeld 2013). English movies and TV series on these outlets are mostly not dubbed but are shown with Greek subtitles. The main language of the print media is Greek, but English often finds its way into it, in particular through code-switching and in magazine titles and headings. Fotiou (2022: 4) rightly argues that this shows that English is used on the island "because it symbolizes progress, success, cosmopolitanism, and exclusivity, and because it indexes knowledge and association with specific domains which are internationally expressed and circulated in English" (see also Fotiou 2017), similar to what has been found for non-postcolonial contexts (see Seiti & Fotiou 2022 on mainland Greece).

In line with current World Englishes research (see Buschfeld & Kautzsch 2017 for a joint theoretical approach to postcolonial and non-postcolonial contexts), this shows how the use of English nowadays is not primarily motivated by former colonialism but by general forces of globalization and the prominent role of English in our modern lives (Fotiou 2022). In addition to that, landscaping studies on the use of English on different types of signs in several larger or touristic cities (Karoulla-Vrikki 2016; Karpava 2022; Kuznetsova-Eracleous 2015) have revealed that English is the most prominent language in this sector of the public sphere, in particular on monolingual signs (see also Fotiou 2022).

However, as pointed out above, in strictly private domains, the use of English by Greek Cypriots is, generally speaking, rather limited. The use of English is mainly, but not completely, restricted to communication with tourists, foreigners, and people of non-Greek or non-Cypriot ethnicity. Still, the use of English in the private domain differs from Greek Cypriot to Greek Cypriot as it depends on a variety of factors: Some Cypriots, for example, grow up in one of the few British — Greek Cypriot mixed families, some have family members living in the UK, the US, Canada, Australia, or South Africa, a number of young Cypriots go to study abroad, and some attend one of the bilingual private schools on the island (for further details on the use of English in the southern part of Cyprus, see Buschfeld

2013). In terms of language use, the situation is therefore heterogeneous, though it is quite clear that nowadays English is mainly reduced to international encounters and acquired through the school system. The study by Buschfeld (2013) has further revealed that, in general, the Cypriot Greek variety and/or Standard Modern Greek are preferred in all domains of daily life and especially the dialect is seen as the marker and carrier of national identity. Therefore, even though people's attitudes towards English are generally positive and English is clearly valued as an important linguistic tool, it does not carry or mark Greek Cypriot identity.

As pointed out in Section 1, some parts of the Greek Cypriot population primarily identify with the Greek people and culture, while others feel and strive for distinct Cypriotness. This ambivalence also finds expression in language use and, in particular, language attitudes and the perception of the linguistic situation in the southern part of the island (Papapavlou & Pavlou 1998; Tsiplakou 2011; for a recent study and references, see Fotiou & Grohmann 2022). Standard Modern Greek is what is often assumed to be spoken in the southern part — and certainly is at least by parts of the population. In addition, the vernacular Cypriot Greek is widely spoken in this part of the island. This has created the idea that the linguistic situation is characterized by diglossia between Standard Modern Greek, officially as spoken in mainland Greece, and Cypriot Greek. However, this clearcut distinction of a sociolinguistically H(igh) and a L(ow) variety does not seem to reflect current linguistic realities. In fact, "Standard Greek in particular is not spoken as a native language in Cyprus except by Greeks who are either permanent residents (2.5% of the population, according to the 2001 census) or reside in Cyprus for limited periods of time (such as students at the University of Cyprus, teachers, army officers)" (Arvaniti 2010: 18).

Even more importantly, however, "Standard Greek as used in Cyprus has been increasingly diverging from Standard Greek as spoken in Greece to the point that it is now recognizably different from it" (Arvaniti 2010: 16). Subsequently, Arvaniti labels this variety — or rather lect (see Rowe & Grohmann 2013) — 'Cypriot Standard Greek', which has been influenced through language contact between the Standard Greek, English, and Cypriot Greek. With the decline in the use of English in many official and semi-official domains and the emergence of new domains of language use such as modern media and advertising, the emergence of Cypriot Standard Greek can be attributed to an increasing need for a standard in particular in semi-formal domains. This, however, cannot be the standard of mainland Greece, mainly for reasons of speaker proficiencies and the negotiation of intricate identity conceptions pertaining to the ambivalence described above. Still, most speakers appear to be unaware of the existence of Cypriot Standard Greek or reluctant to accept its existence, again for reasons of complex identity (for details, see Arvaniti 2010). The relationship between what has often simply been referred to as Standard Modern Greek and Cypriot Greek is thus more complex than long assumed and rather a case of a lectal continuum than a diglossic situation (Arvaniti 2006; for further discussion, see Rowe & Grohmann 2014; Tsiplakou & Armostis 2020). We will briefly return to the issue of bilectalism in Section 3.4.

Next to these 'majority languages', Cypriot Arabic and Armenian are spoken by members of the officially recognized minorities. Another adstrate language widely spoken in the southern part is Russian, the language of the largest group of immigrants (Kuznetsova-Eracleous 2015; Hadjioannou et al. 2011; Karpava 2015). These languages all have entered the linguistic ecology of the southern part of the island and, ultimately, of the island as a whole, as will be discussed in Section 4.

What can be concluded from this sociolinguistic overview is that, even though English had a much stronger prominence in the years immediately following British colonization and prior to the 1974 division of the island, it has found a stable position as an important additional language, in particular in the southern part of the island (see Section 3.3 for details on the northern part) and is spoken to different degrees of fluency and regular use in a considerably multilingual and multilectal context.

3.3 English in the northern part

For reasons illustrated in Section 2.2, there has been little contact between Greek Cypriots and Turkish Cypriots for decades. Almost 30 years of closed borders (1974–2003) and the installment of the Green Line, a demilitarized buffer zone between the two parts that is supervised by the United Nations (UN), solidified the separation of the two groups. Due to the lack of contact and the different political and economic partners and dependencies, the southern and northern parts of Cyprus have developed more or less independently from each other. While the RoC is a member of the European Union, only the southern part of the island executes this membership as we sketched in Section 3.2. The self-declared TRNC is less well-connected to the world, as it is only recognized by Turkey, and it is subject to travel and trade embargos.

Since its declaration in 1983, Turkish has been the sole official language of the TRNC. (Cypriot) Greek is on its way to extinction in Northern Cyprus due to the relocation of Greek Cypriots to the South and new waves of Turkish immigrants who brought new varieties of Turkish to the North (Kappler & Tsiplakou 2018). While English also lost much of its contexts of use, it is still present as a remnant of British colonialism and is used for specific functions, especially to ensure communication with the UN and, most importantly and recently again, between the two parts of Cyprus (Hadjioannou et al. 2011; McEntee-Atalianis & Pouloukas

2001). In addition to Standard Turkish and Cypriot Turkish, a newly emerging *koiné* of the two is used in Northern Cyprus (Kappler & Tsiplakou 2018, following Demir & Johanson 2006). To truly understand the linguistic situation in Northern Cyprus, however, we disentangle the population structure in the TRNC using a language ecology approach.

In the years after the island's separation, migrants from mainland Turkey settled in Northern Cyprus. These settlers and their descendants currently outnumber Turkish Cypriots in Northern Cyprus (Research Centre on Multilingualism 2004). While this group as well as Turkish Cypriots are citizens of the TRNC, only Turkish Cypriots are also citizens of the RoC and can, at this point, cross the inner Cypriot border freely; 'non-RoC' citizens must apply for a visa. Since Turkish migrants brought their linguistic repertoires to the island, Turkish language use in Northern Cyprus is marked by contact between Cypriot Turkish and other varieties of Turkish. The most prominent example of such contact is the above-mentioned new *koiné* that is emerging in Northern Cyprus and increasingly used in communication between (former) Turkish immigrants and Turkish Cypriots (Kappler & Tsiplakou 2018). The emergence of this mixed variety is not rooted in balanced numbers of speakers of the involved varieties — speakers of Cypriot Turkish are a minority and their convergence towards non-Cypriot varieties of Turkish could have been expected. Furthermore, Turkish Cypriots also speak Standard Turkish, since it is the language of media and education. These factors could have resulted in the local variety of Cypriot Turkish disappearing. However, the new *koiné* seems to be a result of the Turkish Cypriots' continued use of their variety to distinguish themselves from the Turkish immigrants and might, furthermore, reflect a change of identification of the (former) Turkish immigrants as becoming 'more Cypriot' (see also Vida-Mannl 2022). Speaking the same variety represents group belonging for current citizens of the TRNC and might reduce the continued differentiation between inhabitants of Cypriot origin and those of mainland Turkish origin (Kappler & Tsiplakou 2018). Although the attitudes towards the Cypriot Turkish variety used to be rather negative and denigrating (Çavuşoğlu & Evripidou 2018; Evripidou & Çavuşoğlu 2015), Cypriot Turkish as well as the emerging variety are now perceived as rather prestigious (Demir & Johanson 2006; Kappler & Tsiplakou 2018). In addition to these varieties of Turkish, English is used in the TRNC. In contrast to the newly emerging *koiné*, the use of English has been found to separate the two major inhabitant groups of Northern Cyprus as the use of English is often understood as a remnant of British rule in Cyprus which only Turkish Cypriots have experienced.

Since the Turkish settlers arrived in Cyprus after its independence from the British Empire, they and their descendants do not have any (colonial) bonds to the UK but oftentimes have maintained their strong ties with Turkey. Turkish

Cypriots in the TRNC, on the other hand, tend to have close ties with the UK and/or their expatriate communities in other English-speaking countries such as the US, Canada, and Australia (Selvi & Silman-Karanfil 2022). Some even have British citizenship and are bilingual speakers of (Cypriot) Turkish and English. These differences obviously affect the linguistic profiles of the two groups. While the use of English is a marker of their Cypriot identity for Turkish Cypriots, for descendants of Turkish immigrants, English serves as a foreign language that is a sign of their level of education and rarely used in private contexts.

English is widely used in (higher) education and tourism. As higher education is a considerable source of income for the TRNC (Vida-Mannl 2022), it is an essential part of Northern Cyprus. In general, attitudes towards English are mostly positive, especially amongst young people in the TRNC, but vary depending on speaker groups, domains of use, and location. For example, Turkish Cypriots' attitudes towards English are generally positive, whereas older inhabitants of Turkish descent in rural areas sometimes show negative attitudes towards the use of English – or the non-use of Turkish in general (Vida-Mannl 2022).

While English in Northern Cyprus is assumed to be based on British English rather than representing a variety of English in itself, there has not yet been a structural investigation of its linguistic characteristics (Buschfeld & Vida-Mannl forthc.). The most recent census has unveiled that besides Cypriots and Turkish citizens, a growing community of foreign nationals, predominantly from Nigeria, Iran, Pakistan, Bulgaria, and Zimbabwe (Hatay 2017), has made Northern Cyprus their home. As these speakers brought their home languages to the TRNC, languages such as Urdu, Persian, and African varieties of English are also locally used in private or informal contexts but rarely noticed in the public domain (Vida-Mannl 2022).

3.4 Bilectalism in the multilingual ecologies of Cyprus

In the earlier sections, we have alluded to the multilingual realities of Cyprus through time. This section addresses a further important aspect of the multilingual ecologies of Cyprus, namely the local vernacular varieties in contrast to as well as alongside Standard Modern Greek in the southern part and Standard Turkish in the northern part. Emphasis will be put on Greek for the simple reason that there is a more solid knowledge base to work from – especially as far as academic language research is concerned, including our own, viz. grammatical, developmental, psycholinguistic, pathological, and sociolinguistic studies carried out within the Cyprus Acquisition Team (the CAT Lab, under the direction of Grohmann).

Drawing our discussion on Rowe & Grohmann (2014), it had at different times been suggested that Cyprus provides evidence for *de facto* trilingualism in Greek, Turkish, and English or 'bilingualism' in Standard Modern Greek and Cypriot Greek in the Greek Cypriot part, or 'bidialectism' in Standard Modern Greek and Cypriot Greek — possibly with its respective counterparts in the northern part (Çavuşoğlu & Evripidou 2018; Demir & Johanson 2006; Evripidou & Çavuşoğlu 2015; Georgiou-Scharlipp & Scharlipp 1998; Imer & Celebi 2006; Kappler 2008). In an attempt to streamline the characterization between vernacular and standard, Grohmann (2011) introduced the cover term 'bi-x' as a descriptive umbrella term. Following Rowe & Grohmann (2013) and much subsequent research in the CAT Lab (Antoniou et al. 2016; Grohmann & Kambanaros 2016; Grohmann et al. 2016; Leivada et al. 2017), we specified bi-x as '(discrete) bilectal', since in diglossic societies, speakers cannot be assumed to be 'bi*dialect*al'; after all, the H variety should by definition be a language proper. This could be Standard Modern Greek, some local form such as Cypriot Standard Greek, or other points on a dialect continuum.

In fact, Arvaniti (2006:26) already draws a revealing comparison between characterizations of 'diglossia' in Cyprus and those that assume a 'dialect continuum' or 'bilingualism'. In her words, although the characterization diglossic "appears clear to some researchers […,] it is not shared by all; many scholars describe the linguistic situation in Cyprus as a 'dialectal continuum' of some sort […] or as bidialectalism." In addition, despite being the L variety, Cypriot Greek has found its way over the past two decades into domains "in which its presence was perhaps unconceivable in the past" (Fotiou & Ayiomamitou 2021:3, see also Fotiou & Grohmann 2022, who present a recent study on language attitudes and perceptions by Greek Cypriots), such as the media, the arts, and the linguistic landscape of the southern part. Furthermore, many studies have demonstrated that Cypriot Greek, in spite of official policies, is also used from pre-primary to tertiary education along with Standard Modern Greek (Ioannidou 2009; Sophocleous & Ioannidou 2020; Tsiplakou 2007; see also Leivada et al. 2020).

Adding to the references to research on Cypriot Turkish provided in Section 3.3 and the before-mentioned gap between research and insights on the interrelation of Cypriot Greek and Standard Modern Greek and Cypriot Turkish and Standard Turkish, as Arvaniti (2006) continues, the relationship between Cypriot Turkish and Standard Turkish in Northern Cyprus exhibits interesting parallels to what we find in Southern Cyprus with respect to 'bi-x'. The final verdict on the form, use, and function of the two Cypriot L varieties and their speakers' exact lingualities in either or both communities has important consequences for an accurate analysis of the linguistic ecologies of Cyprus.

4. Discussion: The current linguistic ecology of Cyprus

As we developed in the previous sections, the linguistic ecology of Cyprus is quite complex. Cyprus is a linguistically, socially, and ethnically diverse country and, for reasons specified in Section 3, the different inhabitant groups make use of various languages depending on the communicative scenario at hand. To understand the linguistic landscape of Cyprus as a whole, and of both of its parts individually, assessing individual languages does not suffice. Implementing an ecological approach that includes and relates all relevant languages in a certain context has shown to be more fruitful. Using Haugen's (1972) parameters for an ecological approach enables a more fine-grained understanding of the languages of Cyprus and the circumstances of their use. These parameters include (1) the classification of the most important languages in relation to each other; (2) the respective user groups and (3) domains of use; (4) the degree of bilingualism amongst users and (5) of language-internal variation; (6) the respective written tradition and (7) the degree of the standardization of this tradition; (8) the influence of institutions on its (non-)use; and (9) the attitudes of language users towards the respective language. Most of these parameters have been discussed in the previous sections in some detail. We discuss and relate the most important of these findings regarding Haugen's parameters in the following.

The RoC has two official languages, Greek and Turkish. In general, however, Cypriots are not bilingual speakers of these languages. The Cypriot people consist of Greek and Turkish Cypriots, and each group speaks one of the official languages of Cyprus. The Greek Cypriots are primarily speakers of Greek and its local variety Cypriot Greek, while Turkish Cypriots primarily speak Turkish and its local variety Cypriot Turkish. The standard variety is mostly used in official and public domains; in turn, the local varieties are more common in private, informal conversations. Furthermore, both groups have continued to speak English, though under different circumstances. In addition to inhabitants of Cypriot ethnicity, Greeks reside in the southern part of Cyprus, while Turks migrated to the North. Both groups tend to not speak the respective local variety and do not share the colonial experience with their respective (Greek or Turkish) Cypriot peers. While this assessment is true, it is a simplification of the complex and evolving linguistic realities in both parts of Cyprus.

Regarding the southern part, we have shown that most inhabitants are bilectal and often multilingual speakers of Standard Modern Greek, Cypriot Greek, and English. Which language or variety is used depends on the context and conversational partner(s), as attitudes towards all options are generally positive. Cypriot Greek might represent Cypriot identity, while Greek might show a high level of education and English might reflect internationality. Although Greek and Turkish are the official languages of Cyprus, official signage in the southern part is often in Greek and English (Vida-Mannl 2022). English is a language of high prestige in Southern Cyprus and its status has developed from emerging ESL to EFL (Buschfeld 2013). It is very commonly used in speaking and writing and it is a language of the media, education, and business. In addition to these three languages, Russian can be widely seen in the public domain, as it is the language of the biggest migrant group in the southern part of Cyprus. Due to the numbers and economic influence of Russian speakers, the prestige and importance of Russian has been constantly increasing. Other, official or unofficial, minority languages are primarily used in the private domain. While English has clearly developed from the colonizer's language to functioning as the global *lingua franca*, the status and prestige of Greek as the language of the motherland, especially in comparison to Cypriot Greek, as a marker of Cypriotness, is more complex and dependent on the individual speaker.

In the TRNC, Turkish has been postulated as the sole official language. The majority of inhabitants in the TRNC, however, are not Cypriot but Turkish and speak a variety different from either Cypriot or Standard Turkish. While Turkish Cypriots understand 'their' variety of Turkish, i.e., Cypriot Turkish, and speak English as a marker of their Cypriot identity and have often maintained close ties with the UK and Turkish Cypriot communities in other (often English-speaking) countries, the descendants of Turkish migrants, who have been living in Cyprus since the island's separation, do not share this identification with English nor Cypriot Turkish. However, it has been found that a new variety of Turkish is emerging in the TRNC which might represent a marker of a shared identity for all Turkish-speaking inhabitants of Northern Cyprus. Due to the complex political situation as an unrecognized country and the structure of its society consisting mainly of ethnic Turks, societal multilingualism is not very common in the TRNC and official language use is often limited to (Standard) Turkish. While varieties of Turkish are primarily used in the public domain, contexts of higher education serve as an exception to this rule. As higher education is a major source of income in the TRNC, international students are attracted by English-medium study programs. Although English is a prestigious international language, it is not widely used in public domains in Cyprus but limited to private contexts that include (British-)Turkish Cypriots and higher education settings. In addition, English also serves as the language of choice in case of interaction between Greek and Turkish Cypriots. While Turkish Cypriots were often bilingual in Cypriot Greek and Cypriot Turkish — both before and during British rule — Turkish Cypriots no longer learn Greek and thus have to rely on English as their bi-communal *lingua franca*. In contrast, English might have been seen as a threat during British rule, currently many Cypriots expect it to be the language of a unified Cyprus.

5. Conclusion

This chapter has approached the complex linguistic reality of the divided island of Cyprus from the perspective of an 'ecology of language' (Haugen 1972). The long history of the island's continued and changing occupations sketched in Section 2 paints a clear picture of a multilingual community of communities. That is, the many linguistic speaker groups that inhabit the island (and, in many cases, have done so for centuries) hail from different ethnic, religious, and social backgrounds. There were times of peaceful cohabitation, there were times of strife and even full-on war, and there were and are times of mutual tolerance.

Our main goal was to bring together pieces of historical and linguistic relevance that help us situate the languages and dialects spoken on Cyprus into its multilingual context through a linguistic ecologies approach. In addition to English, we focused on the two main languages spoken on the island, (Cypriot) Greek in the Greek Cypriot controlled southern two-thirds of the island and (Cypriot) Turkish in the occupied one-third of Northern Cyprus (see also Rowe 2024 with relevance to the 'Cyprus Problem'). This made it necessary to discuss the role of the local vernaculars, dialects, or better perhaps 'lects', as linguistic varieties different from but very much related to the standard languages, Standard Modern Greek and Standard Turkish, respectively. We followed the tradition that started with Grohmann (2011) and Rowe & Grohmann (2013) by identifying Greek Cypriots as bilectal speakers of Cypriot Greek (L variety) and Standard Modern Greek (H variety) or some version thereof (such as Cypriot Standard Greek, as suggested by Arvaniti 2010). Arguably something very similar may hold for the North as well between Cypriot Turkish and Standard Turkish, though research is rather sparse for the time being.

Adding English to the mix, there may have been a time when the linguistic situation in Cyprus could actually be described as (potentially) *de facto* trilingual. English may have played the role of a frequently used link language between Greek and Turkish Cypriots prior to the separation of the island, while today it is mainly used in its function as a global lingua franca. Apart from very little progress on the 'Cyprus Problem', i.e., the problematic political situation of *de facto*-divided Cyprus, the island has also experienced several large waves of migration for a number of reasons and from quite a number of geographic, religious, social, and, of course, linguistic backgrounds. Against these factors, in particular the unresolved issue of a Cypriot reunification, the development of English and the general linguistic ecology of Cyprus is currently unpredictable and it remains to be seen which roles, functions, and purposes the many languages spoken in Cyprus will hold in the future.

References

Annual Colonial Reports for the Social and Economic Progress of the People of Cyprus 1909–1936. 1937. London: His Majesty's Stationary Office.

Antoniou, Kyriakos, Kleanthes K. Grohmann, Maria Kambanaros & Napoleon Katsos. 2016. The effect of childhood bilectalism and multilingualism on executive control. *Cognition* 149: 18–30.

Arvaniti, Amalia. 2006. Erasure as a means of maintaining diglossia in Cyprus. *San Diego Linguistic Papers* 2: 25–38.

Arvaniti, Amalia. 2010. Linguistic practices in Cyprus and the emergence of Cypriot Standard Greek. *Mediterranean Language Review* 17(2006–2010): 15–45.

Browning, Robert. 1980. Byzantium and Islam in Cyprus in the Early Middle Ages. Ἐπετηρίς τοῦ Κέντρου Ἐπιστημονικῶν Σπουδῶν 9(1977–1979): 101–116.

Browning, Robert. 1983. *Medieval and Modern Greek*, 2nd edn. Cambridge: Cambridge University Press.

Buschfeld, Sarah. 2013. *English in Cyprus or Cyprus English: An Empirical Investigation of Variety Status*. Amsterdam: John Benjamins.

Buschfeld, Sarah & Alexander Kautzsch. 2017. Towards an integrated approach to postcolonial and non-postcolonial Englishes. *World Englishes* 36(1): 104–126.

Buschfeld, Sarah & Manuela Vida-Mannl. Forthcoming. English in Cyprus. In Raymond Hickey (ed.), *The New Cambridge History of the English Language*, Vol. 4. Cambridge: Cambridge University Press.

Çavuşoğlu, Çise & Dimitris Evripidou. 2018. "I don't think Turkish used here is normal": Language attitudes of Turkish university students towards Cypriot Turkish. *Quality & Quantity* 52(Suppl. 2): 1151–1166.

Demir, Nurettin & Lars Johanson. 2006. Dialect contact in Northern Cyprus. *International Journal of the Sociology of Language* 181: 1–9.

Dietzel, Irene. 2014. *The Ecology of Coexisting and Conflict in Cyprus*. Berlin: De Gruyter Mouton.

Ekici, Tufan. 2019. *The Political and Economic History of North Cyprus: A Discordant Polity*. Cham: Palgrave Macmillan.

Evripidou, Dimitris & Çavuşoğlu, Çise. 2015. Turkish Cypriots' language attitudes: The case of Cypriot Turkish and Standard Turkish in Cyprus. *Mediterranean Language Review* 22: 119–138.

Fotiou, Constantina. 2017. English–Greek code-switching in Greek Cypriot magazines and newspapers – An analysis of its textual forms and functions. *Journal of World Languages* 4(1): 1–27.

Fotiou, Constantina. 2022. English in Cyprus. *English Today* 39(4): 257–263.

Fotiou, Constantina & Ioli Ayiomamitou. 2021. "We are in Cyprus, we have to use our language, don't we?" Pupils' and their parents' attitudes towards two proximal linguistic varieties. *Linguistics and Education* 63(2021): 100931.

Fotiou, Constantina & Kleanthes K. Grohmann. 2022. A small island with big differences? Folk perceptions in the context of dialect levelling and koineization. *Frontiers in Communication* 6: 770088.

Georghiades, Antonios. 1963. *Die Zypernfrage*. Bonn: H. Bouvier.

Georgiou-Scharlipp, Kyriaki & Wolfgang E. Scharlipp. 1998. Three examples of a Turkish Cypriot dialect. *Mediterranean Language Review* 10: 169–178.

Grohmann, Kleanthes K. 2011. Some directions for the systematic investigation of the acquisition of Cypriot Greek: A new perspective on production abilities from object clitic placement. In Esther Rinke & Tanja Kupisch (eds.), *The Development of Grammar: Language Acquisition and Diachronic Change*, pp. 179–203. Amsterdam: John Benjamins.

Grohmann, Kleanthes K. & Maria Kambanaros. 2016. The gradience of multilingualism in typical and impaired language development: Positioning bilectalism within comparative bilingualism. *Frontiers in Psychology: Language Sciences* 7: 37.

Grohmann, Kleanthes K. & Natalia Pavlou. 2021. Heritage languages in south-eastern Europe. In Silvina Montrul & Maria Polinsky (eds.), *The Cambridge Handbook of Heritage Languages and Linguistics*, pp. 69–90. Cambridge: Cambridge University Press.

Grohmann, Kleanthes K., Maria Kambanaros, Evelina Leivada & Charley Rowe. 2016. A developmental approach to diglossia: Bilectalism on a gradient scale of linguality. *Poznań Studies in Contemporary Linguistics* 52(4): 629–662.

Hadjioannou, Xenia, Stavroula Tsiplakou & Matthias Kappler. 2011. Language policy and language planning in Cyprus. *Current Issues in Language Planning* 12(4): 503–569.

Hatay, Mete. 2017. Population and politics in north Cyprus — An overview of the ethno-demography of north Cyprus in the light of the 2011 census. *PCC REPORT 2/2017*. Friedrich-Ebert-Stiftung and Peace Research Institute Oslo (PRIO). http://library.fes.de/pdf-files/bueros/zypern/14903.pdf (20 February 2023).

Haugen, Einar I. 1972. The ecology of language. In Anwar S. Dil (ed.), *The Ecology of Language: Essays by Einar Haugen*, pp. 328–339. Stanford, CA: Stanford University Press.

Horrocks, Geoffrey. 1997. *Greek: A History of the Language and its Speakers*. London: Longman.

Imer, Kamile & Nazmiye Celebi. 2006. The intonation of Turkish Cypriot dialect: A contrastive and sociolinguistic interpretation. *International Journal of the Sociology of Language* 181: 69–82.

Ioannidou, Elena. 2009. Using the "improper" language in the classroom: The conflict between language use and legitimate varieties in education. Evidence from a Greek Cypriot classroom. *Language and Education* 23(3): 263–278.

Joseph, Joseph S. 2006. The political context and consequences of the London and Zurich Agreements. In Hubert Faustmann & Nicos Peristianis (eds.), *Britain in Cyprus: Colonialism and Post-Colonialism 1878–2006*, pp. 453–472. Mannheim: Bibliopolis.

Kaikitis, Lambros. 1998. *Zypern und die Europäische Union. Erwartungen und Probleme einer eventuellen Vollmitgliedschaft Zyperns*. Aachen: Alano Herodot.

Kappler, Matthias. 2008. Contact-induced effects in the syntax of Cypriot Turkish. *Turkic Languages* 12: 203–220.

Kappler, Matthias & Tsiplakou, Stavroula. 2018. Two Cypriot *koinai*? Structural and sociolinguistic considerations. *Mediterranean Language Review* 25: 75–96.

Karoulla-Vrikki, Dimitra. 2004. Language and ethnicity in Cyprus under the British: A linkage of heightened salience. *The International Journal of the Sociology of Language* 168: 19–36.

Karoulla-Vrikki, Dimitra. 2016. English as a lingua franca: The linguistic landscape in Lidras and Onasagorou Street, Lefkosia, Cyprus. In Natasha Tsantila, Jane Mandalios & Melpomeni Ilkos (eds.), *ELF: Pedagogical and Interdisciplinary Perspectives*, pp. 145–154. Athens: Deree – The American College of Greece.

Karpava, Sviatlana. 2015. *Vulnerable Domains for Cross-linguistic Influence in L2 Acquisition of Greek*. Frankfurt: Peter Lang.

Karpava, Sviatlana. 2022. Multilingual linguistic landscape of Cyprus. *International Journal of Multilingualism* 21(2): 823–861.

Karyolemou, Marilena. 2005. From linguistic liberalism to legal regulation: The Greek language in Cyprus. In Andreas N. Papapavlou (ed.), *Contemporary Sociolinguistic Issues in Cyprus*, pp. 27–50. Thessaloniki: University Studio Press.

Ker-Lindsay, James. 2011. *The Cyprus Problem: What Everyone Needs to Know*. Oxford: Oxford University Press.

Kızılyürek, Niyazi. 2005. The Turkish Cypriot Community and Rethinking of Cyprus. In Michalis Michael (ed.), *Cyprus in the Modern World*, pp. 228–2247. Thessaloniki: Vanias.

Kızılyürek, Niyazi & Sylvaine Gautier-Kızılyürek. 2004. The politics of identity in the Turkish Cypriot community and the language question. *International Journal of the Sociology of Language* 168: 37–54.

Kuznetsova-Eracleous, Natalya. 2015. Linguistic Landscape of Limassol: Russian Presence. M.A. thesis, University of Cyprus.

Leivada, Evelina, Maria Kambanaros, Loukia Taxitari & Kleanthes K. Grohmann. 2020. (Meta)linguistic abilities of bilectal educators: The case of Cyprus. *International Journal of Bilingual Education and Bilingualism* 23(8): 1003–1018.

Leivada, Evelina, Elena Papadopoulou, Maria Kambanaros & Kleanthes K. Grohmann. 2017. The influence of bilectalism and non-standardization on the perception of native grammatical variants. *Frontiers in Psychology: Language Sciences* 8: 205.

Ludwig, Ralf, Peter Mühlhäusler & Steve Pagel. 2018. Linguistic ecology and language contact: Conceptual evolution, interrelatedness, and parameters. In Ralf Ludwig, Peter Mühlhäusler & Steve Pagel (eds.), *Linguistic Ecology and Language Contact*, pp. 3–42. Cambridge: Cambridge University Press.

McEntee-Atalianis, Lisa J. 2001. Language use and attitudes towards the Greek-Cypriot dialect, Standard Modern Greek, and English in the Greek-Cypriot community of Nicosia, Cyprus. In Yoryia Agouraki, Amalia Arvaniti, Jim Davy, Dionysios Goutsos, Marilena Karyolemou, Alexia Panayotou, Andreas N. Papapavlou, Pavlos Pavlou & Anna Roussou (eds.), *Proceedings of the 4th International Conference on Greek Linguistics, Nicosia, September 1999*, pp. 408–415. Thessaloniki: University Studio Press.

McEntee-Atalianis, Lisa J. 2004. The impact of English in postcolonial, postmodern Cyprus. *International Journal of the Sociology of Language* 168: 77–90.

McEntee-Atalianis, Lisa J. & Stavros Pouloukas. 2001. Issues of identity and power in a Greek-Cypriot community. *Journal of Multilingual and Multicultural Development* 22: 19–38.

Newton, Brian. 1972. *Cypriot Greek: Its Phonology and Inflections*. The Hague: Mouton.

Papapavlou, Andreas N. 2001. The spread of English worldwide and the situation in Cyprus: Growing concerns. In Yoryia Agouraki, Amalia Arvaniti, Jim Davy, Dionysios Goutsos, Marilena Karyolemou, Alexia Panayotou, Andreas N. Papapavlou, Pavlos Pavlou & Anna Roussou (eds.), *Proceedings of the 4th International Conference on Greek Linguistics, Nicosia, September 1999*, pp. 431–438. Thessaloniki: University Studio Press.

Papapavlou, Andreas & Pavlos Pavlou. 1998. A review of the sociolinguistic aspects of the Greek Cypriot dialect. *Journal of Multilingual and Multicultural Development* 19: 212–220.

Pavlou, Pavlos & Jim Davy. 2001. Is Cyprus an ESL country? In Thanasis Georgakopoulos, Theodossia-Soula Pavlidou, Miltos Pehlivanos, Artemis Alexiadou, Jannis Androutsopoulos, Alexis Kalokairinos, Stavros Skopeteas, Katerina Stathi (eds.), *Proceedings of the 12th International Conference of the Greek Applied Linguistics Association*, pp. 185–201. Berlin: Edition Romiosini/CeMoG.

Persianis, Panayiotis. 1996. The British colonial education "lending" policy in Cyprus (1878–1960): An intriguing example of an elusive "adapted education" policy. *Comparative Education* 32(1): 45–68.

Poew, René. 2007. *Der Beitritt Zyperns zur EU – Probleme des Völkerrechts, des Europarechts und des zypriotischen Rechts. Leitideen für die Entwicklung eines zukünftigen reorganisierten gesamtzypriotischen Staates.* Hamburg: Lit Verlag.

Rappas, Alexis. 2008. The elusive polity: Imagining and contesting colonial authority in Cyprus during the 1930s. *Journal of Modern Greek Studies* 26: 363–397.

Research Centre on Multilingualism. 2004. *Euromosaic III – Cyprus*. https://publications.europa.eu/en/publication-detail/-/publication/4dc487cf-3c39-40ac-9b97-c55110263a56 (14 February 2019).

Richter, Heinz A. 1997. Historische Hintergründe des Zypernkonflikts, In *THETIS – Mannheimer Beiträge zur klassischen Archäologie und Geschichte Griechenlands und Zyperns*, Band 4, pp. 309–318. Mannheim: Rutzen Verlag.

Richter, Heinz A. 2006. Benevolent autocracy 1931–1945. In Hubert Faustmann & Nicos Peristianis (eds.), *Britain in Cyprus. Colonialism and Post-Colonialism 1878–2006*, pp. 133–149. Mannheim: Bibliopolis.

Rowe, Charley. 2024. Di(a)glossia and political ideology in grecophone Cyprus: Moribundity resistance, diglossic nostalgia, and a sociolinguistic "buffer zone". In Natalia Pavlou, Constantina Fotiou & Kleanthes K. Grohmann (eds.), *Heritage Languages and Variation*, pp. 128–152. Venice: Venice University Press.

Rowe, Charley & Kleanthes K. Grohmann. 2013. Discrete bilectalism: Towards co-overt prestige and diglossic shift in Cyprus. *International Journal of the Sociology of Language* 224: 119–142.

Rowe, Charley & Kleanthes K. Grohmann. 2014. Canaries in a coal mine: Native speakerhood and other factors as predictors of moribundity, death, and diglossic shift in Cypriot Greek. *Mediterranean Language Review* 21: 121–142.

Schwenger, Klaus Peter. 1964. Selbstbestimmung für Zypern: Die Prinzipien von Selbstbestimmung und Schutz der Nation in ihrem Einfluß auf die Entstehung der Republik Zypern. PhD dissertation, Julius-Maximilians-Universität, Würzburg.

Seiti, Ioanna & Constantina Fotiou. 2022. 'Instafashion', 'adeventures' and 'gals on the go': The creative use of English in Greek fashion magazines. *Journal of World Languages* 8(1): 56–82.

Selvi, Ali Fuad & Leyla Silman-Karanfil. 2023. English in Northern Cyprus: A sociolinguistic profile. *World Englishes* 42(4): 679–697.

Sophocleous, Andry & Elena Ioannidou. 2020. Young children performing linguistic varieties: Comparing classroom and play-time language use in the bidialectal context of Cyprus. *Language and Education* 34(4): 345–362.

Terkourafi, Marina. 2007. Perceptions of difference in the Greek sphere: The case of Cyprus. *Journal of Greek Linguistics* 8: 60–96.

The Zurich and London Agreements. 1959. http://www.cyprus-conflict.net/Treaties%20-1959-60.html (31 October 2012).

Tsiplakou, Stavroula. 2006. Cyprus: Language situation. In Keith Brown (ed.), *Encyclopedia of Language and Linguistics*, pp. 337–339. Amsterdam: Elsevier.

Tsiplakou, Stavroula. 2007. Linguistic variation in the Cypriot language classroom and its implications for education. In Andreas N. Papapavlou & Pavlos Pavlou (eds.), *Sociolinguistic and Pedagogical Dimensions of Dialects in Education*, pp. 236–264. Newcastle upon Tyne: Cambridge Scholars.

Tsiplakou, Stavroula. 2009. English in Cyprus: Outer or expanding circle? *Anglistik* 20(2): 75–87.

Tsiplakou, Stavroula. 2011. Linguistic attitudes and emerging hyperdialectism in a diglossic setting: Young Cypriot Greeks on their language. In Corey Yoquelet (ed.), *Berkeley Linguistic Society 29. Special Volume: Minority and Diasporic Languages of Europe*, pp. 120–132. Berkeley, CA: Berkeley Linguistics Society.

Tsiplakou, Stavroula & Spyros Armostis. 2020. Survival of the "oddest"? Levelling, shibboleths, reallocation and the emergence of intermediate varieties. In Massimo Cerruti & Stavroula Tsiplakou (eds.), *Intermediate Language Varieties: Koinai and Regional Standards in Europe*, pp. 203–230. Amsterdam: John Benjamins.

Vida-Mannl, Manuela. 2022. *The Value of the English Language in Global Mobility and Higher Education: An Investigation of Higher Education in Cyprus*. London: Bloomsbury.

Voegelin, Charles F. & Florence M. Voegelin. 1964. Languages of the world: African fascicle one. *Anthropological Linguistics* 6(6): 1–149.

CHAPTER 9

English in the Kurdistan Region of Iraq
Historical background, new status, and future implications

Ludwig Paul & Zana Ibrahim
University of Hamburg | University of Kurdistan Hewlêr

This article aims to give an account of the language situation in the Kurdistan Region of Iraq (KRI), with a focus on the use and position of English within the KRI's linguistic ecology. As an autonomous region, the KRI tries to navigate its way through a volatile time in a politically instable area. It has to cope with constraints and pressure from the Iraqi government, and from neighboring countries like Turkey and Iran. The KRI's cultural and language policies, and the development of the linguistic situation, can only be understood against the overall political situation, with its specific historical background. The article contains also a state of the art about English in the KRI, which is only about to emerge as a field, and a series of interviews with educational experts and policy makers, on the linguistic situation.

Keywords: autonomy, educational system, Kurdistan, multiethnic, surge of English

1. Introduction

The Kurdistan Region of Iraq (KRI) is an autonomous region of northern Iraq with ca. 7 million inhabitants whose political status is disputed. A referendum held in September 2017 yielded a clear vote for independence, but was rejected by the Iraqi central government and most other neighbouring states. The KRI's ethnic-linguistic composition is complex and includes a Kurdish majority (of over 80%) and Turkmen, Assyrian, and Arab minorities, with religious subdivisions (Aziz 2011). To understand the KRI's linguistic ecology, it is necessary to consider the historical background, and the contemporary political, social, and economic situation of the region.

In the last two decades, English has made a significant shift in the KRI from a foreign language to a powerful language of business and communication, education, and access to higher studies and employment opportunities. From a language of little daily utility value up to 10–15 years ago, it has now become one of the major spoken and used languages in the Region. Although this could partly be due to the increasing dominance of English globally, that a language can rapidly establish itself in a foreign society is perhaps somewhat unusual. Therefore, this rapid change in status is a linguistically and socially interesting phenomenon which deserves to be studied. Currently, English is a main requirement for almost all white-collar jobs and postgraduate admission for all programmes of study at universities in the KRI. The view that English is paramount for economic progress and prosperity is shared by the Region's officials and the majority of the public. Therefore, English-medium instruction (EMI) private schools are on the rise, leaving the impression that for a brighter future for their children, parents need to invest in their education by enrolling them in such schools. This has also raised the issue of social inequality manifested in the affordability of EMI for families. Cultural and identity-related consequences of EMI and the ever-growing prominence of English are also another serious pitfall in the near future, especially with the wide perception of the public that Kurdish, the mother tongue of the majority of the Region's population, is of little utility although it is an official language of Iraq alongside Arabic.

So far, little if any work has been done to account for such a rapid change in the position of English and its potential impact on the status of Kurdish. Apart from a few master's theses which are mainly on English-medium instruction in schools, very few studies have considered how English has gained a new status in the KRI community, including possible social, educational, political, and economic factors, and what the societal, educational, and linguistic implications of this status could be. This study therefore has the following objectives. First, it aims to give an account of the general historical background and the present situation that is necessary to understand the linguistic situation of Kurdish and other languages in the present-day KRI. Then, the state of the art on the linguistic situation of the KRI, and the status of English, will be explained. Then, an overview will be given of the linguistic situation and status of English in the KRI, especially with respect to its use as a medium of instruction. Lastly, we will try to highlight the current and future position of English in the KRI's society by examining how the wider public including education officials and language policy stakeholders view the unprecedented position of English. As an appendix, qualitative data will be provided through interviews with educational experts and policy makers. This should give a first impression of what the region aims for by opting to attribute such a powerful role to English across educational and public domain spheres, how this new linguistic reality has impacted the local language and culture, and how this current policy might affect the language ecology of the region in the future.

2. The historical background

Kurds have inhabited their present regions for a long time, but probably their expansion took place from east (Western Iran) to west (Central Kurdistan) in the pre-Islamic period (Minorsky 1986: 447). From early Islamic times onward, Kurds have played an important role as a military force in various Islamic empires. Some local dynasties are of Kurdish origin, e.g., that of the Marwānīds (in the area of Diyarbakır, 990–1085 CE; Bosworth 2004: 89). For pre-modern times, one should not assume any kind of ethnic homogeneity for the Kurds, or the regions they inhabited. Kurds were often organized in tribal confederations, which could include also non-Kurdish speaking and even non-Muslim elements, sometimes more loosely associated with the tribe (van Bruinessen 1989: 69–70, 136–137). Aside from this, in classical Arabic sources, *Kurd* (pl. *Akrād*) was not used as an ethnic term in the modern sense, but could be used as a cover term for nomadic groups in general. During the 16/17th centuries CE, the area of the present-day KRI was disputed between the competing Ottoman and Safavid Empires. Following the peace treaty of Qasr-e Šīrīn (1639), it became part of the Ottoman Empire, and remained so up to the latter's dissolution after the 1st World War. During this time, the area was governed, under Ottoman supremacy, by local petty dynasties like the Bābān or Sorān. In the late 19th century, the Ottoman government transformed the area of the (present) KRI, together with neighbouring areas like Kirkuk and Mosul, to the new administrative unit, named "Vilayet Mosul".

After the 1st World War, the Ottoman Empire's Anatolian areas were occupied by, and distributed among, the allied forces. In the Lausanne peace treaty of 1920, the Kurds were promised an independent state on the territories of the Ottoman Empire. This was nullified by the newly-organized Turkish army that regained, in 1921/22, what it defined as the central area of the future Turkish nation state. The Turkic Republic that was founded shortly after in 1923 tried to get back the rest of the Kurdish-inhabited areas of the former Ottoman Empire, namely the Vilayet Mosul, to incorporate it into the Turkish nation-building project, but the League of Nations rejected this claim in 1925. The oil resources that were found in this area were probably one important reason for the British to keep the Kurdish regions within the Iraqi monarchy, which they had just created artificially, and which they continued to dominate politically as a Mandate area until 1932.

However, when one thinks about the Kurds' claims for independence and statehood from 1920 up to this day, one must say that despite the 1920 Lausanne promise, reality stood in their way from the beginning. The Kurds had neither a history of statehood to refer to, nor was there any powerful state that was fully committed to the Kurdish cause. Although a Kurdish nationalism evolved after the Young Turk revolt of 1908, it always remained weak against its Turkish adversary. Among the Young Turks, there were influential personalities of Kurdish origin that, by their mere existence, relativized Kurdish nationalism. Aside from this, the Turkish national movement continued to "play the Islamic card" in Eastern Anatolia to integrate the local (Kurdish) elites in the ongoing conflict against possible Armenian territorial claims, and against colonial powers like Great Britain (Behrendt 1993: 344–346). For many Kurds in Eastern Anatolia, including those who protested against the new Turkish nation state and its grip over the Kurdish people, the bygone Caliphate (dissolved in 1924 by the Turkish government) continued to be more real and important than a secular Kurdish nationalism.

During the Iraqi monarchy (1921–58), the Kurds waged repeated local and regional uprisings especially under the charismatic leader Mustafa Barzani (1903–1979), who had to go to exile from 1945 until 1958. After the establishment of the Republic in 1958, negotiations alternated with new armed confrontations, which claimed thousands of lives especially on the Kurdish side, but the Iraqi State was unable to secure permanent control over the Kurdish regions. In 1970, new negotiations ended with a historic peace treaty that, for the first time, granted the Kurds cultural and political autonomy although this did not stop the conflict altogether. In the following years, especially since 1980, the Kurds suffered enhanced persecution, dislocation, and destruction of villages. These culminated in the *Anfāl* campaign (1986–89) that aimed at Arabizing strategic parts of the Kurdish-inhabited areas like Kerkuk, and claimed more than 100,000 casualties among Kurdish civilians.[1]

3. The present times

For the Kurds of Iraq, the present times start in 1991. Following the Iraqi invasion of Kuwait in July 1990 and the defeat of the Iraqi army by the US-led International Coalition forces in spring 1991, the Kurds started an extensive uprising against Saddam Husain's regime and the Iraqi State. To protect the Kurds against the revenge of the Iraqi armed forces, a no-fly-zone was established over northern (Kurdish) Iraq in April 1991 by the Coalition forces, which effectively secured Kurdish military supremacy in the northern regions, and has been the basis for the autonomous status of the Kurdish Region of Iraq since then.

---

1. See, e.g., the detailed description in McDowall (1996: 343–367), or Waisy, Ramli & Hung (2014: 193).

In 2003, a US-led Coalition invaded Iraq and defeated the Iraqi military forces, based on allegations that Iraq continued to manufacture weapons of mass destruction — which proved to be erroneous later. The Coalition toppled Saddam Husain's government and installed a US-friendly regime. In 2005, the weakened Iraqi State accepted (in the new constitution) Kurdish autonomy in the northern part of Iraq, in what has been called *Heremê Kurdistān* in Kurdish and *Iqlīm Kurdistān* in Arabic (i.e., the Kurdistan Region) since then. A Kurdish parliament was constituted in Erbil (Kd. *Hewlêr*), and the Kurds developed their military power and political autonomy upon their own military forces, the *Pêşmerga*. The US-led invasion and subsequent policy, especially of dissolving the Iraqi army, created a political and military vacuum which partly contributed to an unstable situation in Iraq. The victory of a Shi'i-dominated government in the elections of 2005 in the aftermath of a total Sunni abstaining from the post-Saddam political era, and anti-American sentiments especially among Sunni Iraqis caused a sectarian civil war with many thousand casualties every year, in which Shi'i and Sunni militia played an important role. After 2011, when the US-led forces had finally left Iraq, the 'Islamic State' (IS) that had established itself in neighboring Syria, gained control over much of Iraq, also of regions (like Nineva) that were partially controlled by the Kurds.

In 2014 and 2015, the Kurds successfully conquered back Mosul and Kirkuk from the IS, and proved instrumental as local partners of the Coalition forces in their fight against the IS. They now controlled a larger area of northern Iraq than ever before, and seemed to become masters of their own destiny and future. Unfortunately, reality again turned against them. In a bid to secure and expand their political autonomy, they held a referendum about statal independence in September 2017, which was accepted by almost 93% of the voters; however, ethnic minorities like the Arabs living in the region hardly took part. The Iraqi State had declared the referendum illegal, and neither the neighbouring states of Iran and Turkey, nor powerful international actors like the USA or Russia, supported the Kurdish claim for independence. Following the vote, the Iraqi armed forces conquered back the cities and areas of Mosul and Kirkuk from the Kurds, which had been ethnically mixed for a long time, and were important economically (e.g., Kirkuk) because of their oil fields.

The current situation of the KRI is difficult. Since the declared victory on IS, the governments in Baghdad have asserted continuous political and economic pressure on the Kurdistan Regional Government, and despite promises in the annual budgets approved by the Iraqi Parliament, the Region's share of the budget has not been properly allocated. More recently and in March 2022, the Iraqi government halted the Region's independent exporting of oil through Turkey, which has left the Region without a major financial lifeline which started in 2014. As a consequence of Iraqi and Iranian influence on the KRI, but also of KRI-internal political division (Stansfield 2006), the KRI's economic situation, which was quite good in the early 2010s, has been deteriorating since 2014. The KRI's security and economic situation is, however, still much better than in the rest of Iraq, where many militias act beyond the control of the Iraqi State. This and the provision of better public services have led to massive Arab migration from southern Iraq to the northern regions of the KRI, especially to the city of Erbil, where Iraqi Arabs, but also Arabs from other crisis-stricken countries like Syria and Lebanon, seek employment and a better life. In effect, Erbil has become a mixed Kurdish-Arabic city nowadays, with many young Kurds, who have not learnt Arabic well at school, having difficulty to communicate, e.g., with Arab waiters in restaurants. This has created concerns amongst the locals about potential Arabization, which the local authorities have been trying to encounter such as by issuing directives for more Kurdish to be used such as in shop names and especially in the tourism sector.

4. State of the art

Very little has been published, so far, on the status of English, and its relation to local languages like Kurdish, in the KRI. To understand this relation, basic works on the overall situation of Kurdish are important, e.g., the comprehensive article by Öpengin (2015) that gives a socio-linguistic account of the history of Kurdish in Iraq, comparing it to Turkey. A recurrent topic in works on Kurdish is the endangerment of Kurdish, or its linguicide, through the nationalist states in which most Kurds are living. The 'classic' article on this is Skutnabb-Kangas & Bucak (1994). Salih (2019) claims that in Iraq, one can also speak of a linguicide, even if on the surface, the situation of Kurdish has often been better than in Turkey.

On the development of teaching English in the KRI, or more generally in Iraq, likewise, little has been published, e.g., Abdul-Kareem (2009) who explains that in the 1970s, for the first time, locally produced syllabuses of English were used in Iraqi schools, or Altae (2020), who distinguishes five phases in the development of English teaching in Iraq for the years 1921–2020. Ahmed, Puteh-Behak & Sidek (2015) explain the important new approach to English teaching, Communicative Language Teaching (CLT), used in the KRI since some time ago. Hassun (2022) is a recent study on private schooling in the KRI. It contains a useful overview of the KRI's educational history and system (7–22), and focusses on socio-economic aspects of private schooling. Since English being the language of teaching is the main distinguishing factor of private and public schools, the work is however also relevant for the spread of English in the KRI (there are also public schools that teach in English, but their number is low, and it is generally believed that the level of their English lessons is lower).

In view of the low number of publications on English in the KRI, several M.A. theses that have been submitted in recent years at various universities of the KRI provide welcome and important additions to the state of art. For example, at the private University of Kurdistan Hewlêr (UKH) in Erbil, seventeen M.A. theses have been written in Applied Linguistics since 2019, several of which relate to English and its status in the KRI. To introduce just a small selection of them, Ahmed (2021) critically deals with central issues of English as a Medium of Instruction (EMI) in the KRI, showing that contrary to the people's (and parents') expectations, EMI as such does not guarantee a higher quality of learning; the success of private EMI schools is rather due to the additional resources that are available in such schools. Ahmed (2021) also points to the social inequality issue that is bound to EMI private schooling in the KRI.

Rahman (2021) studies the implementation of EMI at state universities, explaining various factors that negatively affect its implementation, e.g., the low level of knowledge of English of the students. Sofi-Karim (2015) shows that the *Sunrise* programme, started in 2007 to improve the method of EMI in the KRI, has largely failed to raise the communicative skills of students. Two theses (Fateh 2022; Amin 2022) deal with linguistic landscape, i.e., with the visibility of the three main languages used in the KRI, Kurdish, Arabic, and English, on billboards and advertising posters in shopping streets; the second thesis is on Kirkuk, a mixed Kurdish-Arabic-Turkmen town in the 'contested area' outside the KRI. In Erbil, Kurdish dominates in a traditional, but English in a modern shopping street. In Kirkuk, however, Arabic dominates in all the three streets that were studied. The proportion of the languages depends on various factors, like the neighbourhood, or the 'modernity' of the goods or services that are offered.

Lastly, two doctoral dissertations should be mentioned by Saeid (Vienna 2014) and Mustafa (Bamberg 2023). They provide important data for an understanding of the KRI's language ecology by studying the inner-Kurdish dialectal split of the area into a northern (Badini) and southern (Sorani) dialect area. This dialectal split further contributes to the complex linguistic situation of the KRI today. Mustafa includes also English in some of her interviews.

5. The linguistic situation: A historical overview

According to Abdul-Kareem (2009), teaching English as a subject in public schools in the area of the present-day KRI goes back to the year 1873. While it was taught from the first year of joining primary schools under the British occupation in the aftermath of the 1st World War, it was then changed to start from year 5 of primary school education as a school subject all the way to graduation from high school. In the mid-20th century, English was also changed from a second to a foreign language (Abdul-Kareem 2009: 4). Ever since, English has had no official status in Iraq as a whole other than a foreign language, but is the only compulsory foreign language taught in schools (Altae 2020: 1). In Kurdistan, schooling was mainly in Arabic as the only official language of Iraq, and therefore a major demand of the Kurdish political struggle was for Kurdish to receive some official recognition. In an historic agreement in March 1970, the Iraqi State granted the Kurds a number of cultural and educational rights, including the right for children in the Kurdish-populated areas to be schooled in Kurdish, in place of Arabic (Waisy et al. 2014; see also Öpengin 2015: 4). At this time, a Kurdish Language Academy was also founded by the Iraqi State (Blau 2006: 109–110).

After the Iraqi invasion of Kuwait, and the First Gulf War in 1991, followed by the uprising of the Kurdish people, which resulted in a semi-autonomous de-facto status for Kurdistan, schooling in Kurdish was further strengthened and established. Kurdish replaced Arabic as the main official and working language in the region, being used as the primary language in public and governmental institutions, media, and other domains. During this period, there was a public interest and motivation to promote Kurdish along with strong political sentiments for freedom and autonomy. The local language had been marginalized and a systematic process of Arabization had been taking place by the previous Iraqi regime (Salih 2019: 38–39). English continued to be studied as a school subject, but was seen as a foreign language throughout the 1990s. However, with pro-Western attitudes shared by the majority of the Iraqi Kurds in the aftermath of the Coalition Countries' support for a no-fly-zone (1991) and other protective resolutions and measures from the United Nations, English gained a more prestigious position in the eye of the public. Additionally, this decade witnessed the advent of many humanitarian and international organizations that hired specifically those who had an acceptable command of English. Proficient English speakers were mainly graduates of English language departments of local universities, who had opportunities to be hired by those organizations as translators, interpreters, and in other office worker positions. Yet, because of the dire economic situation due to the international embargo on Iraq and the failing Iraqi currency, being appointed at international organizations was considered as highly lucrative because the pay was in US dollars. Though these two factors helped English to be seen as a valuable asset, it did not translate into widespread use or teaching and learning of the language.

The Iraq war in 2003 changed the status of English from a foreign into a functional language in Iraq as a whole. With American and British military and other service members in the country, English was regarded as the language of the invaders by many Iraqis — for the majority of the Kurds, however, it was the language of the liberators. Additionally, the country opened to a flux of international organizations and multinational companies whose language of operation was primarily English. Inevitably, Iraq has also been impacted by globalization in the last two decades, and with the advent of widespread communication technology, English is seen as being of more significance, especially for trade and economic opportunities. Yet, English remains a foreign language in Iraq as a whole, and does not enjoy the degree of popularity it does in Kurdistan. Unlike the rest of Iraq, the period from 2003 to the present day has witnessed a gradual but rapid change of status and presence of English in the Kurdistan Region. However, this new status was rather not due to the new political and economic parameters which the country witnessed in the aftermath of a new political system, but in large part because of how policy makers and the general public viewed the language. As will be discussed in the next section, English has recently gained an unprecedented level of popularity and dominance in Kurdistan which is somewhat unusual for a small entity, especially because this is not the case in the wider region including the neighboring countries.

6. Current status of English in the KRI[2]

The last two decades have been a golden era for English in the KRI. Although it does not enjoy any official status in Iraq or Kurdistan, English is seen by many as an indispensable skill without which many doors remain locked. This perception is almost equally shared by the majority of the public, evidenced by the rise of English-medium schools, popularity of English learning courses, and by a number of institutional regulations which have incorporated English as a requirement for employment and higher education opportunities. In the sections below, the manifestation of the newly acquired status of English will be presented.

Up until two decades ago, there were no English-medium schools in the Region. In 2021, there were 35 English-medium public schools and 209 English-medium private schools in the Region — a figure which does not include nurseries and kindergartens, which also include EMI ones.[3] Not all private schools offer EMI, a small number of private schools teach in Kurdish or Arabic. While the pub-

---

[2]. This chapter is based partly on general observations of the co-author, who has been following the developments very closely for a long time; it also draws upon the three interviews he held.

[3]. According to the figures as given by Ahmed (2021: 44). Hassun (2022: 2) gives a number of 144 private schools in the KRI for the year 2017/18.

lic EMI schools implement a local curriculum of the Ministry of Education, a number of private EMI schools follow a foreign curriculum, usually imported from an English-speaking country or system. It is believed that thousands of students from elementary and secondary levels study in those EMI schools nowadays, where all subjects are studied in English except Kurdish, Arabic, and Religious Studies which are in Kurdish and Arabic-Kurdish, respectively. EMI private schools usually charge anywhere between USD 2,000 to 8,000 as tuition fees per student per year. In addition to EMI schools, a limited number of schools primarily instruct in French and German. They also include English as a language of schooling, but only for the subject 'English'.

There do not seem to be any regulations within the Ministry of Education in regard to schools operating in English. According to Law No. 13 of 2022, which is the latest approved law for education in Kurdistan, Kurdish is the official language of instruction in all educational institutions in the Kurdistan Region; however, schooling is also allowed in the language of other minorities such as Turkmens, Assyrians, Chaldeans, Armenians, and Arabs, who can study in their mother tongues. Additionally, the Law indicates that other schools can also be allowed to instruct in other languages. However, in a section specific to schooling in languages other than Kurdish, Section 3 of Article 31 in the Law states the following: "Based on the provisions of this law, the Ministry can open public kindergartens, schools and educational and professional institutions in world languages, with abiding them to also include Kurdish language teaching".

The Ministry of Education has set up a directorate for private schools, which is in charge of all private and EMI schools. Since EMI schools usually instruct most subjects in English and have an English subject as well, there is a concern about the status of Kurdish in those schools. These concerns are shared by Ministry officials and parents (Ahmed 2021). Recently, the Ministry imposed that all students in what is called international schools undergo a Kurdish literacy test. The Minister himself announced the results of the test which was conducted on April 3, 2023, and in which 151 schools and 7,359 fifth graders participated. 6,196 students, that is 84.2 percent of those who took the test, had passed. While announcing those results, the Minister acknowledged the concerns about Kurdish in the international, mainly EMI, schools, and explained the Ministry's plan to address those concerns through more work on improving Kurdish proficiency in those schools.[4] Included in addressing the issue of Kurdish being marginalized is also the Ministry's decision to discard the current practice in the twelfth grade national exams system which allows these students the option to not include their grades in the

---

4. Published on a Kurdistan TV channel website on 5 December 2023 (https://kurdistantv.net/ku/news/193517; 04 December 2004).

Kurdish subject in their accumulated average, which determines which programme of study they can join. This reformist decision is set to take effect in 2026.

Although originally the decision to allow EMI schools was in part to accommodate Kurdish returnees from overseas and children of expats who entered the country in larger numbers in the second half of the 2000s, there is also a recognition from officials, educators, and the wider public that in today's globalized era, English is essential to ensure a brighter future especially in regard to employment opportunities (Ahmed 2021). This is part of the perception that English leads to a better future for students. This especially resides in parents who are willing to pay for their children's tuition fees whereas they can enroll them in public schools which are free of charge. However, because public schools do not usually produce graduates with acceptable English proficiency skills, parents find EMI as an alternative to provide an environment in which students can develop their English without necessarily being superior in otherwise educational merits or standards (Ahmed 2021).

Appendix: Interviews with educational experts and policy makers

For preparing this article, interviews with three academic experts and policy makers, and with a number of Kurdish students were held in Erbil in October 2023, from which the article gained its insights. In the following, one of the three interviews with an expert in Applied Linguistics about the status of English in the Kurdistan Region of Iraq (KRI) will be given in full, and two interviews, held with high-ranking officials at the Ministry of Education, will be summarized.

Interview 1: (with an applied linguist, male, around 40 years of age; the interview was held via email and the answers were received in writing via email as well, in English)

Question 1: *What has caused the recent ever-increasing interest in English in the Kurdistan Region of Iraq?*

I think this has to do with the general linguistic ecology in the Kurdistan Region. Under the Kurdistan Regional Government (KRG), especially since 2003, English has been promoted as the major second language in the Kurdistan region, with a view to replace Arabic of previous decades. In the new language constellation Kurdish and English compete for certain social domains which were traditionally reserved to Kurdish and Arabic, such as education, institutions, and recently also home. With a view to integrate the KRG to the western world, the educational system heavily prioritizes English education, with a sizeable portion of private and some public schools in all levels running in English as the medium of education. In such EMI-based schools the position of Kurdish in terms of class hours is marginal while the quality of curriculum is often criticized by students and other stakeholders for not meeting the international curricula followed for other subject matters.

The same political-economical westernization framework leads to a similar relegation of Kurdish and prioritization of English in the more modern workplaces domains, such as NGOs, tech-based companies, etc.

Often high-level political figures also complain about their children's lack of skills in Kurdish as English has become their major medium of socialization and consumption of popular culture. This is further proof that it is the linguistic ecology, or the constellation of language roles and perceptions in favour of English, that work for the promotion and strengthening of English while downplaying the role of Kurdish to compete in such areas. This fact becomes also apparent in the inconsistency between the Kurdish nationalistic discourse and the actual picture, because Kurdish has historically been a major claim of all Kurdish nationalist discourses and struggles but in the current context of KRG the parents who can afford — mostly former political leaders and nationalist elites — disfavour Kurdish education in favour of EMI-based schools.

Question 2: *Is the society in Kurdistan naturally receptive to other languages and cultures and hence English?*

I do not think it is "natural", but it can be claimed that the Kurds are relatively more receptive to other languages due to their status as a minority under the dominance of more powerful larger society and the dominant national languages, such as Arabic, Turkish, Persian. On the flip side, this may have hindered the formation of a positive perception of their own language as capable of competing with such national and international languages for education and other more public uses.

Question 3: *From a sociolinguistic perspective, has there been justification for this interest in English at many public levels? How is the heavy presence of English explained from a somewhat total absence two decades ago to its powerful presence today?*

I shared my ideas about this in Q1.

Question 4: *What do you foresee the role of English would be in the near and distant future?*

I think English will continue to enjoy a major role in the region, however the extent to which it will proceed to replace and marginalize Kurdish in the education, work, and home domains depends on the measure and language policies that the government and other stake-holders will pursue.

Question 5: *Can English maintain its current status or will it expand it even further?*

I do not think there is any risk for English to lose its prestigious status in the region. It can at best be stabilized as one major language alongside an enhanced and prestigious Kurdish.

Question 6: *Has the expansion of English been at the expense of Kurdish? Does English pose a risk on the Kurdish language, culture and identity?*

It seems that in the KRI the English language is coded and presented as the sole important language for progress and socio-economic mobility. The schools and business sector designed along such lines will inevitably foreground the English and relegate Kurdish, which in turn results in younger generations' favoring English in most of their dealings and communication.

This Englishization is also observed in the linguistic landscape of Erbil. An M.A. student of mine conducted a study on the use of languages in the shop signs and official signs in the Citadel and Bakhtiyari streets of Erbil. Sparing you from the details, while Kurdish has a fair share of use in Citadel area, it is the third language in Bakthiari with only around 30% while English is used in around 60% of all signs.

One other outcome of this heavy emphasis on English and relegation of Kurdish is unequal competence in Kurdish and English in young bilinguals. By being fully educated and entertained in English, they have very limited exposure to Kurdish, only with their family members. This creates an imbalance in their competence in the two languages. And they inevitably favor English because it turns out to be the language in which they can express and achieve more. We tend to think that we store languages in our brain in separate locations, but the most recent psycholinguistic approaches to bilingual brain show that there is actually no such thing, we have one 'linguistic repertoire', so it is very easy to be tempted to use the language that is most active and in which we are proficient in our daily life and dealings.

We may idealize the language as the core component of identity but actually it does not have to be, a Kurdish identity can be formed regardless of the language. It is just that do we want such a language-less Kurdishness?

The example of other countries shows us that English-medium instruction does not have to pose a threat to the mother tongue. For instance, Turkey has had private schools teaching entirely in English since mid 20th century. The famous Robert College is one example. Or the highly prestigious Bogazici University. These are entirely in English with obligatory Turkish language-literature and history courses. Throughout their history, these institutions have greatly enhanced the status of the Turkish language as many highly influential artists, writers, translators, politicians in Turkey are graduates of these institutions. The EMI education in Turkey contributes to the development of Turkish language and culture, it does not replace them with English language and culture.

I believe that a better-informed approach to language planning in KRI is urgently needed.

Interview 2: (with a high-ranking educational official, male, about 50 years of age; the interview was held face-to-face in Kurdish)

English in KRI's Education sector

In Iraq and the Kurdistan region, students often graduate high school without being fluent in English, which makes it hard for them to get jobs or study the subjects they want. However, things are getting a bit better because of language learning apps, websites, and English-medium instruction (EMI) schools. There aren't many full English schools in the public sector, but private EMI schools are allowed, and there's hope that their number will increase because English is becoming more important for work and further education.

Teachers in Kurdistan need better training to teach English effectively. They should be more aware of new teaching methods to improve their skills. Right now, the lack of qualified teachers is a big problem, and it's something that the government and educational institutions need to work on.

Parents in Kurdistan really believe in the power of English for their children's futures, even to the point of borrowing money to send them to EMI schools. They think it will give their kids better chances to study abroad and develop a broader perspective on life.

In the future, English is expected to play a bigger role, with more people learning it outside of school using online tools. But the current school programs don't really help because they don't have the right teachers or updated courses that match the local culture and needs.

It is important for all educational sectors to understand how crucial English is because it opens so many resources in various fields. Knowing English from an early age can help students avoid difficulties later on in their studies.

Interview 3: (with educational supervisor at Ministry of Education, female, 50 years of age; the interview was conducted face-to-face and mainly in English, although at times she gave answers in both English and Kurdish via code-switching)

There are two types of schools which instruct in English: some public but mostly private schools. There are some public schools that consider themselves as English medium, but primarily they only teach science and math in English and the rest in Kurdish. Private and public schools are different. Also, international schools are mostly just English medium, but local private schools offer a mix of languages as they have different classes about languages such as Arabic.

The official status of English is determined by whether or not the Ministry of Education grants permission to open schools with English as the medium of instruction. In total, there are about one hundred English-medium schools in the country, containing both local and foreign private schools where English is the primary language of instruction. Due to its global dominance as well as high demand, the Ministry of Education allows the opening of English-medium schools without any limitations.

Financial issues are what motivates school directors. They are aiming for more students and, in turn, increased income. There is concern that increasing usage of English might cause disappearance of Kurdish identity and cause problems in communication with future generations. More English-medium schools are expected to open due to high demand and few restrictions. The need for learning English has been fueled by the belief that knowing the language effectively is essential for the success of students in the future.

According to parents, education in English improves their children's chances of finding better jobs and developing international communication skills. The satisfaction levels of schools are different. For example, international schools indicate a high level of satisfaction, evident by the large number of students they take in. As English is becoming more and more prevalent in our society, more and more people desire to learn it. Concerns about the erosion of Kurdish language and culture due to the rising popularity of English-medium schools.

Some actions are needed to preserve Kurdish language such as limiting English school openings, supporting Kurdish schools, improving teaching methods, and training teachers for better language education.

References

Abdul-Kareem, Natiq Taha. 2009. A survey study of the syllabuses of English used in Iraq (1873–3003 A.D.). *Diala, Jour* 34, [14 p.].

Ahmed, Hamsa Hameed, Fariza Puteh-Behak, Harison Mohd Sidek. 2015. Examining EFL secondary reading curriculum in Iraqi Kurdistan: A review. *Journal of Applied Sciences* 15: 377–391.

Altae, Mayamin. 2020. An overview of te stages of development of the Iraqi English language curriculum. *Social Sciences & Humanities Open* 2: 1–5.

Aziz, Mahir A. 2011. *The Kurds of Iraq: Ethnonationalism and national identity in Iraqi Kurdistan*. London: I. B. Tauris.

Behrendt, Günter. 1993. *Nationalismus in Kurdistan. Vorgeschichte, Entstehungsbedingungen und erste Manifestationen bis 1925*. Hamburg: Deutsches Orient-Institut.

Blau, Joyce. 2006. Refinement and oppression of Kurdish language. In Faleh A. Jabra & Hosham Dawood (eds.), *The Kurds: Nationalism and politics*, pp. 103–112. Beirut: Saqi.

Bosworth, Clifford Edmund. 2004. *The New Islamic Dynasties*. Edinburgh: Edinburgh University Press.

Hassun, Hishyar. 2022. *Private Schools in the Kurdistan Region of Iraq. An Evidence Based Approach on Their Functions*. Bamberg: University of Bamberg Press.

McDowall, David. 1996. *A modern history of the Kurds*. London: I. B. Tauris.

Minorsky, Vladimir. 1986. Kurds, Kurdistān. iii. — History. In Clifford Edmund Bosworth, Bernard Lewis, Charles Pellat & Emeri Johannes van Donzel (eds.), *The Encyclopaedia of Islam*, Vol. V (Khe-Mahi), pp. 447–464. Leiden: Brill.

Öpengin, Ergin. 2015. The changing status of Kurdish in Iraq and Turkey: A comparative assessment. *Singapore Middle East Papers* 8(3): 1–27.

Salih, Kaziwa. 2019. Kurdish Linguicide in the 'Saddamist' State. *Genocide Studies International* 13(1): 34–51.

Skutnabb-Kangas, Tove & Sertaç Bucak. 1994. Killing a mother tongue – how the Kurds are deprived of linguistic human rights. In Tove Skutnabb-Kangas, Robert Phillipson (eds.), *Linguistic Human Rights. Overcoming Linguistic Discrimination*, pp. 347–370. Berlin: Mouton de Gruyter.

Stansfield, Gareth. 2006. Finding a dangerous equilibrium: Internal politics in Iraqi Kurdistan – Parties, tribes, religion and ethnicity reconsidered. In Faleh A. Jabar & Hosham Dawood (eds.), *The Kurds: Nationalism and Politics*, pp. 258–276. Beirut: Saqi.

van Bruinessen, Martin. 1989. *Agha, Scheich und Staat. Politik und Gesellschaft Kurdistans*. Berlin: Edition Parabolis.

Waisy, Karwan Salih, Rashila Haj Ramli, Helen Ting Mu Hung. 2014. Mullah Mustafa Barzani and the United States 1960–0975. *Journal of Islamic and Human Advanced Research* 4(4), 179–199.

Theses

Ahmed, Yaseen Shamsaddin. 2021. EMI in Kurdistan's Basic Schools: Motives, Quality of Education, and Attitudes. M.A. thesis, University of Kurdistan Hewlêr, Erbil.

Amin, Hazhar Jalal. 2022. The Linguistic Landscape of Kirkuk: An Empirical Study on Multilingualism and Ethnolinguistic Vitality. M.A. thesis, University of Kurdistan Hewlêr, Erbil.

Fateh, I. 2022. Multilingualism and the Place of English in the Linguistic Landscape of Erbil: A Comparative Study of Language Use on the Signs of the Two Socio-economically Diverse Commercial Streets. M.A. thesis. University of Kurdistan Hewlêr, Erbil.

Mustafa, Baydaa Mohammed Saeed. 2023. An Empirical Intergenerational Study of Language Choice and Language Attitudes among the Kurdish Population in the Multilingual Governorate of Duhok. P.h.D.dissertation, Universität Bamberg.

Rahman, Jihad Shwan. 2021. The Policy of EMI from the Perspective of Lecturers at an HEI in the Kurdistan Region of Iraq: A Case Study. M.A. thesis. University of Kurdistan Hewlêr, Erbil.

Saeid, Moslih Aowni. 2014. Two Varieties of Kurdish in Competition: The Problematic of Modelling a Language of Instruction in Iraqi Kurdistan. P.h.D.dissertation, Universität Wien.

Sofi-Karim, Mahdi. 2015. English Language Teaching in the Kurdistan Region of Iraq. M.A. thesis University of Kurdistan Hewlêr, Erbil.

PART III

Case studies

CHAPTER 10

English in the linguistic landscape(s) of rural Tanzania

Amani Lusekelo & Roland Kießling
University of Dar es Salaam | University of Hamburg

The linguistic macroecology of Tanzania is characterized by multiple interactions of languages that can generally be summarized as 2 + 1 out of many, involving the national official language Swahili, the ex-colonial and elitist (co-official) language English, and a panoply of 120+ vernacular languages, broadly forming a triglossia. While Tanzania's Swahilisation policy during the Ujamaa socialist era (1967–1985) aimed at restricting public domains of English usage, the turn towards economic, cultural, and educational liberalization since the 1990s and the impact of internationalization, globalization, and the spread of new media of communication have come to boost the image of English considerably (Blommaert 2014; Legère 2006; Lema 2021). Its growing prestige is not only reflected in attitudes (Mohr 2018; Mohr, Lorenz & Ochieng 2020), but also in a surge of English-sourced items surfacing at various levels, e.g., in the urban juvenile stylects of Swahili known as Lugha ya Mitaani (Reuster-Jahn & Kießling 2022), in various terminological registers of standard Swahili (Lupapula 2021; Legère 2006), and in Tanzania's linguistic landscapes at large. The present contribution provides a case study of the visual public presence of English at the Tanzanian grassroots level, e.g., in official signboards and private shop signs found in two remote areas of the Tanzanian Rift valley, i.e., Mkalama district (Singida region) and Mbulu district (Manyara region). By tracing the forms in which English penetrates into the remote corners of the Tanzanian rural linguistic landscapes, the contribution complements existing studies on the linguistics of Tanzanian cityscapes (Bwenge 2009; Chul-joon 2014; Peterson 2014; Mdukula 2018; Lusekelo & Alphonce 2018; Lusekelo & Mdukula 2021). At the same time, the chapter illustrates how English forms are appropriated, manipulated, and creatively adapted to local needs and aspirations in the process of translocation as exponents of global culture.

Keywords: linguistic landscapes, rural areas, Swahili, Tanzania

https://doi.org/10.1075/hsld.9.10lus
Available under the CC BY-NC-ND 4.0 license.
© 2025 John Benjamins Publishing Company

1. Introduction

English occupies an ambivalent position in Tanzania's linguistic macroecology. As ex-colonial and elitist (co-official) language it competes with the national official language Swahili, both being used on top of a mosaic of 120+ vernacular languages (Eberhard, Simons & Fennig 2023), broadly forming a triglossia (Abdulaziz Mkilifi 1972; Lema 2021).

Despite globalization, "English is perceived as more foreign in Tanzania than in "truly" Anglophone or Commonwealth countries" (Schmied 2012: 454), due to the prior phase of Swahili promotion under German colonial rule. While Swahili is the L1 of about 10 percent of the Tanzanian population (Petzell 2012; Rubagumya 1991) with a countrywide distribution as lingua franca (Batibo 2005; Lema 2021), English has virtually no L1 speakers and exhibits typical characteristics of a vertical medium of communication (Heine 1979). It is acquired via formal education at primary school level and becomes a medium of instruction in secondary schools, replacing Swahili in this role.

Tanzania's official language policy successfully promoted Swahili for several decades after independence (Tanganyika 1961; Zanzibar 1963) as a central component in the doctrine of *elimu ya kujitegemea* 'education of/for self-reliance' during the Ujamaa socialist era (1967–1985), with no particular regard to the vernacular languages (Petzell 2012: 139) and with an effort towards relegating English to international communication and secondary and tertiary segments of the education system (Batibo 1995; Blommaert 2014). Corpus planning, as steered by institutions such as *Baraza la Kiswahili la Taifa* (BAKITA) 'National Swahili Council', *Taasisi ya Uchunguzi wa Kiswahili* (TUKI) 'Institute of Swahili Research', and *Taasisi ya Taaluma za Kiswahili* (TATAKI) 'Institute of Swahili Studies', followed and still follows a moderately puristic course, i.e., terminology management favors coinage of Swahili-based terms and when it comes to loanword incorporation, English as donor language ranks low in the hierarchy, beneath Bantu, Arabic, and other Tanzanian languages (Lupapula 2021). Yet, throughout this phase of Swahilization, English always retained its prestigious position in the Tanzanian macroecology as a hallmark of higher education and upward social mobility (Schmied 1985a, 1985b, 1990), although it was largely inaccessible to major parts of a mainly rural population.

In the 1990s, the government took measures to officially discard the doctrine of English containment inherited from the Ujamaa policy and allowed for liberalization of the use of English in the domains of culture, education, and training (United Republic of Tanzania 1995, 1997) in order to boost the dissemination of English in Tanzanian society. Its degree had been increasingly felt as unsatisfactorily low and a hindrance to technological advancement, modernization, information flow, and internationality (Batibo 2005: 20). For instance, due to insufficient skills in English, a vast majority of 97 percent of primary school leavers in the 1980s were not qualified to advance to secondary education (Rubagumya 1991) when the switch in medium of instruction from Swahili to English happened (see also Petzell 2012; Roy-Campbell & Qorro 1997; Schmied 2012). The turn towards liberalization in the national policy indeed contributed to the penetration of English into larger portions of Tanzanian society (Lema 2021; Ochieng 2015) with secondary education expanding in the 2000s whereby more primary school leavers were allowed to proceed to secondary education with English as medium of instruction (United Republic of Tanzania 2013).

In a wider perspective, political liberalization and the impact of internationalization, globalization, and the spread of new media of communication (esp. mobile phones and the internet) has boosted the image of English considerably. Thus, in a contemporary Tanzania embracing neoliberalism, English has become yet more strongly associated with social achievement and success and is seen as a highly desirable commodity (Roy-Campbell & Qorro 1997; Blommaert 2014; Legère 2006; Lema 2021; Rubagumya 2003). In the perception of educated Tanzanians, English occupies an ambivalent position in its relation to Swahili: It is regarded as superior to Swahili in terms of its absolute prestige, i.e., when seen as detached from practical needs of real-world communication and when membership of a global language community is claimed; but when it comes to practical needs of communication in the concrete linguistic environment and when identification with the norms of the smaller (national) community is at stake, it is the relative prestige of Swahili that overrides the supremacy of English.

It is this ambivalence in the distribution of labor between English and Swahili in Tanzania which has also spurred scholars to argue for or against one or the other language (Lema 2021; Mohr & Ochieng 2017; Ochieng 2015). Over the past two decades this debate has expanded to include the ethnic community languages, due to increasingly positive attitudes towards them (Lema 2021; Mohr et al. 2020).

The present contribution explores the forms of English diffusion into the linguistic landscapes of public spaces in rural Tanzania, generally reflecting an ongoing process of translocation of symbols of modernity. Following this introduction, Section 2 provides a brief synopsis of the characterization and some structural aspects of Tanzanian English as articulated by Schmied (2004a, 2004b, 2012). Section 3 interrogates the existing literature that covers the position of English in linguistic landscapes of multilingual Anglophone settings in East Africa, before zooming in on an overview of the linguistic landscapes in Tanzania as evidenced in cityscapes of Dar es Salaam and Dodoma as well as in social media and digital telecommunication (see Section 3.1). The aim is to highlight linguistic situations in which English prevails in East African public spaces. Section 3.2 focuses on signage in the linguistic landscapes of rural Tanzania and generalizations that can be drawn with respect to the diffusion of English in bottom-up signage deployed by private agents in signboards and shop signs found in two remote areas of the Tanzanian Rift valley. Section 4 contextualizes the discussion by pointing out what the study of linguistic landscapes can tell us about the dynamics of Tanzanian language ecologies and the underlying driving forces, which leads to the conclusion in Section 5.

2. Tanzanian English?

Regarding structural aspects, Schmied (2012: 8–9) concludes that Tanzanian English "is not even a semi-independent variety; it only has its preferences in some predictable areas where English displays internal variation anyway". Furthermore, its grammatical system is categorized as "instable and fuzzy [...] maybe more than most other national systems".

Major parameters in which Tanzanian English deviates from Standard English, as pointed out by Schmied (2004a), relate to the morphological and the phonological level: disregard of the distinction of count vs. non-count nouns manifest in overgeneralization of the plural suffix -s, omission of articles and other determiners, neutralization of the contrast of /r/ vs. /l/ and dissolution of consonant clusters either by deletion of consonants or insertion of epenthetic vowels.

As for the phonological phenomena, it remains to be explored to which extent they are actually restricted to L1-speakers of particular languages that lack precisely these features or whether indeed these phonological deviations have become established in an emergent Tanzanian English by mediation of a demographically dominant substratal impact. While it is true that the majority of Tanzanian Bantu languages lack a phonological contrast of liquids /r/ and /l/, most of the Tanzanian non-Bantu languages actually show this particular contrast, e.g., all Southern Cushitic languages (Iraqw, Gorwaa, Burunge, Alagwa), all Nilotic languages (Datooga, Maasai, Luo), and Sandawe. Phonotactic restrictions to open syllables are common in Bantu languages, but again it is not clear whether this actually holds for the (demographic) majority of Tanzanian languages.

The morphological peculiarities are doubtlessly triggered by the general incongruence of English morphological structures vs. morphological structures of many Tanzanian languages. Thus, articles seem to be simply non-existent in most Tanzanian languages, i.e., the plain form of the noun is ambivalent with respect to definiteness and/or specificity, which does not exclude the presence of dedicated markers for precisely these functions. Plural as an independent nominal category is almost non-existent in the Bantu languages, since the concept of plural is usually conflated with the grammatical category of noun classes.

The inroads that English has made into Tanzanian society, e.g., via technologies associated with the internet, social media, and mobile phones (Ilonga & Mapunda 2022; Mapunda & Ilonga 2022; Mapunda & Rosendal 2021), are also paved with various forms of deliberate linguistic hybridity, e.g., Swahili-English code-mixing and English loanwords, more or less conventionalized, more or less adapted, as in Swahinglish (Higgins 2007) or in the stylects of the Tanzanian urban youth subsumed under the label *lugha ya mitaani* (Reuster-Jahn & Kießling 2006).

3. English in East African linguistic landscapes

In the linguistic landscapes of Anglophone East Africa, English surfaces either in monolingual or in multilingual signage where it combines with national and major ethnic community languages such as Chewa, Lozi, Tonga, and Tumbuka in Malawi (Visonà 2017), Kinyarwanda and Swahili in Rwanda (Rosendal 2011), Luganda, Swahili, Acholi, and Runyankore in Uganda (Rosendal 2011), Bemba and Nyanja in Zambia (Costley, Kula & Marten 2022; Banda & Jimaima 2017).

While the complexities of linguistic landscapes in East African ecologies remain to be explored systematically to a larger extent, the patchy evidence gathered so far allows for the generalization that English dominates the scene with national languages coming in to various degrees, depending on their local status and the urban or rural character of the area. Thus, different patterns unfold in the linguistic landscapes of metropolitan and rural East Africa (Banda & Jimaima 2017), as briefly exemplified for Zambia and Rwanda (and Uganda), before we turn to Tanzania in Section 3.1.

Rosendal (2011) reports a dominance of official ex-colonial languages in the linguistic landscapes of Uganda (English) and Rwanda (French and English). In the case of Rwanda, the comparatively minor role of Kinyarwanda even in private signage is remarkable, given the fact that Kinyarwanda has "a potential of reaching practically all citizens" (Rosendal 2011: 299) due to its wide spread as L1 in Rwanda. This shows that language choice in private shop signs and billboards is determined to a large extent by the prestige, modernity, and importance attributed to the imported European languages (mastered by only a marginal part of the population), rather than by practical considerations concerning the potentially broader outreach (Rosendal 2011: 300–301).

Linguistic landscapes of Zambia have been dominated by English, the sole official language and major medium of business and education. While spoken as

L1 by only a small fraction of society, it is still the main language of the media, the internet, and computer applications as well as the major language of newspapers, magazines, and television programs available in Zambia. However, Bemba and Nyanja, the major national languages, are increasingly used in bilingual signs combined with English in urban areas such as Ndola City (Costley et al. 2022), Livingstone, and Lusaka (Banda & Jimaima 2017). Moreover, minority languages such as Toka-Leya, Tumbuka, Namwanga, and Mambwe also make their way into signage and have "found a niche in the social structuring of language outside their place of origin" (Banda & Jimaima 2017: 621).

3.1 Urban Tanzania

Both English and Swahili feature prominently in the urban linguistic landscape of Tanzania, as widely attested in previous studies (Bwenge 2009, 2012; Chul-joon 2014; Ilonga & Mapunda 2022; Mapunda & Ilonga 2022; Legère & Rosendal 2019; Lusekelo & Alphonce 2018; Lusekelo & Mdukula 2021; Mdukula 2018; Steiner-Anthony 2012). The competition of English and Swahili enshrined in Tanzania's language policy is clearly visible in public spaces. In the linguistic landscape of Dodoma city the distribution of both languages seems balanced (Lusekelo & Mdukula 2021). In the case of Dar es Salaam, more fine-grained documentation allows for making more precise distinctions regarding the type of signage and its place in the urban agglomeration. Thus, the transition from the metropolitan center to the suburbs seems to correlate with a cline of frequency in that English is more prominent in the center while Swahili takes over in the periphery (Bwenge 2009). However, a differentiation of signage for its direction[1] may yield different results, e.g., even in the metropolitan area of Dar es Salaam Swahili seems to be preferred over English in bottom-up signage installed by private vendors for advertising their commodities (Peterson 2014). According to common practice, names of brands and products to be marketed are provided in English while

---

1. Following Ben-Rafael et al. (2006: 14), the direction of communication in written messages of the linguistic landscape invokes a hierarchy of "officiality". Thus, inscriptions are categorized according to whether they are authored by governmental or private agents, ranging from an official "top", i.e., the state or local government bodies, to the non-official "bottom", i.e., shop owners or private businesses. More specifically, top-down oriented inscriptions are usually issued by public institutions (religious, governmental, municipal — cultural and educational, medical) and include public signs of general interest, public announcements and signs of street names. Bottom-up oriented inscriptions on the other hand are authored by private agents and include shop signs (e.g., clothing, food, jewellery), private business signs (offices, factories, agencies, companies), private announcements ('wanted' ads, sale or rental of flats or cars) and graffiti.

explanation on utilities is offered in Swahili (Peterson 2014). Still, other factors may also come into play. Thus, the abundance of English usage in bottom-up commercial signage in Arusha and Manyara regions of northern Tanzania seems to be motivated by the intention to attract tourists and international customers (Lusekelo & Alphonce 2018).

As observed outside linguistic landscaping in Tanzanian popular culture (Reuster-Jahn 2014a) and in linguistic landscapes elsewhere in Africa, English is used for indexing modernity, e.g., for the sake of demonstrating the superior quality of commodities in competition to locally made items (Lanza & Woldermariam 2014; Legère & Rosendal 2019).

Public advertisements in urban Tanzania and in Tanzanian internet spaces abound with English-Swahili code-mixing, as reflected in English sourced items fully integrated into a Swahili inflectional matrix, e.g., by the Swahili infinitive prefix *ku-* in *ku-chat* 'to chat' (Ilonga & Mapunda 2022: 96), or even fully Swahilized on all structural levels, e.g., *kistaa* 'like a star', *smatika* 'be smart' and *ji-giftishe* 'give yourself a gift' (Mapunda & Ilonga 2022: 121–122), in which the prefix of noun class 7 *ki-* is used to adverbialize 'star' and the suffixes *-ik* (neutro-passive) and *-ish* (causative) are used for deriving verbs from the English items 'smart' and 'gift', respectively, while the inflectional prefix *ji-* marks the reflexive. These are indeed common strategies of morphological adaptation of English to Swahili observed in oral language use elsewhere.

Languages other than Swahili have also been reported from urban linguistic landscapes, e.g., Arabic, Persian, Hindi, and Chinese (Peterson 2014) and ethnic community languages which tend to be limited to emblematic proper names (Lusekelo & Buberwa 2021).

English, as imposed by British colonial administration prior to independence, has not only become localized in the sense that it is part of Tanzania's macro-ecology (Legère & Rosendal 2019), it is still expanding in an ongoing process of appropriation. Its progressive translocation from urban spaces to the remotest rural corners can be retraced in bottom-up signage of the rural linguistic landscape. The next section embarks precisely on this topic in an effort to complement existing studies on the linguistics of Tanzanian cityscapes outlined above.

3.2 Rural Tanzania

The rural areas under investigation are Mkalama district (Singida region) and Mbulu district (Manyara region). They represent two different microecologies located in the Tanzanian Rift Valley area that is characterized by the convergence of languages from four phyla, namely Niger-Congo (Isanzu, Nyaturu, Nilamba, and Sukuma), Afroasiatic (Alagwa, Burunge, Gorwaa, and Iraqw), Nilo-Saharan

(Datooga and Maasai), and Khoisan (Sandawe) plus the linguistic isolate Hadza (Kießling, Mous & Nurse 2008: 187). In addition, the official languages English and Swahili are used in formal settings in the area.

The first site of data collection is in and around Mwangeza village in Mkalama District of Singida region. Its linguistic microecology is dominated by Bantu groups, i.e., Isanzu, Nilamba, and Sukuma, with marginal presence of Hadza (Languages of Tanzania Project 2009: 110). The Bantu speaking groups are agro-pastoralists living in the village, while the Hadza are hunter-gatherers confined to the bushland at Munguli and Kipamba settlements. All places form the catchment area of the primary schools of Midibwi, Mwangeza, and Munguli where Swahili and English are introduced (see Figure 1).

Figure 1. Midibwi primary school in Mwangeza Ward, Mkalama District, northern Tanzania (March 2020)

The second site of data collection is along the surface road from Dongobesh through Bashay to Yaeda Chini in Mbulu District of Manyara region. The linguistic microecology of this area differs crucially from the previous one in that, instead of Bantu speaking groups, it is rather primarily populated by Iraqw (Southern Cushitic), Datooga (Southern Nilotic), and Hadza (Languages of Tanzania

Project 2009: 52). The Iraqw dominate Bashay and Dongobesh, while Datooga and Hadza inhabit the Yaeda Chini Valley. Dongobesh is a mixed semi-urban village, while Bashay and Yaeda Chini are agro-pastoral rural villages. Numerous secondary schools are established in this area (see Figure 2).

Figure 2. Signpost for Yaeda Chini Secondary School in Mbulu District, northern Tanzania (March 2020)

Generally, the language distribution in top-down signage issued by governmental agents, e.g., road signs and school signboards, aligns with official language policy. Thus, signposts of primary and secondary schools, abundant in both areas, clearly reflect the Tanzanian regulations of official language use in the educational sectors: While primary school signposts are exclusively in Swahili (see Figure 1), signboards of secondary schools are bilingual in both Swahili and English (see Figure 2). Instead of top-down signage, though, the focus in the following will rather be on bottom-up signage installed by private agents for advertising their respective business enterprises, e.g., commercial shops, dispensaries, restaurants, and guest houses. These signs reflect less rigidity in language use, matching with the general trend towards a greater degree of linguistic liberty in private signage (Rosendal 2011).

Translocation of the metropolitan culture into rural Tanzania is achieved by exploiting the alluring cosmopolitanism of English, while the ways it is adopted and integrated reveals a certain degree of creativity.

A local food vending spot at the Dongobesh bus terminal in Mbulu Rural area (see Figure 3) is named "Coco Beach", adopted from a very popular urban place at Msasani Peninsula in Dar es Salaam, "a 2 kilometres coastal stretch consisting of a 1.5 kilometers beach fronting the Indian Ocean bordered by impressive cliffs in both the north and the south direction" (Karlsson & Maniette 2015: 45). Both coconut plants and oceanic beaches are amiss in Dongobesh. Yet, the authors of the signage draw on the cosmopolitan air that the name owes to its English components to boost the restaurant's image and to attract customers.

English components even start seeping into signage that is typically exclusively in Swahili, as in the case of a signpost in Mwangeza village (see Figure 4) that advertises various services and commodities. The top lines PATA PETROL HAPA GAMBASIMBO '(you can) buy petrol here at Gambasimbo's' contains the English word 'petrol', otherwise adapted as *petroli* to conform with the open syllable constraint of Swahili.[2] In the bottom lines FUNDI SIM, REDIO, VIATU 'craftsman for telephones, radio, shoes', the item SIM refers to Swahili *simu* 'telephone' rather than to the English-based SIM (card).

The signpost advertising a dispensary near Bashay village in Mbulu district (see Figure 5) is predominantly in English. There is only one component pointing to Swahili substratal influence, i.e., the placement of the quantifying item before its head in the distance specification KM 1,5 which follows the head initial order of Swahili rather than the quantifier-initial order of English. Otherwise, the use of English-based abbreviations such as P.O. Box for 'Post Office' and R.C. for 'Roman Catholic' is common practice and widely familiar in Tanzania. The same also holds for the English item DISPENSARY which is used instead of the Swahili term *zahanati* denoting a small health facility.[3]

The English-based term DISPENSARY — instead of Swahili *zahanati* — is also used in signage that is otherwise entirely framed in Swahili, as displayed on the

---

[2]. In Tanzania, the Swahili word *mafuta* 'fuel, gas' is commonly used for kerosene as *mafuta ya taa* but *petroli* has reference to fuel.

[3]. In Tanzanian English, the term dispensary for a small health facility contrasts with hospital for a larger health facility, adopted as *hospitali* in Swahili, and with clinic which is dedicated to maternity services.

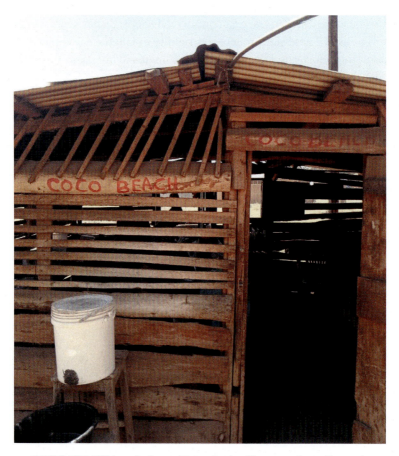

Figure 3. COCO BEACH inscription at Dongobesh village, northern Tanzania (October 2020)

signpost at Maretadu Chini village in Mbulu Rural area (see Figure 6). Swahili framing is manifest in the usage of the abbreviation S.L.P for *sanduku la posta*, the Swahili equivalent of 'P.O. Box' and the distance specification MT. 300 which follows the Swahili order as already described for Figure 5 above, in contrast to what is found in English word order in noun phrases (see Figure 9).

Another translocation can be seen in the name RIVER PARK HOTEL, referring to a guest house in a small township in Mkalama area (see Figure 7). The name does not refer to any local attraction, since no river can be found nearby. Instead it has been adopted from the global name of internationally established 'River Park Hotels', translocated from metropolitan Dar es Salaam to this rural area in Tanzania. While most of the signpost seems to be in English at the surface, four peculiarities can be detected. The term *simu* 'telephone' and the order of quantifier and head in the specification of distance KM. 1 reflect Swahili influence

Chapter 10. English in the linguistic landscape(s) of rural Tanzania 219

Figure 4. PETROL and SIM in signpost in Mwangeza village, northwestern Tanzania (December 2020)

directly. The use of the word 'container' in SELF CONTAINER ROOMS presents a Tanzanianism, i.e., a semantically localized English item, commonly found all over Tanzania for 'self contained rooms'. The term 'hotel' itself is rather misleading in the local context, since in Tanzanian English it refers to a restaurant, i.e., a place that provides food and drink services, but no accommodation, as is also reflected in the Swahili adaptation of the term as *hoteli*. People in Tanzania are generally aware that *hoteli* is derived from the English 'hotel', but they may be much less aware of the semantic shift the term has undergone in Tanzanian English and when it became integrated into Swahili.

In contrast to hotels, a café such as the LYAMBA LYA MFIPA CAFÉ (see Figure 8) serves breakfast (mainly tea, soda, and snacks) and lunch (mainly rice, boiled banana, and stiff porridge) only. The English based term *café* – which has undergone semantic change in the Tanzanian context, similar to *hotel* (Schmied

Figure 5. R.C. DISPENSARY in English-framed signpost at Bashay village in Mbulu District, northern Tanzania (October 2020)

2004a) — has been chosen here instead of the Swahili term *mgahawa* 'restaurant' (see Figure 9 below). The name LYAMBA LYA MFIPA has been borrowed from the name of a place in Rukwa Region in the west of Tanzania which is also the name of a hotel in Mpanda town located in that region. The name means 'mountain of the Fipa person' in the local Fipa language.

The bilingual advertisement of the WASAFI MGAHAWA 'restaurant' in Mwangeza village includes three types of references to popular metropolitan culture used in an effort to upgrade the place's attractiveness and allure customers. First, the name WASAFI is taken from WASAFI media, a popular label of Bongo Flava music, owned by Nasibu Abdul Juma Issack a.k.a. Diamond Platnumz, "who currently is the biggest Bongo Flava star in Tanzania and beyond. Diamond Platnumz has risen to international fame, particularly in Africa, and thus has become a model for many Tanzanian artists" (Reuster-Jahn 2014b: 16). Indeed, translocations of metropolitan culture to rural areas are powerfully mediated by Bongo Flava music throughout Tanzania, especially among the youth (Reuster-Jahn 2014a).

Chapter 10. English in the linguistic landscape(s) of rural Tanzania   221

Figure 6. DISPENSARY in Swahili-framed signpost at Maretadu Chini village in Mbulu Rural area, northern Tanzania (October 2020)

Second, the items advertised, i.e., MASOTOJO[4] which refers to a kind of nice (tasty) food, BAGA 'burger', and PIZA 'pizza', present food types which are emblematic of metropolitan lifestyle. Apart from orthographical adaptations, the point is that these items are unlikely to be obtained here. In fact, the restaurant sells staple food, i.e., rice, cooked banana, and *ugali*, a type of stiff porridge "made from cassava, maize, sorghum and millet flours, either singly or mixed" (Forsythe et al. 2017: 6). None of these items appear on the menu at the restaurant though. Indeed, the alluring terms of metropolitan food have been placed to attract the attention of the passers-by because the restaurant sells breakfast, lunch, and supper. Even the expression KAMA YOTEE 'each and everything plentifully' also reflects metropolitan usage.

Finally, the expression IN GOD WE TRUST borrows the air of big business, since it is common in many large business establishments in urban areas countrywide. While most Tanzanians may not know its meaning, they will immediately

---

4. The term has been coined by Bongo flavour artist Inspector Haroun of Gangwe Mobb in Dar es Salaam. Channel Ten Television station in Dar es Salaam runs a cooking program with the name MASOTOJO. While the term may ultimately include an adoption of French *sauté* 'briefly fried', its exact etymology remains to be confirmed.

Figure 7. RIVER PARK HOTEL in English-framed signage with Swahili structure at Mkalama, northwestern Tanzania (December 2020)

Figure 8. Wall inscription of the term CAFE in Mkalama District in Tanzania (December 2020)

Figure 9. WASAFI restaurant in bilingual signage at Mwangeza village, northern Tanzania (December 2020)

grasp its indexical reference to big business — similar to how Chinese characters have become indexical of Chinese firms in Zambian linguistic landscapes (Banda, Jimaima & Mokwena 2019).

With respect to syntax, the placement of the quantifier before its head noun (50 m) conforms to English word order in noun phrases, contrary to the substratal Swahili influence found in Figures 5–6.

Creative adaptations of English can also be found in signage of small-scale businesses such as the guest house at Mwangeza village in Figure 10. The word in the inscription BAFU 'bathroom' is a fully established borrowing of English 'bath', whereas TOY is a creative clipping of 'toilet', replacing Swahili alternatives such as *choo* or *msala*.

Other lexical borrowings from English have been spread in the rural linguistic landscape with the advent of mobile phones, as is the case with the verb *chaji* 'charge' in the inscription CHAJI SIMU YAKO HAPA 'recharge your telephone here' (see Figure 11), phonotactically and orthographically fully adapted to Swahili standards. Actually, in the mobile telephone industry, the loanword tends to refer to 'recharge' as in the collocation *chaji simu* 'recharge your phone'.

Figure 10. Door inscriptions at a guest house in Mkalama District, northern Tanzania (March 2020)

Figure 11. Loanword CHAJI in rural signage in Mbulu District, northwestern Tanzania (October 2020)

4. English in Tanzanian language ecologies

Linguistic landscapes can be viewed as visual manifestations of the underlying forces that shape linguistic ecologies at large (Mühlhäusler 1996) by virtue of the ecological parameters of graphemicization and institutional support (Haugen 1972). The fact that some languages in a given multilingual setting are equipped with a long tradition of a written standard empowers them to conquer and dominate the visual medium and domains of usage that go with it, bluntly revealing macro-socioeconomic power relations. In most postcolonial states, the ex-colonial languages take over this role. As detailed in Section 1, the 'triglossic' situation in Tanzania is more complex, due to the presence of the fully standardized autochthonous language Swahili that competes with English in many domains of official language use. This is vividly reflected in Tanzania's linguistic landscapes by the co-existence of English and Swahili signage and the combination of both languages in bilingual inscriptions, while the 120+ national languages remain almost invisible, marginalized as languages of informal oral communication at home (Batibo 2005; Petzell 2012) in spite of the fact that many of them presently undergo standardization or have already become standardized in the meantime.

Remarkably, as shown in Section 3.2, the use of English signage is not at all restricted to the cityscapes of Dar es Salaam, Dodoma, and Arusha. Chunks of English can be seen to seep into the linguistic landscapes of rural Tanzanian outbacks in spite of the fact that the majority of the rural population may only have a very rudimentary grasp of English, if at all. The reason for this must be sought in aspirations of local entrepreneurs to link up with cosmopolitan culture associated with the use of English, which underlies the translocations of English terms discussed in Section 3.2. Thus, the study of rural linguistic landscapes provides indirect access to language attitudes, since it reveals a positive inclination towards the emblematic use of English in spite of an extensive absence of English proficiency.

In a wider perspective, the English presence and its forms in rural linguistic landscapes result from three processes: localization, translocation, and creative appropriation. Localization concerns the adaptation of international goods associated with modernity, first introduced in the urban centers. In the study of linguistic landscapes, localization is also observed in the way English names for commodities are adapted in national languages such as Chinese in China and Amharic in Ethiopia (Shohamy & Gorter 2009). Translocation refers to the dissemination of linguistic materials from the urban centers to rural areas. The present analysis of English items in the linguistic landscapes of Tanzania demonstrates the fluctuation from metropolitan areas such as Dar es Salaam, the hub of modernization, to villages even in remote rural backwaters — a process that has also been observed with the diffusion of music (Reuster-Jahn 2014b). In the process of localization and translocation, English material undergoes various formal and semantic transformations that index creative adaptations and appropriations to the local context. Primarily, creative adaptation such as this is applied to material from ex-colonial languages, as widely observed in African urban youth languages (Kießling & Mous 2004) or stylects (Hurst-Harosh 2020) generally and in Tanzanian *lugha ya mitaani* in particular (Reuster-Jahn & Kießling 2006, 2022). But it may also go the other way round, i.e., English affecting the specific forms of idioms in Swahili as observed by Higgins (2007) and Reuster-Jahn (2014b).

5. Conclusion

English presence in bottom-up signage in rural Tanzania results from the translocation of linguistic materials from Tanzanian metropoles where it has originally been introduced and localized, i.e., appropriated and eventually transformed. It takes a variety of forms. Apart from English Tanzanianisms such as *self container rooms*, English sourced loanwords such as *chaji* '(re)charge' and *bafu* 'bathroom' have become fully swahilized, both phonotactically and orthographically. Initial placement of quantifiers in nominal phrases of Swahili-framed signage reflects an alignment to English syntax. Other inscriptions present emblematic English sourced phrasings such as 'In God we trust' and widely known popular names such as 'River Park Hotel' and 'Coco Beach' that can be categorized as translocations from metropolitan to rural areas in the sense of Banda & Jimaima (2015, 2017). While most of them are centered on food services and accommodation facilities, all of them reflect the effort to exploit the cosmopolitanism of English and adopt it as an index of modernity.

References

Abdulaziz Mkilifi, M. H. 1972. Triglossia and Swahili-English bilingualism in Tanzania. *Language and Society* 1: 197–213.

Banda, Felix & Hambaba Jimaima. 2015. The semiotic ecology of linguistic landscapes of rural Zambia. *Journal of Sociolinguistics* 19(5): 643–670.

Banda, Felix & Hambaba Jimaima. 2017. Linguistic landscapes and the sociolinguistics of language vitality in multilingual contexts of Zambia. *Multilingua* 36(5): 595–625.

Banda, Felix, Hambaba Jimaima & Lorato Mokwena. 2019. Semiotic remediation of Chinese signage in linguistic landscapes of two rural areas of Zambia. In Ari Sherris & Elisabetta Adami (eds.), *Making Signs, Translanguaging Ethnographies: Exploring Urban, Rural and Educational Spaces*, pp. 74–90. Bristol: Multilingual Matters.

Batibo, Herman M. 1995. The growth of Kiswahili as language of education and administration in Tanzania. In Martin Pütz (ed.), *Discrimination through Language in Africa? Perspectives on the Namibian Experience*, pp. 57–80. Berlin: Mouton de Gruyter.

Batibo, Herman M. 2005. *Language Decline and Death in Africa: Causes, Consequences and Challenges*. Clevedon: Multilingual Matters.

Ben-Rafael, Eliezer, Elana Shohamy, Muhammad Hasan Amara & Nira Trumper-Hecht. 2006. Linguistic landscape as symbolic construction of the public space: The case of Israel. In Durk Gorter (ed.) *Linguistic Landscape: A New Approach to Multilingualism*, pp. 7–30. Bristol: Multilingual Matters.

Blommaert, Jan. 2014. *State Ideology and Language in Tanzania*. Edinburgh: Edinburgh University Press.

Bwenge, Charles. 2009. Language choice in Dar es Salaam's billboards. In Fiona McLaughlin (ed.), *The Languages of Urban Africa*, pp. 152–177. London: Continuum.

Bwenge, Charles. 2012. English in Tanzania: A linguistic cultural perspective. *International Journal of Language, Translation and Intercultural Communication* 1(1): 167–182.

Chul-joon, Yang. 2014. Shifting agency in shaping linguistic landscape: Evidence from Dar es Salaam, Tanzania. *The Sociolinguistic Journal of Korea* 22(2): 45–64.

Costley, Tracey, Nancy Kula & Lutz Marten. 2022. Translanguaging spaces and multilingual public writing in Zambia: Tracing change in the linguistic landscape of Ndola on the Copperbelt. *Journal of Multilingual and Multicultural Development* 44(9), 773–793.

Eberhard, David M., Gary F. Simons & Charles D. Fennig (eds.). 2023. *Ethnologue: Languages of the World*, 26th edn. Dallas, TX: SIL International. http://www.ethnologue.com (11 October 2024).

Forsythe, Lora, Maria Njau, Adrienne Martin, Aurelie Bechoff & Keith Tomlins. 2017. *Staple Food Cultures: A Case Study of Cassava Ugali Preferences in Dar es Salaam, Tanzania*. Natural Resources Institute and CGIAR Research Program on Roots, Tubers and Bananas (RTB). RTB Working Paper.

Haugen, Einar. 1972. The ecology of language. In Anwar S. Dil (ed.), *The Ecology of Language. Essays of Einar Haugen*, pp. 325–339. Stanford, CA: Standford University Press.

Heine, Bernd. 1979. *Sprache, Gesellschaft und Kommunikation in Afrika: zum Problem der Verständigung und sozio-ökonomischen Entwicklung im sub-saharischen Afrika*. München: Weltforum Verlag.

Higgins, Christina. 2007. Shifting tactics in intersubjectivity to align indexicalities: A case of joking around in Swahinglish. *Language in Society* 36: 1–24.

Hurst-Harosh, Ellen. 2020. *Tsotsitaal in South Africa: Style and Metaphor in Youth Language Practices*. Köln: Rüdiger Köppe.

Ilonga, Emmanuel & Gastor Mapunda. 2022. Complementarity of communicative modes on meaning making in Tanzania's digital telecom marketing: A social semiotic multimodal perspective. *South African Linguistics and Applied Language Studies* 40(1): 87–99.

Karlsson, Mina & Emelie Maniette. 2015. COCO BEACH — From City Dump to Paradise: A Design Proposal for a Public Beach in Dar es Salaam, Tanzania. M.A. thesis, Uppsala University.

Kießling, Roland & Maarten Mous. 2004. Urban youth languages in Africa. *Anthropological Linguistics* 46(3): 303–341.

Kießling, Roland, Maarten Mous & Derek Nurse. 2008. The Tanzanian Rift Valley area. In Bernd Heine & Derek Nurse (eds.), *A Linguistic Geography of Africa*, pp. 186–227. Cambridge: Cambridge University Press.

Languages of Tanzania Project. 2009. *Atlasi ya lugha za Tanzania*. Dar es Salaam: University of Dar es Salaam.

Lanza, Elizabeth & Hirut Woldermariam. 2014. Indexing modernity: English and branding in LL of Addis Ababa. *International Journal of Bilingualism* 18(5): 23–49.

Legère, Karsten. 2006. Formal and informal development of the Swahili language: Focus on Tanzania. In Olaoba F. Arasanyin & Michael A. Pemberton (eds.), *Selected Proceedings of the 36th Annual Conference on African Linguistics*, pp. 176–184. Somerville, MA: Cascadilla Proceedings Project.

Legère, Karsten & Tove Rosendal. 2019. Linguistic landscapes and the African perspective. In Martin Pütz & Neele Mundt (eds.), *Expanding the Linguistic Landscape: Linguistic Diversity, Multimodality and the Use of Space as a Semiotic Resource*, pp. 153–179. Bristol: Multilingual Matters.

Lema, Benedict P. 2021. The triple linguistic heritage in Tanzania: Opportunities and challenges. *Journal of Education, Humanities and Sciences* 10(1): 57–76.

Lupapula, Abel. 2021. Terminological Development in Tanzania: An Analysis of the Bantu-sourced Loanwords in Standard Kiswahili Terminology. P.h.D. dissertation, University of Hamburg.

Lusekelo, Amani & Chrispina Alphonce. 2018. The linguistic landscape in urban Tanzania: An account of the language of billboards and shop-signs in district headquarters. *Journal of Language, Technology and Entrepreneurship in Africa* 9(1): 1–28.

Lusekelo, Amani & Adventina Buberwa. 2021. Swahili and English sell; but what about Iraqw and Sukuma? Tanzanian native languages and ethnic affiliations in bottom-up commercial signage. *Tanzania Journal of Humanities and Social Sciences* 10(1): 73–103.

Lusekelo, Amani & Paschal C. Mdukula. 2021. The linguistic landscape of urban Tanzania in Dodoma City. *Utafiti Journal of African Perspectives* 16(1): 63–94.

Mapunda, Gastor & Emanuel Ilonga. 2022. Lexical innovation through Swahilisation of English lexicon in online advertisement. *Utafiti* 17(1): 107–129.

Mapunda, Gastor & Tove Rosendal. 2021. Imagined futures and new technology: Youths' language attitudes in Songea, Tanzania. *Language Matters* 52(1): 92–112.

Mdukula, Patrick C. 2018. Linguistic Landscape of Public Health Institutions in Tanzania: The Case of Muhimbili National Hospital. P.h.D. dissertation, University of Dar es Salaam.

Mohr, Susanne. 2018. The changing dynamics of language use and language attitudes in Tanzania. *Language Matters – Studies in the Languages of Africa* 49(3): 105–127.

Mohr, Susanne & Dunlop Ochieng. 2017. Language usage in everyday life and in education: Current attitudes towards English in Tanzania. *English Today* 33(4): 12–18.

Mohr, Susanne, Steffen Lorenz & Dunlop Ochieng. 2020. English, national and local linguae francae in the language ecologies of Uganda and Tanzania. *Sociolinguistic Studies* 14(3): 371–394.

Mühlhäusler, Peter. 1996. *Linguistic Ecology. Linguistic Change and Language Imperialism in the Pacific Region*. London: Routledge.

Ochieng, Dunlop. 2015. The revival of the status of English in Tanzania: What future does the status of the English language have in Tanzania? *English Today* 31(2): 25–31.

Peterson, Rhoda. 2014. Matumizi na dhima za lugha katika mandhari-lugha ya jiji la Dar es Salaam. P.h.D. dissertation. University of Dar es Salaam.

Petzell, Malin. 2012. The linguistic situation in Tanzania. *Moderna Språk* 1: 136–144.

Reuster-Jahn, Uta. 2014a. Antivirus: The revolt of bongo fleva artists against a media-and-entertainment empire in Tanzania. In Matthias Kings & Utah Reuters-Jahn (eds.), *Bongo Media Worlds: Producing and Consuming Popular Culture in Dar es Salaam*, pp. 43–78. Cologne: Rüdiger Köppe.

Reuster-Jahn, Uta. 2014b. English versus Swahili: Language choice in bongo flava as expression of cultural and economic changes in Tanzania. *Swahili Forum* 21: 1–25.

Reuster-Jahn, Uta & Roland Kießling. 2006. Lugha ya mitaani in Tanzania: The poetics and sociology of a young urban style of speaking – With a dictionary comprising 1100 words and phrases. *Swahili Forum* 13: 1–196.

Reuster-Jahn, Uta & Roland Kießling. 2022. Tanzania: Lugha ya Mitaani. In Heike Wiese & Paul Kerswill (eds.), *Urban Contact Dialects and Language Change: Insights from the Global North and South*, pp. 167–185. London: Taylor & Francis.

Rosendal, Tove. 2011. *Linguistic Landscapes: A Comparison of Official and Non-official Language Management in Rwanda and Uganda, Focusing on the Position of African Languages*. Köln: Rüdiger Köppe.

Roy-Campbell, Zaline M. & Martha Qorro. 1997. *The Language Crisis in Tanzania: The Myth of English Versus Education*. Dar es Salaam: Mkuki na Nyota Publishers.

Rubagumya, Casmir M. 1991. Language promotion for educational purposes: The example of Tanzania. *International Review of Education* 37(1): 67–85.

Rubagumya, Casmir M. 2003. English Medium Primary Schools in Tanzania: A new "linguistic market" in education? In Birgit Brock-Utne, Saline Zubeida & Martha Qorro (eds.), *Language of Instruction in Tanzania and South Africa*, pp. 149–169. Dar es Salaam: E&D Limited.

Schmied, Josef. 1985a. Attitudes towards English in Tanzania. *English World-Wide* 6: 237–269.

Schmied, Josef. 1985b. *Englisch in Tansania. Sozio- und interlinguistische Probleme*. Heidelberg: Groos.

Schmied, Josef. 1990. Language use, attitudes, performance and sociolinguistic background: A comparison of English in Kenya, Tanzania and Zambia. *English World-Wide* 11: 217–238.

Schmied, Josef. 2004a. East African English (Kenya, Uganda, Tanzania): Morphology and syntax. In Bernd Kortmann & Edgar W. Schneider (eds.), *A Handbook of Varieties of English: Morphology and Syntax*, pp. 930–947. Berlin: Mouton de Gruyter.

Schmied, Josef. 2004b. East African English (Kenya, Uganda, Tanzania): Phonology. In Bernd Kortmann & Edgar W. Schneider (eds.), *A Handbook of Varieties of English: Phonology*, pp. 918–929. Berlin: Mouton de Gruyter.

Schmied, Josef. 2012. Tanzanian English. In Bernd Kortmann & Kerstin Lunkenheimer (eds.), *The Mouton world Atlas of Variation in English*, pp. 454–465. Berlin: Mouton de Gruyter.

Shohamy, Elana & Durk Gorter (eds.). 2009. *Linguistic Landscape: Expanding the Scenery*. London: Routledge.

Steiner-Anthony, Nathalie. 2012. Linguistic Landscape: Schriftlicher Sprachgebrauch im Stadtbild Daressalaams (Tansania). M.A. thesis, University of Hamburg.

United Republic of Tanzania. 1995. *Education and Training Policy*. Dar es Salaam: Ministry of Education and Culture.

United Republic of Tanzania. 1997. *Sera ya utamaduni (Cultural policy)*. Dar es Salaam: Ministry of Education and Culture.

United Republic of Tanzania. 2013. *Basic Education Statistics in Tanzania (BEST)*. Dar es Salaam: Ministry of Education and Vocational Training.

Visonà, Mark. 2017. Language attitudes and linguistic landscapes of Malawi. *Texas Linguistics Forum* 60.

CHAPTER 11

The Zanzibari tourist space as a multilingual language ecology

Susanne Mohr
Norwegian University of Science and Technology

Across East Africa, English is used extensively in urban areas, especially in official domains, while Kiswahili serves as intranational lingua franca, and local autochthonous languages are employed in less formal communication. However, it has been shown that due to globalization, English can be an important part of local multilingual language practices in less urban areas as well. This emphasizes the fact that language practices need to be analyzed locally to assess language ecologies. This chapter discusses a relatively under-researched East African region, i.e., Tanzania's semi-autonomous archipelago Zanzibar, regarding the use of English. The analysis focuses on tourist spaces on Unguja island. English has been discussed as the default choice and an important commodity in these spaces, especially for Zanzibari hosts. Based on ethnographic data (i.e., observations, questionnaires, and interviews), this chapter situates English in its multilingual ecology by analyzing language repertoires, greetings, and subsequent interactions between tourists and hosts. Practical reasons and the enactment of social roles, especially in higher end establishments, emerge as reasons for English being the default choice in tourist spaces in general. This is in contrast to the use of Kiswahili and a simplified, pidginized version of it called 'Hakuna Matata Swahili', which is used in a tokenistic fashion, mostly in greetings in open spaces, to authenticate less expensive establishments and the Zanzibari tourist space. Altogether, the chapter demonstrates that, while English is used more widely in Zanzibar than in mainland Tanzania, it remains lingua franca-reminiscent, a 'multilingua franca' in a highly multilingual ecology.

Keywords: communicative interaction, English as multilingua franca, Kiswahili, Tanzania, tourism, Zanzibar

https://doi.org/10.1075/hsld.9.11moh
Available under the CC BY-NC-ND 4.0 license.
© 2025 John Benjamins Publishing Company

1. Introduction

In large parts of East Africa, English is a language used extensively in urban metropolises, especially in official domains, while Kiswahili serves as intranational lingua franca, and local autochthonous languages are employed in less formal communication (Isingoma 2017). However, there are exceptions to this oft-stipulated triglossic language situation. Importantly, Uganda seems to diverge from this pattern in that the role of Kiswahili is notably different as compared to, for example, Kenya and Tanzania. In Uganda, Kiswahili does not have the same status as intranational lingua franca since other autochthonous languages, especially Luganda, retained their important status in the country (Lorenz 2019; Mohr, Lorenz & Ochieng 2020; see also Meierkord, Isingoma & Namyalo 2016). Further, due to globalization, English can be an important part of local, informal multilingual language practices in less urban areas in Tanzania and Uganda (Mohr et al. 2020). This emphasizes the fact that the dynamics of language practices need to be analyzed locally in order to assess specific language ecologies (Haugen 1972; Pennycook 2010).

This chapter discusses an as yet under-researched East African region with regard to the use of English, i.e., Tanzania's semi-autonomous archipelago Zanzibar. The discussion focuses on tourist spaces on Unguja island, which are potentially highly multilingual given the number of native languages of tourists and hosts that come into contact. However, English has been discussed as a central, default choice in these spaces and an important commodity, especially for Zanzibari hosts working in tourism (see Mohr 2021a on Zanzibar in particular and Heller 2003 on the commodification of language in general). The Zanzibari situation is contextualized in relation to previous descriptions of English and other language use in Tanzania, showing that while there are similarities, there are also certain differences between these language ecologies. Based on ethnographic data (i.e., observations, questionnaires, and interviews) collected between 2017–2019, the place of English in Zanzibar's multilingual language ecology is discussed, especially vis à vis Kiswahili (see Sections 4.1–4.3). A potential variety of English in Zanzibar is considered (see Section 4.4) based on the description of particular language practices salient in the tourist space's language ecology, including the use of a pidginized form of Kiswahili, greetings, other interactions, and attitudes towards English.

Altogether, the chapter aims at contributing to the linguistic description of the tourist space of Zanzibar, as well as English(es) on the archipelago. The differences that emerge between Tanzanian and Zanzibari Englishes, which nominally form part of the same country, emphasize the need to move away from analyzing English in relation to nation states.

2. Multilingual language ecologies in Tanzania

Tanzania is a country in East Africa formed after independence from the British in 1964, out of the territory of Tanganyika and the archipelago of Zanzibar. A British protectorate from 1890 until 1963, Zanzibar experienced several massive political changes after independence, among others the Zanzibar revolution, all culminating in the merger of Tanganyika with Zanzibar. Zanzibar remains a semi-autonomous region, in which (mass) tourism became the main economic sector since the end of socialism in the 1990s (Keshodkar 2013).

Tanzania is highly multilingual, with 129 living languages recorded (Eberhard, Simons & Fennig 2023). Kiswahili (a language of the Bantu family) is the *de facto* national language with ca. 15 million native and 32 million non-native speakers reported in 2022 (Eberhard et al. 2023), and hence the language of the masses (Bwenge 2012). However, even though this amounts to more than 80 percent of the population, competence in Kiswahili has been reported to vary: in rural areas it is rather limited (Brock-Utne & Qorro 2015), while in Zanzibar it is widespread with many native speakers, and the "standard" variety of Kiswahili, Kiunguja, being spoken there as well (Möhlig 1995). Many of the participants in the present study also mentioned repeatedly and proudly that "the best Kiswahili" is spoken in Zanzibar.

Within this multilingual context, English is the *de facto* national working language with ca. 2.6 million non-native speakers, i.e., 4.5 percent of the population. For this reason, some have claimed that English, and not the various autochthonous languages spoken in the country, is Tanzania's real minority language, without a functional role in everyday life (e.g., Brock-Utne & Qorro 2015; Legère & Rosendal 2015; Vuzo 2010). However, globalization has "create[d] pockets away from [...] urban centers where English is an integral part of local linguistic practices" (Mohr et al. 2020: 372). In the following, some examples of such pockets are outlined. In the analysis, this is discussed with special reference to Zanzibar and tourism.

2.1 Language policies and use in Tanzania

As outlined above, Tanzania is a highly multilingual country. The Swahilization policy of the Nyerere era after independence clearly favored Kiswahili as the language of emancipation (Bwenge 2012), and it was implemented as medium of instruction (MoI) in primary education (Mohr 2018). Even during that period, plans for implementing Kiswahili as MoI in secondary education were never put into effect, however, and English was maintained as a sign for quality education

(Bwenge 2012). Generally, language policies, also after the end of that era, remained vague and often contradictory, especially regarding language use in education.

Especially the abrupt switch from Kiswahili to English when entering secondary school means that many Tanzanian students have problems understanding lessons and following teaching (Petzell 2012). This has also been reported for Zanzibar (Mohr 2021a), where those who want to learn English fluently, and to a level that they are eligible to work in the tourist industry, have to take paid tuition classes after school. As in many other African postcolonial countries, the main problem seems to be the lack of or insufficient representation of the pupils' home languages at school (Kamwangamalu & Tovares 2016), but also large class sizes, lack of teaching materials, and lack of knowledge of English among teachers (Mohr 2018; Schneider 2016). The use of Tanzania's autochthonous languages apart from Kiswahili has also been found to be very much necessary and sought after for more sustainable higher education in the country (Ulmer, Divine & Wydra 2023). Thus, attitudes towards autochthonous languages in (higher) education seem to be changing, even though English has repeatedly been reported to hold the highest instrumental value and considerable market force (Babaci-Wilhite 2010; Mohr 2018; Schmied 1991). For the time being, it seems to remain a language of the elites.

Given its official status as *de facto* working language of the country and its widespread use in education, English in Tanzania should belong in the Outer Circle of Kachru's (1985) three circles model. It should be a second rather than a foreign language given its many intranational functions. However, some (e.g., Mohr 2022; Schmied 1991) have criticized this classification as unrealistic viewed the small number of language users and its restriction to elite circles. Indeed, the fact that English still does not seem to fulfill identity-providing functions, especially at national level (Mohr 2018), implies that Tanzania exhibits an English-in-Tanzania rather than a Tanzanian English situation as per Schneider's (2007) model. However, similar to the situation concerning Kiswahili described above, this seems to vary depending on different regions throughout the country, where those with increased touristic activity exhibit more widespread and higher proficiency in English among locals.

2.2 Tourism and language use in Tanzania

Globalization and the increased movement of people around the globe have created interesting new social conditions and sociolinguistic phenomena (Blommaert 2010). As a result of globalization, tourism accounts for one of the largest movements of people across cultures and represents an ideal space for the commodification of language in the new economy (Heller 2003). The study of tourism focusing on sociolinguistic contexts and pragmatic practices emerged rather recently as compared to other areas of tourism research related to geography or anthropology, for instance. Dann's (1996) work is one of the first pertinent analyses, but a plethora of sociolinguistic and pragmatic studies appeared subsequently, discussing, for instance, salient touristic language practices such as greetings and welcomings (e.g., Jaworski 2009, 2015), linguistic practices related to photo-sharing online (e.g., Thurlow & Jaworski 2003, 2011), or the sociolinguistics and semiotics of tourism in general (e.g., Jaworski & Thurlow 2010; Thurlow & Jaworski 2010, 2014). One issue that emerges from these studies is the centrality of the commodification of language, language choices and interactions, which become performative and 'spectacular', especially where otherwise phatic communication is concerned (Heller 2003; Jaworski 2015). In East Africa, Kenya has been paid special attention to, particularly concerning language use among (package) tourists in beach resorts, and some of these tendencies were equally observed there (e.g., Nassenstein 2016, 2019; Storch & Mietzner 2021).

In Tanzania, there are many touristic sights, and the country is a popular destination for safari tourism, which is the main attraction for tourists to Africa in general (Sarmento & Rink 2016). There are several national parks in Tanzania, including Mount Kilimanjaro National Park, home to Mount Kilimanjaro, Africa's highest mountain. Tourism and tourist hotspots seem to further more widespread competency in English than in other parts of Tanzania, usually brought about by informal language learning. For instance, one of Schneider's (2016) examples of grassroots Englishes in tourism stems from an expedition up Mount Kilimanjaro. Among the locals working there, Schneider (2016: 7) reports, English is a prerequisite for a promotion from porter to guide, a fact that emphasizes the economic value that is attributed to English in this economic sector (see also Mohr 2021a). The guides in his study had apparently learnt English from interaction with tourists (Schneider 2016: 8). He further comments on the comparatively high fluency in English of these Tanzanian hosts as compared to the Indian and Indonesian hosts in his study. The widespread use of English in that area of Tanzania also became apparent in language attitude and use studies (Mohr 2018; Mohr et al. 2020), which were based on data from Arusha, which is the starting point for many Kilimanjaro expeditions.

Zanzibar is another popular Tanzanian tourist destination, for instance among safari tourists, who look for a few relaxing days on the beach after their stay on the mainland. It is also popular among package tourists who go straight from the airport to their hotel, do not leave it for the entire duration of their stay, and then return home (see also Storch & Mietzner 2021 for a description of similar tourists in Kenya). And some tourists come for 'active' holidays, involving kite surfing or diving, and there is a fair amount of voluntourists, i.e., tourists combining voluntary work in, e.g., NGOs, and holidays, as well. As mentioned above, tourism is the main economic sector in Zanzibar (Keshodkar 2013) and has been shown to have considerable influence on the use and acquisition of English. English usage is widespread, and English usually acquired via the "grassroots" practices referred to by Schneider (2016), too. Mohr (2021a) outlines that interaction with tourists furthers language learning but that private, paid tuition classes are one of the main means to improve English competence among many Zanzibari hosts. With regard to the multilingual ecology surrounding English in Zanzibar, Mohr (2019) shows that generally, language choices in tourism in Zanzibar are differently motivated, i.e., usefulness or practicality is important when choosing English for both tourists and hosts, while signaling wealth is a crucial factor related to using the tourists' native languages among the hosts. A critical factor in this regard is the performance of social roles in tourist spaces, highlighted by Jaworski & Thurlow (2010). Tourism offers an important space for the negotiation and performance of these roles, and some language practices, greetings in particular, have been shown to imply different types of social personae (Duranti 1997: 89). This warrants a closer look at greetings in the Zanzibari tourist space, and their integration into local English language use in a multilingual context in this chapter.

Given the widespread and high proficiency in both Kiswahili and English among local Zanzibaris as outlined here, mixed with the languages the tourists bring with them, tourist spaces on the Zanzibar archipelago are particularly interesting with respect to English in its multilingual ecologies in general. The aims of the analysis are hence to shed further light on the multilingual ecology of English in Zanzibar, with specific reference to language repertoires (see Section 4.1), language choices and their functions in greetings (see Section 4.2) and interactions at large (see Section 4.3), in order to discuss the status of English(es) in Zanzibar as a whole (see Section 4.4).

3. Methods and data

3.1 Locations of data collection

The analysis presented here is based on ethnographic data, i.e., participant observation and interviews, as well as (short) questionnaires for tourists. While these methods bear the disadvantage of not generating spontaneous speech data, they provide insight into attitudes towards language use, as well as possible conventions of linguistic behavior among tourists and hosts. Observations were conducted for four weeks on Unguja island in three locations (see Figure 1).

These sites were chosen to collect data from different tourist groups. Stone Town is the old part of Zanzibar City and a UNESCO World Heritage Site. Nungwi

Chapter 11. The Zanzibari tourist space as a multilingual language ecology 237

Figure 1. Unguja Island of Zanzibar, image is public domain from: https://commons.wikimedia.org/w/index.php?curid=821055 (04 December 2024)

is a village in the North of the island visited by many package tourists who go there to lie on the beach. Paje is a small village on the East coast and is mainly popular among kite surfers. Some interviews were also conducted in Jambiani, a neighboring village which was less touristy at the time. In their variety, these locations are well suited to provide a broad picture of tourists and their language use in Zanzibar. Further, data could be collected in different settings such as large hotels and small guest houses, restaurants and bars, different kinds of shops, on the beach, and in the streets of Stone Town.

Encounters in enclosed (hotels, restaurants) and open (streets, beaches) spaces were observed. Table 1 provides an overview of the different enclosed spaces in which observations and interviews took place. Price levels were determined according to ratings/stars on tripadvisor.com. However, these are given according to Western standards; many Zanzibaris would not be able to afford visiting them. Only at Zanzibar City Restaurant[1] locals could be met frequently and for Eid al-Adha festival, some afforded a visit to Equator Bar. There are more restaurants and hotels in

---

1. All establishment names used in this chapter are pseudonyms.

Stone Town included in the sample than in Nungwi, Paje, or Jambiani. This reflects the number of inhabitants and demand among tourists.

Table 1. Restaurants and hotels considered in the study

Name	Location	Price level
Zanzibar City Restaurant	Stone Town	€€-€€€
Equator Bar	Stone Town	€€-€€€
Jahazi Restaurant	Stone Town	€€-€€€
Tanzania Hotel (restaurant & bar on premises)	Stone Town	****
Taarab Hotel (restaurant on premises)	Stone Town	****
Diamonds Hotel	Stone Town	****
Freedom Hotel (restaurant on premises)	Stone Town	**
Mango Bar	Nungwi	€€-€€€
Hakuna Matata Guest House (restaurant & bar on premises)	Nungwi	***
Karibu Hotel (restaurant on premises)	Paje	No stars
Seaweed Hotel (restaurant on premises)	Jambiani	***

Observations were recorded as field notes similar to communicative diaries (see Lawson & Sachdev 2000). This method has the advantage of coming relatively close to the recording of spontaneous data, whose collection was impossible due to ethical considerations.

3.2 Interviews

Interviews were semi-structured, one-on-one interviews conducted by the author in a location of the participants' choosing to provide as comfortable and secure an environment as possible (Mohr 2021b: 538). Several of the interviews were not audio-recorded because the participants felt more comfortable with written notes. All participants gave informed consent. Topics discussed focused on language use in tourism and extended to other cultural practices such as dhow[2] building or taarab music, which is popular in Zanzibar. The main language of the interviews was English.

The interviews were conducted with Zanzibaris working in different areas of tourism, such as hospitality and service, tour guiding but also education and training as lecturers in tourism programs at university or non-profit organiza-

---

2. Dhows are traditional wooden sailing boats used throughout the Indian Ocean region.

tions. Altogether, 13 interviews were conducted and approximately 4.5 hours of recordings were collected. Most of the data stem from men, as Zanzibari women are often discouraged from working in tourism for religious reasons (Keshodkar 2013; see also Mohr 2019, 2021a, 2021b). An average age cannot be determined, as several of the participants did not feel comfortable sharing this information. Most of the participants were highly educated and spoke several other languages besides their mother tongue, and Kiswahili (which was their mother tongue in some cases), and English (see Mohr also 2021a, 2021b).

The data was transcribed orthographically based on the transcription guidelines developed for the "Studying English as a Lingua Franca" project (SELF 2009) at the University of Helsinki. All transcriptions were cross-checked by at least two transcribers. The transcription conventions relevant for this chapter can be found in Appendix 1.

3.3 Questionnaires

46 questionnaires were collected among tourists, 17 male and 29 female, with an average age of 33, of different nationalities from Europe, North America, Asia, and Australia. Their mother tongues were diverse, including for example Basque, Dutch, French, German, Hebrew, Japanese, Russian, and Tagalog. All except for one tourist spoke English, the questionnaire was translated into German for them ad hoc by the researcher.

Specifically, tourists were asked where they had acquired their English and Kiswahili skills, and to rate both on a four-point Likert scale (can hardly speak x – able to communicate with some problems – easily able to communicate – fluent). Besides questions targeting the languages spoken by the tourists, questions concerning (a) which language they use for communication with Zanzibaris generally, (b) possible communication problems during their trip, and (c) how they would greet a Zanzibari, were included. All of these items were open-ended, allowing the tourists as much freedom and creativity concerning their answers as possible. Finally, the questionnaire included questions concerning the duration of their stay, reasons for choosing Zanzibar as their destination, sights visited/planned to visit and previous experience with holidays in Africa. Altogether, the questionnaire had 18 questions and took tourists about 5–10 minutes to fill in; they signed an informed consent form as part of the questionnaire.

4. Language practices and attitudes in the multilingual language ecology of touristic Zanzibar

4.1 Linguistic repertoires and language choices

Language choices are dependent on participants' linguistic repertoires, which were investigated on the basis of different questions in the interviews and questionnaires. Participants were asked about their mother tongue(s), English skills, Kiswahili skills, and other foreign language skills. Especially the hosts were asked about the language(s) they prefer for communication in Zanzibar, use most with tourists and the language(s) they identify with.

As mentioned in Section 3.2, all hosts spoke English and the interviews were conducted mainly in English. This indicates that the participants' proficiency in English was high. However, this assessment sometimes diverges from self-assessment, as shown in (1).

(1) Abdalla:[3] tour guide and part time lecturer, Stone Town
Abdalla: i even find one here uh in this conference […] she is PhD holder she is a […] lecturer at university but yeah her English is like mine or maybe less so
Interviewer: but your English is good i think […]
Abdalla: struggling all the time @@@   (Mohr 2017, Abdalla #13:17-13:46#)

These negative feelings concerning own and other Zanzibaris' English competence might explain the contrast between the language preferred by locals — as out of six hosts who commented on the question only three reported English (with one person being undecided between English and Kiswahili) — and the language used most with tourists, being English. This is indicative of a mainly practical motivation for choosing the language, as suggested by Mohr (2019). Among the tourists, 13 (28.3%) reported to be able to communicate in English with problems only and 12 (26.1%) to be easily able to communicate while not rating their own competence as "fluent". This is interesting, as nevertheless almost all tourists ($n=41$, 89.1%) reported using English, or "English and body language" to communicate with hosts. While self-assessments are subjective and might not be completely applicable as shown in Example (1), they convey the participants' feelings concerning their own language skills and the nature of communication in English in this space. The disparity between language use, competence and preference

---

3. The participant names used here are also pseudonyms and were previously used in Mohr (2021a, 2021b).

further emphasizes the merely instrumental value of English in the tourist space as a multilingual language ecology.

Another very prominent language of the Zanzibari language ecology is Kiswahili, given that it is the mother tongue of most Zanzibaris. The participating hosts confirmed that it is indeed the language they use most in public, with the exception of Ali, who claimed that he uses English and Kiswahili equally frequently. It is invariably the language the Zanzibari participants identified with, except for Mikidadi, who had lived in the UK for 20 years. Among the tourists, however, only five claimed to speak (some) Kiswahili, two "a/very little" only. Three said they would be able to communicate with problems only. This is in line with other studies showing very limited knowledge of Kiswahili among tourists in Zanzibar (e.g., Wockelmann 2020). This lack of knowledge of the local language among the tourists does not seem to cause them many communication problems however, probably due to the aforementioned frequent use of English. Most of the tourists ($n=32$, 69.6%) reported that there had been no communication problems during their stay. 14 (30.4%) claimed to have had "a few" problems. One tourist reported to have had problems only in remote areas, one only with young children. The Zanzibaris did not report many problems either. Hussein, a reception manager at Tanzania Hotel in Stone Town, mentioned there would usually be staff speaking additional European languages in case communication problems occurred.

Most Zanzibari participants indeed spoke at least one other foreign language apart from English to accommodate tourists, and several European languages were on display in the linguistic landscape in many hotels and restaurants. This includes especially Italian and Russian, thus catering for some of the largest tourist groups in Zanzibar at the time. This is similar to what Nassenstein (2019) reports for Kenya. Almost all Zanzibari participants also mentioned that they spoke Arabic, probably for religious reasons. Other foreign languages frequently mentioned by the hosts were French, Spanish, and Italian, again catering for large tourist groups.

In contrast to the relatively large linguistic repertoires of the hosts, most tourists reported to speak their mother tongue and English only. Exceptions were an Austrian tourist who claimed only to speak German and five British tourists who only spoke English. Apart from those, there were 17 tourists (36.9%) who spoke at least three languages. Figure 2 provides an overview of the languages in the linguistic repertoires of tourists and hosts.[4] Proficiency in individual languages was not assessed, if the participants found their competency to be good

---

4. This does not include a later fieldwork phase using different methods of data collection (reported in Mohr 2019, for instance), where even more language practices were mentioned.

enough to mention the language, it was included. The aim was thus to let the participants define their own language biography (Pavlenko 2007). This also means that the languages included as "shared" in Figure 2, might not necessarily be shared fully and by all tourists and hosts, although the majority of hosts indeed mentioned to speak them. In this context, "shared" is supposed to emphasize the relatively high possibility of these languages chosen in interactions. In Figure 2, bold print indicates that Kiswahili is spoken by all hosts, additional capitals signify that English is the language spoken by everyone. The rectangles around the languages are not intended to represent them as bounded entities but were chosen for graphical reasons.

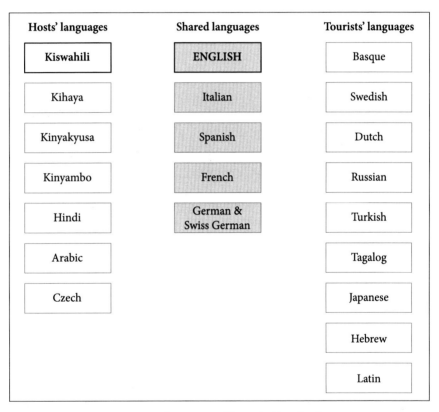

Figure 2. Linguistic repertoires of tourists and hosts in Zanzibar[5]

Figure 2 summarizes the findings presented in this section. It illustrates the multilingual nature of the Zanzibari tourist space and its language ecology, in which it would theoretically be possible to choose any of the languages mentioned

---

5. German and Swiss German were conflated for graphical reasons.

for communication, especially the shared languages. English, however, is the shared language of all participants and thus the most likely choice for communication, a "multilingua franca" (Jenkins 2015) in a multilingual space, despite the reservations that some participants have with regard to their own language competence. Kiswahili, on the other hand, does not come up on the tourists' side of Figure 2, emphasizing the more marginal role it plays in tourists' linguistic repertoires. It does however play an important role in the tourist space in general, especially in phatic communication such as greetings.

4.2 Greetings

As outlined by Jaworski (2009, 2015), greetings are salient in tourist spaces and fulfill purposes beyond their usual phatic function of moving interlocutors into shared interactional space (Duranti 1997). That is why they are often among the only "chunks" of foreign language acquired by tourists (Blommaert & Backus 2011), and also frequently occurred in a language other than English in the Zanzibari tourist space.

The tourists were specifically asked about greetings in the questionnaire. Two of them did not indicate any specific greeting they would employ with Zanzibaris. One tourist, who had reported to speak French and English, mentioned only *hello*. Interestingly, Kiswahili seems to play a more important role in greetings as compared to general communication. The remaining 43 (93.5%) tourists reported to use Kiswahili (sometimes in combination with English) to greet Zanzibaris. The greetings they mentioned are provided in Table 2. The total number amounts to more than 43, as multiple answers were possible. Note that none of these are responses to greetings but only first pair parts.

As indicated, many of the greetings that were mentioned are variants of the same greeting formula. Thus, *jambo, jamboo, djambo, jumbo,* and *ujambo* are all variants of *-jambo-*. The fact that so many different spellings exist is possibly due to most tourists not having learnt Kiswahili formally, nor learnt to write it. The respective mother tongue of the tourists seems to influence their idea of spelling, for example French in the case of *djambo* or English for *jumbo*. The same applies to *habari-*. The insecurity concerning especially the spelling of *jambo* might also stem from the fact that it is not a standard Kiswahili greeting. It is part of the simplified Hakuna Matata Swahili (HMS), the regular Kiswahili greeting being formed with negated subject markers, i.e., *hujambo* and the corresponding response *sijambo* (Nassenstein 2019: 136; see also Wockelmann 2020). *Ujambo* might be a misspelt variant of *hujambo*. While the origin of *jambo* has been discussed in the literature, the Zanzibaris in this study have their own theory (see also Mohr 2019):

Table 2. Kiswahili greetings mentioned by tourists

Greeting	Variants	Times mentioned
-jambo-	!jambo	26 (45.7%)
	jamboo	1 (1.7%)
	djambo	2 (3.5%)
	jumbo	5 (8.9%)
	ujambo	1 (1.7%)
mambo	mambo	13 (22.9%)
habari-	habari	4 (7.1%)
	habarijako	1 (1.7%)
	habaree	1 (1.7%)
salama	salama	1 (1.7%)
shikamoo	shikamoo	1 (1.7%)
asante sana	asante sana	1 (1.7%)
	Total	57 (100%)

(2) Abdalla, Stone Town
Abdalla: i don't know where it started there's like uh now it's like a formal greeting with the tourists [...] they cannot pronounce well how we greeting for example we say <SWAHILI> hujambo </SWAHILI> [...] and then (there) difficult for tourists to say also <SWAHILI> sijambo </SWAHILI> [...] so instead [...] we cut off some [...] and then say <SWAHILI> jambo </SWAHILI> and then they say <SWAHILI> jambo </SWAHILI> so it is easy for them [...] so there's kind of a language [...] very small part of our language that we we we develop for tourist
(Mohr 2017, Abdalla #04:18-05:08#)

As Abdalla explains, *jambo* is a part of Kiswahili that was simplified for tourists; a claim that is in line with Nassenstein's (2019) concept of HMS. The greeting was specifically developed for tourists because they cannot pronounce proper Kiswahili. This is an interesting explanation that is not confirmed by the literature stating *jambo* to have developed in Kenya in the 1970s during political turmoil as an expression to claim Kenya is safe (see Bruner 2001: 892–893). The diverging explanation found in the literature does not preclude that there is some truth to the hosts' explanation, however. Zanzibaris might indeed have encountered tourists who were not able or willing to use the standard form; an explanation that seems likely given the very limited Kiswahili knowledge the tourist participants exhibited. While *jambo – jambo* is certainly a greeting closely related to the tourist sector, it seems to (have) spread beyond that (see Example (3)).

(3) Ali, tour booking clerk, Jambiani
Interviewer: and it would be strange if [you said] it to a zanzibari

Ali: yeah [...] but in nowadays even us we use this [...] a word which is close to me to say this because um because of this environment here [...] for the kids sometimes i can use <SWAHILI> jambo </SWAHILI> [...]

(Mohr 2017, Ali #20:59-21:36#)

As Ali states, *jambo* might in fact be used with other Zanzibaris working in the tourist sector and with children. He even goes on to mention that he believes the greeting will be included in dictionaries (Mohr 2017, Ali). Most Zanzibaris spoken to (in interviews and informally) felt that the greeting is positively connotated, despite its non-standardness. In an art shop in Stone Town, the resident artist, when asked why they used *jambo* on the signs they make, answered "well it's nice, isn't it?".

The ubiquity of the greeting and other HMS iconic expressions like *hakuna matata* in the linguistic landscape of Zanzibar is striking (see also Mohr 2020; Storch 2018). The frequency of the greeting among tourists might in fact be one explanation for its ubiquity on souvenirs (or vice versa): the greeting is commodified (see Heller 2003) and for those who are not satisfied with the greeting itself as a souvenir, being able to buy it on a tangible object is the alternative offered. This is a common phenomenon in tourist contexts (Nassenstein 2019) and the expression's playful character adds to its economic value.

The second greeting that is frequent among tourists as shown in Table 2 is *mambo*. This is in line with the observations made during fieldwork. It is interesting since it is rather colloquial as emphasized by Ali. According to him, it could be considered slang and should only be used with people from one's own peer group (Mohr 2017, Ali; see also Nassenstein 2019). The fact that it is used by tourists reflects their lack of knowledge about and of Kiswahili and register differences within the language. Some hosts use it to greet tourists too, however. The fact that this greeting is used in tourist-host encounters might indicate that familiarity with the tourist is aimed at, with the ultimate goal of selling a good or service. This was also discussed for the participants in Lawson & Jaworski's study (2007), who did not like this attempted familiarity. In their Gambian setting, English was the language of choice, while for greetings in the present study pidginized Kiswahili is preferred. The tourists in Zanzibar might not have been put off by the implied familiarity between the interlocutors because they did not notice the colloquial nature of the expression. This would make the choice of Kiswahili a clever business strategy in line with the commodified nature of many interactions. However, *mambo* seems to imply better language knowledge among tourists than *jambo* for some Zanzibari interlocutors, as it was observed several times that the use of *mambo* by a tourist was reacted to with a flood of other greetings and questions. *Jambo* on the other hand was often followed by the English *how are you?* or an offer of a good or service.

Another greeting that was mentioned in different spellings by the tourists is *habari (yako)*. It can be used with all kinds of interlocutors, mostly from the same age group. Ali classifies it as "good Swahili", similar to *salama* (see Table 2) (Mohr 2017, Ali). The fact that these greetings are only mentioned once each emphasizes that most tourists do not seem to know 'good' Kiswahili. *Asante sana* underscores this as it is not a greeting but a thanking formula.

As outlined here, Kiswahili is dominant in greetings as used by tourists, albeit in touristified, pidginized forms as used by both tourists and hosts, stemming from the lack of knowledge of and about Kiswahili among the tourists (Mohr 2019). This frequency of Kiswahili in greetings is much in contrast to the self-reported language choices of both tourists and hosts for communication in general as outlined in Section 4.1 (see also Mohr 2019). It emphasizes the special status of greetings in the tourist context (Jaworski 2009), but it also raises the question as to why this difference exists. One reason seems to be the commodified nature of greetings, and their performative function of displayed multilingualism, which is common in tourist spaces (Heller 2003; Jaworski 2015).

4.3 Interaction beyond greetings

The performative function that greetings fulfill became especially apparent when considering different types of spaces in which communicative interactions take place. In enclosed spaces, it could be observed that the staff in hotels, restaurants, and bars usually greeted guests in English, sometimes preceded or followed by Kiswahili *karibu* 'welcome'. This was irrespective of the location and price level of the establishment. English is usually not the language Zanzibaris identify with (see Sections 4.1 and 4.4). When greeted in Kiswahili by a tourist entering a restaurant or hotel, staff usually did not reply, or replied in English. This is in line with all hotel staff interviewed stating that the most frequently used language for greeting tourists is also English. Practically, the use of English in greetings and front office matters is enforced. Thus, Diamonds Hotel has English skills as a prerequisite for hiring their front office staff as outlined by the manager. Greetings are executed according to the hotel's own brand standard, which is English. This could be confirmed by observations of their security personnel who used an English greeting adjusted to the time of day and the phrase *how are you today?* every time they were observed. Taarab Hotel and Tanzania Hotel seemed to have similar policies, albeit without brand standards. Altogether, this is in line with Nassenstein's (2016: 121) observation that hotel staff in Kenya usually use more formal language with guests as they have to present themselves differently than beach boys, for instance. The same seems to apply in Zanzibar: the hotel and restaurant staff (are required to) represent a certain professional and social persona, which is closely linked to language choices in general (see Jaworski & Thurlow 2010).

Despite the preferred use of English in greetings, the use of Kiswahili was in fact encouraged for interaction with staff once inside an enclosed space, by providing translations of 'important words' into Kiswahili on menus, for instance. An example from Seaweed Hotel's restaurant is provided in Figure 3.

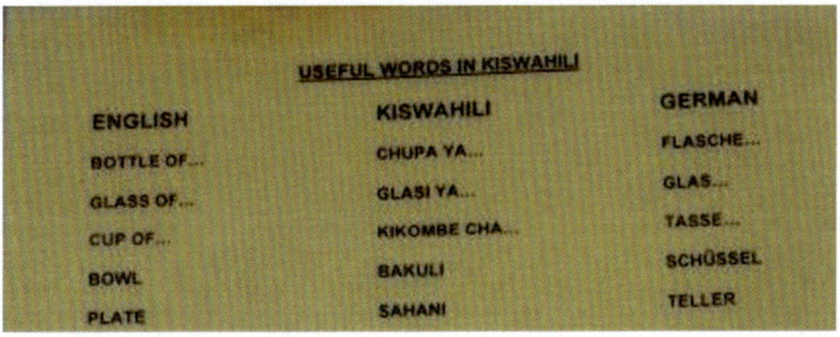

USEFUL WORDS IN KISWAHILI		
ENGLISH	KISWAHILI	GERMAN
BOTTLE OF...	CHUPA YA...	FLASCHE...
GLASS OF...	GLASI YA...	GLAS...
CUP OF...	KIKOMBE CHA...	TASSE...
BOWL	BAKULI	SCHÜSSEL
PLATE	SAHANI	TELLER

Figure 3. Kiswahili translations of "useful words" on a menu at Seaweed Hotel

Kiswahili skills were encouraged during ordering too, i.e., during the transactional part of an encounter. A group of tourists at Zanzibar City Restaurant placed their order in a mix of Kiswahili and English, using Kiswahili numerals and English words for drinks and dishes: "moja coffee, moja tea na tatu cups", 'one coffee, one tea and three cups'. This is an interesting example of foreigner talk and shows the limited Kiswahili knowledge of the tourists, as agreement of the Kiswahili numerals with the nouns was not formed and word order reversed. In Kiswahili, the noun would precede the numeral, resulting in *vikombe vitatu*, lit. 'cups three' (for similar examples see Nassenstein 2019; Wockelmann 2020). Still, the waiting staff seemed to appreciate the effort and reacted in a friendly way.

The apparent difference in language choices in hotels and restaurants, preferring English for the opening part of encounters and some Kiswahili for transactional talk, confirms Duranti's (1997: 89) claim that greetings imply social personae. In restaurants and hotels, greetings have representational character and Zanzibaris seem to want to convey their professionalism using English. This is rather different from the connotations of the frequently used *jambo*, which plays a more important role in encounters in open spaces.

Open spaces in this study were the streets, mainly of Stone Town, where vendors display souvenirs, food, and drinks. This also includes the owners of small shops, who display a large part of their wares outside and who often sit there to talk to neighbors or passing tourists. Another service that is often sold in the street is guided tours or taxi rides. The beach is another open space where shop owners and beach boys sell souvenirs, snacks, drinks, and tours. Street vendors in Stone Town often did not greet tourists using any of the English or Kiswahili greetings mentioned above but called out *karibu* 'welcome' combined with a pointing gesture directed at their stalls. In this case, *karibu* fulfilled the function of a greeting, as it was supposed to move the shop owner and the tourists into mutual interactional space (Duranti 1997). It makes the commodified nature of this 'greeting' very apparent. Different from Lawson & Jaworski's (2007) investigation, where they argued that the initiation of friendly chats did not constitute a "ticket" for interaction in European terms, the intention of these vendors in Zanzibar is more obviously economic in nature. They invite tourists into their shops or to their stalls, with the clear intention of a transaction. The greeting thus seems to go beyond its phatic function, similar to the *where are you going?* greeting in Samoan (Duranti 1997).

The same holds true for (un)official tour operators offering their services in the street and on the beach. As many of them do not work for an official agency with an office, they need to sell their services by proactively approaching potential customers. As opposed to the street vendors, they usually did so by greeting the tourists *jambo*, often followed by phrases in different languages that might be the mother tongues of the tourists, such as German *alles klar*. As outlined in Section 4.1, guides often speak several European languages and Nassenstein (2016: 120) argues that his participants in Kenya did so to win the tourists' trust, and successfully sell their goods or service. If the Zanzibari hosts were not successful at guessing the tourists' mother tongue, they followed their greeting by *where are you from?*.

Finally, the same applies to the beach: vendors and beach boys in Nungwi, Paje, and Jambiani usually greeted tourists using *jambo*, followed by greetings in different languages, a case of displayed multilingualism typical of tourist spaces (Jaworski 2015). Another phrase described as "general phatic marker" by Nassenstein (2019) was ubiquitous, specifically in Nungwi, namely *hakuna matata*. This has been mentioned to be part of HMS too and has a similar history as *jambo* (see Bruner 2001). The more standard form would be *hakuna matatizo*, or in colloquial non-tourist related language *hakuna* or *hamna shida* (Nassenstein 2019: 136). However, as *hakuna matata* is known to most tourists due to its presence in Western popular culture, it is preferred over its more standard forms. The use of this phrase, similar to the fun *jambo*, conveys a relaxed lifestyle that fits perfectly into the tourists' holiday environment (Mohr 2019). It serves to initiate a friendly conversation, ultimately leading to the consumption of a good or service, stressing its commodified nature (Heller 2003). Like *karibu*, *hakuna matata* is not originally a greeting. It might be compared to English *how are you?* in that it is relatively ritualized in a greeting context. Importantly, it illustrates the function of Kiswahili greetings in the tourist space clearly. It represents its user as a certain social persona (relaxed) in a specific situational context (the beach), very different from hotels or restaurants where the staff must use English.

Generally, in interactions in open spaces, where customers must be acquired with greetings before any transaction can take place, Kiswahili seems to function as a promotional feature (see Jaworski 2015), selling the host's service and closely linking it to Zanzibar as a tourist space. The choice of expressions that are not originally greetings and the different speech acts they are associated with emphasize this commodification of language even more (see also Heller 2003).

The English greetings in enclosed spaces like restaurants or hotels seem to serve as markers of professionalism. They are not needed to acquire customers, who have already chosen to consume a certain service or good there. For the transaction itself however, Kiswahili is appreciated, possibly emphasizing Zanzibari culture as an important part of the tourist experience.

Altogether, this section has shown that language choices are not only influenced by the part of an interaction (greetings vs. further interaction) as outlined in Section 4.2 but also by the nature of the space (open vs. enclosed) where a communicative interaction takes place. In enclosed spaces, English is preferred in greetings while Kiswahili is encouraged in further transactions such as ordering. This is different in open spaces, where Kiswahili greetings are more prominent and used to acquire customers, who then interact with hosts in English. Besides the enactment of social personae, this type of language use also authenticates the Zanzibari tourist space.

4.4   Zanzibari English(es)?

As the previous sections have shown, English is closely intertwined with the many languages it comes into contact with in the tourist space of Zanzibar. This applies especially to the local language Kiswahili, as shown here and in previous research (Mohr 2019, 2021a, b; Storch 2018; Wockelmann 2020). HMS seems to merge with English in some spaces and situations, rendering a distinct Zanzibari variety different from English on the mainland. At the same time, it possibly adds "authenticity"[6] (Jaworski 2015) to Zanzibar as a holiday destination. It has also become apparent that general competence in English is higher and its use more frequent than in mainland Tanzania, and perhaps also as compared to tourism on the mainland. The first is underscored by the interview data, in which Abdalla, for

---

6. "Authenticity" is put in quotation marks here to indicate that the concept is problematic in tourist contexts because it is part of the performance and staging of the destination (see also Jaworski 2015). It is beyond the scope of the chapter to discuss this in detail, however.

instance, claims that there is no connection with English in the streets of mainland cities like Dar es Salaam (Mohr 2017, Abdalla 1). The latter would need to be confirmed by dedicated studies on this topic (see also Mohr et al. 2020; Schneider 2016 on English in touristic areas). It was also shown here that the use of English is differently motivated in different participants in the tourist space, such as practicality or expressing specific social personae.

A question that has not been addressed thus far is the possibility of a — or several — Zanzibari Englishes. This would include the presence and usage of distinctive linguistic features and practices on the one hand (linguistic developments and structural effects in Schneider's 2007 model), and an awareness of and identification with Zanzibari English among its speakers on the other (sociolinguistics of use and attitudes in the model). With regard to specific language practices, the systematic use of various greetings and interactional routines was demonstrated in Sections 4.2 and 4.3. Moreover, Mohr (2021b) analyzed the use of the discourse markers *you know* and *I think* among Zanzibaris. The study concluded that based on the data (which was the same as the data used for this chapter), it is difficult to determine the variety status of English as used by Zanzibaris clearly. However, there are several indications of an English as a lingua franca (ELF) type (Mohr 2021b), and no distinct, Zanzibari variety.

Secondly, a closer look at awareness of and identification with a supposed Zanzibari English variety suggests itself. In Example (1), Abdalla said that he thinks his English is not fluent and that many Zanzibaris do not speak the language well, thus demonstrating his attitude towards English as used by Zanzibaris. This perception of own language skills is corroborated by the interview with Ali, who claimed that he is still learning the language (Mohr 2017, Ali). The perception of and attitude towards other Zanzibaris' skills seems to focus on spoken language, as mentioned again by Abdalla, saying that Zanzibaris "cannot speak" (Mohr 2017, Abdalla 1).

This is similar to what Mohr (2018) describes in terms of domains of English usage on the mainland, where English is often restricted to official, written language-based contexts. At the same time, spoken English must be and is used by hosts in the Zanzibari tourist space, but only by a group of people that can afford paying for additional, extramural tuition in English (Mohr 2021a). Interestingly, this situation does not seem to have existed forever, as Abdalla describes in (4).

(4) Abdalla, Stone Town
Abdalla: in zanzibar we are very poor in english not not not before because uh duri-during colonial time the actual zanzibaris they are studying with uh same uh syllabus with cambridge [...] if you go to our fathers uh forefathers the english they speak it was <SMACKING SOUND> and but now is very poor very poor
(2017, Abdalla 1 #45:36-46:00#)

Chapter 11. The Zanzibari tourist space as a multilingual language ecology

As can be seen here, some Zanzibaris seem to feel that there has been a decline in English standards since colonial times – this is underscored by Abdalla mentioning in a second interview that standards were much higher when there were still more native speaker teachers around or when Zanzibaris got scholarships to go to Britain to learn English (Mohr 2017, Abdalla 2). This exonormative orientation towards native English-speaking cultures or native English speakers in general is typical of EFL contexts, as speakers often demonstrate a certain norm-dependency that would be less present in a second language environment.

Some of the reasons for choosing English (or Kiswahili) were touched upon in Section 4.1. They are related to the attitudes of Zanzibaris towards English: it is generally not perceived as a language that they identify with, as Kiswahili fulfills that function. Abdalla claims that this is due to little English culture being present in Zanzibar anymore (see Example (5)), again relating to a certain nostalgia with regard to colonial times and possibly another indication of linguistic norm-dependency.

(5) Abdalla, tour guide and part time lecturer, Stone Town
Abdalla: language always [...] is attached <BEATING BENCH> with the with the culture <BEATING BENCH> [...] of people with their life <BEATING BENCH> with the history <BEATING BENCH> [...] like if if i be more in english than i i'd be attached with more, english things   (2017, Abdalla 2 #17:39-18:04#)

Kiswahili, however, has strong identity-providing function in Zanzibar, where "we are prouding of the language", as Abdalla says (Mohr 2017, Abdalla 2 #10:13#). This is different from mainland Tanzania, where Blommaert (2014) claimed that Kiswahili does not fulfill that same identity providing function, at least not on a national level. Thus, attitudes towards Kiswahili differ between the mainland and Zanzibar, too. English can be an object of pride in Zanzibar too, but this is rather limited to educational contexts and the related upward social mobility granted by English securing good chances on the job market. This is corroborated by the interview with Maburuki, in which he links English to book knowledge:

(6) Maburuki, tour guide, Stone Town
Maburuki: i like english because i have so many books every time i read books so

Interviewer: okay [...] but are there books in, there are books in [...] swahili i know

Maburuki: swa- yeah there are swahili books but i prefer english book-
     (2017, Maburuki #08:44-08:56#)

Abdalla, too, states that learning English in school made him feel like he was "actually" studying (Mohr 2017, Abdalla 2), a statement that emphasizes the strong link of the language with education, books, and its status as a language of the public domain. Altogether, the attitudes towards English and the lack of identification with it outlined here suggest that there is no communal sense of a Zanzibari English, similar to what has been found for mainland Tanzanian English (Babaci-Wilhite 2010; Bwenge 2012; Mohr 2018). In this regard, Zanzibar does not seem to be different from mainland Tanzania and the English spoken there, respectively. However, there are distinct differences in the use of English and its features (incorporation of pidginized Kiswahili, specific greeting formulae), which do suggest that Englishes as spoken in mainland Tanzania and in Zanzibar are in fact different.

5. Conclusion

This chapter explored English as it is used in tourist spaces on the Zanzibar archipelago. As was shown based on the various types of ethnographic data employed, English co-exists with many different languages used by the local hosts, i.e., first and foremost Kiswahili, and the various languages spoken by the tourists. This results in highly diverse repertoires and a highly multilingual language ecology, in which the term "English as a multilingua franca" (Jenkins 2015) is very apt. Focusing on language choices and motivations for them, it was outlined that English is the default choice as means of communication in the tourist space, usually for practical reasons and to fulfill social roles associated with the tourist industry. The commodification of language plays an important role as well. This becomes even more evident in the analysis of greetings and subsequent communicative interactions, where English serves as status marker for more expensive establishments and as marker of professionalism for their staff, while Kiswahili or HMS greetings identify hosts and their establishments as less expensive and lower in status. The tourists' foreign languages also feature as status symbols in this context (see also Nassenstein 2016). HMS greetings are mostly used in spaces where customers need to be acquired — this is not the case in expensive establishments in enclosed spaces where customers have already chosen to consume a good or service. In less formal spaces, HMS emphasizes a tourism imaginary (Salazar 2012) of Zanzibar and its culture, i.e., a romanticized and simplified image of the archipelago, that tourists with little to no knowledge of Zanzibar, its culture and language practices, maintain. It provides exactly the right amount of "authenticity" and exoticism, which do not alienate tourists (see also Bruner 2001).

English as a multilingua franca with a distinct Zanzibari character due to HMS might qualify as one — or several — distinct variety/ies of English based on Schneider's (2007) model. Usage patterns of the language and the number of speakers were also shown to be different, i.e., there is more widespread competence as compared to mainland Tanzania. However, attitudes towards and identification with English in Zanzibar among the participants of this study still imply that Zanzibari English(es) are not a significant part of Zanzibaris' identities and there does not seem to be a "Zanzibari English" acknowledged in its own right. There is still a certain nostalgia associated with English competence during colonial times, which is indicative of an exonormative orientation of speakers. This is in line with previous claims that English(es) spoken in Zanzibar (Mohr 2021b) might be ELF varieties.

All of the data presented here then indicates that English(es) as spoken in Zanzibar are not easily classifiable as a second language variety, a label that has, inappropriately, often been used for Tanzanian English. Some characteristics point towards an ELF or EFL variety, but other labels, like "grassroots English", have been discussed as well (Mohr 2021a, b). In line with Mohr (2021a), I maintain that an unequivocal classification of Zanzibari English(es) might not be possible,[7] nor is it in fact desirable. Rather, in a highly multilingual space like the tourist space of Zanzibar, it is important to document English(es), their use and motivations for that usage, attitudes towards the variety/ies and possible features, especially those emerging from language contact, in order to comprehend the dynamics of this, and possibly other Englishes, in their multilingual ecologies.

Funding

The fieldwork for this project was funded by a research grant from the North Rhine-Westphalian Academy of Sciences, Humanities and the Arts, and by a Feodor-Lynen grant from the Alexander von Humboldt Foundation.

Acknowledgements

I would like to thank all my participants, who took the time to answer my questions. I am deeply indebted to Abdulsatar Ali Mohammed who showed me around Stone Town and introduced me to many people. Judith Rauland and Sarah Lapacz deserve mention for their help with transcribing the interview data.

---

7. Especially not based on data stemming from a qualitative study like the present one.

Transcription conventions

<Sx>	beginning of speaker's turn
</Sx>	end of speaker's turn
(text)	uncertain transcription
@	laughter
,	brief pause (2–3 sec.)
.	longer pause (3–4 sec.)
[text]	overlapping speech
[...]	Speech not relevant for the analysis and left out
<CAPITALS>	non-speech related but relevant information, for example background noise, tone of voice etc.

References

Babaci-Wilhite, Zehlia. 2010. Why is the choice of the language of instruction in which students learn best seldom made in Tanzania? In Zubeida Desai, Martha Qorro & Birgit Brock-Utne (eds.), *Educational Challenges in Multilingual Societies*, pp. 281–305. Cape Town: African Minds.

Blommaert, Jan. 2010. *The Sociolinguistics of Globalization*. Cambridge: Cambridge University Press.

Blommaert, Jan. 2014. *State Ideology and Language in Tanzania* 2nd edn. Edinburgh: Edinburgh University Press.

Blommaert, Jan & Ad Backus. 2011. Repertoires revisited: 'Knowing language' in superdiversity. *Working Papers in Urban Language & Literacies* 67: 1–26.

Brock-Utne, Birgit & Martha Qorro. 2015. Multilingualism and language in education in Tanzania. In Androula Yiakoumetti (ed.), *Multilingualism and Language in Education: Current Sociolinguistic and Pedagogical Perspectives from Commonwealth Countries*, pp. 19–30. Cambridge: Cambridge University Press.

Bruner, Edward M. 2001. The Maasai and the Lion King: Authenticity, nationalism, and globalization in African tourism. *American Ethnologist* 24(4): 881–908.

Bwenge, Charles. 2012. English in Tanzania: A linguistic cultural perspective. *International Journal of Language, Translation and Intercultural Communication* 1(1): 167–182.

Dann, Graham S. 1996. *The Language of Tourism. A Sociolinguistic Perspective*. Wallingford, Oxon: CAB International.

Duranti, Alessandro. 1997. Universal and culture-specific properties of greetings. *Journal of Linguistic Anthropology* 7(1): 63–97.

Eberhard, David M., Gary F. Simons & Charles D. Fennig (eds.). 2023. *Ethnologue: Languages of the World*, 26th edn. Dallas, TX: SIL International. https://www.ethnologue.com/ (3 February 2023).

Haugen, Einar. 1972. The ecology of language. In Anwar S. Dil (ed.,) *The Ecology of Language. Essays by Einar Haugen*, pp. 325–339. Stanford, CA: Standford University Press.

Heller, Monica. 2003. Globalization, the new economy, and the commodification of language and identity. *Journal of Sociolinguistics* 7(4): 473–492.

Isingoma, Bebwa. 2017. Languages in East Africa: Policies, practices and perspectives. *Sociolinguistic Studies* 10(3): 433–454.

Jaworski, Adam. 2009. Greetings in tourist-host encounters. In Nikolas Coupland & Adam Jaworski (eds.), *The New Sociolinguistics Reader*, pp. 662–679. Houndmills: Palgrave Macmillan.

Jaworski, Adam. 2015. Welcome. Synthetic personalization and commodification of sociability in the linguistic landscape of global tourism. In Bernard Spolsky, Ofra Inbar-Lourie & Michal Tannenbaum (eds.), *Challenges for Language Education and Policy. Making Space for People*, pp. 214–231. London: Routledge.

Jaworski, Adam & Crispin Thurlow. 2010. Language and the globalizing habitus of tourism: Toward a sociolinguistics of fleeting relationships. In Nikolas Coupland (ed.), *The Handbook of Language and Globalization*, pp. 255–286. Chichester: Wiley-Blackwell.

Jenkins, Jennifer. 2015. Repositioning English and multilingualism in English as a lingua franca. *Englishes in Practice* 2(3): 49–85.

Kachru, Braj B. 1985. Standard, codification and sociolinguistic realism: The English language in the Outer Circle. In Randolph Quirk & H. G. Widdowson (eds.), *English in the World: Teaching and Learning the Language and Literatures*, pp. 11–30. Cambridge: Cambridge University Press.

Kamwangamalu, Nkonko M. & Alla Tovares. 2016. English in language ideologies, attitudes, and educational practices in Kenya and South Africa. *World Englishes* 35(3): 421–439.

Keshodkar, Akbar. 2013. *Tourism and Social Change in Post-Socialist Zanzibar*. Plymouth: Lexington Books.

Lawson, Sarah & Adam Jaworski. 2007. Shopping and chatting: Reports of tourist-host interactions in The Gambia. *Multilingua* 26: 67–93.

Lawson, Sarah & Itesh Sachdev. 2000. Codeswitching in Tunisia: Attitudinal and behavioural dimensions. *Journal of Pragmatics* 32(9): 1324–1361.

Legère, Karsten & Tove Rosendal. 2015. National languages, English and social cohesion in East Africa. In Hywel Coleman (ed.), *Language and Social Cohesion in the Developing World*, pp. 75–91. Colombo: British Council/Deutsche Gesellschaft für Internationale Zusammenarbeit.

Lorenz, Steffen. 2019. Living with Language. An Exploration of Linguistic Practices and Language Attitudes in Gulu, Northern Uganda. P.h.D. dissertation. University of Cologne.

Meierkord, Christiane, Bebwa Isingoma & Saudah Namyalo (eds.). 2016. *Ugandan English. Its Sociolinguistics, Structure and Uses in a Globalising Post-Protectorate*. Amsterdam: John Benjamins.

Möhlig, Wilhelm J. G. 1995. Swahili Dialekte. In Gudrun Miehe & Wilhem J. G. Möhlig (eds.), *Swahili Handbuch*, pp. 41–62. Cologne: Köppe.

Mohr, Susanne. 2017 (collection date). *Language Repertoires in Tourism in Zanzibar. Unpublished Corpus of (Transcriptions of) Interviews*. Bonn: University of Bonn.

Mohr, Susanne. 2018. The changing dynamics of language use and language attitudes in Tanzania. *Language Matters: Studies in the Languages of Africa* 49(3): 105–127.

Mohr, Susanne. 2019. Assembling concourse material and selecting Q-samples on the sociolinguistics of tourism discourse in Zanzibar. *Operant Subjectivity* 41(1): 65–82.

Mohr, Susanne. 2020. The "I" in sociolinguistics: The role of subjectivity in ethnographic fieldwork. *The Mouth. Critical Studies on Language, Culture and Society* 6: 101–118.

Mohr, Susanne. 2021a. English language learning trajectories among Zanzibaris working in tourism. In Christiane Meierkord & Edgar. W. Schneider (eds.), *World Englishes at the Grassroots*, pp. 70–90. Edinburgh: Edinburgh University Press.

Mohr, Susanne. 2021b. You know and I think in English(es) in Zanzibar. *World Englishes* 40(4): 534–547.

Mohr, Susanne. 2022. *Nominal Pluralization and Countability in African Varieties of English*. New York, NY: Routledge.

Mohr, Susanne, Steffen Lorenz & Dunlop Ochieng. 2020. English, national and local linguae francae in the language ecologies of Uganda and Tanzania. *Sociolinguistic Studies* 14(3): 371–394.

Nassenstein, Nico. 2016. Mombasa's Swahili-based 'Coasti Slang' in a superdiverse space: languages in contact on the beach. *African Study Monographs* 37(3): 117–143.

Nassenstein, Nico. 2019. The Hakuna Matata Swahili: Linguistic souvenirs from the Kenyan Coast. In Angelika Mietzner & Anne Storch (eds.), *Language and Tourism in Postcolonial Settings*, pp. 130–156. Bristol: Channel View.

Pavlenko, Aneta. 2007. Autobiographic narratives as data in applied linguistics. *Applied Linguistics* 28(2): 163–188.

Pennycook, Alastair. 2010. *Language as Local Practice*. London: Routledge.

Petzell, Malin. 2012. The linguistic situation in Tanzania. *Moderna Språk* 106(1): 136–144.

Salazar, Noel. 2012. Tourism imaginaries: A conceptual approach. *Annals of Tourism Research* 39(2): 863–882.

Sarmento, João & Bradley Rink. 2016. Africa. In Jafar Jafari & Honggen Xiao (eds.), *Encyclopedia of Tourism*, Vol. 1, pp. 14–17. Cham: Springer.

Schmied, Joseph. 1991. *English in Africa*. London: Longman.

Schneider, Edgar W. 2007. *Postcolonial English. Varieties Around the World*. Cambridge: Cambridge University Press.

Schneider, Edgar W. 2016. Grassroots Englishes in tourism interactions: How many speakers acquire 'grassroots English' in direct interactions, and what this may mean to them, and perhaps to linguists. *English Today* 32(3): 2–10.

Storch, Anne. 2018. Linguistic landscapes of tourism – A case study from Zanzibar. In Klaus Beyer, Gertrud Boden, Bernhard Köhler & Ulrike Zoch (eds.), *Linguistics Across Africa. 40 Jahre Afrikanistik*. Köppe: Cologne.

Storch, Anne & Angelika Mietzner. 2021. *The Impact of Tourism in East Africa: A Ruinous System*. Bristol: Channel View.

Studying English as a Lingua Franca (SELF) project. 2009. *SELF Transcription Guide*. https://www2.helsinki.fi/sites/default/files/atoms/files/self_transcription_guide.pdf (17 February 2023).

Thurlow, Crispin & Adam Jaworski. 2003. Communicating a global reach: Inflight magazines as a globalizing genre in tourism. *Journal of Sociolinguistics* 7(4): 581–608.

Thurlow, Crispin & Adam Jaworski. 2010. *Tourism Discourse: Language and Global Mobility*. London: Palgrave MacMillan.

Thurlow, Crispin & Adam Jaworski. 2011. Banal globalization? Embodied actions and mediated practices in tourists' online photo sharing. In Crispin Thurlow & Kristine Mroczek (eds.), *Digital Discourse. Language in the New Media*, pp. 220–250. Oxford: Oxford University Press.

Thurlow, Crispin & Adam Jaworski. 2014. "Two-hundred ninety-four": Remediation and multimodal performance in tourist place-making. *Journal of Sociolinguistics* 18(4): 459–494.

Ulmer, Nico, Ntiokam Divine & Kerstin Wydra. 2023. Lost in translation? Tanzanian students' views on sustainability and language, and the implications for the pledge to leave no one behind. *International Journal of Sustainability in Higher Education* 24(7): 1381–1397.

Vuzo, Mwajuma. 2010. A comparative appraisal of teaching and learning resources in private primary schools in Tanzania: Implications for teaching and learning. In Zubeida Desai, Martha Qorro & Birgit Brock-Utne (eds.), *Educational Challenges in Multilingual Societies*, pp. 254–280. Cape Town: African Minds.

Wockelmann, Deborah. 2020. Language and tourism in Zanzibar: An analysis of Othering, authenticity and power relations in tourists' encounters. Special Issue of *The Mouth. Critical Studies of Language, Culture and Society* 3: 8–108.

CHAPTER 12

The sociolinguistics of English in the plurilingual ecology of Lagos (Nigeria)
A pilot study on class, ethnicity, and entrepreneurship

Henning Schreiber & Mirjam Möller Nwadigo
University of Hamburg | Lund University

Nigeria as a country is characterized by a highly diverse language ecology. In Nigerian mega-cities such as Lagos, English is the official language and dominant in media and education. Language attitudes and choices in Nigeria follow particular trends (Igboanusi 2008). However, language dominance patterns and the functional roles of Nigerian English varieties are still subject of research. Altogether, rather few sociolinguistic studies relate linguistic dominance of English in specific domains of urban settings and its relation to social transformation to social parameters from the perspective of urban ethnography. The paper presents results from an interview survey on English in Lagos among small and medium enterprises (SMEs) ($n = 43/+10$ test group) from the perspective of social factors, including class, ethnicity, and economic activity. Business is an omnipresent cultural theme in Nigeria and communication is one of the entrepreneurial skills needed for successful entrepreneurship in Nigeria (Inyang & Enuoh 2009). It is likewise the driving force behind social transformation and the emergence of social class identity. To determine the impact of sociolinguistic parameters on language choices, semi-randomly chosen participants located in Lagos were asked about their origin, social and economic status, business activities, and language attitudes towards English — in contrast to other Nigerian business languages. The study examines whether H varieties of English constitute a major factor in social transformation and entrepreneurial orientation and further provides insight into whether the SMEs sector of Lagos should be regarded as a domain in which 'levelled' English emerges continuously as a marker of an economic middle class, backgrounding origin and ethnicity.

Keywords: entrepreneurship, ethnicity, Lagos, language attitudes, Nigerian English, social class

https://doi.org/10.1075/hsld.9.12sch
Available under the CC BY-NC-ND 4.0 license.
© 2025 John Benjamins Publishing Company

1. Introduction

The current paper deals with language ecology and economy in one of the most challenging urban and culturally diverse settings of Africa, Lagos (Nigeria), with a particular focus on English varieties. The growing influence of English in Lagos seems to go hand in hand with urbanization, social transformations in the context of linguistic diversity, and plurilingualism. Although Lagos is still perceived as a Yoruba city, and Yoruba is one of the majority languages, its status as a lingua franca is questionable. English has without doubt the highest prestige and functional value of all languages in Lagos and is the global language in international business.

Nigerian English and Englishes in Nigeria are widely researched topics, and learner-varieties have been much studied at Nigerian universities. In the World Englishes framework, Nigerian Standard English (NSE) is regarded as a cluster of sub-varieties (Gut 2008) showing language contact from various autochthonous Nigerian languages ('indigenized Englishes'; Mufwene 2015). Corpus data of Nigerian varieties are made available in the Corpus of Nigerian English (ICE; Wunder, Voormann & Gut 2010). As argued in the literature, NSE has developed into a stable postcolonial variety and it is seen as being at the stage of endonormative stabilization (Ugorji 2015) in terms of the five-stage model of Schneider (2003, 2007) – although delimitation of NSE is still a matter of debate when it comes to common features of NSE (Gut 2012). However, the linear nature of the five-stage model is questioned in the literature. Given the high level of social complexity in African urban settings, it may well be assumed that different stages of NSE co-occur depending on the respective social and multilingual microecologies in Lagos. Fluidity and complexity may, moreover, be obscured by ethno-sociolinguistic categorizations, which are more often based on individual emblematic constructions than on isoglossic sets of linguistic traits. The perceived variation does likely differ from what is actually found in language corpora.

In the urban linguistic ecology of Lagos, NSE plays a central role in the domains of media, business, and administration. Due to the strong international networks of Nigerian elites, US and UK varieties are also present in the upper social milieus (Jowitt 2019: 33). Thus, NSE competes with the dominant languages Yoruba, Hausa, and Igbo across functional domains, but also with varieties of Nigerian Pidgin English (NPE). As shown by Deuber (2005), an 'educated' Nigerian Pidgin register has also emerged, which reflects the linguistic practices of the Lagos population. NPE spreads by linguistic solidarity (Schreiber, Odoje & Obot 2012/2017), and, in contrast to acrolectal NSE, NPE is an anti-language in Lagos' vibrant subculture and among students (Akande & Salami 2010). Nevertheless, language diversity and dominance patterns are distinct even within Lagos' Local

Government Areas (LGAs) due to differences in urbanization processes and settlement (see Adedun & Shodipe 2011).

What is certain is that economic success is by large the most pertinent factor in migration and urbanization, and communicative skills (in acrolectal English varieties, NSE, and RP) are seen as one major component in theories about entrepreneurial success. In the globalized world, general sociolinguistic trends and shifts in language repertoires are often driven or initiated by business. By the same token, social transformations are intrinsically connected to changes in the economy, although the question of social class transformation in Africa is controversially disputed. The strong economy of Lagos State is expected to create a large (lower) economic middle class and to attract many upward-oriented people engaged in all kinds of businesses (see also Section 2.3). Social transformations in the course of urbanization and the high degree of linguistic diversity would assign English a particular position in the linguistic ecology of Lagos. However, at the same time it seems that class consciousness is less pertinent for social identity construction, and traditional lifestyles and languages continue to play an important role in affluent traditional milieus. Like in other African metropolises, ethnicity maintains its important function of solidarity in an environment defined by social hardship. Moreover, the strong impact of ethnicity in Nigeria and the reported importance of ethnicity in entrepreneurial success in the area of trust and customer relations make the absolute dominance of English in the economy questionable. As a result, competition between ethnic languages and English varieties in the same sociolinguistic domain of economy is expected.

Research on language attitudes of entrepreneurs is thus of major interest in the study of language repertoires in highly urbanized settings. How people communicate and negotiate language, but also the symbolic value of language choices is of central interest to sociolinguistics. In this sense, the role and function of English in Lagos is somewhat unclear. In contrast to ethnic languages, it is not a shared language that could trigger trust by activation of an emotion of commonness for the great majority of people in business. Moreover, even if English has become a first language for many, it is not necessarily a language that binds people by common social belonging and triggers homophily (McPherson, Smith-Lovin & Cook 2001), a feeling of social "sameness". Concerning repertoires and choices on a broad scale, the question arises which parameters impact language use and "language work" in a given urban setting such as Lagos.

In this paper, we will include the emic perspectives (Pike 1967) with a focus on liberal language choices in the home and entrepreneur domain, in contrast to the domain of education in which status planning and persistent language ideologies restrict speakers in their repertoires. The argument will be that liberal choices better reflect the dynamics and current social and sociolinguistic changes.

The structure of the paper is as follows. The next section will give a general overview of Lagos, its linguistic ecology, and social stratification with a focus on linguistic diversity and English varieties in Lagos. In the second part, the questionnaire and research methodology are presented. The results of the data collection are presented in Section 3 followed by a discussion of some basic statistical correlations between aggregated factors that display entrepreneurial orientation, social status, success, and language attitudes of the participants in Section 4. The paper concludes with a summary and outlook to further research.

2. The setting: Lagos

The African mega-city Lagos (Nigeria) is characterized by a high level of social and ethnic diversity. Based on a projection of data from the 2006 census (Lagos State Bureau of Statistics 2013: 4), the population of Lagos state is estimated to be 23 million, the biggest urban population in Nigeria. The city, being Nigeria's central economic and commercial hub with 25 percent of Nigeria's GDP being generated there, is appealing to business and triggers labour mobility from all parts of Nigeria, West Africa, and Africa as a whole with such a strong economy. The pace of urbanization in Lagos is high and the search for economic success is the driving motor for incoming city dwellers. Consequently, Lagos' linguistic ecology is highly complex and dynamic in terms of internal sociolinguistic stratification (Schreiber, Odoje & Obot 2012/2017).

However, Lagos is less a city than a large urbanized area or urban agglomeration of 20 Local Government Areas (LGA), subdivisions of the state. Living standards and quality of infrastructure are highly stratified, as is the level of urbanization in Lagos' LGAs and the rate of ethno-linguistic diversity. Lagos' economy is equally dependent on LGAs, which show specific socio-economic features and different conditions for business and trade. For example, Apapa is known for its port, Ikeja is the administrative centre of Lagos State and therefore the capital of the state, and Eti-Osa has been referred to as the business and financial centre of Lagos state which shelters both domestic and international businesses in its area.

2.1 A brief note on Lagos' history and its languages ecologies

Nigerians belong to an estimated number of 500 different ethno-linguistic groups (Eberhard, Simons & Fennig 2023), most of which are represented in Lagos. Some individuals from minority groups may not permanently reside in Lagos, but travel to the urban area for jobs and business for a shorter or longer period of time. Nigerians also have a variety of religious beliefs and groups; the majority of them can be grouped belonging to either Christianity, Islam, or African Traditional Religion shaping linguistic repertoires. Ethnic and religious identities have often been the source of civil conflicts in history and they still are a political factor of major importance in Nigeria's democracy at present. Mixed with educational, economic and social inequalities among the ethnic and religious groups, the multilingual context of Nigeria as a whole is quite unique in its complexity.

Present-day Lagos is a conurbation that emerged out of a British colony on the ground of formerly Edo and Yoruba dominated settlements. Lagos' linguistic ecology is shaped by a complex settlement history, rapid urbanization, and integration of former hinterland towns into a metropolitan area. English in Lagos is, on the one hand, related to colonial expansion and more of the type of trade colonization (Mufwene 2001). Alhough speakers of British English were rather few, the installation of missionary education (CMS Schools) and the need to recruit clerks working for the colonial administration likely integrated English into the early ecology in the Lagos Island settlements in particular. On the other hand, NSE should also be viewed from the perspective of globalization. Since colonial times, and to a large extent in recent decades, migration has further brought English varieties to Lagos from all over Nigeria and other African countries, such as Ghana. The history of English in Lagos is perhaps much more impacted by a 'migration strand' than by other factors.

Moreover, Dominant Language Constellations (Aronin 2019) in present Lagos differ at large from one LGA to another. The formerly independent town of Mushin, for example, hosts predominantly Yoruba speakers. Other LGAs are more multi-ethnic and include large communities of heritage language speakers like the Hausa inhabitants in Agege, who have their own traditional Hausa ruler, "Sarkin Hausawa of Agege" (Tijani 2008). The ethnic profiles of LGAs are also related to economic activities. Agege is known as the centre for kolanut trade, while local commercial enterprises are prominent in Mushin, which also hosts a large marketplace of agricultural products ('food stuff'). Commercial activities are connected to modern constructs of ethnicity. According to some common stereotypes, people from the Niger Delta are active in motor-business, Hausa do trade and agricultural commerce. These 'ethno-economic' constructs impact also Dominant Language

Constellations, as such economic specializations must be regarded as sociolinguistic domains. However, English seems to be an integral part of all LGA ecologies.

Regarding contact-induced variation, proficiency in NSE and the level of L1 interferences is related to different lengths of exposure to English in the education system (Gut & Fuchs 2013). Thereby, the impact of education on NSE variation can be roughly estimated by the factors of education quality and exposure, based on data for Lagos. As indicated by the Literacy report 2011 (Lagos State Government 2011: 10), literacy of household members in English stretches from 80 to 93 percent. The high level of informal English learning in some LGAs such as Badagry suggests, however, that learner varieties and NPE play also a dominant role in some settings. Moreover, ethnicity is likewise a factor in NSE variation and in phonology in particular (see Gut 2008).

In the literature (see Schreiber, Odoje & Obot 2012/2017), the presence of NPE is often motivated by the strong influx of people from Delta state where NPE creole communities live. Another view is that West African Pidgin English creole varieties (see Huber 1999; Peter & Wolf 2007) were likely present in an early period as Lagos attracted freed slaves and people from Sierra Leone ('Sarro') who settled in the quarter of Olowogbowo and formed part of the local administrative elite. Afro-Latin Aguda ('Brasilians') of Popo Aguda, a group practising Catholicism and worshipping Afro-Latin Orishas with strong relations to Yoruba culture, likewise formed an early 'bourgeoise' speaking either Yoruba, Spanish, or Portuguese. However, creole English may have also played an important role in their repertoires as intermarriage between Spanish, Portuguese, and NPE speaking families occurred in the course of resettlements. The portion of Afro-Latin lexis in Nigerian Pidgin may be taken as linguistic evidence for the use of Nigerian Pidgin by Afro-Latin groups interacting with other elites like the Sarro. "Though Afro-Atlantic communities spoke in the idiom of locality, it was the transnational, polylingual nature of these conversations that allowed for their distinct modes of perpetuation and reinvention" (Otero 2010: vii). In Lagos' linguistic ecology, NSE is — at least by speakers — distinguished from American (AE) and British English (BE), which are very present due to global media consumption and by strong personal relationships to the diaspora in the UK and the US (see Awonusi 1994).

In sum, the level of diversity of English varieties in Lagos is assumedly rather high. From the acrolectal to the basilectal level, all kinds of Englishes, distinct stable varieties, fossilised learner language, and ethnic 'lects', stand in sociolinguistic competition and in contact with each other. Yet, most upward-oriented people coming to Lagos are Nigerians. Many who engage as entrepreneurs in the SMEs sector use NSE on a daily basis but come from different educational backgrounds. As English proficiency becomes a form of communication capital, the dominance of H varieties and dialect levelling of ethnic varieties are expected in the multilingual SMEs sector. However, very little is known empirically about English in Lagos as social capital and about language attitudes as a factor of entrepreneurial orientation.

2.2 English and entrepreneurship in Lagos

In this research, we relate theories about social transformation and entrepreneurial success with language attitudes and linguistic repertoires. Apart from the media and the educational setting, the work and business domain are another area in which linguistic accommodation but also negotiations of language attitudes occur, and language ideologies of personal success and language emerge.

Sociolinguistic theory and social capital theory (Clark 2006) somehow imply at first sight a rather self-evident high status of NSE and a dominance of English in entrepreneurship. English is generally regarded as an important asset for success in life and business. However, English must not necessarily create a feeling of sameness, common social belonging, and trust. Quality in education, mechanisms of social exclusion (Bamgbose 2000), migration as well as ethno-linguistic vitality may act as counter-effects to the spread of English in Lagos' linguistic ecology.

In the literature, communication in Nigerian work- and marketplaces has been the subject of several studies through the years (inter alia, Alo & Soneye 2014; Ayeni 2020, 2021; Ayoola 2009). These studies show that NSE does not dominate absolutely. Code-switching, or interlanguaging, are practiced to accommodate or distance oneself from the other. In the business world, the reasons for code mixing or switching vary with the role of the speaker. As a vendor, one reason for code mixing can be to accommodate and include the customer, whereas as a customer, the same speaker can use code mixing and switching to get a good bargain. This leads to the assumption that not proficiency as such, but an elaborate repertoire is needed. Although actual practices and required proficiencies will depend on the business setting and domain, mastering English is important for entrepreneurial success. However, the role of NSE, AE/BE, and NPE are not yet clear.

3. Project description and methods

The purpose of this pilot study was to collect data by interviews to gain insight in linguistic repertoires according to the interviewee's own assessment. Apart from this, the objective of the study was to do a test questionnaire which can be used to develop a more detailed questionnaire for a future study.

Lagos' population is diverse and a group such as middle-class entrepreneurs is very heterogeneous. The entrepreneurial domain is particularly interesting because it attracts people from all socioeconomic backgrounds and requires interaction across social class and ethnic groups. Therefore, the questionnaire includes questions from four sections/domains: the interviewee's living situation, their self-identity, their linguistic repertoire, and their business. The questions were designed to collect demographic data about the participants, either directly (for example age), or by asking for detailed single questions and statements which were later aggregated into scores like the entrepreneurial orientation score (see Section 3.2).

3.1 Socioeconomic background

The first section focuses on general questions concerning the person's origin, age, and residence in Lagos. As people's linguistic behaviour is influenced by many factors, e.g., socioeconomic background, education, ethnicity, among others, we needed to include questions that could indicate a person's socioeconomic status without relying on self-assessment of social status alone.

Economists traditionally measure middle class based on income. But there is no single definition of the middle class which applies to the middle class in developing countries. Measurement of socioeconomic status in developing countries is a much-debated issue in economic theory. Based on the researchers' ethnographic knowledge and on consensus analysis with people from Lagos, we therefore researched single specific living standard criteria (scaled) that are regarded as indicative of the middle class in Lagos. In order to get information about participants' socioeconomic background we inquired into their current living situation: whether they rent or own their accommodation, what they pay in rent, the size of their accommodation, if they live alone or with family, if they own an inverter/solar, have health insurance, own a car, and employ security staff. Then we also investigated their preferred means of transport among the following options: a private driver, drive yourself, use of taxi services (e.g., Uber, Bolt), use of *bus* (minibus), *keke* (motor-tricycle), or *okada* (motorbike-taxi). Each reply was assigned a score between 1 and 4 depending on the estimated cost of that specific feature. For statistical analysis, the data was then aggregated into a Living Standard Score (see Section 3.2).

3.2 Social and self-identity

Social belonging and self-identity, as strong motivating factors for language choice, affects a person's linguistic solidarity and their attitudes towards other languages. Moreover, common ethnicity creates trust and its impact on entrepreneurship is thus to be expected. We gave the interviewee the task to sort themselves into three categories using the following items: *Nigerian, Lagosian, my ethnic group, religious belonging*, or any *other* label. How interviewees rank their three preferred labels can indicate whether they prefer to identify as Nigerian or a Lagos metropolitan before their ethnic identity. In the same section we also asked the interviewee's own perception of social status, whether he/she perceives him/herself to belong to the lower middle-class, middle middle-class, upper middle-class, or any other preferred economic status category. We were not interested in an objective self-assessment of class, but we rather wanted to know about the interviewees' imagined class identity.

3.3 Educational background

This factor matters in regard to linguistic repertoire, as it can give an indication about a person's exposure to NSE. Thus, we included one question about whether the interviewee has a higher education diploma, has taken professional courses (e.g., training for a specific profession outside academic institutions), or has their A-level diploma.

3.4 Linguistic repertoire

The section focusing on the interviewee's linguistic repertoire determined what languages they speak and to what degree of proficiency, according to following descriptions: fluent, speaks it but not fluently, understands it, knows some phrases, does not speak it at all (see Figure 1). The interviewees were required to rank the language(s) they use with their immediate family or persons living in their household. Furthermore, the interviewees were asked what languages they use: with members of their extended family, in the neighbourhood, in their business, at church/mosque/religious activity, in the market, at the bank/office settings, with their house staff. In this pilot study we also wanted to get a hint of interviewees' attitudes towards NSE, NPE, as well as AE/BE. The questionnaire therefore included a number of statements to which the interviewee could agree, disagree or choose to answer neutral. For statistical analysis, language attitudes towards the varieties were later aggregated into a NSE Affinity score, AE/BE Affinity score, and NPE Affinity score. This section also included an open question about how the interviewee perceives the differences between NSE, NPE, and AE/BE.

Chapter 12. The sociolinguistics of English in the plurilingual ecology of Lagos 267

What language do you speak?	Fluently	I speak it but not fluently.	I understand it.	I know some phrases.	I don't speak it.
Nigerian English	☐	☐	☐	☐	☐
American/British English	☐	☐	☐	☐	☐
Nigerian Pidgin	☐	☐	☐	☐	☐
Yoruba	☐	☐	☐	☐	☐
Hausa	☐	☐	☐	☐	☐
Igbo	☐	☐	☐	☐	☐
Other	☐	☐	☐	☐	☐

Figure 1. Linguistic repertoire questions

3.5 Economic success and language use in business

One section aimed to answer questions about their business, the language(s) used in the business, and if linguistic repertoire, according to the interviewee, has had an impact on their business success. The first questions collected answers to: what type of business the interviewee owns, number of employees, what year they started, how much sales they make on average per year (not gain, just sales). Inspired by a model of the relationship between entrepreneurial orientation and business performance (Krauss et al. 2005), we chose two categories which can be applied to linguistic repertoire and business success: learning orientation and autonomy orientation. We included six statements to which the interviewee could agree, disagree or choose a neutral response. This section also gathered answers to what language(s) they use within the business and with whom: permanent staff, ad hoc employees, business partners, enterprise clients, private clients, dealers, and officials. In order to get a hint of interviewees' attitudes towards NSE, NPE, other Nigerian languages, as well as to AE/BE, we included six statements to which the interviewee could agree, disagree or choose a neutral response. The last question assembled answers to the open question: *How has learning different languages been important in your business?*

	Agree	Neutral	Disagree
Speaking several languages is important for business success in Nigeria.	☐	☐	☐
Speaking AE/BE helps me reach certain clients in my business.	☐	☐	☐
To not speak AE/BE would limit me in my business.	☐	☐	☐
Not speaking a Nigerian language has limited me in my business.	☐	☐	☐
I prefer hiring staff who in addition to NSE also speak AE/BE.	☐	☐	☐
Learning different languages has been important to my business success.	☐	☐	☐

Figure 2. Statements about linguistic repertoire in business

3.6 Data collection

The questionnaire was implemented online to offer participants the opportunity to participate on their own. The same schema was also used for data collection of telephone interviews. We collected data from 33 entrepreneurs through interview sessions conducted via telephone and recorded for future reference. In addition, we had 10 entrepreneurs who replied to the same questionnaire on their own. This resulted in 43 forms completed. The participants were selected by semi-random sampling through friends and contacts in Lagos, who then in turn provided other contacts in their network. The sampling process was therefore not entirely random but still avoided any bias of the interviewer in the selection process. We further collected data for a test group of 10 people living outside of Lagos in Yoruba-dominated adjacent states for the sake of comparison.

4. Results

In this section, we will first examine the descriptive statistical results and later discuss some correlations related to the rationale of the paper and data exploration. We will also highlight some results, which appear of particular interest to the research questions raised.

Among the 43 responses by 23 male and 20 female entrepreneurs, a majority, 27 participants, were from the age group 30–39 years, 9 participants were 40+, and

7 participants were of the age 20–29. Among the 43 responses, 19 described themselves as Igbo, 14 as Yoruba, and 10 as from other ethnic groups in Nigeria (e.g., Edo, Idoma, Itsekiri). However, none of the participants identified themselves as ethnic Hausa. We established three groups of ethnic belonging: Igbo, Yoruba, and a group of other 'Minorities'. Moreover, participants were from a total of 13 different states of origin, only 2 reported Lagos as their state of origin. When participants state their origin, they often refer to the state of their father. A person can be born in Lagos and still consider his state of origin as the origin where his father originally is from. All participants reside permanently in Lagos, in 11 different LGAs, but a majority, 26 participants, reside in Oshodi-Isolo.

4.1 Living situation and education

When asked about their own socio-economic group, a majority (30) responded that they identify as 'middle class'. How the majority of the participants identify as middle class corresponds to some extent with their living standards, although some participants may have a perception of belonging to a higher or lower section of middle class than the score they got in this study suggests. Participants were also asked to choose among the 'preferred identity' labels: Nigerian, Lagosian, Ethnic group, religious identity, or other. In the sample, 23 participants chose to describe themselves firstly as 'Nigerian'. As a second option, 17 participants identify as their ethnic belonging. As a third option, 13 participants chose to describe themselves with their religious identity. Moreover, only 18 participants describe themselves as Lagosians (see Figure 3).

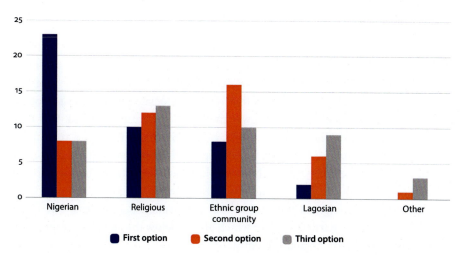

Figure 3. Rankings of participants' identity as Nigerian, ethnic group, religious group, and other

Concerning education, a majority of participants (30) have a higher education degree. 6 participants had taken professional training whereas 3 had stopped their education at A-levels and 4 participants had stopped after completing their O-level (see Figure 4).

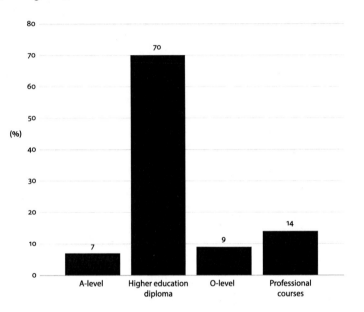

Figure 4. Educational background among the participants

4.2 Linguistic repertoire

Concerning the language use and proficiencies, all participants report that they are highly proficient in NSE.[1] 32 participants report that they are fluent in NPE, whereas 10 participants report that they do not speak it well. The reported lower competence in NPE compared to NSE could possibly be influenced by the low status associated with NPE. The fact that NPE is associated with lower socioeconomic background could result in fewer participants wanting to admit that they are proficient in speaking NPE. However, both NSE and NPE play a role in the participants' repertoire. Moreover, 33 participants report that they are also competent in one of the three official Nigerian languages. A total of 10 participants reports not speaking any of the three official Nigerian languages: Hausa, Igbo, and Yoruba. 12 participants report that they are proficient in at least one other Nigerian language. 5 participants (of which all are below the age of 40) report not speaking any Nigerian language fluently.

---

1. One could expect that some participants reported that they speak NSE, but not quite fluently.

Chapter 12. The sociolinguistics of English in the plurilingual ecology of Lagos   271

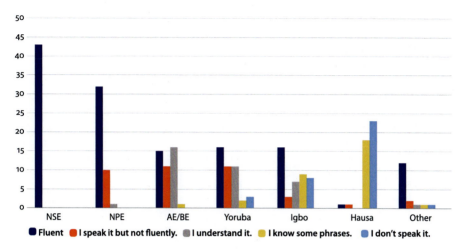

Figure 5. Language dominance among the participants

4.2.1 Home language

When participants report on the languages they speak at home, it is clear that NSE is the dominant first language. 21 participants report NSE as their first language at home, of which 4 participants report it as their only language at home. The 4 participants that reportedly speak NPE as their first language at home are from the states Abia, Anambra, and Edo. Interestingly, there are 10 participants that state using Yoruba as their first language at home, whereas only 3 participants reportedly use Igbo as their first home language, and only 4 indicate using another Nigerian language as their first language at home. The fact that Lagos is a city indigenous to the Yorubas, making Yoruba one if not the most dominant Nigerian languages in the state, could be a reason why Yorubas find it easier to speak their mother tongue at home compared to speakers of other Nigerian languages.

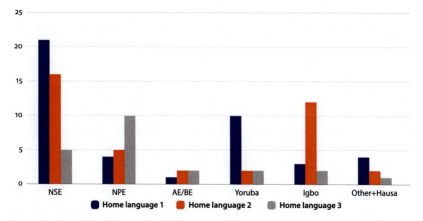

Figure 6. Language dominance at home

The participants were also asked to testify about different contexts in which they chose to use the languages in their repertoire. A majority indicates NSE as their preferred language choice within all contexts. NPE is the preferred choice only in the marketplace.

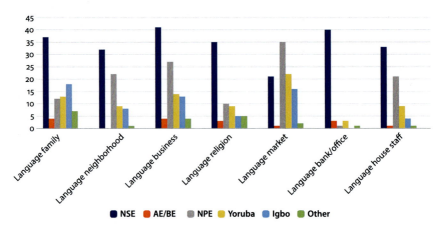

Figure 7. What language is used in different domains

As shown in Figure 6, only 15 participants described themselves as competent in AE/BE. Although 28 participants admit that they are not proficient in AE/BE, only 5 agree with the statement that they *lack confidence when speaking AE/BE*. Moreover, 21 participants agree with the statement that individuals who speak AE/BE are educated, while only 9 agree with the statement that *I respect people who speak AE/BE more than I respect individuals who don't*. Although 21 participants associate *AE/BE* with higher education, 30 participants disagree with showing more respect to a person based on them using AE/BE.

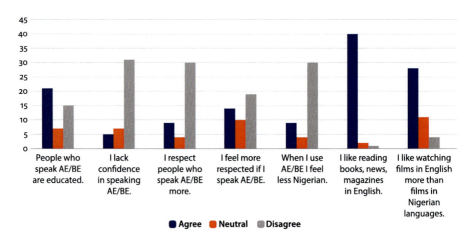

Figure 8. Statements about AE/BE

4.2.2 Language in business and entrepreneurship

Among the different categories of businesses that participants are engaged in, a majority (26) is engaged in buying and selling goods. The duration of how long the participants have been into entrepreneurship varies from 2 to 20 years. 18 of the participants reported that they started their business before 2015, another 9 participants started theirs between 2015 and 2018, while 16 participants started their business in 2019.

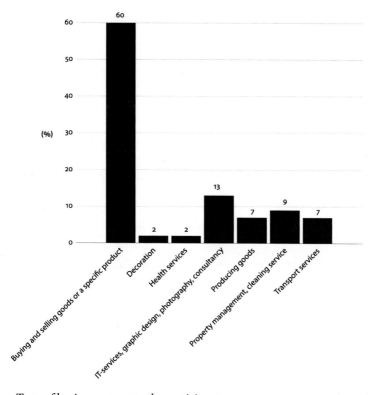

Figure 9. Type of businesses among the participants

The average sales per year for the majority does not exceed 5 million Nigerian Naira. The average sales in a business are affected by what type of goods you sell or what services are offered. Another indication for long-term growth and success can be the number of persons that a business employs as permanent staff. Half of the participants (22) reported having none or only one employee. 15 participants reported having 2–5 employees, and 6 participants reported having 7–10 employees. The low average of sales per year along with the fact that the businesses employ none or a low number of permanent staff, reflect that the businesses are smaller businesses.

In measuring the participants' entrepreneurial orientation and autonomy, we asked them whether they agreed or disagreed with five statements relating to independence versus collaboration, willingness to take on a salary job or not, etc. 21 participants report that they would not take a salary job even if they were paid well. This indicates that there are other factors for having a business besides making a living. Such factors could be, e.g., time-management, independence, and that these entrepreneurs are motivated by opportunity rather than necessity only.

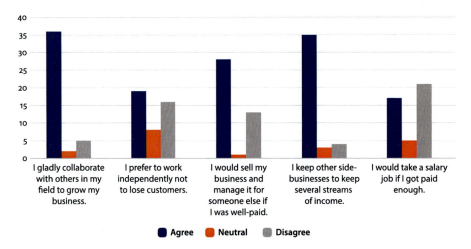

Figure 10. Entrepreneurial orientation

Regarding language dominance in economic activities, first, second, and third language are reportedly used in their business. A majority (32) reports NSE as their first and main language used.

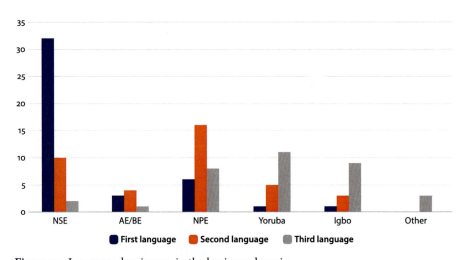

Figure 11. Language dominance in the business domain

Chapter 12. The sociolinguistics of English in the plurilingual ecology of Lagos   275

When asked about what language the participants use in different contexts relating to their business there is a clear preference for using NSE across all contexts. However, when dealing with providers and private clients, NPE is viewed as an option by half of the participants.

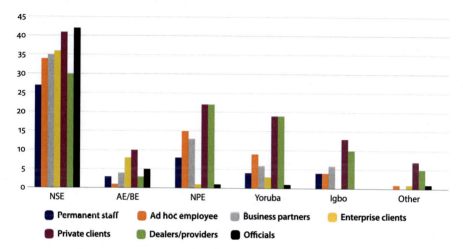

Figure 12. Language dominance in business contexts

Participants were lastly asked to relate to six statements concerning the importance of language learning in relation to business in Lagos. A majority (36) agrees that speaking several languages is important for business in Lagos. And a majority (28) agrees that not speaking AE/BE does not limit them in their business relations.

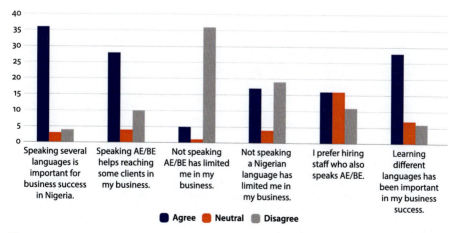

Figure 13. Statements on importance of language learning

4.3 Data aggregation

In multivariate studies, multiple testing of various independent variables on one dependent factor must be avoided. Principal Component Analysis and clustering are statistical techniques to reduce the number of and to show inherent relationships between independent variables. However, principal components are sometimes hard to interpret. Variable aggregation is a qualitative approach to reduce the number of analyses and a way to avoid type-1 errors. Based on the original data, we have aggregated single responses into scores and established groupings based on empirical distributions.

The Living Standard Score (LSTSc) aggregates scaled data from different questions about the participants' socioeconomic status into a standard of living score. Each reply to questions (see Table 1) was assigned a score between 1–4 depending on the estimated cost of that specific feature.

Table 1. Scores given for each living standard factor

Living situation	#	Annual rent	#	Living standards	#	Transport	#
Own an apartment/house	4	1 million+	3	Employ security staff	4	Private driver	4
Live within an estate	4	500k–1 million	2	Health insurance	3	Drive yourself	3
2 bedroom +	3	Below 500k	1	Own an inverter/solar	2	Using taxi services	2
1 bedroom flat	1			Own a car	2	Keke/Okada/Bus	1
Live alone	3						
Live with family	2						

This measure follows a normal distribution (mean = 16, SD = 4.95; Shapiro-Wilks: W = 0.97313, p-value = 0.40). Based on this observation, we divided the total score of the participants into three sub-groups (corresponding to the self-assessments): 16 participants scored 8–13 (below 33%), 16 participants scored 14–18 (below 66%), and 11 participants scored 19–28 (below 100%). In the test group, the scores are expectedly much lower, and 6 persons are classified as lower (5.7), one as middle (7.9), and 3 as upper middle class (9.16). As shown in Figures 11 and 12, the groupings between self-assessed social status and the three groups derived from the living standard score overlap only partly.

The Entrepreneurial Orientation Score (EOSc) aggregates data based on the participants' replies. We gave each participant a score reflecting their entrepreneurial orientation. The empirical distribution is not normal (mean = 6.7, SD = 2.04). For further analysis, we categorized the participants into four groups according to the EOSc quantiles (see Figure 12).

Chapter 12. The sociolinguistics of English in the plurilingual ecology of Lagos

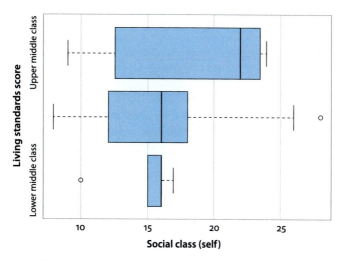

Figure 14. Self-assessed social class and aggregated living standard score

Table 2. Scores given for entrepreneurial orientation

Entrepreneurial orientation score	Agree	Neutral	Disagree
I gladly collaborate with others in my field to grow my business.	2	2	0
I prefer to work independently.	0	1	2
I would sell my business if I was given a good offer:	0	1	2
I keep other side businesses to maintain several streams of income.	2	1	0
I would take a salary job if I was paid enough.	0	1	2

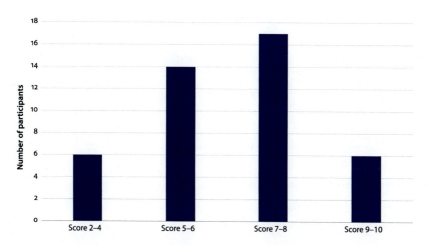

Figure 15. Groups of entrepreneurial orientation based on quantiles

4.4 Dominance scores

The preference of a language in a certain domain gave that language a score that translated into a total score for NSE, NPE, and AE/BE which indicated if the participant had a preference for one over the other (see Table 3).

Table 3. Scores given for language dominance

Language dominance score for NSE, NPE, and AE/BE	Scoring
I speak the language fluently.	2
I speak it but not fluently.	1
I understand the language.	0
First language used at home, first language used in the business.	3
Second language used at home, second language used in the business.	2
Third language used at home, third language used in the business.	1
Each domain/context where the interviewee reported to use the language.	1

Data exploration by plots and test for normality both show that the distributions of these scores are all rather skewed and non-normal. This also holds true for their log-transformed counterparts. As a consequence, standard ANOVA cannot be applied, and non-parametric tests had to be used in the analysis.

Special attention was given to language attitudes towards AE/BE. For statistical analysis, language attitudes towards the varieties were aggregated into ABESc (AE/BE Affinity score). Based on their replies (see Figure 8) we aggregated responses according to the participants' positive attitude towards AE/BE. A higher score indicates that the participant gives high status to the language (see Table 4).

Table 4. The affinity scores given for attitudes towards AE/BE

Attitudes towards AE/BE	Agree	Neutral	Disagree
People who speak AE/BE are educated.	2	1	0
I lack confidence in speaking AE/BE.	0	1	2
I respect people who speak AE/BE more (than I respect people who don't speak AE/BE).	2	1	0
I feel more respected when I speak AE/BE.	2	1	0
When I use AE/BE I feel less Nigerian.	0	1	2
I like reading books, news, magazines in English.	2	1	0
I prefer watching films in English rather than Nigerian languages.	2	1	0

Chapter 12. The sociolinguistics of English in the plurilingual ecology of Lagos

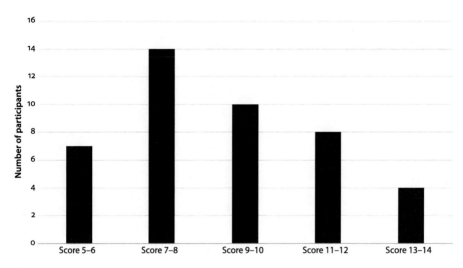

Figure 16. Calculated score of positive attitudes towards AE/BE

Based on their replies we gave each participant a score (Language Learning Score, LLSc) reflecting how they value language learning in relation to their business (see Table 5). This measure follows a normal distribution (mean = 6.89, $SD = 4.95$; Shapiro-Wilks: $W = 0.97$, p-value = 0.47).

Table 5. Importance of language learning in business

Language learning impact on business success	Agree	Neutral	Disagree
Speaking several languages is important for business success in Nigeria.	2	1	0
Speaking AE/BE helps me reach certain clients in my business.	2	1	0
To not speak AE/BE would limit me in my business.	2	1	0
Not speaking a Nigerian language has limited me in my business.	2	1	0
I prefer hiring staff who in addition to NSE also speaks AE/BE.	2	1	0
Learning different languages has been important to my business success.	2	1	0

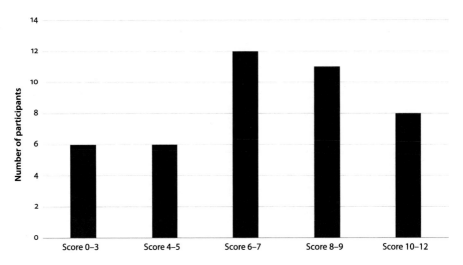

Figure 17. Categorization of language learning based on LLSc

4.5 Test group

The test group consisted of 10 participants who filled in the questionnaire online. 9 of the 10 participants were Yoruba who reside in other Yoruba states. It was therefore interesting to compare the Yoruba entrepreneurs in Lagos to the Yoruba entrepreneurs who reside in other states. When looking at the sample means for the language dominance score, there is a tendency for AE/BE to be used more among the Yorubas in Lagos (mean = 3.5) compared to the Yorubas residing elsewhere (mean = 2.6). The difference between the two groups was also seen in the score for use of NSE, where Yorubas residing in Lagos have a higher mean (17.5) than the test group (10.6). Also, NPE has a higher average dominance score among Yorubas residing in Lagos (mean = 5.7) compared to the test group (mean = 1.6). While only one Yoruba participant in Lagos reportedly does not use NPE, four participants from the test group reported not using NPE at all. The two groups differ insignificantly in their AE/BE affinity scores (Yorubas in Lagos: mean = 10, versus Yorubas in the test group: mean = 9). The rating for importance in language learning indicates that there is a tendency for Yorubas residing in Lagos to value language learning higher (mean = 7.2) than Yorubas residing in other states where Yoruba is the dominant language (mean = 4.8).

5. Trends and results

After exploring descriptive data, we tested correlations between social factors and language attitudes such as language dominance and adherence to multilingualism, and self-reported language use. Based on the observations of the descriptive statistics as outlined above, it appears that further hypothesis testing is warranted for the following observations: NSE is overall dominant in both the business and household sectors, NPE appears as a second language in the home domain and AE/BE affinity is only visible in economic domains. This section will focus on correlations between aggregated scores of language attitudes and sociodemographic factors using statistical tests to examine these impressionistic differences between groups.

Our strategy involves categorizing social groups based on demographic data, specifically on attributes, as described in Section 2.3. The following factors are considered: (a) social class (aggregated LSTSc), (b) ethnicity (original questionnaire data), (c) age, and (d) entrepreneurial orientation (aggregated EOSc). The dependent variables will be: (i) aggregated language dominance, (ii) aggregated language AE/BE affinity, and (iii) aggregated multilingual language learning orientation. We applied parametric and non-parametric tests depending on the empirical distributions. Because the sample size was small and the normality assumption was not met for language dominance and language affinity scores, we utilized a Kruskal-Wallis Test to compare multiple independent groups. ANOVA was applicable only to the LLSc.

5.1 Language dominance (Kruskal-Wallis)

NSE is, as shown in Section 3, the dominant business language in Lagos. Nonetheless, it remains unclear if some socio-demographic factors favour language dominance more than others. We have tested differences between language dominance and social class, ethnicity, and entrepreneurial orientation: None of the tested factors showed statistically significant correlations. While the data suggest, e.g., that the mean of the NSE dominance increases with social class, the Kruskal-Wallis did not indicate significant differences. This holds true for the aggregated LSTSc and self-assessed social class.[2] Still, this result demonstrates that NSE is the dominant business language in Lagos among all socio-economic classes.

In the data, NPE dominance looks at first sight the highest for the socio-economic middle class (LSTSc) but neither the self-assessed class nor the aggre-

---

2. The same holds true for regression analysis of the two continuous LSTSc and NSEDom variables, which shows no strong relationship.

gated score exhibits any valid and significant statistical correlation. Nevertheless, ethnicity has a distinct impact on NPE. We see a significant difference between Yoruba and other speakers (Kruskal-Wallis, $p = 0.0064$): NPE dominance is much lower among Yoruba speakers. The post-hoc Pairwise Wilcox Test shows that the difference is significant between Yoruba and Igbo ($p = 0.008$) with a large effect size (Wilcox Effectsize = 0.52).

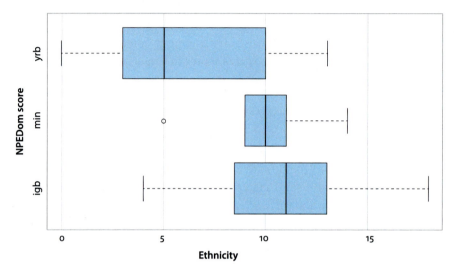

Figure 18. Language dominance and ethnicity

A similar situation is observed for entrepreneurial orientation groups where NSE dominates and no significant differences exist regarding NPE attitudes. In sum, language use of English varieties and language attitudes — except for NPE among Yoruba — are rather coherent and converging in the highly diverse linguistic setting of Lagos.

5.2 AE/BE Affinity (AEBSc) (Kruskal-Wallis)

To measure the influence of class, ethnicity, and entrepreneurial orientation, we tested the AEBSc affinity score against social class getting a significant result (Kruskal-Wallis; $p = 0.031$) for class — while testing the AE/BE affinity score against the other factors showed no significant outcome. A post-hoc pairwise comparison using t-tests with pooled SD data revealed a significant difference between lower and upper middle class ($p = 0.028$). However, the Wilcox Effectsize (0.49) is only moderate. In sum, positive attitudes towards exonormative varieties correlate with socioeconomic class (see Section 5).

Chapter 12. The sociolinguistics of English in the plurilingual ecology of Lagos **283**

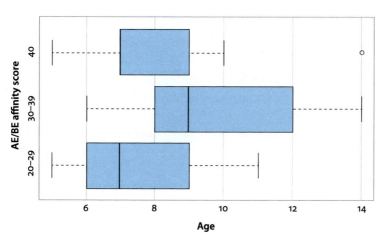

Figure 19. AE/BE affinity and age

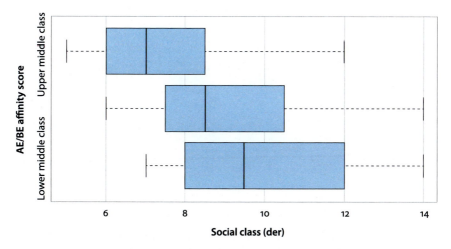

Figure 20. AE/BE affinity and aggregated social class

5.3 Tests for Language Learning Score (LLSc) (ANOVA)

In contrast to the other aggregated scores, one-way ANOVA can be used for statistical testing as the LISc score is normally distributed (Shapiro-Wilks; $W=0.97$, $p=0.47$). The ANOVA tests show significant differences for age ($F(2,40)=3.331$, $p=.045$)) and social class ($F(2,40)=3.331$, $p=.045$)). However, Tukey's HSD Test for multiple comparisons found that the mean value of LISc was not significantly different between age groups 30–39 and 20–29 ($p=.08$, 95% C.I.$=-0.24, 4.65$).

Nonetheless, the same test demonstrates a noteworthy disparity in the mean value of LISc between upper middle class and lower middle class ($p=.02$, 95%

C.I. = −4.75, −0.27). ANOVA for Ethnicity shows almost a significant result ($F(2,39) = 36.85$, $p = .052$)) and further testing revealed a significant result in the Tukey's HSD Test between the groups of "Minorities" and Yoruba ($p = .04$, 95% C.I. = 0.081, 5.09). Thus, older upper middle-class individuals prioritize language learning more than younger speakers from a lower socio-economic status, and the Yoruba have a more positive attitude towards language learning than the other groups. However, the analysis did not reveal a statistical correlation for the factors entrepreneurial orientation and learning orientation.

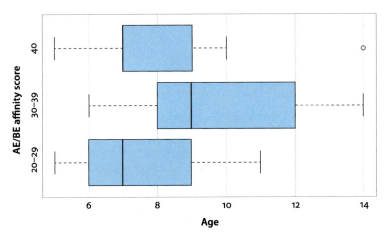

Figure 21. AE/BE affinity and age

6. Discussion

In the current sample data, the dominance of NSE in Lagos and in all business-domains can be shown. English, as a trend, is much more than a 'second language' and its use has fully stabilised in the LGA Oshodi Lagos setting. With regard to languages used at home, Yoruba show a more conservative preference for their ethnic language, while Igbo and 'Minorities' equally use NSE more often in the home domain. The process of 'nativization' is thus at a much-advanced stage if language dominance is taken as an indicator, but it is likewise related to sociolinguistic parameters having progressed more among Lagos' latecomers. NPE plays an important role as well. However, the data suggest to analyse NPE as the L variety and NSE as the H variety of Nigerian English based on the observation that Yoruba attitudes towards NSE run parallel to those towards NPE. It is thus necessary to study in more detail the linguistic features of what is taken as NPE in Lagos and whether the 'ethno-sociolinguistic' categorisation of 'Broken' refers more to a vernacular NSE, the Delta creole or an accommodated koiné. The perceived categories of NSE and NPE may both cover a wide range of un-recognized linguistic variation. This is to say that the empirical variation in the data may differ from the variation perceived by speakers, also related to their proficiency or familiarity with English varieties.

The analysis of sociolinguistic parameters indicates that ethnicity is an important factor in the Lagos setting. The 'first-comer' Yoruba show differences in language use, attitudes, and learning orientation while the 'late-comer' Igbo and 'Minorities' are much more similar in terms of dominance patterns and language attitudes. Ethno-linguistic identity impacts language attitudes but, underlyingly, it is not a difference in ethnicity but more of a 'traditional firstcomer' identity that explains a more conservative and distanced attitude towards all varieties of English among the Yoruba including the most 'nativized' NPE. However, Yoruba in Lagos and those from the test group show differences in, e.g., NSE language dominance (see 'test group' above). Taking the Yoruba sub-group alone, sociolinguistic factors such as class show larger effects than in other ethnic groups.

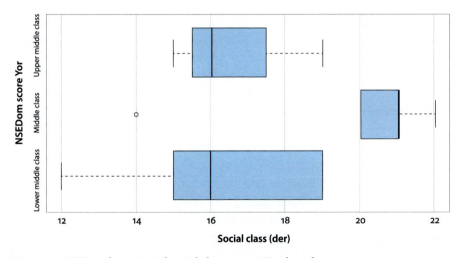

Figure 22. NSE and aggregated social class among Yoruba sub-group

The affinity towards AE and BE indicates a mismatch between self-assessed social class membership and measured socio-economic class. There is a significant difference for the measured socio-economic class but not for self-assessed social class, although the aggregated score indicates that socio-economic class is related to social structure and shared language attitudes towards AE/BE English. This leads to a paradoxical situation in which the impact of social class can be identified by socioeconomic parameters and shared values (language attitudes), but no corresponding construction of social identity is practiced. Conscious social identity is seemingly more determined by ethnicity than by social class. Class seems, nevertheless, to be a 'covert category' without conscious symbolic interaction. That is to say there is no feeling for common social class identity although people share world views, social norms and values. This suggests that commonness in social values and language attitudes does not necessarily shape a common sense of sameness and a common social identity, but an ideological construction of identity and a "mental [model] that people use to determine their behavior" (Hanappi & Hanappi-Egger 2021: 125).

Thus, social class in Lagos must be considered as more of a covert category that impacts language attitudes, use, choices, and language learning, albeit on a subconscious level. Moreover, the impact of age on language attitudes and the preference of older participants for English accents is also found in other studies on NSE (Oyebola & Gut 2020).

On the one hand, interaction and common social practice in business has not led to a common entrepreneur identity in the case of Lagos. On the other hand, communities of practice apparently disseminate language ideologies among people of distinct social identities, but more on a subconscious level. Concerning entrepreneurship, English, and business success, there are no clear differences between the groups of entrepreneurial orientation and the status of NSE. As expected, English proficiency is seen as a form of communicative capital by all social, ethnic, and economic groups. Nevertheless, the dominant H variety is NSE while AE/BE play at best a minor role. NPE as the L variety is likewise present in all business domains and in the more informal settings.

Language learning is moreover considered important in the multilingual SMEs sector. There is a tendency for entrepreneurs to recognise the importance of language flexibility in business relations, but AE/BE has no significant role in any business relationship within our group of entrepreneurs.

The present data suggest that, despite the high level of linguistic diversity in Lagos, language use of English varieties appears to be rather coherent regarding language attitudes. However, the perceived categorizations of English varieties of NSE and NPE do much likely diverge from those of sociolinguists. In a similar way, the data show a mismatch between conscious and subconscious categorization when it comes to social categories. This situation thus asks for more research and a refined methodology.

7. Limitations of the study and outlook

This study indicates that there are trends in communication practices and language dominance constellations. Given the small dataset and the focus on middle class business, the results of this study cannot be used as a representation of language choices of Lagosians in general. In the data there are various biases due the mode of collection. Education levels are highly similar and research in other LGAs would lead to different results. However, even for the most represented LGA Oshodi, the results are far from being representative. The low number of participants in this study is not statistically representative of entrepreneurs in Lagos as a whole, either.

7.1 Methodological issues

We experienced some difficulties during the collection of data by telephone interviews. Conducting data collection at a distance is not optimal for many reasons. Many factors are involved in finding participants to share their experience in entrepreneurship, one key factor being trust. We found that there was little or no previous experience with similar research questionnaires among the participants and there was a general suspicion towards anything that requires you to fill in personal information online, not least with the high level of scams that are widespread in Nigeria. Future research would allow to visit a well-known market, or to conduct data collection in settings such as offices or interviews in the private environment. Meeting with entrepreneurs in person would have helped establish trust for the research project and the purpose of collecting reliable data. Besides not finding entrepreneurs willing to participate in this study, it was also a challenge to get a wide range of sampling. Among the participants we noticed a tendency to interact with people from their own ethnic group, and/or their own area of residence in Lagos, which made it more difficult to find participants from a wide range of characteristics and backgrounds.

7.2 Outlook

Apart from sample size, the high degree of complexity of factors demands more randomized sampling and, e.g., the inclusion of customers. Testing the effect of LGA as a contextual factor would be of interest as well. The same holds true for other domains with a more outwards oriented profile such as tourism and hotels. Moreover, self-assessed categorizations are problematic, as argued above. Experimental research on linguistic categorization of English varieties such as matched guise testing of ethnic NSE varieties is needed. In addition to questionnaires, observational data and language perception tests could provide more insights into the process of stabilization and language levelling of NSE and NPE in particular.

The questionnaire should be revised with the aim of getting more normal data. While data aggregation worked quite well for social status, questions targeting entrepreneurial orientation would profit from a more profound reception of entrepreneur theory and personal interviews and researcher observation. More ethnographic work in Lagos will likewise be needed to refine the section on language attitudes and aggregation into language dominance scores.

Data and questionnaire data replies

[DOI: 10.5281/zenodo.13907238]

References

Adedun, Emmanuel & Mojisola Shodipe. 2011. Yoruba-English bilingualism in central Lagos — Nigeria. *Journal of African Cultural Studies* 23(2): 121–132,

Akande, Akimande T. & L. Oladipo Salami. 2010. Use and attitudes towards Nigerian Pidgin English among Nigerian university students. In Robert McColl Millar (ed.), *Marginal Dialects: Scotland, Ireland and Beyond*, pp. 70–89. Aberdeen: Forum for Research on the Languages of Scotland and Ireland.

Alo, Moses A. & Taiwo O. Soneye. 2014. Haggling as a socio-pragmatic strategy in selected urban markets: An amalgam of English and Nigerian languages. *Marang: Journal of Language and Literature* 24: 12–20.

Aronin, Larissa. 2019. Dominant language constellation as a method of research. In Eva Vetter, Ulrike Jessner (eds.), *International Research on Multilingualism: Breaking with the Monolingual Perspective* (Multilingual Education 35), pp. 13–26. Cham: Springer.

Awonusi, Victor O. 1994. The Americanization of Nigerian English. *World Englishes* 13(1): 75–82.

Ayeni, Bartholomew. 2020. Winning the customers over and again: Investigating discourse features in Nigeria banking interactions. *International Journals of English Language Studies* 2: 89–101.

Ayeni, Bartholomew. 2021. Language choices and its effect in a culturally diversified Nigeria Business Places: Adopting Giles' Communication Accommodation Theory. *International Journal of Applied Linguistics and English Literature* 10(1): 80–88.

Ayoola, Kehinde. 2009. Haggling exchanges at meat stalls in some markets in Lagos, Nigeria. *Discourse Studies* 11(4): 387–400.

Bamgbose, Ayo. 2000. *Language and Exclusion: The Consequences of Language Policies in Africa*. Münster: LIT Verlag.

Clark, Tom. 2006. Language as social capital. *Applied Semiotics= Semiotique Appliquee* 18: 29–41.

Deuber, Dagmar. 2005. *Nigerian Pidgin in Lagos: Language Contact, Variation and Change in an African Urban Setting*. London: Battlebridge.

Eberhard, David M., Gary F. Simons, & Charles D. Fennig (eds.). 2023. *Ethnologue: Languages of the World*, 26th edn. Dallas, TX: SIL International. http://www.ethnologue.com (12 October 2024).

Gut, Ulrike. 2008. Nigerian English: Phonology. *Varieties of English* 4: 35–54.

Gut, Ulrike. 2012. Standards of English in West Africa. In Raymond Hickey (ed.), *Standards of English: Codified Varieties around the World* (Studies in English Language), pp. 213–228. Cambridge: Cambridge University Press.

Gut, Ulrike & Robert Fuchs. 2013. Progressive aspect in Nigerian English. *Journal of English Linguistics* 41(3): 243–267.

Hanappi, Hardy & Edeltraud Hanappi-Egger. 2021. Social identity and class consciousness. *Forum for Social Economics* 50(1): 124–151.

Huber, Magnus. 1999. *Ghanaian Pidgin English in its West African Context: A Sociohistorical and Structural Analysis*. Amsterdam: John Benjamins.

Igboanusi, Herbert. 2008. Changing trends in language choice in Nigeria. *Sociolinguistic Studies* 2(2): 251–269.

Inyang, Benjamin J. & Rebecca O. Enuoh. 2009. Entrepreneurial competencies: The missing links to successful entrepreneurship in Nigeria. *International Business Research* 2(2): 62–71.

Jowitt, David. 2019. *Nigerian English*. Berlin: De Gruyter Mouton.

Krauss, Stefanie I., Michael Frese, Christian Friedrich & Jens M. Unger. 2005. Entrepreneurial orientation: A psychological model of success among southern African small business owners. *European Journal of Work and Organizational Psychology* 14(3): 315–344.

Lagos State Bureau of Statistics. 2013. *Digest of Statistics 2013*. Lagos: Ministry of Economic Planning and Budget.

Lagos State Government. 2011. *Lagos State Literacy Report 2011*. Lagos: Ministry of Economic Planning and Budget/Lagos State Agency for Mass Education.

McPherson, Miller, Lynn Smith-Lovin, James M. Cook. 2001. Birds of a feather: Homophily in social networks. *Annual Review of Sociology* 27(1): 415–444.

Mufwene, Salikoko S. 2001. *The Ecology of Language Evolution*. Cambridge: Cambridge University Press.

Mufwene, Salikoko S. 2015. Colonization, indigenization, and the differential evolution of English: Some ecological perspectives. *World Englishes* 34(1): 6–21.

Otero, Solimar. 2010. *Afro-Cuban Diasporas in the Atlantic World* (Rochester Studies in African History and the Diaspora 45). Martlesham: Boydell & Brewer.

Oyebola, Folajimi & Ulrike Gut. 2020. Nigerian newscasters' English as a model of standard Nigerian English? *Poznan Studies in Contemporary Linguistics* 56(4): 651–680.

Peter, Lothar & Hans-Georg Wolf. 2007. A comparison of the varieties of West African Pidgin English. *World Englishes* 26(1): 3–21.

Pike, Kenneth L. 1967. Etic and emic standpoints for the description of behavior. In Kenneth L. Pike, *Language in relation to a unified theory of the structure of human behavior* (2nd revised edn), pp. 37–72. The Hague: Mouton.

Schneider, Edgar W. 2003. The dynamics of New Englishes: From identity construction to dialect birth. *Language* 79(2): 233–281.

Schneider, Edgar W. 2007. *Postcolonial English: Varieties Around the World*. Cambridge: Cambridge University Press.

Schreiber, Henning, Clement Odoje & Djeneba Obot. 2012/2017. Linguistic solidarity against ultra-hyper-diversity: Nigerian Pidgin in Lagos. In Klaus Beyer & Raija Kramer (eds.), *Language Change under Multilingual Conditions* (Frankfurter Afrikanistische Blätter 24), pp. 51–72. Köln: Rüdiger Köppe.

Tijani, Abdulwahab. 2008. The Hausa community in Agege, Nigeria 1906 – 1967. *Journal of Social Sciences* 17(2): 173–180.

Ugorji, Christian U.C. 2015. Nigerian English in Schneider's dynamic model. *Journal of English as an International Language* 10(1): 20–47.

Wunder, Eva-Maria, Holger Voormann & Ulrike Gut. 2010. The ICE Nigeria corpus project: Creating an open, rich and accurate corpus. *ICAME Journal* 34: 78–88.

CHAPTER 13

The role of English in the linguistic ecology of Northeast India

Robert Fuchs, Caroline Wiltshire & Priyankoo Sarmah
University of Bonn | University of Florida | Indian Institute of Technology Guwahati

India is the world's most populous country and a hub of linguistic diversity. Within this diverse country, India's Northeast is a region that is historically, geographically, religiously, and linguistically more distinct from the rest of India than probably any other region, but it has received scant attention from academic research. As a locus of contact and exchange between South Asia, Southeast Asia, and East Asia, it is one of the linguistically most diverse regions in the world. Many of its states lack a single local majority language, potentially contributing to the more widespread use of English as a lingua franca in these states. We examine both the general linguistic diversity and the knowledge of English in the Northeast using the latest Census data (2011). We borrow the concepts of alpha and gamma diversity and the measure of diversity *Simpson's D* from the study of ecology and apply them to the analysis of linguistic ecology, confirming that the population of Northeast India is characterized by a greater diversity of local languages than the remainder of India; we also find that knowledge of English is more widespread in four of eight states. Furthermore, we examine the potential for Assamese, Hindi, and English to all serve as local linguae francae and discuss the limitations of Census data as a source, ending with proposals of methods with the potential to contribute to a more comprehensive understanding of the role of English in the linguistic ecology of the Northeast.

Keywords: diversity index, lingua franca, linguistic ecology, Northeast India

1. Introduction

India is a country of considerable global importance. It is the world's most populous country, with more than 1.4 billion residents (United Nations 2022), and the fifth largest economy, with substantial economic growth projected for the next few years (International Monetary Fund 2023). In this multilingual country, English

https://doi.org/10.1075/hsld.9.13fuc
Available under the CC BY-NC-ND 4.0 license.
© 2025 John Benjamins Publishing Company

is used as a national lingua franca by the elite and fulfills many official and public functions (Wiltshire 2020: 6–7). We focus on an area of India that has received scant scholarly attention, its Northeast, and whose linguistic ecology arguably exceeds in complexity that of the rest of the country.

This area is historically, geographically, religiously, and linguistically more distinct from the rest of India than probably any other region (De Maaker & Joshi 2007; Dikshit & Dikshit 2014). As a locus of contact and exchange between South Asia, Southeast Asia, and East Asia, it is one of the linguistically most diverse regions in the world. Because of this linguistic diversity, unlike other Indian territories, the states in the Northeast often lack a single local majority language, which may contribute to a more widespread use of English as a lingua franca. Whereas English is a language of the elite in most regions of India, in the Northeast it potentially fulfills broader functions for the general population. This unique linguistic ecosystem has so far received negligible attention in linguistic scholarship, and the existing literature focuses mainly on individual languages, rather than considering their complex interplay.

The present chapter will draw on and critically discuss the available evidence in order to contribute to a better understanding of the sociolinguistic complexities of Northeast India and the role that (Indian) English(es) play in it. We will first review the historical context for the linguistic diversity of the area, including the arrival and establishment of English, to provide a basis for exploration of the current linguistic ecology of the area. We then analyze data from the 2011 Census of India in order to measure the degree of linguistic diversity and the reported knowledge of English among speakers of the Northeast, in comparison to other regions of the country. Finally, we discuss the limitations of the analysis here and what avenues future research should explore in order to provide a more comprehensive picture of Northeast India's linguistic ecology.

2. India, Northeast India, and the role of English

2.1 Northeast India within the Republic and the wider region

The Republic of India emerged in 1947 as a result of the decolonization of British India. This process, locally known as 'Partition', divided the former colony into Hindu-majority India and Muslim-majority Pakistan. The new state of Pakistan consisted of two non-contiguous areas to the west of the Republic of India (later Pakistan proper) and to its east, which in turn gained independence in 1971 as the new country of Bangladesh. Partition fundamentally reshaped the Indian subcontinent and was accompanied by a breakdown of public order, large pogroms, and the (often forced) migration of people who suddenly found themselves in the 'wrong' country (Bharadwaj, Khwaja & Mian 2008). The particular effect on the geopolitics of Northeast India was to render its position precarious. Previously a "key hub of capitalist extraction" in British India (Baruah 1999: xix), it suddenly found itself connected to mainland India (a term that in this context is often used to refer to the rest of India; Sarma & Saharia 2019: 370; Sharma 2018: 258) merely by the 'chicken neck' at Siliguri, a corridor bordering Nepal, Bangladesh, and Bhutan that is only 22 kilometers wide at its narrowest section (Middleton 2019). Today, the Northeast comprises the seven so-called 'sister' states of Arunachal Pradesh, Assam, Manipur, Meghalaya, Mizoram, Nagaland, and Tripura, as well as the 'brother' state of Sikkim, which is non-contiguous with the other Northeastern states and situated to the north of the Siliguri corridor (see Figure 1).

Figure 1. Northeast India with its constituent states (in italics) and neighboring countries (smaller, regular font style). Map adapted from https://commons.wikimedia.org/wiki/File:SevenSisterStates.svg (Furfur, CC BY-SA 3.0 https://creativecommons.org/licenses/by-sa/3.0, via Wikimedia Commons; 03 December 2024)

The perilous geopolitical situation of Northeast India, all too easily cut off from the mainland in case of war, gave rise to a sustained interest of the Indian Army in this region. Border conflicts with neighboring countries, such as a border war with China in 1962, as well as extensive local rebellions and independence movements (Sharma 2018: 258) reinforced the continued presence and local influence of the Army. In addition, state control over land and people has often been precarious in the large mountainous and inaccessible parts of the wider Himalayan region (Scott 2009). A large part of the population of the Northeast belongs to so-called 'scheduled tribes', i.e., 'tribes' that are accorded special status by virtue of being enumerated in an annex ('schedule') of the Indian constitution (Ziipao 2020).[1] These communities were traditionally characterized by their exclusion from the caste system governing social relations for mainstream Indian society, and the term 'tribe' has often been used pejoratively "in manifestations of extreme cultural racism" (see Ziipao 2020: 2 for an overview). The role of the Northeast in the Indian national psyche has been characterized as that of 'the other' (Sharma 2018: 258); on the one hand, a tourist destination seen as a "quaint virgin land" of natural beauty, "camouflaged by [...] mysticism [and] geographical seclusion" (Sarma & Saharia 2019: 370) and, on the other hand, dismissed as remote and backward, a "zone of war, conflict [and] unrest" (Sharma 2018: 257–258). Despite or perhaps because of this ambivalence, the Northeast has until recently been neglected by academic studies and has remained marginalized in journalistic and public discourse in India (Sharma 2018: 257–261).

With some 98 percent of its border shared with the countries of Bhutan, China, Tibet, Myanmar, and Bangladesh (Ziipao 2020), the Northeast has a long history of migration of people and their languages. As a consequence, the current linguistic ecology of the Northeast includes languages from the Indo-Aryan, Tibeto-Burman, and Austro-Asiatic families, as well as English. Many of these languages have coexisted in the region for centuries. Speakers of Tibeto-Burman languages arrived over 2000 years ago (Post & Burling 2017) and probably displaced Austro-Asiatic languages (Masica 1991); of which the main surviving members in this part of India are the Khasian languages in Meghalaya. Speakers of Tibeto-Burman languages used to occupy the entire Assam valley, as well as parts of Bengal (Chatterji 1926 as cited in Masica 1991), and developed enormous diversity within the family, resulting in "anywhere from 100 to 300 individual languages" (Post & Burling 2017). However, large communities continue to speak Tibeto-Burman L1s across all Northeastern states. At the beginning of the 4th cen-

---

[1]. The proportion of the population belonging to scheduled tribes is, by state, Mizoram 94.4%, Nagaland 86.4%, Meghalaya 86.1%, Arunachal Pradesh 68.8%, Manipur 35.1%, Sikkim 33.8%, Tripura 31.8%, and Assam 12.4% (Ziipao 2020: 3).

tury CE, waves of migration of Eastern-Indo-Aryan speakers from the Jamuna/Padma delta region overwhelmed parts of the Northeast, particularly the states now called Assam and Tripura (Baruah 1960 as cited in Post & Burling 2017). The Ahoms, a more recent arrival to the area and speakers of a Tai language, ruled Assam from the 13th century to 1826. They left behind only place names, including *Assam* and the name of the modern local Indo-Aryan language *Assamese*, closely related to Bengali. Immigration continues to the present day, primarily from within India and from Bangladesh, adding to the presence of Indo-Aryan languages such as Hindi, Bengali, and Nepali, and introducing Dravidian languages. Furthermore, the Northeast has developed an extended pidgin/creole of its own named Nagamese, whose lexifier is primarily Assamese. Bhattacharjya (2001) traces its origins from a pidgin in the late 1800s to its expansion and development into a widely-used extended pidgin, especially in Nagaland; he furthermore documents its development into a creole on the basis that it is used as an L1 by a small community in Dimapur. Nagamese has so far not been recognized as a language in the Census.[2]

The English language arrived in the Northeast in both British and American forms in the 1820s and 1830s. The British assumed nominal control of the people and resources of the region from 1826, while American Christian missionaries tried to win hearts and minds, building churches and establishing schools in the area, including in Assam (1836) and Nagaland (1838) (Barpujari 1986). As of 1813, the British East India Company's charter included a duty to educate the local population and to support missionaries in their attempts at education, and both American and later British missionaries were quite successful in large parts of the Northeast. The 2011 Census reports Christianity as the dominant religion in Nagaland (88%), Mizoram (87%), and Meghalaya (75%), compared to the 2.3 percent rate of Christianity in India as a whole. Missionary goals, as stated in contemporaneous documents from 1837 onwards as cited in Barpujari (1986), included the translation of religious works into local languages. However, their schools also provided instruction in English, and one report from 1867 commented that "the desire among the natives for an English education is quite surprising" (1986: 121), noting that some feared that it may be prompted by the usefulness of knowing English in organizing a rebellion against the British.

British control of some of the territory of the current Northeast of India began with the signing of the Treaty of Yandabo at the end of the first Anglo-Burmese War in 1826. Before the arrival of the British, the territory of the Northeast included kingdoms and village republics as well as tribes with their own

---

2. Due to its role as a pidgin for most speakers and a creole for just a few, we refer to Nagamese as 'pidgin/creole' in this chapter.

forms of self-governance (Ziipao 2020). The treaty between the Kingdom of Ava and the British East India Company did not involve the participation of the various local forms of sovereignty within the territory, which resulted in years of shifting degrees of British and local control, as well as shifting administrative borders. After the initial treaty provided British India with parts of Assam, Manipur, and Tripura, British territory gradually expanded to include the remainder of the current Northeast, culminating with the annexation of the Naga Hills in 1866. British assertions of control in the region, including road building, resource extraction, and military expeditions were "often greeted with stiff resistance", especially by tribes in the hill territories (Ziipao 2020: 5).

After India's independence, the Northeast, then known as Assam Province, was gradually carved into the current set of the seven 'sister' states, beginning with the formation of Nagaland as a state in 1963 and ending with Arunachal Pradesh in 1987; Sikkim, although in some respects a part of British India, gained independence as a sovereign state in 1947, and did not join India until 1975. The newly formed Northeastern states were sometimes aligned with the distribution of particular linguistic groups but also sometimes based on political or cultural organization. While most Indian states were constructed so that native speakers of a single language dominate (e.g., Tamil in Tamil Nadu), the divisions of the Northeast resulted in states with no single language spoken by a majority of the population and groups of speakers of the same language present in more than one state. Given this linguistic diversity, three of the Northeastern states have adopted English as their only official language (Arunachal Pradesh, Meghalaya, Nagaland), and two consider it a co-official language (Mizoram and Sikkim); furthermore, two of the other three officially recognize two languages, one Indo-Aryan and one Tibeto-Burman (Assam — Assamese and Bodo, Tripura — Bengali and Kok-Borok). As the constitution of India mentions Hindi as the official language of the country and English as a language that can be used for official purposes, the fact that no Northeastern state proposes Hindi as a state language is meaningful; though the Northeast is diverse in many ways, a uniting factor has been resistance to the central Indian government, often symbolized by resistance to Hindi and its speakers.

The central government of India sets the policy for language education in public schools and, as recommended by the Kothari commission of 1964–66, follows a three-language policy of primary education in the local language, followed by the introduction of a second language (English or Hindi) between the third and sixth grade, and a third language taught from sixth grade. States can modify this formula to introduce languages earlier and to choose which language will be second or third; the government of Assam, for example, decided in 2007 to introduce English as a subject from first grade (age 6) in Assamese-medium schools. Children who speak a minority and non-official state language at home, such as the Rabha speakers in Assam, may need to learn four languages: Rabha, Assamese, English, and Hindi. Overall, policies on language education are likely to exert considerable influence on the spread and maintenance of linguae francae.

2.2 Indian English(es) and the Northeast

The scholarship on postcolonial varieties of English has enjoyed considerable interest in the last few decades (e.g., Schneider 2007) and Indian English is in all likelihood one of the more widely studied varieties. In addition to several monographs on Indian English as a whole (e.g., Lange 2012; Sailaja 2009; Wiltshire 2020), research, much of it empirically based, has explored its syntax (Sharma 2005; Rautionaho 2014), semantics, lexis (Lambert 2012; 2014), pragmatics (Fuchs 2012; Larina & Suryanarayan 2023), phonetics and phonology (Fuchs 2016; Maxwell & Fletcher 2009; Wiltshire & Harnsberger 2006), and sociolinguistics (Fuchs 2021; Lange & Leuckert 2021). Other studies have explored its historical development (Fuchs 2020; Lambert 2014; Mukherjee 2007) as well as its role as a local linguistic 'epicenter', influencing neighboring varieties of English (Fuchs 2023; Hoffmann, Hundt & Mukherjee 2011; Parviainen & Fuchs 2019), as well as the internal differentiation of how English is spoken in India. In particular, the question of the unity and diversity of English in India continues to be debated, with some evidence of a focused educated variety having emerged (Lange 2012). This variety has few markers of regional differentiation at the formal end of a stylistic continuum, while there is more differentiation in less formal and/or less educated socio- and regiolects (Leuckert et al. 2023).

As part of the debate on regional differentiation, a few studies have started to explore the characteristics of English in Northeast India (Sarmah & Wiltshire 2024; Wiltshire 2005; Wiltshire & Sarmah 2021). However, as yet there is no comprehensive analysis of the relationship between Indian English(es) as a whole and English in Northeast India. In particular, there is a lack of scholarship on the linguistic ecology of India, the role of English vis-a-vis other languages, and to what extent these dimensions vary between Northeast India and the Indian mainland. In this chapter, we aim to make a contribution towards filling this research gap and make use of a rich, yet under-used, font of data on the linguistic ecology of India — the Indian Census.

2.3 The Indian Census

The first modern Indian Census was concluded in 1872 and has since been taken every decade, with the exception of the 2021 Census, which was postponed due to the Coronavirus pandemic (Registrar General 2023: 15–27, 239). In the present analysis, we rely on data from the most recent Census from 2011. Its "Household Schedule" comprised 29 items, of which items 10 and 11, "mother tongue" and "other language known" (with up to two answers recorded for the latter, as "subsidiary languages"), are of interest for our analysis (Registrar General 2021). While the household is the "operational unit of enumeration" of the Census, it aims to gather data from individuals (Registrar General 2023: 39). For the 2011 Census, this information was gathered, except for some mountainous areas, in February 2011 by 2.7 million census functionaries who visited all households and the homeless population (Registrar General 2023: 177, 188). The Census manual was available in 18 languages (Registrar General 2023: 195–156).

3. Methods

This chapter will provide an exploratory account of the linguistic diversity and linguistic ecology of Northeast India, which we will compare in a contrastive analysis with data for the rest of India ("mainland India"). The analysis relies on data series C16 (Population by mother tongue) and PC01/C17 (Population by Bilingualism and Trilingualism), for which we downloaded separate tables for all 35 Indian states and Union territories (henceforth just "states") from the Indian Census database[3] and collated them into a single table each for further analysis in R/RStudio.

The analysis of L1 ("mother tongue") focused on entries classified as languages in the Census and ignored possible subclassification into dialects. The first step of the analysis focused on the state level, whereas in the second step we looked at the smallest territorial unit at which this data was available, variously labeled as town, village or 'tahsil' in the Census terminology. The data used in this second step also permitted a differentiation by urban/rural location and respondent gender. In addition, data on population numbers of states and towns/villages was derived from these tables.

In order to analyze linguistic diversity in this data, we borrow two analytical tools from the study of ecology. First, the analysis of linguistic diversity at the local level and the state level can be related to the concepts of alpha diversity (or local diversity) and gamma diversity (or non-local diversity), respectively (Jurasinski, Retzer & Beierkuhnlein 2009; Whittaker 1972). Second, in order to quantify linguistic diversity, we use Simpson's diversity index, or Simpson's D (Simpson 1949;

---

[3]. Available online at https://censusindia.gov.in/nada/index.php/catalog/ (04 December 2024).

sometimes called the Gini-Simpson index), which is widely used in the area of ecology (e.g., Morris et al. 2014), but, to our knowledge, has not been applied to the analysis of linguistic ecology as yet (but has been considered as a measure of lexical diversity, see Jarvis 2013). Simpson's D was designed to provide a straightforward quantification of the ecological diversity of a habitat in terms of the number of individuals of extant species. The intuition behind the index is that a habitat with a large number of species, each of which has a small percentage of individuals, is more diverse than a habitat with a small number of species that each represent large percentages of individuals or one with a large number of species but dominated by one or a few species that are relatively numerous. The index ranges from 0 to 1, with 1 representing a notional habitat in which there is one individual of each species (the highest possibly diversity), and 0 representing a habitat in which all individuals belong to a single species (the lowest possible diversity). The index can be further interpreted in terms of the odds that two randomly selected individuals belong to the same species. A Simpson's D of 0 obtains when the odds are 1 in 1, i.e., the two individuals are guaranteed to belong to the same species. By contrast, Simpson's D of 1 indicates that the odds that two random individuals belong to the same species is 0. Finally, values between 0 and 1 represent habitats with varying odds. For example, an index of 0.33 indicates that there is a 1 in 3 chance that two random individuals belong to a different species, while an index of 0.5 indicates that the odds are 1 in 2. In our analysis, we compute Simpson's index with the *abdiv* package in R (Bittinger 2020).[4]

Apart from analyzing linguistic diversity as indicated by self-reported L1, we also contrast rates of reported knowledge of English and selected other languages as an L1, L2, or L3 ("mother tongue" and "subsidiary languages" in the Census terminology). Note that the Census only provides information on which languages respondents claim they speak, not at what level of proficiency. Moreover, individuals under 6 years of age were deemed to have knowledge of only a single language and no information on possible L2s or L3s is available. For this part of the investigation, we removed all entries for other reported languages from the data and then computed the totals of all respondents reporting knowledge of English and selected other languages for each state. These numbers were then divided by the population reported in the Census in order to obtain state-wise percentages of the population reporting knowledge of English.

In addition to data from the Census, we further enrich the analysis by means of the Human Development Index (HDI) for all Indian states in order to account for disparities in social and economic conditions between Indian states (data

---

4. Note that terminology varies between implementations such that the scale of Simpson's D may be reversed. We follow the implementation provided in the abdiv package.

retrieved from the Subnational HDI Database of the Global Data Lab, https://globaldatalab.org/shdi/, version v7.0, Smits & Permanyer 2019; 04 December 2024). The HDI is a measure published by the United Nations Development Programme that accounts for levels of education, health, and standard of living in a society and was devised as a more comprehensive measure of development than purely economic indicators such as Gross Domestic Product per capita.

Finally, the statistical treatment of the data is shaped by the nature of the data provided by the Census, which aims to account for the entire population of India (notwithstanding the possibility that any census may miss a small number of inhabitants). Unlike in most linguistic research, where a sample of the underlying population is taken and differences between groups or conditions are subjected to statistical tests in order to determine the validity of possible inferences to the underlying population, in the present study the Census data itself represents the population. We therefore do not make use of significance tests, but report mean and median values as well as standard deviations.

4. Results

4.1 Linguistic diversity

We first analyze linguistic diversity in claimed L1 at the state level (gamma diversity). Linguistic diversity is much greater across the Northeastern states with a mean Simpson's D of 0.67 (median = 0.68, SD = 0.16) than in mainland India, with a mean of 0.35 (median = 0.27, SD = 0.20). This result suggests that when two people are chosen at random within a Northeastern state, there is a two in three chance that they speak different L1s, whereas in mainland India the odds are roughly halved, i.e., there is a one in three chance that the two individuals speak different L1s. Linguistic diversity is greatest in the Northeastern state of Nagaland (Simpson's D 0.93) and lowest in the state of Mizoram (Simpson's D 0.46). Notably, notwithstanding the considerable variation in linguistic diversity in both groups of states, all Northeastern states have a greater linguistic diversity than the median mainland state. These results are illustrated in Figure 2 at an aggregate level (where circles represent individual states and their size indicates population numbers) and Figure 3 in relation to economic and social development as measured by the Human Development Index (HDI), with circle size again indicating population number. Overall, the Northeastern states have an HDI on par or slightly below average to the populous mainland states, but much higher linguistic diversity.

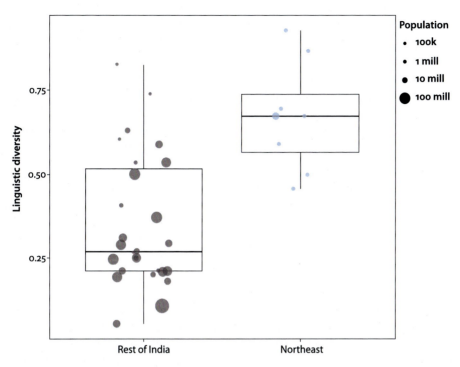

Figure 2. Linguistic diversity in Northeastern states compared to mainland Indian states

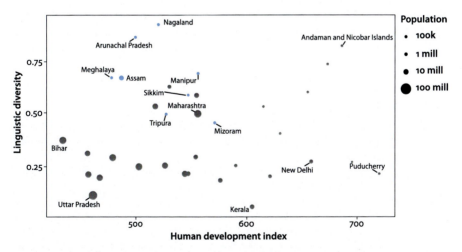

Figure 3. Linguistic diversity in Northeastern states (blue) compared to mainland Indian states (grey), in relation to economic and social development

While the state-level results presented so far are instructive, they are open to interpretation as to the social and geographic nature of linguistic diversity and to what extent the Northeastern and mainland states differ in this regard. More specifically, it is conceivable that linguistic diversity in some states is of a segregated nature, with speakers of one language concentrating in one part of the state and speakers of another language in a different part. By contrast, in other cases, speakers of different languages might intermingle relatively evenly across all parts of a state. In terms of the concepts borrowed from the study of ecology, mentioned in Section 4 above, it is conceivable that gamma (or non-local) linguistic diversity exceeds alpha (or local) linguistic diversity, and it is possible that Northeast India and the rest of India vary in this regard.

In order to explore linguistic diversity at the local level, we now turn to a comparison of Northeastern and mainland states in this respect. Overall, the analysis indicated that linguistic diversity as measured by Simpson's D is much lower at the local level than at the state level, indicating that speakers of particular L1s are likely to concentrate within certain parts of a state. This in itself is hardly surprising, given the fact that shared L1s may give rise to social identities. Moreover, in the long run, dispersed linguistic groups are also more likely to be subject to language shift than contiguous settlement areas of speakers of a particular language.

What is of interest in regard to the aims of the present chapter is that the Northeast still has a much greater linguistic diversity (mean 0.36, median 0.34) than mainland India (mean 0.20, median 0.13) when analyzed at the local level (see Figure 4). Moreover, this holds both for urban and rural locations as well as for women and men (see Table 1 and Figure 5). For example, Northeastern urban localities have a median Simpson's D of 0.45 while mainland urban localities have an index of 0.19. In other words, two randomly chosen individuals in a Northeastern town have an almost even chance of speaking different L1s, while the odds are 1 in 5 in mainland towns. Linguistic diversity is overall lower in rural areas, but again much higher in the Northeast (median Simpson's D 0.32) than in mainland India (Simpson's D 0.10).

Finally, we also tested for the influence of the population size of the statistical catchment areas on linguistic diversity. For reasons of space, we can only report the main results of this analysis. The results indicate a positive influence of catchment area population size on linguistic diversity in rural locations in the Northeast, i.e., more populous rural catchment areas have more linguistic diversity. Intriguingly, this was not the case in mainland India, where linguistic diversity remains at a low level regardless of rural catchment area size. Under the assumption that statistical catchment area boundaries represent localities with geographical, social, and historical ties, this finding further underscores the vitality of the Northeast's linguistic diversity. However, given the fraught relationship

Chapter 13. The role of English in the linguistic ecology of Northeast India **303**

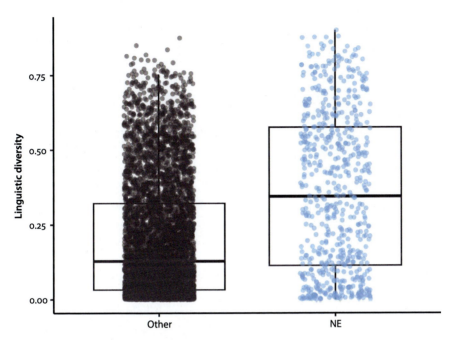

Figure 4. Linguistic diversity in Indian towns and villages in mainland India (left) and Northeast India (right)

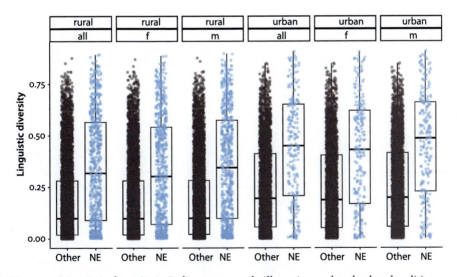

Figure 5. Linguistic diversity in Indian towns and villages in rural and urban localities, separately for female (f), male (m), and all inhabitants, in mainland India (grey circles), and Northeast India (blue circles)

of the Northeast to mainland India and its history of external political interference, we cannot exclude the possibility that in some cases the statistical catchment areas in the Northeast are less reflective of local conditions (i.e., related to geographical, social, and historical ties) than those in mainland India, perhaps sometimes lumping together linguistic communities that might otherwise be situated in separate catchment areas.

A further finding of the analysis of the influence of catchment area population size on linguistic diversity is that in some very large urban catchment areas (several million inhabitants) in mainland India that are regarded as a single unit in the survey, linguistic diversity is very high. This finding likely reveals the melting pot function of these urban centers, which attract migrants from various parts of the country. The Northeast lacks populous urban areas of such considerable size; its largest city, Guwahati, Assam, had a population of 968,549 in the 2011 Census, making it 47th in size in India.

Overall, this analysis of linguistic diversity provides empirical evidence on a large scale that India's Northeast is linguistically much more diverse in terms of self-proclaimed L1s than mainland India. This result holds at the state and the local level and is valid for both female and male inhabitants.

Table 1. Linguistic diversity in Indian villages (rural) and towns (urban) by gender and location (Northeast vs. mainland India). (Number = Number of local statistical catchment areas, i.e., town/village/tahsil)

Urban/rural	Gender	Location	Mean	Median	SD	Number
all	all	Mainland	0.20	0.13	0.2	5338
all	all	Northeast	0.36	0.34	0.26	645
all	f	Mainland	0.20	0.13	0.20	5338
all	f	Northeast	0.34	0.32	0.26	645
all	m	Mainland	0.20	0.13	0.20	5338
all	m	Northeast	0.37	0.37	0.26	645
rural	all	Mainland	0.18	0.10	0.19	5237
rural	all	Northeast	0.34	0.32	0.26	640
rural	f	Mainland	0.18	0.10	0.19	5236
rural	f	Northeast	0.33	0.30	0.26	640
rural	m	Mainland	0.18	0.10	0.19	5237
rural	m	Northeast	0.35	0.34	0.26	640
urban	all	Mainland	0.25	0.19	0.21	3043
urban	all	Northeast	0.44	0.45	0.26	226
urban	f	Mainland	0.24	0.19	0.21	3043
urban	f	Northeast	0.42	0.43	0.26	226
urban	m	Mainland	0.25	0.20	0.21	3043
urban	m	Northeast	0.45	0.49	0.26	226

4.2 Knowledge of English

The linguistic diversity of Northeast India may have promoted the use of English as a local lingua franca and its spread beyond an economic and educational elite towards a larger part of the population. Most Indian states have a single language that is claimed as an L1 by a large part of the population, often an overwhelming majority. In fact, modern Indian state boundaries were reorganized in 1956 precisely out of a popular demand for an alignment of linguistic areas and state borders, superseding the earlier, very different colonial administrative boundaries; however, the reorganization left Assam Province largely intact, separating only Tripura and Manipur as distinct territories. The state boundaries for the mainland have remained largely stable since 1956, notwithstanding limited changes over time, mainly in the form of the creation of two or more new states out of what was a single state. By contrast, India's Northeastern states, many of which were officially formed between 1963 and 1987, largely lack a single majority L1, potentially giving more prominence to English to avoid giving preference as well as economic and social privileges to a particular L1 group.

English is claimed as an L2 or L3 (and rarely as an L1) overall more frequently in Northeastern states (mean of all states 16.3%, median 14.0%, $SD=10.1$) than in mainland India (mean 14.8%, median 12.4%, $SD=7.4$; see Figure 7). Across all states, there appears to be a moderate correlation with economic and social development (HDI, see Figure 6), except for a few less populous states. This positive relationship is plausible given that knowledge of English is imparted in India in large part through the education system; greater economic prosperity and access to formal education might be the causal mechanism behind a considerable part of the variation between states in the knowledge of English. What is noteworthy is that some states, especially Nagaland and Manipur, and to some degree Arunachal Pradesh and Sikkim, have greater rates of claimed knowledge of English than would be expected by their HDI. Comparing these results to language policies across these states, it is evident that rates of self-reported knowledge of English do not necessarily correspond to the status of English as official in the states, as the examples of Manipur (not official but high rate) and Mizoram (co-official but lower rate) show.

Overall, claimed knowledge of English appears to be slightly more widespread in India's Northeast than the mainland. However, the difference is small when seen on its own and is mainly noteworthy when seen against the background of a slightly below-average economic and social development compared to the rest of India. When the Northeastern states are compared to mainland states of a similar HDI, it becomes clear that higher rates of knowledge of English obtain in four of the eight Northeastern states.

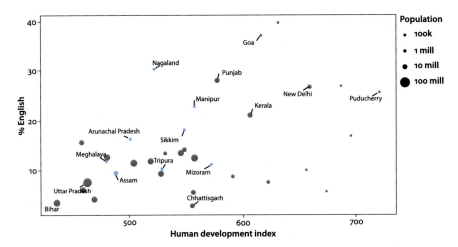

Figure 6. Percentage of residents claiming English as an L1, L2, or L3 in Northeastern states (blue) and mainland Indian states (grey), relative to economic and social development

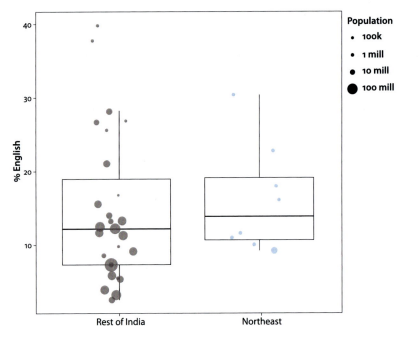

Figure 7. Percentage of residents claiming English as an L1, L2, or L3, in Northeastern states (right) and mainland Indian states (left) (circles represent individual states)

4.3 Other linguae francae in Northeast India

So far, the findings suggest that English may fulfill the function of a local lingua franca in four of the eight Northeastern states. However, it is not the only language of regional importance. This subsection turns to an analysis of the most widely spoken languages in the Northeast and the question of which of these languages might serve as local linguae francae. In terms of total numbers of L1, L2, and L3 speakers combined, the Census data indicates that Assamese is most widely spoken (18.8 million), followed by Bengali (12.6 million), Hindi (8.0 million), English (5.4 million), Manipuri (1.8 million), Bodo (1.3 million), Nepali (1.3 million), and Khasi (1.2 million), with other languages spoken by fewer than 1 million people. Another language that is potentially relevant is the pidgin/creole Nagamese (see Section 2.1 above), which does not enjoy official status and is not counted in the Census, so that we lack any data on it. Of these eight languages, only Assamese, English, and Hindi are spoken by at least 10 percent of the population in at least three states.

These three regional linguae francae are not spoken to the same extent across the Northeastern states (see Table 2 and Figure 8). While in some states two or even three of the linguae france are widely spoken, in others, local languages dominate. We therefore refine our analysis of linguistic diversity and its association with lingua franca usage and focus on the three regional linguae francae for which we have data.

Table 2. The three most widely spoken languages (sum of self-reported L1, L2, L3) across the Northeastern states according to the Census (2011), with the regional linguae francae Hindi, English, and Assamese shown in bold print

State	Rank 1	%	Rank 2	%	Rank 3	%
Arunachal Pradesh	**Hindi**	41.1	**Assamese**	17.2	**English**	16.2
Assam	**Assamese**	57.5	Bengali	29.7	**Hindi**	19.0
Manipur	Manipuri	56.1	**English**	22.9	**Hindi**	13.8
Meghalaya	Khasi	38.4	Garo	25.3	**English**	11.8
Mizoram	Lushai/Mizo	66.8	**English**	11.1	Bengali	8.0
Nagaland	**English**	30.4	**Assamese**	24.8	**Hindi**	15.0
Sikkim	Nepali	74.9	**Hindi**	31.7	**English**	18.1
Tripura	Bengali	75.1	Tripuri	22.5	**English**	10.2

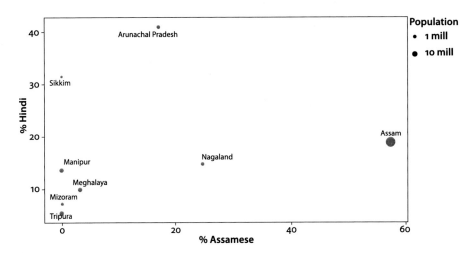

Figure 8. Percentage of residents claiming Assamese (horizontal axis) or Hindi (vertical axis) as an L1, L2, or L3, in Northeastern states

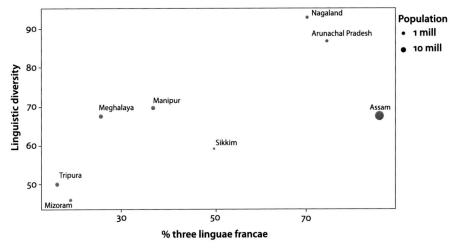

Figure 9. Percentage of residents claiming Hindi, English, or Assamese as an L1, L2, or L3, in Northeastern states, relative to linguistic diversity

This association can indeed be shown (see Figure 9) with less linguistically diverse states such as Tripura and Mizoram (15.8% and 18.8% of lingua franca usage, respectively), while states with high linguistic diversity show high rates of lingua franca usage (Nagaland and Arunachal Pradesh, 79.2 and 74.6%, respectively). Assam seemingly bucks this trend with high lingua franca usage but moderate linguistic diversity, compared to the other states. However, in this state, Assamese is widely used as an L1 so that it serves both as an L1 and as a lingua franca.

In summary, this subsection has uncovered a complex constellation of linguistic diversity, locally dominant L1s, and at least three regional linguae francae. Of these linguae francae, one is relevant to Northeast India only, while English and Hindi also function as linguae francae of India as a whole, but play very different roles in different parts of the country. Moreover, in the Northeast, linguistic diversity on the state level (gamma diversity) appears to be associated with lingua franca usage. The more linguistically diverse a state is, the more the linguae francae are used by the population.

5. Discussion

While India as a whole is a country characterized by linguistic diversity, the present analysis has revealed that Northeast India is a region of even greater linguistic diversity. At the state level, the odds that two randomly selected inhabitants speak different L1s is two in three in the Northeast, while in mainland India it is 'just' one in three. Unsurprisingly, at the local level, linguistic diversity is lower, but even through this analytical lens the remarkable linguistic diversity of the Northeast is confirmed and can be contrasted with the Indian mainland. Returning once again to the concepts of alpha (local) and gamma (regional) diversity, the analysis revealed that gamma diversity in the linguistic ecology of India is greater across the board and that Northeast India exceeds the rest of the country in both alpha and gamma diversity.

We next asked whether the Northeast's linguistic diversity might be associated with a more widespread knowledge of English compared to the rest of India. This turned out to be true for four of the eight Northeastern states, but not for the region as a whole. Instead, there appears to be a complex interplay of the three linguae francae, Hindi, English, and Assamese. The first two of these are used across India as linguae francae and are not widely spoken as an L1 in the Northeast. By contrast, Assamese is widely spoken as an L1 in the Northeastern state of Assam (which accounts for a sizable part of the population of the region) and is also used as a lingua franca in the region. Yet these three linguae francae are not used equally widely across the Northeast. Instead, it appears that the more linguistically diverse a state is, the more widely one or more of the linguae francae is used.

In addition to the results regarding linguistic diversity and the linguistic ecology of Northeast India, the present chapter also demonstrated how the concepts of alpha and gamma diversity as well as Simpson's diversity index, which are widely used in ecology, can be fruitfully applied to linguistic data. We submit that this index provides an easily interpretable and valid quantification of linguistic diversity. In particular, its results lend themselves to a straightforward interpretation of the odds that two randomly selected people speak the same language. This is of course an abstraction — many human encounters are not random, but facilitated by social networks in which people with some degree of a shared background interact. However, for survey and census data, this index provides a useful analytical tool. Moreover, acknowledging the utility of Simpson's D index for the analysis of linguistic diversity does not preclude a recognition of a need for more involved and targeted research that can provide a fuller account of the linguistic ecology of Northeast India.

Before exploring implications for the study of linguistic ecology, the discussion turns to a critical appraisal of the data used in the present chapter. The analysis relies heavily on data from the Government of India's 2011 Census. This source yields empirical evidence on all but a small percentage of Indians not captured by the Census, putting this analysis on a much sounder footing in quantitative terms than the survey-based research that linguists, including ourselves, would usually engage in for such purposes. However, using census data also comes with a number of important caveats. More specifically, collecting information on "mother tongues" and other languages is known to have limitations that undermine the validity of the source data under any circumstance and likely even more so in the Indian context. There are two types of issues: determining the language(s) of the speakers and determining the extent of multilingualism.

First, the sheer number of languages reported raises issues for tabulating the results (Kohli 2017). For example, speakers report the names of their mother tongue using a variety of local terms, resulting in an abundance of names which may reasonably be judged to refer to the same language. While 10,400 mother tongue names were returned, the Census report reduced these terms to 3,372 names of languages, of which 1,576 were classified and 1,796 left unclassified (Kohli 2017: 19, citing Bhattacharjya 2001: 57–58). Furthermore, the Census results do not include the names of languages claimed by fewer than 10,000 speakers. These small languages, of which there might be a great number, are only listed as "other" in the Census. The "Language Atlas of India 2011" (Singh & Nakkeerar 2011), the main Census-related publication on the languages of India, is silent on questions of the identification and demarcation of languages and dialects and we are not aware of what guidelines were used to resolve such questions.

Second, the accuracy of the speakers' responses may be problematic in the sense that the information provided by individual respondents may not always correspond to the scholarly definition of native language. In the Indian context, the term 'mother tongue' (rather than 'native language' or other terms) is used in general discourse in English, and it is this term, and translations of it, that the Census used. Interpretations of this term in the Indian context may depart from the linguistic understanding of a native language and respondents could interpret it as referring to the primary language of their mother or the primary language of their ethnic group, rather than to a language that the speaker learned first or knows best. Some speakers may also report the name of their ethnic group or caste, even when that is not the name of a language. Such concerns are somewhat mitigated by the soundness of the definition of 'mother tongue' used in the Indian Census since 1971, which is "the language spoken in childhood by the person's mother to the person or mainly spoken in the household", or, if the mother died when the child was in infancy, "the language spoken in the person's home in childhood" (Singh & Nakeerar 2011: viii). However, since Census data was gathered by volunteers, who in turn relied on self-reporting by respondents, it seems likely that the identity function that the category 'mother tongue' bears in the Indian context influenced the results to some degree. Thus, information on 'mother tongue' may on occasion elicit information that relates to ethnic identity rather than native or first language.

Moreover, there is reason to believe that the way the Census captures linguistic information is likely to misrepresent, to a certain degree, the multilingual repertoire of speakers and to present a selective picture of the linguistic ecology of the country. Linguistic repertoires are captured in terms of mother tongue (L1) and subsidiary languages (L2 and L3), and children below the age of six are deemed to know just a single language. This scheme ignores the ramifications of language acquisition in linguistically complex societies, such as the possibility that speakers may use multiple languages during childhood, in effect having multiple native languages or 'mother tongues' (Genesee & Cenoz 2001), which is likely to be relevant for a large number of people in India. In the Census data, speakers (except for children under 6) with two native languages are likely to have chosen one language to be recorded as their L1 and the other as their L2, which is reductive but retains the information on these two languages. The Census also ignores (i) any languages beyond the three that can be listed, which is likely to be relevant for a substantial number of Indians, and (ii) does not account for variation in proficiency or otherwise more nuanced information on a speaker's language knowledge. Some of these caveats might conceivably affect the accuracy of the Census data more for the Northeast than for mainland India. Specifically, in a highly multilingual region such as the Northeast, a larger proportion of individuals would be likely to report a repertoire of more than three languages if given the chance compared to regions such as many northern states, where the national language Hindi is spoken widely. Moreover, given the widespread use of English in some Northeastern states, there are probably more children with knowledge of English in addition to at least one other language. Overall, this suggests that the already substantial linguistic diversity and rates of knowledge of English that the Census data reports for the Northeast are in fact underrepresentations of their true extent and that the contrast between Northeastern and mainland India is in fact even greater than the data suggests.

Third, while the Census asks speakers to report any second or third languages they know, these self-reports may be incomplete. The 2011 report calculated bilingualism rates of 26 percent and trilingualism at 7.1 percent; Commenting on earlier Census data, Sridhar (1989), argued convincingly that these numbers might be too low, as speakers may not report a language unless they are literate in it or unless it is considered prestigious; furthermore, speakers may consider some languages to be merely dialects, not worth reporting separately. The limit of three languages might also depress reported rates of claimed knowledge of English, in cases where respondents who speak English prioritized providing three other languages out of their linguistic repertoire.

Finally, the Census provides no indications of domains of use of any of the reported languages, making it difficult to determine not only the current extent of use but also the trajectory of language shift. In order to understand the linguistic ecology and the place of English within it, more information than that provided by the Census will be required.

Notwithstanding these limitations, the Census still provides the most comprehensive empirical and nation-wide source of data on multilingualism in India. With respect to the aims of the present chapter, some of the Census' limitations are attenuated by the broad perspective we have adopted in this chapter. Specifically, while detailed linguistic analysis may open up to controversy about what is counted as a language in the Census and what is classified as a dialect (and thus not counted separately in the Census), these classifications will have been applied with a certain degree of uniformity across the entire country. Similarly, the threshold of 10,000 speakers to be included as a language in the Census applies uniformly to the entire body of data. Consequently, the results of a broad analysis such as the one presented here are probably not unduly influenced by such considerations, at least where different parts of the country are compared. Nevertheless, as far as comparisons with data from other countries are concerned, the 10,000 speaker limit necessarily leads to an underestimation of the linguistic diversity of India and the role that less widely spoken languages play in it. This underestimation might affect the data for a linguistically diverse region such as the Northeast to a greater extent than for mainland India.

A more substantial drawback of the Census' reliance on self-reports is a possible bias against less prestigious languages and a bias towards languages that sustain ethnic or other group identities. Even more important for researchers who would like to go beyond an analysis of multilingualism towards an exploration of the whole linguistic ecology of Northeast India is the lack of information on domains of use and attitudes. To be fair, it would be unrealistic to expect a general

Census to provide such information in a comprehensive manner. In the future, we will therefore engage in fieldwork in order to provide a holistic account of the linguistic ecology of Northeast India.

6. Conclusion

Our analysis of the Census data indicates that English plays an important role among the linguae francae of Northeast India, the most linguistically diverse area of an already diverse country. While some aspects of the complex linguistic ecology of Northeast India have been addressed in previous research (DeLancey 2014; Haokip 2011; Kondakov 2013; Morey 2017), the role the English language plays within it has so far hardly been explored (with the exception of limited discussions in Wiltshire 2005, 2020). We conclude with suggestions for how this research gap can be addressed.

First, there is a need for surveys that are better designed and more complete than the Census, in order to elicit the full linguistic repertoires of speakers and the domains of use for each language. Whereas the Census limited the number of potential responses to a single L1 and two additional languages, open-ended questions would enable reports of any language of which speakers have some knowledge, the extent of that knowledge, and how these were acquired/learned. Furthermore, as speakers may not recognize the pidgin/creole Nagamese as a language, targeted questions are needed to determine the extent of its use. Follow-up questions can elicit further details about the contexts in which each of the speaker's languages are most commonly used: where, when, with whom, and about which topics. Children should not be limited to reporting a single language and including information on the age of the respondents would enable apparent-time analyses of diachronic change in usage.

Second, self-reporting is a technique limited not only by the survey instruments but also by the self-awareness and honesty of the respondents. Observation of actual language use in natural contexts, including the initial negotiation between interlocutors of which language to speak and any changes in language choice during an interaction, could both verify the survey data and extend our understanding of the role(s) each language plays in the linguistic ecology. Third, our research has been confined to sources written in English, while sources written in local languages may also offer more insights into the language ecology of Northeast India.

Only by drawing on such a level of detail will it be possible to grasp more fully the complexities of the role of English in the linguistic ecology of Northeast India.

References

Barpujari, Heramba Kanta. 1986. *The American Missionaries and North-East India* (1836–6900 A.D.). Guwahati: Spectrum.

Baruah, Kanak Lal. 1960 [1933]. *Early History of Kāmarupa, from the Earliest Times to the End of the Sixteenth Century*. Guwahati, IN, Lawyer's Book Stall.

Baruah, Sanjib. 1999. *India against Itself: Assam and the Politics of Nationality*. Philadelphia, PA: University of Pennsylvania Press.

Bharadwaj, Prashant, Asim Khwaja & Atif Mian. 2008. The big march: Migratory flows after the partition of India. *HKS Working Paper No. RWP08-829*.

Bhattacharjya, Dwijen. 2001. The Genesis and Development of Nagamese: Its Social History and Linguistic Structure. P.h.D. dissertation, City University of New York.

Bittinger, Kyle. 2020. *abdiv: Alpha and Beta Diversity Measures*. R package version 0.2.0, https://CRAN.R-project.org/package=abdiv (12 October 2024).

Chatterji, Suniti Kumar. 1926. *The Origin and Development of the Bengali Language*, 3 Vols. Calcutta. Repr. London: Allen & Unwin.

De Maaker, Erik & Vibha Joshi. 2007. Introduction: The Northeast and beyond: Region and culture. *South Asia: Journal of South Asian Studies* 30(3): 381–390.

DeLancey, Scott. 2014. Sociolinguistic typology in North East India: A tale of two branches. *Journal of South Asian Languages and Linguistics* 1(1): 59–82.

Dikshit, Kamal Ramprit & Jutta K. Dikshit. 2014. *North-East India: Land, People and Economy*. Dordrecht: Springer.

Fuchs, Robert. 2012. Focus marking and semantic transfer in Indian English: The case of also. *English World-Wide* 33(1): 27–53.

Fuchs, Robert. 2016. *Speech Rhythm in Varieties of English: Evidence from Educated Indian English and British English*. Singapore: Springer.

Fuchs, Robert. 2020. The progressive in 19th and 20th century settler and indigenous Indian English. *World Englishes* 39(3): 394–410.

Fuchs, Robert. 2021. Sociolinguistic variation in intensifier usage in Indian and British English: Gender and language in the Inner and Outer Circle. In Tobias Bernaisch (ed.), *Gender in World Englishes*, pp. 47–68. Cambridge: Cambridge University Press.

Fuchs, Robert. 2023. Colonial lag or feature retention in postcolonial varieties of English. The negative scalar conjunction "and that too" in South Asian Englishes and beyond. In Paula Rautionaho, Hanna Parviainen, Mark Kaunisto & Arja Nurmi (eds.), *Social and Regional Variation in World Englishes: Local and Global Perspectives*, pp. 123–148. London: Routledge.

Genesee, Fred & Jasone Cenoz (eds.). 2001. *Trends in Bilingual Acquisition*. Amsterdam: John Benjamins.

Government of India, Office of the Registrar General & Census Commissioner, India. Ministry of Home Affairs. 2011. *Census of India 2011*. https://censusindia.gov.in/ (15 September 2023).

Haokip, Pauthang. 2011. *Socio-Linguistic Situation in North-East India*. New Delhi: Concept Publishing Company.

Hoffmann, Sebastian, Marianne Hundt & Joybrato Mukherjee. 2011. Indian English an emerging epicentre? A pilot study on light verbs in web-derived corpora of South Asian Englishes. *Anglia* 129(3–4): 258–280.

International Monetary Fund. 2023. *World Economic Outlook database: April 2023*. https://www.imf.org/en/Publications/WEO/weo-database/2023/April/ (April 2023).

Jarvis, Scott. 2013. Capturing the diversity in lexical diversity. *Language Learning* 63: 87–106.

Jurasinski, Gerald, Vroni Retzer & Carl Beierkuhnlein. 2009. Inventory, differentiation, and proportional diversity: A consistent terminology for quantifying species diversity. *Oecologia* 159: 15–26.

Kohli, Vijaya John. 2017. *Indian English? Reframing the Issue*. New Dehli: Pragun Publishers.

Kondakov, Alexander. 2013. Koch dialects of Meghalaya and Assam: A sociolinguistic survey. In Gwendolyn Hyslop, Stephen Morey & Mark W. Post (eds.), *North East Indian Linguistics*, Vol. 5, pp. 3–59. New Delhi: Foundation Books.

Lambert, James. 2012. Beyond Hobson Jobson: Towards a new lexicography for Indian English. *English World-Wide* 33(3): 292–320.

Lambert, James. 2014. Diachronic stability in Indian English lexis. *World Englishes* 33(1): 112–127.

Lange, Claudia. 2012. *The Syntax of Spoken Indian English*. Amsterdam: John Benjamins.

Lange, Claudia & Sven Leuckert. 2021. Tag questions and gender in Indian English. In Tobias Bernaisch (ed.), *Gender in World Englishes*, pp. 69–93. Cambridge: Cambridge University Press.

Larina, Tatiana & Neelakshi Suryanarayan. 2023. Address forms in academic discourse in Indian English. In Nicole Baumgarten & Roel Vismans (eds.), *It's Different With You. Contrastive Aspects on Address Research*, pp. 142–170. Amsterdam: John Benjamins.

Leuckert, Sven, Asya Yurchenko, Claudia Lange & Tobias Bernaisch. 2023. *Indian Englishes in the 21st Century: Unity and Diversity in Lexicon and Morphosyntax*. Cambridge: Cambridge University Press.

Masica, Colin. 1991. *The Indo-Aryan languages*. Cambridge: Cambridge University Press.

Maxwell, Olga & Janet Fletcher. 2009. Acoustic and durational properties of Indian English vowels. *World Englishes* 28(1): 52–69.

Middleton, Townsend. 2019. Connective insecurities: Chokepoint pragmatics at India's chicken neck. *Ethnos* 88(2): 1–22.

Morey, Stephen. 2017. The sociolinguistic context of the Tangsa languages. In P. S. Ding & J. Pelkey (eds.) *Sociohistorical Linguistics in Southeast Asia*, pp. 169–187. Leiden: Brill.

Morris, E. Kathryn, Tancredi Caruso, François Buscot, Markus Fischer, Christine Hancock, Tanja S. Maier, Torsten Meiners, Caroline Müller, Elisabeth Obermaier, Daniel Prati, Stephanie A. Socher, Ilja Sonnemann, Nicole Wäschke, Tesfaye Wubet, Susanne Wurst & Matthias C. Rillig. 2014. Choosing and using diversity indices: Insights for ecological applications from the German biodiversity exploratories. *Ecology and Evolution* 4(18): 3514–3524.

Mukherjee, Joybrato. 2007. Steady states in the evolution of New Englishes: Present-day Indian English as an equilibrium. *Journal of English Linguistics* 35(2): 157–187.

Parviainen, Hanna & Robert Fuchs. 2019. 'I don't get time only': An apparent-time investigation of clause-final focus particles in Asian Englishes. *Asian Englishes* 21(3): 285–304.

Post, Mark W. & Robbins Burling. 2017. The Tibeto-Burman languages of Northeast India. In Graham Thurgood & Randy J. LaPolla (eds.), *The Sino-Tibetan Languages*, pp. 213–242. London: Routledge.

Rautionaho, Paula. 2014. Variation in the Progressive: A Corpus-based Study into World Englishes. Tampere: Tampere University Press. (P.h.D. dissertation, Tampere University).

Registrar General [Office of the Registrar General & Census Commissioner, India]. 2021. *Census Questions (1872–2011)*. https://censusindia.gov.in/census.website/CENSUS_ques (10 February 2023)

Registrar General [Office of the Registrar General & Census Commissioner, India]. 2023. *A Treatise on Indian Censuses since 1981*.

Sailaja, Pingali. 2009. *Indian English*. Edinburgh: Edinburgh University Press.

Sarma, Prabalika & M. Deepsikha Saharia. 2019. English education and literature in the culture of violence in Northeast India. *International Journal of English Learning & Teaching Skills* 1(4): 368–373.

Sarmah, Priyankoo & Caroline Wiltshire. 2024. Acoustic properties of the monophthongs of Assamese Indian speakers based on medium of instruction. *World Englishes* 43(1): 161–181.

Schneider, Edgar. W. 2007. *Postcolonial English: Varieties around the World*. Cambridge University Press.

Scott, James C. 2009. *The Art of not Being Governed: An Anarchist History of Upland Southeast Asia*. New Haven, CT: Yale University Press.

Sharma, Devyani. 2005. Language transfer and discourse universals in Indian English article use. *Studies in Second Language Acquisition* 27(4): 535–566.

Sharma, Saba. 2018. Framing Northeast India—Perspectives and positions. *Südasien-Chronik-South Asia Chronicle* 8: 257–272.

Simpson, Edward H. 1949. Measurement of diversity. *Nature* 163: 688.

Singh, Kandhai & Nakkeerar, R. 2011. *Language Atlas of India 2011*. Office of the Registrar General & Census Commissioner, India.

Smits, Jeroen & Inaki Permanyer. 2019. The Subnational Human Development Database. *Scientific Data* 6: 190038.

Sridhar, Kamal K. 1989. *English in Indian Bilingualism*. New Delhi: Manohar Publications.

United Nations. 2022. *World Population Prospects 2022*. https://population.un.org/wpp/ (12 October 2024).

Whittaker, R. H. 1972. Evolution and measurement of species diversity. *Taxon* 21(2–3): 213–251.

Wiltshire, Caroline. 2005. The "Indian-English" of Tibeto-Burman language speakers. *English World-Wide* 26(3): 275–300.

Wiltshire, Caroline. 2020. *Uniformity and Variability in the Indian English Accent*. Cambridge: Cambridge University Press.

Wiltshire, Caroline. R. & James D. Harnsberger. 2006. The influence of Gujarati and Tamil L1s on Indian English: A preliminary study. *World Englishes* 25(1): 91–104.

Wiltshire, Caroline & Priyankoo Sarmah. 2021. Voicing contrasts in the stops of Indian English produced by Assamese speakers. *Proceedings of Meetings on Acoustics 179ASA* 42(1): 060003.

Ziipao, Raile Rocky. 2020. Roads, tribes, and identity in Northeast India. *Asian Ethnicity* 21(1): 1–21.

CHAPTER 14

Discourse-pragmatic *like* in East Asian Englishes
Focus on Taiwan

Jakob R. E. Leimgruber & Sofia Rüdiger
University of Regensburg | University of Bayreuth

The multilingual ecology of Taiwan includes the official language Mandarin, the vernaculars Hokkien and Hakka, as well as several Aboriginal Austronesian languages. In this context, English has emerged as an important additional language, not least in the education system. Research on English in Taiwan has thus far largely been restricted to the educational setting (Chen 2006; Chien 2014; Kao & Tsou 2017; Wu & Lau 2019) or to the function of English as an international language (Chen 2006). Some, such as Seilhamer (2015; 2019), have focused on the sociolinguistic realities of English on the island, bringing the issue of language 'ownership' to the foreground. This, combined with recurring proposals to elevate English to co-official status (Chen, Shih, Yeh & Lee 2018), suggests considerable societal importance attached to the language. However, much less is known about the actual form and structure of Taiwanese English. In this chapter, we present data from a 76,000-word pilot version of the Taiwanese Spoken English corpus (TASE, see Rüdiger, Leimgruber & Tseng 2023). Taking previous studies of spoken South Korean English into account (Rüdiger 2019; 2021; Rüdiger, Leimgruber & Tseng 2023), we present a case study of discourse-pragmatic uses of *like* by Taiwanese speakers of English. Our findings suggest that the functional range of *like* is similar in Taiwan and South Korea and that discourse-pragmatic *like* also forms part of Taiwanese English speakers' repertoire.

Keywords: Asian Englishes, discourse-pragmatics, Expanding Circle Englishes, *like*, Taiwan

1. Introduction

Much like in the rest of Asia and beyond, English has become a language to reckon with in the linguistic ecology of Taiwan. The island is no stranger to complex questions of multilingualism: the indigenous Austronesian languages have long been displaced by southern varieties of Chinese, of which Hokkien (Min Nan) and Hakka are the most prominent ones. After 1949, national language status was awarded to Mandarin, spoken by the large number of post-civil war migrants to the island; it soon became the primary language of the island, gradually displacing the older Chinese vernaculars. These latter varieties have, however, retained some identity-bearing functions, particularly in terms of localist orientations in contradistinction to the heavy Mandarin-based national language ideology in Mainland China.

In this multilingual context, the presence of English as a language with high levels of prestige, not least in the education system, raises questions as to its status within the country. In Section 2, we explore these issues in more detail. We then move on to a more central theme of this article, i.e., the question of the actual linguistic form of the putative Taiwanese English. Research on this has been scant, as we will show. In Section 3, we present our dataset before assessing the use of discourse-pragmatic *like* in Section 4. We compare our findings from data provided by Taiwanese speakers of English to previous research from the South Korean context.

2. English in Taiwan

Taiwan is an island located off the southeast coast of Mainland China. Its population is currently around 24 million and tends to cluster in the densely populated urban centers along the (west) coast, particularly in the regions around Taipei in the North and Kaohsiung in the South. Several languages are spoken on Taiwan: The indigenous Formosan (Austronesian) languages, Hokkien, Hakka, and Mandarin being the most often-cited ones, leading Kobayashi (2020: 548), who adds Taiwanese Sign Language (Tai & Tsay 2015) to this list, to call the island's society "multilingual". Mandarin, however, has been promoted so effectively since the 1950s that substantial language shift has taken place, to the extent of Taiwan becoming referred to as "pseudo-monolingual" (Go 2018, as cited in Kobayashi 2020: 548). In this section, a brief overview of language policies in historical context is offered, followed by an assessment of the current situation.

Taiwan's early history includes episodic Western colonial contact, with the Dutch (1624–1662) and the Spanish (1626–1642) being involved with the indigenous Austronesian population. This contact, though, left few linguistic traces beyond the development of romanization systems for Aboriginal languages as part of missionary activities. More impactful were the Qing dynasty policies promoting Chinese as the lingua franca of the island; policies which were, however, interrupted by the loss of the island to the Japanese in 1895. Half a century of Japanization followed, during which the colonial language was heavily promoted in public institutions and education switched entirely to Japanese; the population was actively discouraged from speaking their vernaculars (Hokkien, Hakka, etc.) even in private. This strong presence of Japanese in society led to a certain loss of proficiency in prestigious registers of Chinese, with literacy also suffering. The vernaculars, however, remained the primary first language acquired at home, and the intense contact with Japanese resulted instead in some lexically and grammatically mixed forms of, e.g., Hokkien (Simpson 2007).

The Japanese defeat at the end of World War II put an end to this colonial presence, and the island was returned to China. On the mainland of China, though, civil war was raging between nationalists and communists until 1949, at which point the nationalist camp led by the Kuomintang (KMT), after a continuous loss of ground, retreated to the island of Taiwan as their last military holdout. The KMT would go on to rule Taiwan until 2000, using martial law to cement its power up to 1987. Linguistically, Mandarin was heavily promoted during KMT rule, as well as English language education as a driving force of economic development (Cooper 1990; Chen 2006). The nation-building aspect of Mandarin rather than of Hokkien, Hakka, etc. (Tsao 2018), which was so important immediately post-war, led to significant language shift away from the other languages. This process was only stemmed somewhat with the lifting of martial law and the eventual shift of power from the KMT to the Democratic Progressive Party (DPP) in 2000. A more open economic market changed the population's attitudes towards languages and language policy, with local vernaculars becoming more important in indexing Taiwanese identity and the English language remaining a crucial facilitator for participation in the globalizing economy (Wu & Lau 2019).

Following the election of the DPP into power in 2000, a 'Taiwanization' policy (Wu 2011) in the education system implemented the Local Language in Education (LLE) policy, maintaining the national language Mandarin as a main medium but reducing its hours in the curriculum and, crucially, including the teaching of local vernaculars, primarily Hokkien, in primary schools. Ministry guidelines from 2001 specifically refer to the local vernaculars as central to Taiwanese cultural identities. English language teaching, too, was further promoted for both economic advantage in a globalized world and to respond to "social change and national goals" (Chen 2006: 322). In practice, this means that English was made a compulsory subject in primary schools (starting in year 1 in Taipei and some other cities and in year 3 at the latest elsewhere), and minimum English scores were required for university graduation. Furthermore, English-medium courses were promoted in higher education, with lecturers of such courses being paid more than lecturers teaching in other languages (Kao & Tsou 2017; Wu & Lau 2019). In a more recent policy development, the 2030 Bilingual Nation Development Goal, articulated in 2018, specifically seeks to enhance English proficiency in the population, citing again globalization as a motivation. The scheme focuses on bilingualism in the education system and proposes to extend English to pre-school institutions, making a certain number of English-medium courses obligatory in higher education, providing all-English mass media, and promoting visitor-friendly bilingualism in touristic places (National Development Council 2018).

In terms of languages, the 2020 Population and Housing Census (National Statistics 2020) reports that overall, Mandarin is spoken by 96.8 percent of the population, Hokkien by 86.0 percent, Hakka by 5.5 percent, and Aboriginal languages by 1.1 percent (see Figure 1). These numbers include all speakers of these languages, with widespread bilingualism resulting in total figures over 100 percent. Mandarin is the dominant language of 66.4 percent and an additional language for 30.4 percent of the population. Hokkien is the primary language of 31.7 percent and an additional language for 54.3 percent. Clearly, Mandarin has reached the status of the uncontested national tongue, with Hokkien showing a still relevant presence, even as a (formerly even more) widespread lingua franca. The Census does not name other languages, so there is no nationwide figure of English language use.

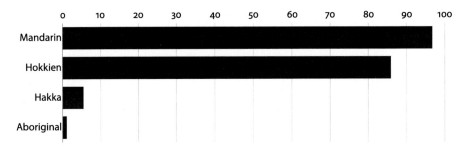

Figure 1. Languages of Taiwan (2020 Census); Percent of population reporting language use

Figure 2 offers an apparent-time view of language shift in Taiwan by showing the dominant languages of age decades above six years of age. It appears that there is a clear shift towards Mandarin, with younger Taiwanese more likely to be dominant in the language than their elders, reaching over 90 percent in the 6 to 14 age group. In the case of Hokkien, the opposite trend is visible: its use as a dominant language drops from 65.9 percent among the 65+ age group to around 7.4 percent in the youngest group. Hakka also experiences a negative shift, but from an already low starting point. The Aboriginal and 'other' languages remain largely stable, never rising above 0.6 percent. These developments are the results of a Mandarin-only language policy put in place by the KMT government after 1945 (Sandel 2003; Scott 2012), with the expressed aim to achieve a shift towards the unifying 國語 *Guoyu* 'national language', Mandarin.[1] The numbers seem to suggest that this aim has been largely achieved.

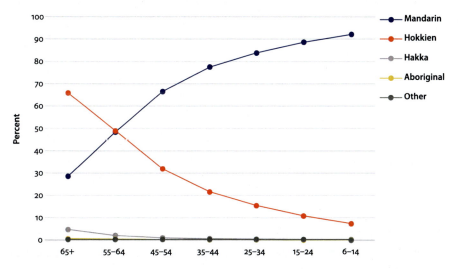

Figure 2. Dominant language (%) by age group; 'Aboriginal' and 'Other' are consistently below 1 percent

These top-down policies notwithstanding, linguistic behaviour on the part of the Taiwanese population always was largely embracing of English. The language had been important in school and the workplace (and, indeed, daily life) even before the 2001 curricular changes (Chen & Tsai 2012). The demands of English proficiency in the education system nonetheless represent a strong motivator (Chien 2014): on top of the regular school system, there is the parallel system of 'cram schools', locally known as *buxiban* (Chou & Yuan 2011), which pupils attend in the afternoons and evenings after regular school to give them a competitive

---

[1] Similar shifts happened elsewhere in the Sinosphere, with Mandarin being heavily promoted by government actors in China (Saillard 2004) and Singapore (Tan 2006; Leimgruber 2013), for instance. For the longer-term, more contemporary effects of these post-war policies, see, e.g., Jiang & Dewaele (2019) for Mainland China and Leimgruber, Siemund & Terassa (2018) for Singapore.

edge in school exams. Found throughout East Asia (Hu & McKay 2012), they are popular with pupils of all academic abilities, and while research suggests a positive correlation between *buxiban* attendance and academic performance among Taiwanese students, less is known about the overall impact of regular schools and cram schools in predicting Taiwanese learners' English proficiency (Chou 2015).

The discourse of the 'bilingual nation' (interestingly always bilingualism in English and Chinese, not, e.g., Mandarin and Hokkien), a status to be achieved by 2030, seems to have had some motivational effect on the learning and teaching of English. Challenges that remain include the lack of sufficiently proficient personnel to teach non-English language subjects through the medium of English, of resources and infrastructure, as well as the issue of linguistic identity, which is already being indexed by a challenging mix of the national language Mandarin and other vernaculars (Ferrer & Lin 2021). Furthermore, the acceptance of local forms of English (e.g., Taiwanese English and East Asian Englishes) remains, as far as we know, low, both in the general population and among policymakers (though there is a lack of systematic studies of language attitudes).

Beyond the education system, of course, English has a strong presence on the island, predominantly in advertising (Chen 2006) and in the media (English-language films being screened in the original with subtitles; cf. also the existence of some entirely English-language newspapers such as the *Taipei Times* and *Taiwan News*). Some sectors of the workplace, such as the medical field, also see a lot of internal communication in English (Bosher & Stocker 2015). In the private context of the home, language use remains under-researched, but there are reports of children using English with parents and peers (Go 2018, as cited in Kobayashi 2020: 548). Most research on English in Taiwan focuses on language planning and policies (inter alia, Simpson 2007; Price 2014) or ELT (Chen & Tsai 2012; Wang & Lin 2013; Chen 2013; Yu 2015; Tsai 2015), and is often outdated (Hsu 1994; Chen 2006). Seilhamer (2015: 376) gives a more recent and more sociolinguistically informed account of the English used by six informants, calling their language use confident and expressing a "sense of ownership" of the language. At the very least, this suggests that for some Taiwanese speakers, English is indeed actively used (see also Seilhamer 2019). In the following, we will offer some insight into the use of a particular discourse-pragmatic item by Taiwanese speakers of English, based on a recent spoken language dataset.

3. Data

In the empirical part of this chapter, we explore the use of discourse-pragmatic *like* by Taiwanese speakers of English. Our data stems from a pilot version of TASE — the Taiwanese Spoken English corpus, which we refer to here as TASE1. TASE1 is part of a larger corpus collection scheme targeting a final corpus size of 300,000 words — in its current state, TASE1 comprizes 76,000 words contributed by 21 speakers of Taiwanese English. All speakers signed an informed consent sheet before data collection started and filled in a short demographic survey. The 13 women and 8 men who are featured in the corpus material were aged between 18 and 27 at the time of data collection (October 2019). All but two of them were students at a major university in Taiwan, with many of the participants enrolled in English studies or related programs.[2] Participants reported limited amounts of international mobility, with 11 participants reporting no stays abroad at all, while 8 were abroad for shorter periods of time (0–6 months), and one each for 7–24 months and more than 24 months. All participants indicated Mandarin/Taiwanese Chinese as their L1.

In order to ensure comparability with another East Asian variety of English, i.e., English in South Korea, we followed the corpus design principles set out for the Spoken Korean English corpus (aka SPOKE).[3] This entailed the use of the same set of interview guidelines following the 'cuppa coffee' framework (Rüdiger 2016) to create a more informal atmosphere with the aim of eliciting conversational material from the participants. Interviews were thus conducted in local coffee shops between the second author of this chapter and one to two research participants at a time. All TASE1 material was collected in October 2019.

A first investigation of TASE1 (Rüdiger, Leimgruber & Tseng 2023) involved a comparison to the South Korean English material in the SPOKE corpus. A keyword analysis using AntConc (Anthony 2018) revealed several lexical items which are key in TASE1 (with SPOKE as reference corpus), among them the item *like* (on rank 3 with a keyness of +344.62 and an effect size of 0.2544; see Rüdiger, Leimgruber & Tseng 2023: 105). Discourse-pragmatic uses of *like* in SPOKE have

---

[2]. The final corpus design envisions a more diverse set of participants in terms of age, profession, and, in case of student participants, study programs.

[3]. We selected South Korean English as a reference point for this study as it is located in the same regional context (i.e., East Asia) and English has had a similar developmental trajectory (i.e., non-postcolonial) and position in present-day society (i.e., acquisition as a foreign language; English bearing social and linguistic capital). In addition, the existence of the SPOKE corpus provides an empirical basis for the comparisons we aim to undertake. For more information on the Korean setting, the reader is referred to Rüdiger (2019).

been investigated in detail in Rüdiger (2021) who found *like* to be an established part of the Korean English repertoire — a finding of particular interest due to the common lack of explicit language instruction in the use of discourse-pragmatic features (cf. Hellermann & Vergun 2007; Gilquin 2016). This of course begs the question of why *like* then shows up in a keyword analysis comparing TASE1 to SPOKE, which we formulated as "an invitation to have a closer look at both corpora" (Rüdiger, Leimgruber & Tseng 2023: 104). In this study, we follow-up on this invitation by providing an analysis of the uses of *like* in TASE1. Our research questions are:

1. What role does *like* (across its functional range) play in the Taiwanese English repertoire?
2. How does this compare to Korean speakers of English, particularly in the realm of discourse-pragmatic uses of *like*?

All instances of *like* in TASE1 were retrieved automatically and subsequently manually tagged regarding their different functional realizations. Following D'Arcy (2017) and corresponding to the categories employed in Rüdiger (2021), these included uses as verb, adjective, noun, preposition, conjunction, comparative complementizer, suffix, approximative adverb, sentence adverb, discourse marker, discourse particle, and quotative. Two additional categories (also present in Rüdiger 2021) were 'repetition' and 'unclear'. The former was used for cases where *like* was repeated (in which case only the last instance was tagged as a specific functional category with all preceding items marked as 'repetition'), and the latter for all cases where a functional category could not be established (usually because of incomplete utterances, etc.). A detailed differentiation between the functional categories can be found in D'Arcy (2017), but important to mention here are the three uses of *like* which we subsume under the discourse-pragmatic heading: discourse marker, discourse particle, and quotative. While discourse marker and discourse particle use of *like* is at times conflated into one category, discourse marker *like* is positioned at the left boundary of utterances and connects the following utterance to the previous discourse. In terms of function, it fulfills specific roles related to the "encod[ing] of textual relations" (D'Arcy 2017: 14), such as exemplification, illustration, elaboration, and clarification; see (1) and (2) for two examples. In (3) and (4), however, we find *like* used as discourse particle. As such, *like* can occur in different positions in the utterance and frequently marks subjectivity (D'Arcy 2017: 15). All examples given here stem from the Corpus of Contemporary American English (COCA; https://www.english-corpora.org/coca/; 04 December 2024); all emphases are ours.

(1) I don't want to work in dating. **Like**, that's just not going to be my future.
(COCA, 2017, Spoken)

(2) Wow, I actually do look like my grandma. **Like**, it's really surprising.
(COCA, 2019, Spoken)

(3) And so when you have a lady drunk, she's often, **like**, failing at that task of taking care of others [...]   (COCA, 2018, Spoken)

(4) And in a lot of ways, these ideas — these principles are what got me through, this idea of, **like**, listen to people more than you talk   (COCA, 2016, Spoken)

Last but not least, quotative *like*, illustrated in (5) and (6), introduces direct speech or thought. Here it is often (but not always) preceded by a verb such as *go* or *be*.

(5) Well, the rest of the class ***went*** **like**, 'Oh, God.' So I said, 'Come up here.'
(COCA, 1996, Spoken)

(6) So my friend Christy had these baby carriers and she ***was*** **like** you can try this if you want. I ***was*** **like**, you know what, we will.   (COCA, 2019, Spoken)

In the following section, we present the results of our corpus analysis, with a particular focus on discourse-pragmatic uses of *like*.

4. Analysis

4.1 Use of *like* across functional categories

Altogether, 1,946 instances of *like* were identified in TASE1. Manual annotation of all instances allowed us to differentiate between its different uses. Table 2 reports the raw frequencies as well as the normalized frequencies per thousand words (ptw) for the different uses of *like* in the TASE1 corpus. The percentage of all instances of *like* is also given. The last column gives the normalized frequency (ptw) and percentage of all instances of *like* for the SPOKE corpus (as reported in Rüdiger 2021).

As demonstrated in Table 2, *like* certainly is part of the English repertoire of the Taiwanese speakers in TASE1 as it is used consistently across functional categories (except as noun and adjective) — apparently even more, at least in terms of frequency, than the Korean English speakers from the SPOKE corpus do, as *like* is used 25.5 times per thousand words by the Taiwanese speakers of English and 15.0 times per thousand words by the Korean speakers. However, for this and all following results, we need to keep in mind that TASE1 is still in its pilot stage

Table 2. The functional ranges of *like* in TASE1 and SPOKE

	Functional category	Raw frequency in TASE1	Normalized frequency (ptw) & % of all instances of *like* in TASE1	Normalized frequency (ptw) & % of all instances of *like* in SPOKE
1	Discourse particle	712	9.3 / 36.7%	7.0 / 46.6%
2	Discourse marker	334	4.4 / 17.2%	1.1 / 7.6%
3	Verb	235	3.1 / 12.1%	2.9 / 19.5%
4	Preposition	174	2.3 / 8.9%	2.2 / 14.4%
5	Approximative adverb	102	1.3 / 5.2%	0.7 / 5.0%
6	Quotative	87	1.1 / 4.5%	0.5 / 3.1%
7	Conjunction	44	0.6 / 2.3%	0.1 / 0.4%
8	Comparative complementizer	40	0.5 / 2.1%	0.1 / 0.9%
9	Sentence adverb	26	0.3 / 1.3%	0.0 / 0.0%
10	Suffix	1	0.0 / 0.1%	0.0 / 0.0%
11	Noun	0	0.0 / 0.0%	0.0 / 0.0%
12	Adjective	0	0.0 / 0.0%	0.0 / 0.0%[4]
13	Repetition	64	0.8 / 3.3%	0.3 / 1.7%
14	Unclear	127	1.7 / 6.5%	0.1 / 0.9%
	Σ	1,946	25.5 / 100%	15.0 / 100%

and is not only much smaller than SPOKE but also reflecting a somewhat different speaker demographic (e.g., the TASE1 speakers are younger, see methodology section; the average age of TASE1 speakers is 20 years whereas the average age of the SPOKE speakers is 27).[5]

---

4. The adjective frequency was originally not listed in Rüdiger (2021) but has been added to this table.

5. However, Rüdiger (2021: 556) found no significant difference in *like* usage between younger speakers (i.e., students) and the slightly older speakers (i.e., early professionals) in SPOKE.

4.2 Discourse-pragmatic uses of *like*

We can also see that the frequencies of use per thousand words are higher for TASE1 in every single functional category (except for nouns and adjectives, where zero instances were observed for both TASE1 and for SPOKE) — in particular for the discourse marker (4.4 vs. 1.1 instances ptw), discourse particle (9.3 vs. 7.0 instances ptw), and unclear (1.7 vs. 0.1 instances ptw) categories. The latter could potentially point to a higher number of incomplete utterances in the Taiwanese data set than in the Korean one, as instances such as (7) and (8) below, where *like* could not be clearly identified due to the fragmented nature of the utterance, were typically tagged as unclear.[6] It remains to be seen, however, whether this hypothesis holds up in follow-up research.

(7) you put it on the stove to **like** (2) is that fried?[7] (TASE1_TW002_2)

(8) yeah a little because I need to **like** (.) I wor- I'm a teacher part time teacher too so (TASE1_TW002_3)

Examples of *like* used by the TASE1 speakers as discourse marker can be found in (9) and (10) and as discourse particles in (11) and (12).

(9) **like** you enroll in those classes (.) like before the major exam (TASE1_TW006_8)

(10) **like** my boss and my colleague sometimes they need to fly to uh Thailand or Vietnam or other country (TASE1_TW019_22)

(11) that movie was big in (.) in **like** Chinese speaking countries (TASE1_TW017_20)

(12) I'm **like** doing a lot of voluntary services (TASE1_TW014_17)

For the SPOKE corpus, Rüdiger (2021) identified four speakers (out of 115) who did not use *like* as discourse marker or discourse particle (nor as quotative) at

---

6. It might also be connected to the tagging procedure, with a student assistant working through the corpus at large first and the researchers only re-tagging problematic cases. However, we went through all cases which the student assistant had marked as unclear and assigned them the correct tags where possible.

7. Speakers from the TASE1 corpus are identified by the name of the corpus followed by interview and participant number (see Section 3 for information on the demographics of our sample). Transcripts are orthographic representations of speech including the following additional information: long pauses marked by brackets including a number giving approximate pause length in seconds, e.g., (2) for a two-second pause; short pauses marked by (.); ? for rising question intonation; incomplete words marked by -, see, e.g., *wor-* in Example (8).

all.[8] No non-users of discourse-pragmatic *like* were found in the TASE1 corpus, though it remains to be seen if this holds for the finalized corpus in its much larger form. There were, however, two participants who either did not use any discourse particle *like* (but did use it as discourse marker) — participant 4 — or, vice versa, did not use any discourse marker *like* (but did use it as discourse particle) — participant 18. Otherwise, we found very different individual preferences for discourse-pragmatic uses of *like*, ranging from 0.5 ptw at the lower end to 11.2 ptw as the maximum for discourse marker *like* and from 0.5 ptw to 34.9 ptw for discourse particle *like*. The highest numbers for both discourse marker and discourse particle usage of *like* (i.e., 11.2 ptw for discourse marker and 34.9 ptw for discourse particle) stem from the same person — participant 17, an 18-year-old male student of English literature, who had dual citizenship with the US where he spent six years of his early childhood, though growing up with Mandarin Chinese as L1. In the SPOKE data, similar tendencies were observed, with the most prolific *like* user being a 24-year-old female student who had spent 8 months in the USA and who had a Korean-American boyfriend. While her discourse marker usage of *like* stayed below the rate by the Taiwanese male speaker mentioned above (11.2 ptw vs. 8.8 ptw), her discourse particle use of *like* is higher: 61.2 ptw vs. the 34.9 ptw by the Taiwanese speaker. What both the prolific Taiwanese user and Korean user of discourse-pragmatic *like* have in common are their particularly strong ties to the US-American setting. Both speakers might contribute to the spread of discourse-pragmatic *like* outside of classroom settings. Nevertheless, it needs to be kept in mind that in both corpora many of the speakers who used *like* as discourse marker and/or particle had less prominent or even no obvious ties to the United States (besides influence from pop culture and English language teaching material).

4.3 Quotative *like*

Besides uses as a discourse marker and discourse particle, we identified 87 instances (1.1 ptw) of quotative *like*, i.e., instances where *like* was used to introduce reported direct speech or thought (see Example (13)). Altogether, 11 of the 21 TASE1 speakers used at least one instance of quotative *like*.

(13)   he saw a picture in the yearbook and he point at me he's **like** well who is she?
(TASE1_TW007_09)

---

8. The four non-users of *like* with discourse-pragmatic function in SPOKE are a 29-year-old male IT-worker, a 26-year-old female youth education student, a 25-year-old male electronics student, and a 21-year-old female business management student (Rüdiger 2021: 554).

The most common introductory element occurring before quotative *like* is a form of *be* (as demonstrated in (13)). Other options chosen by the participants are *ask, introduce, say* (see (14) for an example), and *tell*, but as shown in Table 3, most of these are nonce uses or very rare (e.g., *say* with five occurrences). A small exception can be found in the absence of an introductory element, or, to be specific, the absence of a verbal introductory element (labelled here as 'zero'). In those cases, we usually find a pronoun or noun, followed by *like* and the quotative material respectively. An example of this pattern is given in (15), where the friends of the speaker ("all my friend") are quoted as commenting on a fortune teller's prediction regarding the age when she will meet her boyfriend ("oh that's too old twenty-six").

(14) and then I say (.) ***saying* like** (.) hello what's problem? skin problem or you have fever?   (TASE1_TW009_12) [*say* + *like*]

(15) I mean all my friend **like** oh that's too old twenty-six
                                                   (TASE1_TW017_20) [*zero* + *like*]

It might be interesting to note that nearly none of the cases of the *zero* + *like* pattern are bare as such, as they commonly include the adverb *just* before the quotative *like*, as demonstrated in (16), (17), and (18). One might hypothesize that *just* is used together with *like* before short quotative passages (as seen in (16) and (17)), but this is clearly not the case in instances such as (18).

(16) she'll ***just* like** no   (TASE1_TW009_12)

(17) we saw her we ***just* like** hi   (TASE1_TW009_12)

(18) so he ***just* like** I maybe you can you'll like to have a chat with [name]
                                                         (TASE1_TW010_13)

The speech in (18) is immediately followed by another use of quotative *like*, see (19), and even though here the quoted material is much shorter, no *just* is used. In addition, this demonstrates that the speaker is able to use various quotative *like* patterns and is not restricted to a single usage form.

(19) and I ***was* like** yes of course   (TASE1_TW010_13)

In fact, six of the nine occurrences of zero + *like* in TASE1 include such a use of *just*. While the numbers for this pattern are generally quite low and in need of further investigation in the full TASE corpus upon its completion, we can already comment on this as a potential difference to the way Korean speakers of English use zero + *like* as a quotative. This pattern (i.e., *just* combined with zero + *like*) has not been described in Rüdiger (2021) but going back to the SPOKE data and re-analyzing all zero + *like* instances (*n*=26) for this specific usage pattern revealed a single instance only (occurring in a recollection of the traumatic experience of having been bullied in the past and what the bullies said: "I don't know I don't remember but *just* **like** you're Korean like ah yah (sharp intake of breath)").

Table 3. Verb + *like* combinations in TASE1 (lemmatized)

X + *like*	Raw frequency	% of all quotative *like*
Be	69	79.3%
Zero	9	10.3%
Say	5	5.7%
Ask	1	1.1%
Introduce	1	1.1%
Respond	1	1.1%
Tell	1	1.1%
Σ	87	100%

While quotative *like* seems to form part of at least some Taiwanese speakers' English repertoire, less variety in the use of the introductory elements can be observed when comparing this to the Korean English data from SPOKE; whereas only 47.9 percent of quotative *like* is introduced by a form of *be* in SPOKE, the corresponding percentage in TASE1 is 79.3 percent, pointing clearly towards a less varied usage of introductory elements.

Conspicuously absent in both corpora are any uses of *go* + *like* as found for instance in American English (see (20); see also (6)); *go* + *like* is only attested once for the Korean English data (see (21)) and does not occur at all in TASE1.

(20) I heard his voice and I went, whoa. I *go* **like** who is that?
(COCA, 2011, Spoken)

(21) I I went there and told them like (.) hey that's (.) you know what that's my mum and they *go* **like** (.) that's your mum? cool mum can I have your number?
(SPOKE; Rüdiger 2021: 557)

5. Discussion and conclusion

In this paper, we have shown that the use of *like* as a discourse marker, discourse particle, and quotative is fairly widespread in our Taiwanese English data. A comparison with data from South Korea reveals interesting similarities and differences in distribution: an overall higher rate of *like* use in Taiwan, particularly for discourse markers; and quotative uses collocate more often with *just* in Taiwan than Korea, but both varieties disfavor *go* + *like*.

As highlighted in Rüdiger (2021: 558) for *like* in Korean English, one might also wonder about the considerable frequency of use of this discourse marker/particle in Taiwanese English, seeing as it is not the kind of use typically found in most textbook- and classroom-based teaching activities — especially so in educational settings that prioritize (primarily written) examination preparation rather than naturalistic conversational interaction. Seeing as both the Korean and Taiwanese contexts largely fit that educational ideology, our results may, at first glance, appear surprising. In keeping with Rüdiger (2021), we hypothesize that the widespread use of *like* in these rather more colloquial functions stems from school-external sources of language contact, e.g., in the form of the consumption of (often US-origin) pop-cultural products and media, their use on globalized social media, as well as, potentially, the solidification of such discourse markers through repeated use within the Taiwanese English speech community (subject to its ontological status, see, e.g., Seilhamer 2015). Actual face-to-face contact between Taiwanese (and, indeed, Korean) English speakers and L1 English speakers, in the course of which such features might be transferred in more spontaneous, colloquial forms of speech, is a fringe phenomenon restricted to those with actual travel experience abroad (or English-language tourism encounters in Taiwan) and is therefore unlikely to affect the population at large. It also remains to be seen to which degree other forms of English variety contact (such as, e.g., between Korean and Taiwanese speakers of English who might draw on English as a lingua franca [ELF]; see Lorenz 2022 on the use of *like* by ELF speakers in the United Arab Emirates) play a role in the transmission or solidification of discourse-pragmatic feature use.

The nature of the pilot corpus used in this study means that its size renders more statistically informed comparisons difficult, particularly across demographic groups based, e.g., on gender and age. The first glimpses of the distributional behavior of *like* indicate though that it is a feature worthy of further attention once the complete corpus is available.

In more general terms, while we postulated a US origin for the discourse marker/particle and quotative *like* found in our data, we want to stress that we regard it as a feature firmly entrenched in Taiwanese and Korean English, and, we surmise, in other (East) Asian Englishes. We would like to end this chapter, therefore, with a call for more corpus-based studies of discourse-pragmatic variation in Outer and Expanding Circle varieties of English.

Acknowledgments

The authors gratefully acknowledge the DFG (German Research Foundation) funding for the pilot study (research grant LE3136/4-1 and RU2369/1-1). We are particularly thankful to our hosts and colleagues at Fu Jen University, Taipei, and our interview participants. We would also like to thank Miriam Neuhausen, Franziska Ahlstich, and Lê Đồng Thảo Vy for their help with transcription and tagging.

References

Anthony, Laurence. 2018. *AntConc 3.5.7*. Tokyo: Waseda University. https://www.laurenceanthony.net/software (12 October 2024).

Bosher, Susan & Joel Stocker. 2015. Nurses' narratives on workplace English in Taiwan: Improving patient care and enhancing professionalism. *English for Specific Purposes* 38: 109–120.

Chen, Ai-hua. 2013. An evaluation on primary English education in Taiwan: From the perspective of language policy. *English Language Teaching* 6(10): 158–165.

Chen, Cheryl Wei-Yu. 2006. The mixing of English in magazine advertisements in Taiwan. *World Englishes* 25(3–4): 467–478.

Chen, Christie, Hsiu-chuan Shih, Joseph Yeh & Hsin-Yin Lee. 2018. Government offers vision of English as official language in Taiwan. *Taiwan News*. https://www.taiwannews.com.tw/en/news/3352571 (26 January 2023).

Chen, Su-Chiao. 2006. Simultaneous promotion of indigenisation and internationalisation: New language-in-education policy in Taiwan. *Language and Education* 20(4): 322–337.

Chen, Suchiao & Yachin Tsai. 2012. Research on English teaching and learning: Taiwan (2004–2009). *Language Teaching* 45(2): 180–201.

Chien, Chin-Wen. 2014. Integration of school features into Taiwanese elementary school new English curriculum. *Education 3–13* 42(6): 589–600.

Chou, Chuing Prudence & James K. S. Yuan. 2011. Buxiban in Taiwan. *The Newsletter* 56: 15.

Chou, Mu-Hsuan. 2015. Impacts of the Test of English Listening Comprehension on students' English learning expectations in Taiwan. *Language, Culture and Curriculum* 28(2): 191–208.

Cooper, Robert L. 1990. *Language Planning and Social Change*, 1st edn. Cambridge: Cambridge University Press.

D'Arcy, Alexandra. 2017. *Discourse-Pragmatic Variation in Context: Eight Hundred Years of LIKE*. Amsterdam: John Benjamins.

Ferrer, Alessandra & Tzu-Bin Lin. 2021. Official bilingualism in a multilingual nation: A study of the 2030 bilingual nation policy in Taiwan. *Journal of Multilingual and Multicultural Development* 45(2): 1–13.

Gilquin, Gaëtanelle. 2016. Discourse markers in L2 English: From classroom to naturalistic input. In Olga Timofeeva, Anne-Christine Gardner, Alpo Honkapohja & Sarah Chevalier (eds.), *New Approaches to English Linguistics: Building Bridges*, pp. 213–249. Amsterdam: John Benjamins.

Go, S. 2018. Taiwan ni okeru gengo shiyo no jittai: Kagi-ken kenritsu D shogakko "Kyodo Gengo" rishusha wo jirei ni [*The actual state of language use in Taiwan: A case study of students enrolled in "local language" classes at Chiayi City Municipal D Elementary School*]. https://ir.library.osaka-u.ac.jp/repo/ouka/all/70000/gbkp_2017_hm_019.pdf (12 October 2024).

Hellermann, John & Andrea Vergun. 2007. Language which is not taught: The discourse marker use of beginning adult learners of English. *Journal of Pragmatics* 39(1): 157–179.

Hsu, Jia-Ling. 1994. Englishization and language change in modern Chinese in Taiwan. *World Englishes* 13(2): 167–184.

Hu, Guangwei & Sandra Lee McKay. 2012. English language education in East Asia: Some recent developments. *Journal of Multilingual and Multicultural Development* 33(4): 345–362.

Jiang, Yan & Jean-Marc Dewaele. 2019. Language anxiety in Chinese dialects and Putonghua among college students in mainland China: The effects of sociobiographical and linguistic variables. *Journal of Multilingual and Multicultural Development* 40(4): 289–303.

Kao, Shin-Mei & Wenli Tsou (eds.). 2017. *English as a Medium of Instruction in Higher Education: Implementations and Classroom Practices in Taiwan* (English Language Education 8,. 1st edn. Singapore: Springer.

Kobayashi, Peter Iori. 2020. English in Taiwan. In Kingsley Bolton, Werner Botha & Andy Kirkpatrick (eds.), *The Handbook of Asian Englishes*, 1st edn, pp. 547–567. Hoboken, NJ: Wiley Onle Library.

Leimgruber, Jakob R. E. 2013. The management of multilingualism in a city-state: Language policy in Singapore. In Peter Siemund, Ingrid Gogolin, Monika Edith Schulz & Julia Davydova (eds.), *Multilingualism and Language Diversity in Urban Areas: Acquisition, Identities, Space, Education*, pp. 227–256. Amsterdam: John Benjamins.

Leimgruber, Jakob R. E., Peter Siemund & Laura Terassa. 2018. Singaporean students' language repertoires and attitudes revisited. *World Englishes* 37(2): 282–306.

Lorenz, Eliane. 2022. "We use English but not like all the time like": Discourse marker *like* in UAE English. *Frontiers in Communication* 7.

National Development Council. 2018. *Blueprint for Developing Taiwan into a Bilingual Nation by 2030*. https://ws.ndc.gov.tw/Download.ashx?u=LzAwMS9hZG1pbmlzdHJhdG9yLzEx L3JlbGZpbGUvMC8xMjE2OS9lOWIzZjRkZS05YmZmLTRiNzYtYTBlZS05NzQ5ODU3 MzhmMzkucGRm&n=Qmx1ZXByaW50IGZvciBEZXZlbG9waW5nIFRhaXdhbiBp bnRvIGEgQmlsaW5ndWFsIE5hdGlvbiBieSAyMDMwLnBkZg%3d%3d&icon=..pdf (26 January 2023).

National Statistics. 2020. 109年人口及住宅普查總報告提要分析. *National Statistics, Republic of China*. https://ws.dgbas.gov.tw/001/Upload/463/relfile/11064/230649/b2ae65e2-86fe-416a-b02c-8376e1f4f73d.pdf (3 March, 2023).

Price, Gareth. 2014. English for all? Neoliberalism, globalization, and language policy in Taiwan. *Language in Society* 43(5): 567–589.

Rüdiger, Sofia. 2016. Cuppa coffee? Challenges and opportunities of compiling a conversational English corpus in an expanding circle setting. In Valentin Werner, Hanna Christ, Daniel Klenovšak & Lukas Sönning (eds.), *A Blend of MaLT: Selected Contributions from the Methods and Linguistic Theories Symposium 2015*, pp. 49–71. Bamberg: University of Bamberg Press.

Rüdiger, Sofia. 2019. *Morpho-Syntactic Patterns in Spoken Korean English* (Varieties of English Around the World G62). Amsterdam: John Benjamins.

Rüdiger, Sofia. 2021. *Like* in Korean English speech. *World Englishes* 40(4): 548–561.

Rüdiger, Sofia, Jakob R. E. Leimgruber & Ming-I Lydia Tseng. 2023. English in Taiwan: Expanding the scope of corpus-based research on East Asian Englishes. *English Today* 39(2): 100–109.

Saillard, Claire. 2004. On the promotion of Putonghua in China: How a standard language becomes a vernacular. In Minglang Zhou & Hongkai Sun (eds.), *Language Policy in the People's Republic of China* (Language Policy 4), pp. 163–176. Dordrecht: Springer.

Sandel, Todd L. 2003. Linguistic capital in Taiwan: The KMT's Mandarin language policy and its perceived impact on language practices of bilingual Mandarin and Tai-gi speakers. *Language in Society* 32(4): 523–551.

Scott, Maggie. 2012. Capitalising on the city: Edinburgh's linguistic identities. *COLLeGIUM: Studies Across Disciplines in the Humanities and Social Sciences* 13: 115–131.

Seilhamer, Mark F. 2015. The ownership of English in Taiwan. *World Englishes* 34(3): 370–388.

Seilhamer, Mark F. 2019. *Gender, Neoliberalism and Distinction through Linguistic Capital: Taiwanese Narratives of Struggle and Strategy*. Bristol: Multilingual Matters.

Simpson, Andrew. 2007. Taiwan. In Andrew Simpson (ed.), *Language and National Identity in Asia*, pp. 235–159. Oxford: Oxford University Press.

Tai, James & Jane Tsay. 2015. 32 Taiwan Sign Language. In Julie Bakken Jepsen, Goedele De Clerck, Sam Lutalo-Kiingi & William B. McGregor (eds.), *Sign Languages of the World*, pp. 771–810. Berlin: De Gruyter.

Tan, Charlene. 2006. Change and continuity: Chinese language policy in Singapore. *Language Policy* 5(1): 41–62.

Tsai, Kuei-Ju. 2015. Profiling the collocation use in ELT textbooks and learner writing. *Language Teaching Research* 19(6): 723–740.

Tsao, Feng-fu. 2018. The language planning situation in Taiwan. In Robert B. Kaplan & Richard B. Baldauf (eds.), *Language Planning and Policy in Asia*, Vol. 1, pp. 237–284. Bristol: Multilingual Matters.

Wang, Li-Yi & Tzu-Bin Lin. 2013. The representation of professionalism in native English-speaking teachers recruitment policies: A comparative study of Hong Kong, Japan, Korea and Taiwan. *English Teaching: Practice and Critique* 12(3): 5–22.

Wu, Li-ying & Ken Lau. 2019. Language education policy in Taiwan. In Andy Kirkpatrick & Anthony J. Liddicoat (eds.), *The Routledge International Handbook of Language Education Policy in Asia*, 1st edn, pp. 151–161. London: Routledge.

Wu, Ming-Hsuan. 2011. Language planning and policy in Taiwan: Past, present, and future. *Language Problems and Language Planning* 35(1): 15–34.

Yu, Melissa H. 2015. Developing critical classroom practice for ELF communication: A Taiwanese case study of ELT materials evaluation. In Hugo Bowles & Alessia Cogo (eds.), *International Perspectives on English as a Lingua Franca*, pp. 35–54. London: Palgrave Macmillan.

CHAPTER 15

Translanguaging the hero online
A case study on language ecology in praising Qatar's Emir during the 2017–2021 blockade

Irene Theodoropoulou
Qatar University

This interdisciplinary chapter focuses on the digital translanguaging practices of Qatar-based people's construction of H.H. Sheikh Tamim bin Hamad Al Thani, the current Emir of Qatar, as a hero during the blockade that was imposed on the country in June 2017 and lasted until January 2021. A translingual and multimodal corpus comprising tweets and songs composed and performed by the super-diverse population of Qatar during the first year of the blockade is analyzed in the context of resemiotization, and in an appraisal framework with a focus on attitude, namely the ways whereby feelings are seen as a system of meanings. The findings suggest that Sheikh Tamim is constructed as a political and moral hero (Allison, Goethals & Kramer 2016: 5) via a bottom up translanguaged praise of his agency and communal focus evident in his political and diplomatic actions. This praise is realized via emotional stance (affect), which translates into the expression of positive feelings pertinent to his personality, such as love, appreciation, gratitude, and ethics (judgment). The latter is related to attitudes toward Sheikh Tamim's behavior during the blockade (admiration and praise). At the same time, the role of language ecology including translanguaging in the superdiverse (Vertovec 2007) context of Qatar is examined in the construction of the discourse of Sheikh Tamim's heroism. More specifically, it is argued that, while English is used referentially, in order to refer to Sheikh Tamim's achievements and character, languages like Standard Arabic, and Arabic dialects, are used in a more personalized way to either address him directly or to represent his thoughts in the form of direct speech. In this sense, the chapter suggests a new take on translanguaged ecologies through their association with attitudes.

Keywords: appraisal, language ecology, Qatar, resemiotization, Sheikh Tamim, translanguaging

1. Introduction

The Gulf Cooperation Council (GCC) was established in 1981, and it consists of the six countries of Bahrain, Kuwait, Oman, Saudi Arabia, Qatar, and the United Arab Emirates. The UAE and Qatar have the highest numbers of expatriates at just under 90 percent in both nations, and Oman and Saudi Arabia have the lowest percentages at approximately 45 percent and 33 percent respectively (Hopkyns & Elyas 2022: 19). While Arabic is the official language of the GCC countries, English is the *de facto* lingua franca, and multilingualism — including primarily Malayalam, Urdu, Hindi, Tagalog, and other languages — is the lived sociolinguistic reality of the people who live and work in these countries.

On June 5th, 2017, four countries, Saudi Arabia, the United Arab Emirates, Bahrain, and Egypt, discontinued their diplomatic ties with Qatar. These countries imposed a ban on Qatar from using these countries' respective airspaces and sea routes, as well as land crossing in Saudi Arabia, the only country that shares a land border with Qatar. The aforementioned countries alleged that Qatar supported terrorism, violating a 2014 GCC agreement. Qatar denied any assistance linked to terrorist groups, such as Al-Qaeda or the ISIL/ISIS (Khan 2014).

This crisis became known as the "blockade of Qatar" (Chughtai 2020), the "Gulf crisis", or "Qatar's diplomatic crisis" (Miller 2018). I use the term "blockade" in this chapter, instead of "Gulf crisis", because as a resident of Qatar during that period, I was facing the consequences of this situation at multiple levels, including my personal, social, and professional life, on a daily basis.

Following the blockade, trades were brought to a halt, air and sea travel were banned to and from the countries involved, and there were several other social and political implications as well. For example, Hamad Al-Shamsi of UAE imposed a complete ban of any social media posts or other forms of solidarity or sympathy for Qatar, with a punishment of up to 500,000 dirhams, and/or 3–15 years of imprisonment.[1]

During the blockade, one of the most prominent figures in Qatar was its current leader, H. H. Sheikh Tamim bin Hamad Al Thani, who was appointed as the Emir of Qatar in June 2013 by his father Sheikh Hamad bin Khalifa Al Thani.[2] He serves as the youngest leader in the Gulf, and he is one of the 10 youngest leaders in the world.

During the blockade in Qatar that began in June 2017, Sheikh Tamim bin Hamad Al Thani showed effective leadership. Despite the economic and political

---

1. https://www.aljazeera.com/news/2017/6/7/uae-social-media-users-face-jail-for-qatar-sympathy (29 February 2024).
2. https://www.diwan.gov.qa/hh-the-amir?sc_lang=en#data--- (15 February 2024).

pressures imposed on Qatar by its neighboring countries, Sheikh Tamim focused on finding a peaceful resolution to the crisis. He worked to strengthen Qatar's ties with other countries outside the region, diversifying its economy, and investing heavily in infrastructure projects.

In addition, Sheikh Tamim continued to engage in international diplomacy, traveling to different countries to strengthen Qatar's relations with the rest of the world. He also hosted several high-profile events in Qatar, including the 2022 FIFA World Cup, which helped to showcase the country's resilience and determination in the face of adversity.

Sheikh Tamim attempted to end the blockade on several occasions, through multiple initiatives. In September 2017, he addressed the United Nations General Assembly, calling out the unjust behavior of the four major blockading countries. In his speech, he labeled their behavior as "terrorism-like".[3] His speech gained attention and support both within and outside Qatar. Two examples of international politicians who expressed support to Qatar were the President of Turkey, Recep Tayyip Erdogan, and the then-US President Donald J. Trump. The former urged the countries to lift the "sanctions negatively affecting the living conditions of the Qatari people" (Reinl 2017), while the latter extended his support for resolving the crisis for Qatar, despite having initially supported the Saudi-led coalition (Wintour 2017).

At the same time, this speech also triggered a massive wave of solidarity with Sheikh Tamim and Qatar within Qatar, which had already started on the 5th of June 2017 on social media, but it found its physical expression in the masses of Qataris and non-Qatari citizens, who flocked to Doha's waterfront, known as the Corniche, to greet the Emir as his motorcade passed by (Al Jazeera 2017).

The superdiverse (Vertovec 2007) population of Qatar, consisting of both Qatari nationals and expats, namely non-Qatari workers from various national, ethnic and social class-related backgrounds, expressed their solidarity with Qatar both electronically, i.e., via social and mainstream media, but also physically, through their signing their appreciation to Qatar and to its Emir on gigantic billboards (see Figure 1).

Numerous members of the population of Qatar were observed to be using visual resources depicting Sheikh Tamim in their everyday lives. These include primarily photos of him in formal and more informal contexts, and portraits with or without words of appreciation and wishes for wellbeing. They used them on their cars as markers of love and appreciation, and they also tended to pose in front of them, especially if these visuals were found in the public space as over-

---

3. https://www.gco.gov.qa/en/speeches/his-highness-speech-at-the-72nd-session-of-the-un-general-assembly/ (15 February 2024).

Figure 1. Billboard with written wishes and support to Sheikh Tamim during the blockade. Source: https://thepeninsulaqatar.com/article/03/07/2017/Outpouring-Qatari-love-gives-iconic-Tamim-Al-Majd-a-mass-touch-up-in-Gharrafa (12 October 2024)

sized billboards, and Qatari nationals and residents alike had their personal photo taken and posted on social media.

Other popular ways whereby both Qatari nationals and residents alike expressed their support is through resemiotizing Sheikh Tamim in their tweets and also through the composition and performance of songs dedicated to Sheikh Tamim, which are the focus of this chapter. More specifically, people's translanguaged construction of H.H. Sheikh Tamim bin Hamad Al Thani as a hero is tackled here. Before I proceed with a short discussion of my methodology and data, I provide a discussion of the theoretical framework in which my analysis is embedded with a focus on resemiotization, translanguaging, and appraisal.

2. Resemiotization, translanguaging, and appraisal framework

Resemiotization refers to the process of multimodally changing the meaning or interpretation of a sign, symbol, or communication system by modifying its context or the way it is used (Iedema 2003). This can happen when a symbol or sign is removed from its original context and placed in a new context, or when a new meaning is attached to it through repeated usage or social conventions. Resemiotization highlights the idea that the meaning of a sign is not fixed or inherent but is subject to change based on social and cultural factors.

Such fluidity with regard to semiotic meaning is also at the heart of translanguaging. This term refers to the practice of using multiple communicative repertoires, both in speech and in writing (Blackledge & Creese 2017; Pennycook 2017; Wei 2018). It is a language-based fluid communicative practice that involves the seamless and dynamic use of different languages, dialects, registers, and semiotic resources, such as images, videos, and sound, to communicate and to construct meaning. It is not limited to bilingual individuals, but it can also involve monolingual individuals who use different linguistic resources, such as slang or technical jargon, to communicate (Chan & Chou 2022). It is an approach that has its roots in language teaching and learning (Creese & Blackledge 2015; García & Lin 2017) that recognizes the multilingual competence of individuals and encourages them to draw on their linguistic repertoires to make meaning and communicate effectively.

As such, translanguaging challenges the traditional view of language as a set of discrete and separate systems, and instead sees language as a dynamic and fluid resource that is used flexibly and creatively by multilingual speakers. It involves the use of code-switching, code-mixing, dialect-meshing, and other hybrid language practices to bridge different linguistic and cultural contexts. Nonetheless, it goes beyond code-switching, which is the practice of alternating between languages, and involves using all available linguistic resources to convey meaning (Gardner-Chloros 2009). In translanguaging, the different languages, language varieties, and semiotic modes are not viewed as separate or compartmentalized but are rather seen as part of a fluid semiotic repertoire (Theodoropoulou 2021). Translanguaging is particularly relevant in contexts where there is sociolinguistic diversity, such as Qatar (Hillman & Ocampo Eibenschutz 2018), and where individuals may be bilingual or multilingual. As such, it can be seen as a set of resources, whereby they can take stances, namely how they can be interpersonal in their communication.

Such interpersonality is the focus of evaluation and appraisal. The appraisal system, which is the other theoretical framework in which my analysis is embedded, is a systemic-functional lexical-semantic framework, which is "concerned with the interpersonal in language, with the subjective presence of speakers/writers in texts as they adopt stances towards both the material they present and those with whom they communicate" (Martin & White 2005: 1). In other words, it can help us "understand how speakers/writers approve and disapprove, enthuse and abhor, applaud and criticize, and how they position their readers-listeners to do likewise" (Martin & White 2005: 1) Ultimately, it allows us to interpret how speakers/writers construe for themselves particular authorial identities or personae, with how they align or disalign themselves with actual or potential respondents. The appraisal can be inscribed or invoked (Statham 2022: 67–68). The type of direct evaluation has been directly inscribed in discourse through the use of attitudinal lexis. Nonetheless, evaluation in language can also take place through the use of ideational tokens, namely words or clauses that do not directly construe evaluation but rather imply the emotional response of the speaker. This is known as invoked evaluation (Martin & White 2005: 61).

In light of this, the appraisal framework acknowledges that, through making linguistic choices to evaluate events or people, language users are also addressing actual or potential respondents; speakers are using evaluation to persuade listeners of the legitimacy of their opinion. The two main types of evaluation, which are pertinent to the data at hand, are affect and judgment (Statham 2022: 64–76). Affect refers to how good or bad on a positive/negative spectrum a speaker thinks something is. In other words, it encodes emotions, or the "expressive resources we are born with", in Martin & White's wording (as cited in Statham 2022: 66), while judgments and appreciation recontextualize these emotional feelings to specifically address judgments about behavior and appreciation of aesthetic value.

Judgment refers to evaluation about how people should behave, and in this sense, it codifies ethical or moral reactions. What is judged is morality, ethics, behavior, and, ultimately, the character of a person. There are two main types of judgment: social esteem and social sanction. Social esteem involves admiration and criticism, while social sanction involves praise and condemnation (White 2016). Social esteem includes evaluations of capacity, namely how in/capable someone is, normality, namely how un/usual someone is, and tenacity, namely how ir/resolute someone is. Social sanction includes evaluations of propriety, namely how un/ethical someone is, and veracity, namely how un/truthful someone is.

Against this theoretical backdrop, the guiding research question addressed in this chapter is pertinent to the linguistic and semiotic ways whereby Sheikh Tamim is constructed as a hero during the first year of the blockade. Before my attempt to answer it, though, a brief discussion of my methodology and data is in order.

3. Collecting Sheikh Tamim-related data

In order to understand the ways whereby the diverse population of Qatar has constructed Sheikh Tamim as a hero during the blockade, I compiled a translingual and multimodal corpus comprising photos, tweets from and songs composed and performed by the super-diverse population of Qatar during the first year of the blockade (5 June 2017–5 June 2018). More specifically, I created a visual sub-corpus of approximately 800 images taken by myself in the landscape of Qatar and others fetched from Google Images (using the key words "Sheikh" and "Tamim"), portraying Sheikh Tamim during the first year of the blockade. In addition, I compiled a sub-corpus of approximately 450 tweets that include the hashtag #Tamim and all its variants (e.g., #Tamim_bin_majd, #Tamim_al_thani,

#Sheikh_Tamim, etc.) which contain appraisal of his character, leadership, and initiatives. The decision whether the tweets had appraisal or not was mine and the appraised tweets were also read by native speakers of Arabic to confirm that my reading thereof was accurate.

Hashtags combine "conversationality and subjectivity in a manner that supports both individually felt affects and collectivity" (Papacharissi 2015: 27), hence they were used as a measurement of my data analysis. Also, the examination of hashtags is one of the most convenient means of understanding what users say about a certain topic. The corpus was collected with the help of Twitter's Advanced Search engine, where I defined the exact hashtags and their chronological range. Also, I specified that the tweets should be in English and Arabic. As a result of my search, I received tweets in Arabic, English, and a few tweets that included code-switching between Arabic and English. In the #KullunaTamim Arabic tweet corpus, the majority of tweets contain embedded images and emojis. Anonymity and the sheer volume of visual data that are created, circulated and viewed by unknown audiences make it difficult to perform conventional qualitative visual analysis. This study is based on the underlying assumption that textual and visual data work together to create meaning and that meaning can be extracted from visuals in conjunction with their associated texts (Pennington 2017: 234). This can happen by focusing on "what is physically present in a picture" and as understanding "symbolic or connotative meanings" (Pennington 2017: 237), based on the sociopolitical context of Qatar. Each of the scrutinized tweets was analyzed in terms of its language and/or dialect of Arabic, emotional and epistemic stance taken by the Twitter user.

Regarding ethics when working with data from social media, some scholars (e.g., Fuchs 2018: 390) suggest the omission of Twitter usernames as a good practice, unless the account belongs to a public figure or an institution. Aligning with this practice, I have anonymized all usernames and images in relation to a quotation from a tweet, in order to maintain the anonymity of the owner of the postings. Since it is against Twitter's terms and conditions to display a tweet with modifications to its original content, I have provided screenshots of the analyzed tweets along with their translations in English, where applicable.

Finally, I was able to find 12 songs that were composed to honor Sheikh Tamim for his leadership during the blockade by various artists with lyrics in English, Arabic, Urdu, and Malayalam. Due to the nature of my heroism-related research focus, obviously the data samples I have collected are biased in favor of Sheikh Tamim. Since this chapter focuses on translanguaging, due to word restrictions, I analyze visual data, tweets in Arabic, and the lyrics of a song that contain translanguaging, as defined above.

All of these different types of data are like a digital collection of people paying tribute to Sheikh Tamim as a true leader, who has passed the confines of his political role and reached the level of a hero. Like an ancient Greek hero, Sheikh Tamim is praised for his *aristeia* 'excellence', meant here as his greatest political, diplomatic, financial, social, cultural moments. More specifically, the tweets and songs can be argued to be similar to epic poetry in ancient Greek society. It is a common practice of Qataris, expats, and blue-collar workers alike to attribute any major achievement of society, such as the smooth navigation of the country during the blockade, to the personal breakthrough of a cultural hero who is pictured as having made his monumental contribution at an early stage in during his administration. These tweets have almost created a Qatari myth about Sheikh Tamim by Twitter users, who tend to reconstruct the figure of the current Emir as the originator of the sustainability of Qatar as it evolves. The same sort of evolutionary model may well apply to the figure of Sheikh Hamad as an originator of Qatar's modernization.

4. Resemiotizing Sheikh Tamim

From the first day of the blockade onwards, a unique climate of solidarity was created in Qatar on behalf of the various and diverse social groups that make up the mosaic of the Qatari society (see Table 1). This solidarity, which was personified as social esteem, was directed primarily towards the leadership of Qatar and, above all, to Sheikh Tamim. Qatari artist, Ahmad Al-Maadheed, designed a portrait of the Emir (see Figure 2) with the calligraphically written Arabic name "Tamim al Majd", which means "Tamim the Glorious". It was posted on Twitter a few days after the start of the blockade. Since then, this particular portrait has been reposted, retweeted, and resemiotized so many times that it became the emblematic symbol of solidarity of Qatari society to the country's leader. The main reason why this specific portrait was widely used and circulated both inside and outside Qatar was because one of the basic demands of the blockading countries was for Qatar to change its leader. The people who retweeted and resemiotized Sheikh Tamim's portrait wished for Sheikh Tamim to remain the Emir of Qatar, hence they wanted to side with, express their strong solidarity and full alignment with their leader by praising him through the circulation of that portrait.

Many residents across Qatar stuck the portrait of the Emir (see Figure 3) to their cars, while others wore it as a blouse; at the same time, institutions and compounds had it at the bottom of their swimming pool (see Figure 4), while many buildings and houses both in central Doha as well as on the outskirts posted huge banners bearing this portrait.

Table 1. List of the top nationalities in Qatar. Source: https://www.populationu.com/qatar-population (14 February 2024)

Country	Expat population (in thousands)	Country	Expat population (in thousands)
India	700	Sudan	60
Bangladesh	400	Syria	54
Nepal	400	Lebanon	40
Egypt	300	United States	40
Philippines	236	Kenya	30
Pakistan	150	Iran	30
Sri Lanka	140	United Kingdom	22

Figure 2. Tamim al Majd (Copyright © belongs to Ahmad Al-Maadheed. Source: Google Images)

The main reason behind the resemiotization (Iedema 2003: 30) of this particular portrait, namely the "the social-processual logic which governs how material meanings mutually transform one another," is, I argue, people's need to express gratitude to the current Emir for the fact that, during the blockade their life was not affected, in the sense that they carried on living and working in a safe country, which

Figure 3. The Emir's portrait on a car window (October 2017)

Figure 4. The Emir's portrait at the bottom of the swimming pool at Qatar University (October 2017). Source: https://www.qu.edu.qa/sites/ar_QA/about/newsroom/Qatar-University/Underwater-%E2%80%9CTamim-Al-Majd%E2%80%9D-(Glorious-Tamim)-billboard-launched (29 February 2024)

would provide them with a decent life and also the ability to save money and/or send remittances back home (Theodoropoulou 2020). In this sense, the social esteem expressed through the Tamim al Majd portrait focuses primarily on the capacity of Sheikh Tamim as a skillful and unusual leader, who, despite the multiple challenges during the blockade, was able to navigate Qatar efficiently and to secure people's prosperity, safety, and wellbeing. Noteworthy is the fact that this portrait of the Emir is still present (i.e., as of February 2024) on multiple billboards scattered across Doha, the capital of Qatar, indexing people's steady appreciation of Sheikh Tamim. Whether the choice to leave these billboards is a top-down decision, namely something that stems from the government, is unclear.

The resemiotization of this portrait during the blockade also resulted in the creation of gigantic posters praising Sheikh Tamim, on which the people of Qatar could record their thoughts and feelings. One such poster example is the one foregrounded, which is found in Figure 5. Even though its creator is unknown, contrary to the one in the background, which is the Tamim al Majd one created by Qatari artist Ahmad Al-Maadheed, it contains various support messages written about Qatar and the Emir personally in various languages, such as Arabic fuṣḥá (Modern Standard Arabic), as well as in various dialects, such as Palestinian Arabic, English, French, German, Urdu, Hindi, Persian (Farsi) as well as Turkish. The message that stands out in Figure 5 is written in Standard Arabic and it reads as /kuluna tami:m/, which means "We are all Tamim." It is noteworthy that, yet again, this is a resemiotization of the equivalent hashtag that the diverse population of Qatar used extensively at the beginning of the blockade in June 2017.

Figure 5. "Kuluna Tamim" taken at the Museum of Islamic Art Park in September 2017

This motto indexes a collectivistically framed affective stance that people have taken by associating, bonding and, essentially, identifying themselves with the Emir. Such an affective stance is the underlying premise of a series of resemiotizations of the portrait, which have taken place both in offline and online communication channels within (and outside of) Qatar. One could argue that it echoes the "Je suis Charlie" hashtag, which was used as an index of ecstatic sharing centered on the affective intensity of the here-and-now (Giaxoglou 2018). The difference, however, between the two is that, in the case of "kulluna Tamim", the affective intensity pertains to the popular absolute Muslim monarch of Qatar, and not to the French satirical magazine Charlie Hebdo. In this sense, there is an interesting shift of the meaning of this syntactic formula in the context of Qatar, maybe as an unintended response to the "Je suis Charlie" movement with the goal of restoring the prestige of Islam in the face of Sheikh Tamim. After all, a closer look at the billboard suggests that the vast majority of messages written on it are in Arabic and Urdu, languages that are closely associated with Islam. However, this claim might be seen as far-fetched in the context of Twitter, given that a number of non-Muslim expats residing in Qatar also tweeted by using this hashtag.

The portrait was also resemiotized in a series of medals, awarded in a series of running races, titled QRS Map Challenge, which targets members of the Qatari community. Such use of the portrait underlines the virtuality of the particular portrait and the importance it has in the daily lives of Qatari residents, while, at the same time, it reiterates the importance that Qatar as a country as well as the Emir himself attaches to sports as a driving force behind the country's socioeconomic development and sustainability (Theodoropoulou & Alos 2020). Sport is used by the country as a form of soft political influence in the world, especially in the aftermath of the successful organization of the 2022 World Cup. More specifically, the branding strategy of Qatar with respect to its sports activities is employed to project its political agenda into a vision of a good society (Theodoropoulou & Alos 2020: 26–27). Qatar is one of the three countries in the world (the other two being India and Japan) that have a statutory holiday that is dedicated to sports and is called "National Sports Day." The latter is celebrated every second Tuesday of February and has been instituted by Sheikh Tamim, who is known for his affinity to sports.

In addition to athletic life, the Tamim al Majd portrait also featured in traditional shops in downtown Doha, as is evident in Figure 6.

In this image, there is an interesting semiotic and translanguaged mix of elements that characterize Qatari culture, such as the bisht, which is the traditional male garment worn on official occasions, including weddings. The bisht is knitted by Indian tailors in a men's clothing store in Souq Waqif, which is the traditional Doha bazaar. Such a working relationship reflects metonymically the macro-level financial relationship between Qatar and India, which has been based on trade between the two countries and India's sending blue-collar workers to Qatar, for the latter to construct the country's emerging infrastructure. Indians along with other blue-collar workers from the Indian sub-continent and beyond keep supporting their families and relatives back home with remittances from the money

Figure 6. The Emir's portrait in a clothing store at Souq Waqif, the traditional bazar in Doha

they make in Qatar (Theodoropoulou 2020). A change that has taken place in Qatar after the blockade through bilingual signs in Arabic (official language of the state) and English (the main language of communication in the country) is to encourage the population to buy Qatari products, in order to boost the local economy, as well as products from Qatar-friendly countries, such as Turkey, Iran, and Lebanon. Through these practices, I claim that the concept of solidarity was built in the public sphere, and it was implemented both linguistically and at the discursive level of encouraging consumerist behaviors, which embrace locality and friendly countries. It is also worth noting that Souq Waqif is one of the most popular tourist destinations for Qatari visitors, so Figure 6's translation of the message in English was also targeting an international audience, namely the tourists, who visited the Souq during their stay in Doha, who, in turn, would carry it as a tourist impression to their country.

The Emir's portrait was also placed on traditional souvenirs and gifts sold in Qatar, such as the plaster model of a Qatari door (farhat al bab). Such miniatures of doors, which are characteristic examples of the distinctive architecture of a culture, were (and are currently) also sold as souvenirs in other places, like Zanzibar (Nooter 1984). One could argue that the Emir is constructed metaphorically as an individual who has opened the door of the country (following into the footsteps of his father, Sheikh Hamad bin Khalifa Al Thani, the Father Emir) for Qatar's extrovert investments, in order to secure the sustainability of the country. There was a belief that the international consumers of these products would travel around the world, so people from all over the world would see this particular portrait and they would receive the message that the people of Qatar are united and fully supportive of their Emir. This very same message of solidarity was expressed through another very creative way through this portrait, as shown in Figure 7.

In Figure 7, the negative of the portrait is used against the backdrop of the original Qatari flag, a practice that, according to Article 5 of the Law No. 14 of 2012 Concerning the Qatari Flag,[4] is not allowed. Such a bottom-up resemiotization of the Emir's portrait can be interpreted as an attempt to visualize through it an important part of the Qatari population — both the Qataris and non-Qataris; the latter include, amongst other social and ethnic groups, black people of African descent and people of color originally from the Indian Peninsula (mainly from India, Bangladesh, and Sri Lanka). By identifying themselves visually with the Emir, these Qatari residents can be argued to express their gratitude, and appreciation to the country's leader, who, in their view, has effectively managed the Persian Gulf diplomatic crisis in a beneficial way for Qatar; it is beneficial because, despite the crisis, daily life in Qatar was not significantly affected. Food and medicine were found in abundance, but the only difference compared to the pre-blockade period was that during the blockade these products were either produced within Qatar or they were imported from allies of Qatar. In addition, in spite of the rather negative and precarious political context of the blockade, Qatar in general managed to instill into its citizens and residents alike a feeling of safety. All of these are important achievements that had an impact on numerous people's everyday lives, and they were seen as the outcome of efficient leadership of Sheikh Tamim (Al-Jaber 2021). I am not aware of any potential fines that were imposed to

---

4. https://www.almeezan.qa/LawArticles.aspx?LawTreeSectionID=14593&lawId=4680&language=en (15 February 2024).

Chapter 15. Translanguaging the hero online 349

Figure 7. The Emir's portrait on a negative of the Al-Maadheed portrait

that particular store that has exhibited this alterative flag but, given that this flag has been shown there for quite some time, my guess is that the authorities might have shown some tolerance to this resemiotization due to the positive meaning it has for the Emir of Qatar.

Finally, and in a similar spirit of using the Qatari flag as a background with strong patriotic connotations, the portrait of the Emir is often accompanied by poetic texts, such as that of Figure 8.

In this particular resemiotization of the Emir's portrait against the backdrop of a Qatari flag, there is a poem written in the Standard Arabic language, whose English translation reads as follows:

Figure 8. The Emir's portrait along with a poem

> You are the country
> in the eyes of your people
> oh, Tamim the Glorious

Through this poem, the creator, who is unknown, and all the people that have shared this portrait in both online and offline communication take a strongly positive affective stance vis-a-vis the Emir by identifying him with the people of Qatar. Such expression of solidarity in an absolute monarchical context, such as that of Qatar, is iconic of the affinity, intimacy, and pride that people in Qatar have in their Emir, which is primarily due to his actions, initiatives, and strategies in order to deal with the blockade (Ulrichsen 2018). These in unison have resulted in this multimodal resemiotization of social esteem vis-à-vis the ruler of Qatar.

It is worth noting that before the blockade, the photos and portraits of Sheikh Tamim as well as the Father Emir Sheikh Hamad bin Khalifa al-Thani did not exist in Qatar's public urban landscape as gigantic posters, photos, or stickers. This was in stark contrast to neighboring countries, such as the United Arab Emirates, where photos of the leaders of each Emirate feature prominently all over the country. The reason for this was because the Emir's family has always wanted to maintain a low profile and modesty in all expressions of public life. Images and artwork related to the Emir's family could only be seen in Qatar during the period just before and shortly after Qatar's National Day (al yaoum al watani), which is celebrated every year on December 18th. This Day has been established as a day of celebrations from 2007 and marks the anniversary of unification of all the local tribes of Qatar as well as the country's detachment from British rule, as until 1971 Qatar was a British protectorate (Fromherz 2012).

In conclusion, a combination of resemiotizations of the portrait of Sheikh Tamim along with the use of translanguaging used in the creative reworkings of Tamim al Majd portrait by Ahmad Al-Maadheed in various surroundings and different locations within Qatar epitomizes the ways in which the diverse social segments forming Qatar's population, including Qataris, non-Qataris, blue-collar workers and also middle class expats, express their collective social esteem, admiration of, and solidarity with Qatar's monarch for his leadership abilities as well as his temper. The Emir of Qatar was able to navigate the country successfully during the blockade, something which is evident in the enhancement of its economy (Antoniades, Al-Jassim & Gharatkar 2022) and also the strengthening of its diplomatic position in the global sphere (Al-Muftah 2019).

This constructed solidarity with H.H. Sheikh Tamim, the current Emir of Qatar, by means of analyzing the resemiotization of the Tamim al Majd portrait within Qatar during the blockade offers a systematic look at how an individual leader is treated communicatively in the image-saturated post-modern absolute monarchical context of Qatar. The resemiotization of Sheikh Tamim paves the way for us to understand the daily cross-modal communicative practices in which the diverse population of Qatar participates.

All this semiotic convergence of different people with different interests around the Emir as is evident through the resemiotization of Ahmad Al-Maadheed's portrait of Sheikh Tamim can be argued to create a post-modern global advertising mechanism from the people inside Qatar, inspired by Sheikh Tamim. This mechanism in turn can be argued to reverse the negative image that had been cultivated against the country both because of the blockade (Jones 2019) and earlier through negative publications, primarily in Western mainstream media, regarding the 2022 World Cup. Most importantly, the mechanism is backed up and endorsed by lay people, a phenomenon that is rather rare to find in the contemporary world, where in numerous (for the most part democratic) countries people take a rather negative and, at times even hostile stance against their leaders. In this sense, discourse analysis of a resemiotized portrait constructing solidarity can be used for questioning and, ultimately, attempting to change the existing conditions of subjectivity between a leader and his people; the hierarchy that is to be expected collapsed, at least during the blockade. Such a solidarity-driven collapse of hierarchy has paved the way for the semiotic and translanguaged construction of Sheikh Tamim as a hero.

5. Heroism as political prudence: Sophrosyne

A hero is a person who is ready, willing, and able to act decisively. It is exactly this decisive action which can be seen as the very barrier that holds back distraction; and it is exactly this decisive action that most people are unable or unwilling to take. A hero becomes, thus, the agent of the larger group (Allison et al. 2016). During the blockade, Sheikh Tamim's multidimensional tactical behavior has resulted in outcomes that have been praised by Twitter users based in Qatar as heroic. The ensuing translanguaging and appraisal analysis has taken primarily a situationist perspective towards understanding Sheikh Tamim's constructed heroic leadership as actions taken to reduce the blockade repercussions for the population of Qatar and as a catalyst for socioeconomic transformation in the country.

In Greek epic poetry, artists used vase paintings to reconstruct heroism; similarly, in the contemporary era, I argue that we have a similar type of iconography but on social media, which includes both Sheikh Tamim's pictures, drawings and videos of him, his activities, his speeches, his movements, his behavior, his existence. Sheikh Tamim develops into a hero in the course of the developing story of the blockade as told by people in offline and online worlds, on Twitter and social media in general. On Twitter and Instagram, what we see in Sheikh Tamim's treatment is a very stylized version of sophrosyne (prudence), which is discussed immediately below.

Sophrosyne is a Greek term that refers to the concept of an ideal of self-control, balance, and moderation (Rademaker 2017). It encompasses a sense of sound-mindedness, prudence, and rational thinking, as well as an avoidance of excess and overindulgence in any aspect of life. The term is often associated with the ancient Greek philosopher, Socrates, who believed that self-knowledge and self-control were the keys to living a virtuous life. Today, the term is sometimes used to describe a state of mental and emotional equilibrium or a state of mindfulness and self-awareness.

Among the many themes that were discussed during the initial phases of the blockade was H.H. Sheikh Tamim himself as the Emir of Qatar, his response to the blockade, his initiatives, and, eventually, his personality. Again, such discussions were not usual in the public sphere of social media before the blockade. In a systematic way, people in Qatar — especially Qatari nationals but also other groups of blue-collar workers and white-collar expats — started using the terms "hero" and "heroism" to refer to Sheikh Tamim's leadership and character. An indicative example of this is found in the following tweet:

In this tweet, written in Modern Standard Arabic, which ironically enough was posted 10 days before the beginning of the blockade, the user usefully epitomizes what it means for Sheikh Tamim to be a hero /baTal/. More specifically, he

Chapter 15. Translanguaging the hero online 353

Figure 9. A Qatari male academic's tweet about Sheikh Tamim
Translation: Name of a Qatari male academic
In stories of success, there is always a hero committing himself to the principles and values, facing challenges and paying the price of defending the truth and the honorable people.
25th May 2017
#Tamim_almajd #Tamim_bin_hamad

creates an image of the typical hero in stories that we hear and links it with Sheikh Tamim indirectly using his photo and the hashtag #Tamim_almajed. Sheikh Tamim is constructed in this tweet as hero who is devoted to his values despite the blockade countries' attempts to distort his moral image. He is portrayed as a hero who fights for human rights and goes through hardship for his people. The idea foregrounded here is that of social sacrifice and it translates into Sheikh Tamim being a hero who is ready to face the risk of destroying his social image and reputation for the sake of his own people, and for the sake of people who need help. This tweet hints at the fact that Sheikh Tamim is the leader of a country, which has been labelled as "a terrorist" by the blockading countries. The tweet essentially is used as a logos-based rebuttal to this pathos-based accusation by making the claim that Qatar (through Sheikh Tamim) actually does the opposite by offering help to those in need and by helping and supporting Palestinians financially (Zureik 2018), politically, and diplomatically (Eddin & Rahma 2021). This aspect of political heroism of Sheikh Tamim is a significant dimension of Sheikh Tamim's sophrosyne, which is analyzed immediately below in a song that was composed to praise Sheikh Tamim during the blockade.

6. Sheikh Tamim's heroism as translanguaged honor

Honor demonstrates a status achieved because of a religious or societal preference (Andishan 2019). Sheikh Tamim's multiple aspects of honor are included in a hip-hop song, called *Glorious*,[5] composed by the Qatari-Canadian artist L'Omari. Even though the song lyrics are in English, namely a combination of Standard American English and African American Vernacular English, there are some Muslim keywords in Modern Standard Arabic as well as some intertextual references to the Qatari national anthem, which is titled "as salam al amiri" (= peace to the Emir).

According to the artist, the incentive behind composing and performing this patriotic song was, in his words, "for His Highness and the world to see how much we love and support our Emir. To show the world the actual truth, not the made up and paid media version of what they're saying about Qatar".[6]

The song lyrics of *Glorious* are the following:

1 They know I know (x4)
2 Born as a king
3 Die as a legend
4 They know I know
5 I was born as a king
6 Die as a legend
7 They know I know
8 I was made from sand', ya' I came from nothin'
9 I'm the savior of my land, you can't tell me nothin'
10 If it wasn't part of God's plan, tell me then who is He testin'
11 Tell me (x2)
12 Who's he testin'

---

5. https://www.youtube.com/watch?v=SXBl5aUeLho (15 April 2023).
6. https://www.iloveqatar.net/news/community/lomari-the-glorious-hip-hop-sensation-that-has-taken-qatar-by-storm (15 February 2024).

13 Tell me then who's he testin'
14 Who are you (x2)
15 To say that I ain't glorious
16 Who are you (x2)
17 To say I ain't a warrior
18 Who am I (x2)
19 I'm a son of a king
20 To the throne I'm loyal
21 Who am I (x2)
22 Can't throw dirt on my name when I came from soil
23 When my time's up and it's too late
24 When the whole world is against me
25 When nobody gets me
26 I know God, God got me
27 Qasaman (x2)
28 God got me
29 A yes man to you
30 Is no man to me
31 I did it on my own
32 Respect my sovereignty
33 So what you want from me
34 What you want from me
35 Who are you (x2)
36 To say that I'm incapable
37 Who are you (x2)
38 To say I'm not relatable
39 Who am I (x2)
40 Bloodline traces back to prophecy
41 Who am I (x2)
42 Remember my name cuz I just made history
43 When my time's up and it's too late
44 When the whole world is against me
45 When nobody gets me
46 I know God, God got me
47 Qasaman (x2)
48 God got me
49 Qasaman (x2)
50 God got me
51 One thing that I'll die for

52 Is my dignity and pride
53 What you think that I'm alive for
54 What you got to show for
55 I got my people by my side
56 Down to ride when it's time for war
57 All that I have is my faith in Allah
58 Hamdulillah
59 Inshallah
60 Mashallah
61 I made it this far,
62 So far that I belong with the stars now
63 When my time's up and it's too late
64 When the whole world is against me
65 When nobody gets me
66 I know God, God got me
67 Qasaman (x2)
68 بمن رفع السما
69 قسما
70 You are glorious
71 Qasaman (x2)
72 بمن نشر الضياء
73 قسما
74 You are glorious

67 and 69   /qasaman/ (I swear)
68 /qasaman bi-man rafaʿa s-samāʾ/ (Swearing by the one who raised the sky)
72 /qasaman bi-man našra ḍ-ḍiyāʾ/ (Swearing by the one who spread the light)

The language of the lyrics is predominantly English, even though this is a patriotic song; as such the expectation would be that the lyrics would be in the Qatari dialect of Arabic or, at least, in Modern Standard Arabic. The reason behind the dominance of English is, as I argue, the intended international audience to which L'Omari appeals through his song. In other words, the artist is trying to praise Sheikh Tamim to an international audience, and not just to Arabs, in order to raise global awareness about the value and merit of the current leader of Qatar. In addition, there is African-American Vernacular English used in numerous lines throughout the song (e.g., the words *nothin'*, *testin'*, *ain't*, and *'cuz*) with the goal of vernacularizing Sheikh Tamim's multiple dimensions of constructed heroism.

More specifically, in lyrics 2 and 3, the subject of the lyrics is omitted but it is safe to assume that the lyrics refer to Sheikh Tamim, who in lines 5–6 and 8–9 is stylized by the artist as a moral hero (indexed through the lexical choices "legend" and "savior"), who resists the allegations, and overall pressure that was exercised to him and his country on behalf of the blockading countries, especially at the beginning of the blockade. The structure of the English lyrics is a stylized version of Sheikh Tamim's resisting argumentation against the blockading countries, whereby he tries to defend himself, his country, and his people. He is represented to do this by alluding — through the lexical choices "glorious" in line 15, "warrior" in line 17, and "king" in line 19 — to the admirable fact that his country has transformed into a regional political, military, and diplomatic powerhouse in the Gulf not only due to the discovery of oil and natural gas but primarily due to the efficient and long-term planning-oriented leadership of H.H. Sheikh Hamad, the Father Emir, and his son, Sheikh Tamim, as has been already discussed above.

The societal preference, which is a sine qua non for our understanding of the concept of honor, is given linguistically through the intertextual reference to the word Qasaman, whose literal meaning in the anthem is "we pledge". This Standard Arabic word is also the title of the Qatari national anthem.[7]

The leadership of Sheikh Tamim is also framed religiously in this song through the reference to God in lines 26, 28, 46, and 48, who, according to the lyricist of the song, has understood and approved the leadership choices and has embraced the actions that Sheikh Tamim has taken to defend his country and people during the blockade. This is because, according to line 40, Sheikh Tamim and his bloodline-based tribe, the Al Thanis, are referenced as appointed exemplary individuals, i.e., prophets and messengers, to communicate God's guidance to humanity; this is the essence of prophecy (Arabic: نبوة, /nubuwwah/), the Islamic principle that is mentioned in line 40. What is very interesting is that this religious framing can be seen as the styling of Sheikh Tamim's morality-based heroism, which gets unpacked climactically in the form of a constructed stylization of Sheikh Tamim's voice. Here is the excerpt from the song again:

51 One thing that I'll die /dɑ:/ for
52 Is my dignity and pride
53 What you think that I'm alive /alɑ:v/ for
54 What you gotta show for
55 I got my people by my side /sɑ:d/
56 Down /dɑ:n/ to ride when it's time for war

---

7. https://www.hymne-national.com/en/national-anthem-qatar/ (10 March 2023).

57 All that I have is my faith in Allah
58 Hamdulillah
59 Inshallah
60 Mashallah
61 I made it this far

The two dominant ideas here are self-sacrifice for the country and its people and faith in Allah; the former is encoded in African-American Vernacular English, evident in the phonemically transcribed AAVE words found in lines 51, 53, 54, 55, and 56. The fine line between life and death as well as the popular support to the leader are the two key themes presented as facets of Qatar leader's moral heroism (Allison et al. 2016). Linguistically speaking, the AAVE framing serves the purpose of vernacularizing it, namely constructing it as trendy and cool, and, hence, understandable to a wide range of people, who will listen to the song and will form an opinion about Sheikh Tamim. The leader, in that sense, is constructed as a down-to-earth hero, whose support base is wide, despite the fact that institutionally speaking, he is an absolute monarch, a fact that, at least in Western democracies, is usually treated as a recipe for the people being completely isolated from the leader.

In lines 57–60, there is a climactic construction of stylized Sheikh Tamim's voice, which affirms his faith to Allah. The sociolinguistic resources used here include the Standard Arabic words *hamdulillah*, which is an abbreviated version of *alhamdulillah* ("praise be to God"), *inshallah*, which again is an abbreviated version of *insha'allah* ("God willing"), and *mashallah*, which yet again is an abbreviated version of *masha'allah* ("God has willed it [has happened]"). In line 58, the stylized voice of Sheikh Tamim expresses its praising, appreciation, and gratitude for the creator. At the same time, through this utterance there may be an indirect appreciation made to Allah, that the blockade could have created more and more severe problems to Qatar than the ones it actually did (Albasoos, Hassan & Al Zadjali 2021). The *insha'allah* of line 59 indexes the lyricist's hope that the blockade will soon come to an end, when he was writing the song. The *mashallah* in line 60 is used by the lyricist to praise Sheikh Tamim for his wise leadership during the blockade. The word is used as a way of praising God with a sense of *Du'aa* for a blessing in it attached to it.[8]

Overall, the analysis found above suggests that the issue of faith (religion-based and faith in the leader of the country) has been encoded in Arabic through constructed stylizations and intertextual references to terms that form an indispensable part of the Qatari identity, such as the Islamic expressions and the

---

8. https://islamkazikr.com/mashallah-meaning-in-english/ (10 April 2023).

name of the Qatari national anthem, while the characterization of Sheikh Tamim's actions, character, and personality is encoded in Standard English and African-American Vernacular English as a way to internationalize the leader's image and to raise awareness about the heroic stance that Sheikh Tamim has taken throughout the blockade. In the following section, I conclude the analysis by reflecting on the sociolinguistic ecology and its interaction with attitudes.

7. Conclusion

This interdisciplinary chapter, combining theoretical tools from discourse analysis, classics, and heroism science focused on the digital translanguaging practices pertinent to the State of Qatar, with a special focus on people's translanguaged construction of H.H. Sheikh Tamim bin Hamad Al Thani, the current Emir of Qatar, as a hero during the blockade that was imposed on the country from Saudi Arabia, Bahrain, United Arab Emirates, and Egypt on the 5th of June 2017, which was ended on the 4th of January 2021.

My findings suggest that Sheikh Tamim is constructed as a political and moral hero (Allison et. al. 2016: 5) via a bottom-up translanguaged praise of his character and his agency in his political and diplomatic actions. This praise is realized via emotional stance (affect), which translates into the expression of positive feelings pertinent to his personality, such as love, appreciation, gratitude, and ethics (judgment), which is concerned with attitudes toward Sheikh Tamim's behavior during the blockade (admiration and praise).

The analysis of images, tweets, and songs dedicated to Sheikh Tamim suggests that the ruler of Qatar can be seen as prime cultural hero of Qatari society in the contemporary history of the country, at least during the blockade phase. As it was shown above, it was a common practice for Qataris, expats, and blue-collar workers alike to attribute the smooth navigation of the country during the blockade to the personal breakthrough of a cultural hero who is pictured as having made his monumental contribution at a relatively early stage during his administration (he was appointed as the Emir in June 2013, and the blockade started in June 2017). The analyzed material is indicative of the creation of a Qatari eulogy about Sheikh Tamim which translates into the figure of the current Emir been seen as the originator of the sustainability of Qatar as the country evolves. The same sort of evolutionary model may well apply to the figure of Sheikh Hamad as an originator of Qatar's modernization.

The two most prevalent dimensions of Sheikh Tamim's heroism are political prudence (sophrosyne) and honor, which are constructed both linguistically and semiotically via mediatized vernacularization (Theodoropoulou 2016), namely an unconventional, direct, and (positively) emotionally charged translanguaged style, which is not normally used to address or refer to country leaders. This was shown primarily in Figures 8 and 9, and it was also very evident in the song lyrics analyzed above. Such translanguagedly expressed power in an absolute monarchical state, where usually people do not comment on the personality or political actions of leaders, contributes a constructivist sociolinguistic take to heroism science. More specifically, the latter is premised on the idea that language is understood as "a social practice with speakers drawing on all kinds of linguistic and semiotic (my addition) resources" (Pennycook 2017: 211) to digitally share their folk conceptions of hero.

This translanguaged ecology, examined in the construction of the discourse of Sheikh Tamim's heroism, further suggests that, while varieties of English are used referentially, in order to refer to Sheikh Tamim's achievements and character, linguistic varieties like Standard Arabic and Arabic dialects, are used in a more personalized way to either address him directly or to represent his thoughts in the form of direct speech. In this sense, the chapter suggests a new take on translanguaged ecologies through their association with attitudes. It will be interesting to conduct a larger-scale analysis of translanguaging practices of the people of Qatar (Leimgruber et al. 2022) to see if these initial attitude-based correlations pertain to the aforementioned sociolinguistic resources.

More specifically, the resemiotization of Sheikh Tamim includes visual and linguistic expressions of appreciation. These, in turn, recontextualize the diverse people of Qatar's emotional feelings in the form of praising the leader's strategic and moral behavior against the backdrop of unsubstantiated accusations, stemming primarily from the blockading countries.

Acknowledgments

I would like to thank the editors of this volume and the anonymous reviewer for useful feedback on previous drafts of this chapters. In addition, many thanks are due to Noorin Iqbal and Sara Al-Naimi for their help in data collection. All errors remaining are my own.

References

Al Jazeera. 2017. Thousands welcome back Sheikh Tamim in show of unity. *Al Jazeera Online News*. https://www.aljazeera.com/news/2017/9/24/thousands-welcome-back-sheikh-tamim-in-show-of-unity (2 September 2023).

Al-Jaber, Khalid. 2021. Governance and the state in Qatar. In Mahjoob Zweiri & Farah Al Qawasmi (eds.), *Contemporary Qatar: Examining State and Society*, pp. 23–38. Singapore: Springer.

Al-Muftah, Hamad. 2019. Qatar's response to the crisis: Public diplomacy as a means of crisis management. In Andreas Krieg (ed.), *Divided Gulf: The Anatomy of a Crisis*, pp. 233–250. Singapore: Palgrave Macmillan.

Albasoos, Hani, Gubara Hassan & Sara Al Zadjali. 2021. The Qatar crisis: Challenges and opportunities. *International Journal of Research in Business and Social Science* (2147-7478)10(1): 158–167.

Allison, Scott T., George R. Goethals & Roderick M. Kramer. 2016. Introduction. Setting the scene. The rise and coalescence of heroism science. In Scott T. Allison, George R. Goethals & Roderick M. Kramer (eds.), *Handbook of Heroism and Heroic Leadership*, pp. 1–16. London: Routledge.

Andishan, Hamid. 2019. Honor or dignity? An oversimplification in Islamic human rights. *Human Rights Review* 20: 461–475.

Antoniades, Alexis, Rafia Al-Jassim & Khalique Gharatkar. 2022. The blockade against Qatar: A blessing in disguise? In David Roberts (ed.), *Reflecting on the GCC Crisis*, pp. 107–125. London: Routledge.

Blackledge, Adrien & Angela Creese. 2017. Translanguaging in mobility. In Suresh Canagarajah (ed.), *The Routledge Handbook of Migration and Language*, pp. 31–46. London: Routledge.

Chan, Brian H.S. & Chris I.P. Chou. 2022. Translanguaging practices of Macau junior-one students in a remedial class. *Asian-Pacific Journal of Second and Foreign Language Education* 7(1): 37.

Chughtai, Alia. 2020. Understanding the blockade against Qatar. *Al Jazeera Online Newspaper*. https://www.aljazeera.com/news/2020/6/5/understanding-the-blockade-against-qatar (2 September 2023).

Creese, Adrien & Angela Blackledge. 2015. Translanguaging and identity in educational settings. *Annual Review of Applied Linguistics* 35: 20–35.

Eddin, Lubna N. & Eltigani A. Rahma. 2021. On Qatar's pragmatic foreign policy: The Palestinian case. In Mahjoob Zweiri & Farah Al Qawasmi (eds.), *Contemporary Qatar: Examining State and Society*, pp. 93–116. Singapore: Springer.

Fromherz, Alan J. 2012. *Qatar: Rise to Power and Influence*. London: Bloomsbury.

Fuchs, Christian. 2018. 'Hear Mr. Neo-Nazi, can you please give me your informed consent so that I can quote your fascist tweet?' In Graham Meikle (ed.), *The Routledge Companion to Media and Activism*, pp. 385–403. London: Routledge.

García, Ofelia & Angel M.Y. Lin. 2017. Translanguaging in bilingual education. In Ofelia García, Angel M.Y. Lin & Stephen May (eds.), *Bilingual and Multilingual Education. Encyclopedia of Language and Education*, pp. 117–130. Cham: Springer.

Gardner-Chloros, Penelope. 2009. *Code-switching*. Cambridge: Cambridge University Press.

Giaxoglou, Korina. 2018. #JeSuisCharlie? Hashtags as narrative resources in contexts of ecstatic sharing. *Discourse, Context & Media* 22: 13–20.

Hillman, Sara & Emilio Ocampo Eibenschutz. 2018. English, super-diversity, and identity in the State of Qatar. *World Englishes* 37(2): 228–247.

Hopkyns, Sarah & Tariq Elyas. 2022. Arabic vis-à-vis English in the Gulf bridging the ideological divide. In Sarah Hopkyns & Wafa Zoghbor (eds.), *Linguistic Identities in the Arab Gulf States Waves of Change*, pp. 17–32. London: Routledge.

Iedema, Rik. 2003. Multimodality, resemiotization: Extending the analysis of discourse as multi-semiotic practice. *Visual Communication* 2(1): 29–57.

Jones, Marc O. 2019. The gulf information war| propaganda, fake news, and fake trends: The weaponization of twitter bots in the gulf crisis. *International journal of communication* 13: 27.

Khan, M. U. H. 2014. Qatar: A model of sustained growth. *Defence Journal* 17(6): 70.

Leimgruber, Jakob R. E., Ahmad Al-Issa, Eliane Lorenz & Peter Siemund. 2022. Managing and investing in hybrid identities in the globalized United Arab Emirates. *Journal of Language, Identity and Education*: 1–18.

Martin, James R. & Peter White. 2005. *The Language of Evaluation: Appraisal in English*. New York, NY: Palgrave Macmillan.

Miller, Rory. 2018. International actors and the new balance of power in the Gulf. *Al Jazeera Centre for Studies Report, Doha, Qatar*: 2–3. https://studies.aljazeera.net/sites/default/files/articles/reports/documents/795b6d7f7ee5471e8063d0f5127d305d_100.pdf (15 March 2023).

Nooter, Nancy Ingram. 1984. Zanzibar Doors. *African Arts* 17(4): 34–96.

Papacharissi, Zizi. 2015. *Affective Publics: Sentiment, Technology and Politics*. Oxford: Oxford University Press.

Pennington, Diane R. 2017. Coding of non-text data. In Luke Sloan & Anabel Quan-Haase (eds.), *Social Media Research Methods*, pp. 232–250. London: Sage.

Pennycook, Alastair. 2017. Translanguaging and semiotic assemblages. *International Journal of Multilingualism* 14(3): 269–282.

Rademaker, Adrianne. 2017. *Sophrosyne and the Rhetoric of Self-restraint: Polysemy & Persuasive Use of an Ancient Greek Value Term*. Boston, MA: Brill.

Reinl, James. 2017. Sheikh Tamim takes Gulf crisis to global audience. *Al Jazeera Online Newspaper*. https://www.aljazeera.com/news/2017/9/20/sheikh-tamim-takes-gulf-crisis-to-global-audience (2 September 2023).

Statham, Simon. 2022. *Critical Discourse Analysis: A Practical Introduction to Power in Language*. London: Routledge.

Theodoropoulou, Irene. 2016. Mediatized vernacularization: On the structure, entextualization and resemiotization of Varoufakiology. *Discourse, Context & Media* 14: 28–39.

Theodoropoulou, Irene. 2020. Blue-collar workplace communicative practices: A case study in construction sites in Qatar. *Language Policy* 19: 363–387.

Theodoropoulou, Irene. 2021. Humoristic translanguaging in intercultural communication in Qatar: Merits, limitations, and its potential contribution to policy development. In Kashif Raza, Christine A. Coombe & Dudley Reynolds (eds.), *Policy Development in TESOL and Multilingualism: Past, Present and the Way Forward*, pp. 161–175. Cham: Springer.

Theodoropoulou, Irene & Julieta Alos. 2020. Expect amazing! Branding Qatar as a sports tourism destination. *Visual Communication* 19(1): 13–43.

Ulrichsen, Kristian C. 2018. Lessons and legacies of the blockade of Qatar. *Insight Turkey* 20(2): 11–20.

Vertovec, Steven. 2007. Super-diversity and its implications. *Ethnic and Racial Studies* 30(6): 1024–1054.

Wei, Li. 2018. Translanguaging as a practical theory of language. *Applied Linguistics* 39(1): 9–30.

White, Peter R. 2016. Evaluative contents in verbal communication. *Verbal Communication* 3: 77–96.

Wintour, Patrick. 2017. Donald Trump tweets support for blockade imposed on Qatar. *The Guardian*. https://www.theguardian.com/world/2017/jun/06/qatar-panic-buying-as-shoppers-stockpile-food-due-to-saudi-blockade (2 September 2023).

Zureik, Elia. 2018. Qatar's humanitarian aid to Palestine. *Third World Quarterly* 39(4): 786–798.

CHAPTER 16

English as a lingua franca in Croatia's multilingual ecology

Manuela Vida-Mannl
TU Dortmund University

This chapter offers one of the first assessments of the role of English in Croatia that focuses on non-educational settings. After presenting the linguistic history of Croatia as part of former Yugoslavia, it offers an overview of Croatia's current linguistic ecology. In so doing, the status and role of the most important and most frequently used languages in Croatia are introduced before zooming in on the role and use of English. While English has been part of the linguistic ecology of Croatia in various domains for quite some time already, it has so far predominantly been investigated in educational contexts. This chapter will focus on tourism and discuss how English might be conceptualized in these contexts. Using the framework of *English as a lingua franca* (ELF) to assess linguistic features occurring in oral interview data, the paper shows that tourism in Croatia can be considered to be a context of ELF use. However, the analysis also shows that some characteristics of ELF that are found in the data might also be explained by specific language contact between Croatian and English and that yet other linguistic characteristics might not be accounted for so easily and should hence be further investigated.

Keywords: Croatia, English as a lingua franca, English in tourism, global use of English

1. Introduction

The Republic of Croatia is a small country located at the Adriatic Sea in southeastern Europe. Prior to its independence in 1991, Croatia was one of the six constituent republics of the Socialist Federal Republic of Yugoslavia. While the sole official language of Croatia is Croatian (Bunčić 2008, for a discussion of the nationalization of the Slavic languages), the country's population of less than 4 million people is by no means monolingual (if that even exists). Due to the somewhat turbulent history of foreign rules and powers in Croatia, some areas, such

https://doi.org/10.1075/hsld.9.16vid
Available under the CC BY-NC-ND 4.0 license.
© 2025 John Benjamins Publishing Company

as parts of Istria, are officially bilingual. Furthermore, speaking various (foreign) languages, such as Czech, German, Italian, or French, is desired and considered to be important in Croatia. This has led many Croats across the country to invest in becoming proficient speakers of multiple (additional) languages (Mihaljević Djigunović 2013). Unsurprisingly, one of the languages that is widely spoken and learned as a foreign language by many Croats is English.

English has not been brought to Croatia as the language of a colonial power but functions as an international language. It is used regularly, especially in urban and coastal, i.e., touristic, regions and by younger Croats, and has consequently developed into a salient component of many Croats' linguistic repertoires. English is salient within these linguistic repertoires mainly for two reasons. Firstly, English is very frequently used in the media in Croatia: movies and TV series are oftentimes not dubbed but offered as English original versions with Croatian subtitles. Consequently, many Croats are used to being exposed to English on a daily basis when watching TV or a movie and have developed extensive receptive skills. The exception to this rule might be older Croats or those who consume only Croatian national television, which also offers TV series and movies in Croatian. Furthermore, English is the dominant language on social media platforms (e.g., Vida-Mannl forthc., on Facebook), where users receive and produce content, potentially enhancing receptive as well as productive language skills. Secondly, the English language is in regular use as a lingua franca. In international encounters and conversations in tourism contexts, for example, tourism workers are provided with extensive opportunities to use English. The contribution at hand will present some first insights into the English used as a lingua franca by Croats who work in the tourism sector.

The present chapter will start with an introduction to the languages of Croatia in Section 2. After an overview of the past and present linguistic situation in Croatia in Section 2.1, it will focus on the special role and use of the English language in Section 2.2. Section 3 introduces the data and the methodology implemented before turning to the findings of the data analysis and their discussion in Section 4. Section 5 will summarize the role of English in the multilingual ecology of Croatia.

2. The multilingual ecology of Croatia

Together with Serbia, Slovenia, Bosnia and Herzegovina, Montenegro, and Macedonia, Croatia, or better the then-so-called People's Republic of Croatia (*Narodna Republika Hrvatska*, 1945–1963) or Socialist Republic of Croatia (*Socijalistička Republika Hrvatska*, 1963–1991), constituted the Federal People's Republic and later

Socialist Federal Republic of Yugoslavia (*Federativna Narodna Republika Jugoslavija*, from 1963 *Socijalistička Federativna Republika Jugoslavija, SFRJ*; henceforth Yugoslavia) from 1945 until the independence of Croatia in 1991. Although multilingualism was encouraged and all languages of the above-mentioned member republics of Yugoslavia, i.e., Serbo-Croatian, Macedonian, and Slovenian, had equal rights and institutional support, Serbo-Croatian was promoted as the common language of the various ethnic groups of Yugoslavia (Bugarski 2004). Although Serbo-Croatian was the primary language of approximately 73% of the inhabitants of Yugoslavia, a multilingual approach to education was widely implemented, allowing students to learn and be taught in both their mother tongue and/or Serbo-Croatian (Bugarski 2012; Požgaj Hadži 2014). Serbo-Croatian was conceptualized as a pluricentric language with two main standard varieties (Serbian and Croatian, bureaucratically termed the 'Eastern' and 'Western' variety or the 'Serbo-Croatian' and the 'Croato-Serbian' variety of the 'Serbo-Croatian or Croato-Serbian language') on the federal level and two further standard varieties for the constituent republics of Montenegro and of Bosnia and Herzegovina. In informal situations, Croats, Serbs, Montenegrins, and Muslims spoke mutually intelligible, sometimes even "hardly distinguishable and often identical dialects, and on the standard-language level, a language that was likewise for all practical purposes one and the same in both substance and structure" (Bugarski 2004: 30). As the demise of Yugoslavia in the early 1990s and the respective independence or reformation of its member republics in the years thereafter resulted in significant turmoil and armed conflicts, declaring a unique and independent national language was of importance to these now independent countries. Although the differences between the declared languages are minimal — besides the use of only the Latin alphabet (Croatian and Bosnian) or both the Latin and the Cyrillic alphabet (Serbian and Montenegrin) — they functioned as a sign of each country's close identification with their respective ethnic majority group(s). While Croatia declared their variety to be Croatian, the successor state of Yugoslavia, which comprised Serbia and Montenegro, declared to be speaking Serbian, and the *de facto* official languages of Bosnia and Herzegovina are Bosnian, Serbian, and Croatian (Gröschel 2009). After the dissolution of the State Union of Serbia and Montenegro in 2006, Serbia claimed to speak Serbian, while Montenegro chose Montenegrin as their state language (Požgaj Hadži 2014).[1]

---

1. With special thanks to Daniel Bunčić for his thorough and constructive feedback on an earlier version of this paper.

2.1 Language use and status in Croatia

As mentioned above, since its independence in 1991, the sole official language of Croatia has been Croatian (Bunčić 2008). The South Slavic language is spoken as a first language by the vast majority of the population (95.25% per 2021 census, cf. Croatian Bureau of Statistics 2023). Apart from Croatian, there are several minority languages spoken in Croatia. These languages do not only contribute to Croatia's linguistic diversity and cultural richness; after a period of Croatisation that aimed at linguistic purism immediately after the independence of Croatia, since 2002 these languages are also recognized in and protected by the Croatian Constitution. A recognition as minority language allows for its use in official documents, education, media, and public life within specific regions and communities (Petričušić 2004). Languages can gain or lose minority language status, depending on various factors, most importantly on speaker numbers.

The history as part of Yugoslavia and the mutual intelligibility of the Serbo-Croatian languages, i.e., Croatian, Serbian, Bosnian, and, later, Montenegrin, have facilitated members of other ethnic groups of former Yugoslavia to (continue to) inhabit Croatia. As of 2021, the second and third most commonly spoken first languages in Croatia, after Croatian (95.25%), are Serbian (1.16%) and Bosnian (0.45%). Other minority languages, such as Romani, Albanian, Italian, Hungarian, Czech, German, and Russian (in order of speaker numbers), are each spoken as a first language by less than one percent of Croatia's population (Croatian Bureau of Statistics 2023).[2] In areas in which a significant percentage of other ethnic groups reside, their languages receive the status of an official language in local administration. Therefore, towns in the region of Istria, such as Rovinj, are often bilingual in Italian and Croatian. In this specific case, the Italian-speaking inhabitants result from parts of Croatia having been under Venetian Rule until 1797 (Lampe et al. 2023). Whether a language is considered an official language in local administration, however, is not based on a potential colonial history but on (more or less) current regional speaker numbers. In addition to these official measures, ethnic minorities in Croatia preserve and execute their languages and (cultural) identities through media, e.g., newspapers and radio and TV programs, and cultural institutions. Furthermore, ethnic minority groups have the right to education in their languages (preschool to high school, see European Commission 2022).

---

2. In the 2011 census, the only language that could be chosen in the used questionnaire was Croatian — other languages had to be added manually. (https://web.dzs.hr/Hrv/censuses/census2011/forms/langs/Englezi%20OP.pdf; 12 October 2024). If the elicitation tool had not been revised, the clear dominance of Croatian in the 2021 census is assumed to represent the government's bias rather than accurate speaker numbers.

While the national language Croatian is most widely spoken and used in Croatia, the English language also holds a unique position in Croatia's multilingual ecology as it serves several functions simultaneously: (1) English is the first language of a small minority of inhabitants of Croatia (Croatian Bureau of Statistics 2023) as well as the language of frequently watched movies and TV programs. It is, consequently, a language many Croats are in contact with on a regular, if not daily basis; (2) English is the only foreign language that is obligatory for all students. Foreign language learning starts in the first grade and English is by far the most widely learned and taught foreign language in Croatian first-grade classrooms (85–90%, cf. Medved Krajnović & Letica 2009). In cases in which a student chooses one of the other foreign languages in the first grade, such as German, Italian, French, or Spanish, they are required to start learning English in grade four. For students who took up English in the first grade, an additional foreign language in grade 4 is optional. Secondary education, i.e., in international schools, and a small but increasing number of tertiary education programs are offered using English as the medium of instruction (see, e.g., Drljača Margić & Vodopija-Krstanović 2018, 2020 for an overview); (3) English is the language of communication in international contexts, such as business or tourism. This frequent use of English — mostly with fellow learners of English — caused a difference in how Croats perceive the English language in comparison to other additional languages that are used and learned in Croatia. English is understood as a lingua franca, i.e., Croats tend to not consider English to belong only to its native speakers but see and use it as being a medium of international communication. This has led to a change in their attitudes towards the language as well as towards the language learning process (cf. Mihaljević Djigunović 2013). One of the contexts in which English is very frequently used as a lingua franca is the tourism sector.

Croatia has more than 5,800 kilometers of coastline to the Adriatic Sea, many beautiful islands, as well as stunning mountainous regions. Consequently, Croatia is very popular with foreign and domestic tourists and has been ever since its time as a member republic of Yugoslavia. In 2021, 12.8 million tourists traveled to or in Croatia, 10.6 million of which were foreign. Due to this high number of tourist arrivals, tourism has become one of the major sources of income for the economy of Croatia. In 2021, the tourism sector contributed €9.1 billion to Croatia's GDP (total of €58.2 billion, cf. Croatian Bureau of Statistics 2022a), while providing many locals with tourism-related jobs such as working in hotels, restaurants, and tourist attractions. Most visitors in 2021 were German-speaking, i.e., 2.7 million from Germany and 1 million from Austria, closely followed by just under 1 million visitors from Slovenia (Croatian Bureau of Statistics 2022b). While many Croats that work in tourism are highly multilingual — and speak, for example, Slovenian and German, English serves as the main lingua franca in the tourism industry.

Due to the frequent contact with English-language media, the extensive schooling, and the economic need, Croatians working in tourism are commonly very proficient speakers of English and can cater to international visitors' needs. Comparing countries in Central and East Europe with the Commonwealth of Independent States, the English Proficiency Index of Croatia was the highest in 2022. Croatian participants of an investigation of the proficiency levels of English users in 111 countries reached a CEFR level that is comparable to C1 in 2021 (Education First 2022). The insights of this study, however, are based on a comparably small sample and might, hence, not be representative of the Croatian population.

2.2 English for touristic purposes in Croatia

While some Croats are first-language users of English and others might have no knowledge of it at all, for most Croats English serves as a foreign or additional language (Strang 1970). Consequently, English in Croatia could be considered to have EFL status. As English is primarily learned through formal (school) instruction in Croatia, previous research has been concerned mostly with the methods, tools, and results of English language teaching (Ivanović, Patekar & Košuta 2019; see Vilke 2007 for an overview) as well as with students' attitudes towards English and other foreign languages (see, e.g., Margić & Širola 2014; Mihaljević Djigunović 2013). In addition, scholars have investigated teaching and learning English for Specific Purposes (ESP, see, e.g., Widdowson 1997), such as business and finances (e.g., Paris 2017) or legal communication (Kordić & Cigan 2013; Matijašević 2013). While teaching English for touristic purposes – as a sub-field of ESP – has received some attention in recent years (Ennis & Petrie 2019; Stainton 2019), scholars have rarely focused on Croatia (Kostic Bobanovic & Grzinic 2011). Due to English functioning as a foreign language in Croatia, investigating and improving teaching ESP and EFL is a suitable approach. However, the use of English in tourism contexts is not limited to Croats in Croatia but potentially also includes speakers from various other countries. Its investigation calls for a more inclusive approach.

The use of English by users with multiple and various first languages from different, sometimes very distant communities is at the very heart of tourism. To investigate this complex scenario, multiple frameworks might be helpful. One essential approach is that of *communities of practice* (CoPs). A community of practice depicts "a social grouping not in virtue of shared abstract characteristics (e.g., class, gender) or simple copresence (e.g., neighborhood, workplace), but in virtue of shared practice." (Eckert 2006: 683). Thus, it includes speakers who do not share geographical or social proximity as full members of the respective speaker community (Eckert 2006; Lave & Wenger 1991). Communities of speakers that use English as a global language in international contexts constitute CoPs as they often include speakers from all Kachruvian circles (Kachru 1985) who speak different and often multiple first languages and use English as a first, second, or additional/foreign language for communication. More recently, groups of English users, characterized by a high level of speaker mobility and diversity have also been considered *Transient International Groups* (TIGs, Pitzl 2018). These are speaker groups that interact at least once and do not necessarily share a common practice or interest. Some tourism encounters, which are characterized by being unique in their speaker constellation, might be considered typical encounters by TIGs while more stable groups would be considered CoPs.

Due to the national, social, and linguistic variety of the speakers involved in tourism interactions, scholars have resorted to using the *English as a lingua franca* framework (Jenkins 2000, 2007; Seidlhofer 2004, 2011) when investigating and describing English in tourism. English as a lingua franca (ELF) emerged around the turn of the century and might be defined as "any use of English among speakers of different first languages for whom English is the communicative medium of choice [...]" (Seidlhofer 2011: 7). The initial aim of the ELF framework has been to identify linguistic features that facilitate non-L1 speakers' communication and norms to improve the teaching of English to speakers of other first languages (Jenkins 2000, 2007, see Jenkins 2000 on phonological features and the *Lingua Franca Core*; Cogo & Dewey 2012; Dewey 2007; Mortensen 2013; Seidlhofer 2004, on grammatical features; Jenkins 2006a; Seidlhofer 2004, on teaching ELF, among others). In addition to the educational focus, it also aimed at achieving the acceptance of non-L1 speakers of English as rightful rather than deficient users by claiming that successful communication is more important in the global or international use of English than the approximation of first-language user norms (Jenkins 2007; Seidlhofer 2011). While these aims of ELF are certainly desirable, the exclusion of all conversations that include first-language users of English has quickly been understood as restrictive causing the concept of ELF to widen its scope and include all speakers of English.

> ELF is a social construct adjusting to the needs of its users in individual communicative situations. It is highly flexible, emerging "out of and through interaction" presumably without ever achieving "a stable or even standardized form" (Meierkord 2004: 129), reflecting and accepting "the variable use of English in intercultural communication" (Baker 2015: 7). (Vida-Mannl 2022: 24)

As a result of the extensive research in ELF contexts and despite the flexible, variable, and context-dependent nature of ELF, several linguistic features that diverge from L1-user norms but tend to not hinder successful communication have been identified. On a morpho-syntactic level, these features include (Seidlhofer 2004: 220, italics original):

- "Dropping the third person present tense -s"
- "Confusing the relative pronouns *who* and *which*"
- "Omitting definite and indefinite articles where they are obligatory in ENL, and inserting them where the[y] do not occur in ENL"
- "Failing to use correct forms in tag questions (e.g., *isn't it?* or *no?* instead of *shouldn't they?*)"
- "Inserting redundant prepositions, as in *We have to study about…*)"
- "Overusing certain verbs of high semantic generality, such as *do, have, make, put, take*"
- "Replacing infinitive-constructions with *that*-clauses, as in *I want that*"
- "Overdoing explicitness (e.g., *black color* rather than just *black*)"

While ELF in academic or business contexts has been investigated quite thoroughly (Hynninen 2016; Mauranen 2012 on academic ELF; Gerritsen & Nickerson 2009; Murata 2015 on business ELF), less formal contexts such as tourism have only rarely been investigated (Maci 2018 on written discourse; Vida-Mannl 2024 on pragmatic startegies of ELF in Croatia; Wilson 2018, 2021 on pragmatic strategies). Hence, assessing the morphosyntactic characteristics of ELF in tourism contexts still constitutes a research gap. A first attempt at closing this gap is presented in the paper at hand.

3. ELF in tourism contexts: Methodology and data

The data and findings presented in this chapter are part of a more extensive investigation of multilingualism in tourism interactions in Croatia. The project encompasses three regions in Croatia: The Northwest, specifically the island Krk and the town Rovinj in Istria; Dalmatia, specifically Croatia's second largest city Split; and the capital Zagreb. As part of this large-scale project, the author collected four different types of data, i.e., 104 ethnographic questionnaires, 71 recordings of qualitative sociolinguistic interviews, 74 recordings of conversations between tourist workers and tourists, as well as extensive linguistic landscaping data. The following insights into morpho-syntactic features in the oral production of English by tourist workers in Croatia are based on a randomly selected subset of 10 interviews. These 10 interviews were conducted by the author in Rovinj and Krk in October 2020 and in Split in August 2021. Due to the small size of the subset, the insights in this paper represent an initial, qualitative look into the characteristics of English used by Croats in tourism settings. For a full assessment of English used as a global language in Croatia further analyses are required.

The relevant interviews were conducted in person and with each participant individually. All participants gave informed consent to their participation as well as to the audio recording of the interviews. Due to the prevailing COVID-19 restrictions at the time of the data collection, the interviews were mainly conducted in public places, such as parks, cafes, or restaurants. Empty shops or offices were used in case an interviewee felt more comfortable in a private setting. The interviews were conducted as qualitative interviews, which are "in-depth, semi-structured or loosely structured forms of interview[s]" aiming at "generating qualitative data" (Mason 2002: 62). Their semi-structuredness triggered thematic narratives as well as informal dialogues and ensured a focus on the content — not the form — of the conversations. Having addressed similar topics, as it is common for Labovian sociolinguistic interviews (Labov 1982, 1984), facilitates comparability. The topics discussed included, for example, the reasons the interviewees work in the tourism industry, their experiences with tourists, the impact of the COVID-19 pandemic on their lives and Croatia's tourism industry, as well as their linguistic biography, linguistic repertoires, and language attitudes. The interviews vary in length between 26 and 70 minutes and were all conducted in English.

Regarding the randomly chosen sub-set discussed in this paper, the interviewees' age ranges between 20 and 47 years with an average of 31 years. 60 percent are female and 40 percent male. All but one identify as first-language users of Croatian and two of these participants are bilingual users of Croatian and Italian or Croatian and Bosnian. Interviewee 14 identifies as a first-language user of Serbian, a language very similar to Croatian — but states Croatian is the language they use most often. Most participants hold university degrees (70%). Three interviewees work as tour guides, two hold management positions, and five work as assistants in shops or tourist agencies. The interviews were transcribed orthographically in ELAN (https://archive.mpi.nl/tla/elan; 12 October 2024) based on MacWhinney's (2000) CHAT (Codes for the Human Analysis of Transcripts), as this is a commonly used and accepted format. Due to the focus of this investigation, the guidelines were adapted.[3]

3.1 Morphological features of ELF

As introduced in Section 2.2, Seidlhofer (2004) has suggested several morphological features that commonly occur in ELF users' speech. Although these features diverge from L1-English users' language use, they do not hinder successful communication. The analysis in this section will be guided by the following subset of Seidlhofer's features (Seidlhofer 2004: 220, italics original):

---

[3]. The transcription codes relevant for this chapter are: [/]: retracing without correction; [//]: retracing with correction; [///] retracing with reformulation; [=!text]: paralinguistic material; &: phonological fragment.

- "Dropping the third person present tense -s"
- "Failing to use correct forms in tag questions (e.g., *isn't it?* or *no?* instead of *shouldn't they?*)"
- "Overusing certain verbs of high semantic generality, such as *do, have, make, put, take*"
- "Overdoing explicitness (e.g., *black color* rather than just *black*)"

While the dataset used for the study at hand includes all the chosen features, they occur to different extents.

As expected, the third person singular present tense verbal inflection -s is dropped in all 10 interviews (e.g., Example (1)). Further incorrect agreement of subject and verb, such as plural subjects followed by a verb inflected for singular or vice versa, occurs with marked verb forms (see Example (2) & (3) for the former and Example (4) & (5) for the latter) as well as with unmarked verb forms (see Example (6)) in 7 of 10 interviews.

(1) "Yeah, everybody **speak** English." (Interview2_S, 00:09:59:990–00:09:61:960)

(2) "maybe here **was** more English speaking, uh, guests." (Interview2_S, 00:01:02:480–00:01:06:000)

(3) "This is part of Europe where we talk very similar. Bosnia, Croatia and Serbia **is** very similar. You can [//] I can understad [//] understand them at all." (Interview20_S, 00:01:44:050–00:01:53:580)

(4) "So I [//] she had [//] didn't had problem to talk in Germany, and, uhm the girl she lived with **have** same name as I." (Interview42, 00:12:73:000–00:12:81:840)

(5) "[...] Er, a brother from my boyfriend, he **were** here, he was working and he said, er, here is great, [...]." (Interview14, 00:01:11:700–00:01:31:610)

(6) "I realized that I have a couple of friends who **owns** tourist agencies, and I traveled a lot before that." (Interview21_S, 00:07:09:660–00:07:16:750)

40 percent of the speakers have been found to overuse "certain verbs of high semantic generality" (Seidlofer 2004: 220). Most frequently the verbs *put, make*, and *have* were overused (see Examples (7)–(10)). While the meaning of the individual utterances is always clear, more specific or accurate verbs could have been used. In Example (7), for instance, the interviewee explains that he sometimes speaks English in private contexts. He chooses the verb *put* to articulate choosing 'sometimes' on the respective question in the complementary questionnaire.

(7) "Now, at the moment, [=!exhales] er, we can **put** it 'sometimes', and that's it." (Interview29, 00:23:36:128–00:23:40:910)

(8) "No, no, no, maybe. Well, a lot of people co& [/] come back. I know [=!clucks tongue] when I was working in the [/] in the other agency, like two years ago, they **had** accommodation as well. So they booked accommodation for others."
(Interview22_S, 00:20:42:010–00:20:55:900)

(9) "Sometimes people treat you like a [/] like a slave. And, uh, it's& [//] there is, uh, option to **put**, uh, the boundaries and risk bad reviews."
(Interview21_S, 00:22:68:470–00:22:81:980)

(10) "So we can make this, uhh, uh, meeting very short. [=!laughs] And [/] and all of your study can be **made**, uhh, uh, very short."
(Interview2_S; 00:00:30:000–00:00:41:360)

Finally, the interviews analyzed here do not include traditional tag questions. However, in two instances other particles were used for the same function. In Example (11) the speaker uses *no*, while in Example (12) they use *or* in an interrogative function. Similarly rare in the data at hand is "[o]verdoing explicitness" (Seidlhofer 2004: 220) which was found only once (see Example (13)).

(11) "And, uh, practically, uh, tourist feedback is something which uh, is Ø only [/] only measurement of your success. **No?**"
(Interview21_S, 00:08:18:400–00:08:29:520)

(12) "So, we shall now start with the questionnaire **or?**"
(Interview23, 00:01:24:210–00:01:28:070)

(13) "You know, because I grew up with **double bilingual**. I grew up Croatian and Italian, yes. […]"
(Interview43, 00:11:90:506–00:11:98:141)

In addition to these ELF features, the interviews show some additional features that are not categorized as ELF-specific. Most notable is the use of prepositions. Examples (14) and (15) show a common confusion of the prepositions *in* and *on*. As 'in English' translates to *na engleskom* in Croatian and the Croatian *na* translates to English 'on', this confusion of prepositions might be a transfer feature from the speakers' L1, Croatian. The same holds for Examples (16) and (17). Regarding (16), the literal translation of Croatian *zavisiti od* would be 'depends from'. The literal translation of *ići na večere* is 'go on dinners', in Example (17).

(14) "Well, I [/] I almost [//] I can almost, uh, better communicate in Spanish than **on** Italian or German."
(Interview22_S, 00:05:20:650–00:05:27:650)

(15) Yes, yes, and I have other colleagues, but we talk **on** Croatian."
(Interview42, 00:06:32:940–00:06:36:870)

(16) "[…] this depends **from**, erm, [=!clucks tongue] from, er, type of the accomodation in youth hostels."
(Interview23, 00:04:16:030–00:04:23:680)

(17) "And they like go **on** the dinners and they spend time together."
(Interview2_S, 00:10:12:000–00:10:15:270)

After having discussed features that might be common in ELF use in general as well as those that seem to be transfer features of Croatian on a morphological level, we will now turn to syntactic features found in the dataset.

3.2 Syntactic features of ELF

Similarly to the analysis in Section 3.1 on morphological features, the frame for this section's analysis is Seidlhofer's (2004) commonly used features of ELF users. Specifically, the following four features will be assessed (Seidlhofer 2004: 220, italics original):

- "Confusing the relative pronouns *who* and *which*"
- "Omitting definite and indefinite articles where they are obligatory in ENL, and inserting them where the[y] do not occur in ENL"
- "Inserting redundant prepositions, as in We have to study about…)"
- "Replacing infinitive-constructions with *that*-clauses, as in *I want that*"

This section starts with the most common feature, which is the unconventional use[4] of definite and indefinite articles in L1-Croatian speakers' use of English. As there are no articles in Croatian, their unconventional use is a common feature and occurs in all interviews. Most commonly, speakers omit articles in sentences in which an L1 user would use them. Omitting an article occurs in structures in which an L1 user would use a definite (see Example (11), (18) & (19)) or an indefinite article (see Example (20)–(22)).

(18) "Maybe I was thinking about being a blogger on Ø internet."
(Interview14, 00:04:51:180–00:04:57:140)

(19) "Sunday. You sent it to Ø information office and probably they sent it to our, like, erm secretary," (Interview43, 00:01:91:510–00:01:97:860)

(20) "er, I worked since I was Ø teenager, in youth hostels, so [=!murmurs] it's Ø wonderful experience." (Interview23, 00:03:75:550–00:03:84:210)

(21) "It's Ø stressful situation, yeah." (Interview42, 00:13:10:000–00:13:11:720)

(22) "I don't have Ø problem with that, don't worry."
(Interview20_S, 00:00:00:790–00:00:02:720)

---

4. Following Hülmbauer's (2013) terminology, language use that would not be considered standard for inner-cicle English users is called "unconventional language" rather than "misuse".

Less often — but still in 80 percent of the interviews —, speakers overuse articles. Example (23) shows an instance in which an indefinite article is used although an L1 user would not use one. Equally, Examples (24) and (25) show the use of a definite article in utterances in which an L1 user would have left this position empty.

(23) "er, open, outgoing and [/] and so on, and maybe it was like kind of **a** destiny. And then I went studying, I didn't want to study,"
(Interview43, 00:09:49:441–00:09:58:021)

(24) "Yeah, we had, er [//] on the last year of preschool, we had **the** optional English,"
(Interview23, 00:09:23:413–00:09:29:254)

(25) "It's totally different if you compare it with **the** s& [//] Western or Northern Europe." (Interview21_S, 00:00:47:960–00:00:52:160)

Quite common in the dataset at hand is the confusion of relative pronouns. Speakers confuse the relative pronouns *who* and *which* (see Example (26) & (27)) in 70 percent of the interviews. This might be due to the Croatian relative pronoun *koji* which refers to both animate and inanimate referents and might be translated by 'which.' Example (26), hence, could be a direct translation of *koji*, while (27) might be a hypercorrection of differentiating between 'which' for inanimate and 'who' for animate referents.

(26) "And, uh, I always had a problem with, er, my employees **which** have been talking English exclusively." (Interview2_S, 00:0089:830–00:00:96:770)

(27) "Yeah, they [/] they are trying to get that Croatian-speak language, **who** will be just a local variant of Serb language."
(Interview2_S, 00:09:29:000–00:09:37:270)

Finally, while no instances of inserting redundant prepositions have been found in the data, two instances of replacing infinitive constructions with *that*-constructions were found (Examples (28) & (29)). Example (28) even shows the exact construction used by Seidlhofer (2004: 220), i.e., *want that*.

(28) "You know, but it's in English. And then I translate a little bit. I don't **want that** they feel like," (Interview43, 00:18:73:032–00:18:78:542)

(29) "No problem. I'm **happy that** I can help."
(Interview22_S, 00:00:61:000–00:00:64:680)

After having assessed features that are assumed to be ELF-specific, other features that occur in the dataset might again be specific to L1 users of Croatian and their use of English. In line with the fact that no articles exist in Croatian, the dataset did not only reveal that they are unconventionally omitted and used but also that their form might differ from the one an L1 user of English would employ. Example (30) shows the only instance in the dataset in which the speaker correctly filled the determiner position in the sentence. The use of the quantifier instead of an indefinite article might be a transfer effect from Croatian *jedan* ('one', 'some'). Furthermore, due to a rich case marking in nouns and adjectives, Croatian word order is quite flexible. While the most common sentence structure is SVO, all other orders are also common, depending on the information structure. These structures are sometimes kept when using English (see Example (31)). Furthermore, the order of arguments, which again is quite flexible in Croatian and less so in English, might be transferred into the use of English (see Example (32) & (33)). Last but not least, traces of negation structures used in Croatian can be found in the interviews. In Example (34), the speaker seems to have kept some of the Croatian sentence structure of *to nije bila dobra ideja* (which translates into 'it has not been good idea'). As *nije* means 'not' as well as 'is not', the speaker might have chosen the latter meaning to form "It's not was a good idea [...]" or might have decided to switch from present perfect to simple past mid-sentence with 'It's' as cliticized 'It has'.

(30) "Yeah, there's in my village. It's **one** village close to the seaside."
(Interview2_S, 00:12:24:000–00:12:28:000)

(31) "Slovenia m& [/] much less but, er, **I can** [//] ehm **them understand.** [...]"
(Interview20, 00:01:53:720–00:01:58:640)

(32) "And, uh, Chinese lady working there **was speaking with people Croatian.**"
(Interview 2_S, 00:11:51:640–00:11:55:580)

(33) "But I think it's not, er, I don't know **in which zone is which country** but I think, yes." (Interview22_S, 00:18:84:000–00:18:91:000)

(34) "[=!inhales] w& [///] **It's not was** a good idea to learn German."
(Interview20, 00:0051:720–00:00:55:700)

The potential effects of the presented features on the role of English within the multilingual ecology of Croatia will be discussed in the following.

4. English for touristic purposes in Croatia: Discussion

This paper has shown that English has become an essential part of Croatia's multilingual ecology. While it has been used in the media, education, and tourism for quite some time, it used to just be one of many foreign languages present in Croatia. However, due to the global rise of English as the most important global lingua franca as well as the resulting increase in command of English amongst speakers around the globe, it has become more important and increasingly dominant in international contexts. One of these contexts, which is also of utmost economic importance in Croatia, is the tourism industry. The economic importance of the tourism sector to the Croatian economy has resulted in a focus on tourism already in secondary and tertiary education, i.e., there are tourism high schools and tourism and hospitality study programs across the country. These educational paths include several foreign languages such as German, Italian, and Spanish to reflect these languages' traditional importance within the tourism industry. As English proficiency around the globe has increased — also amongst other Europeans visiting Croatia — the importance of these languages has decreased and English has taken over as the most important language in this sector. Consequently, there has been some research on English in Croatia; however, up until now, it has focused primarily on educational settings.

This paper has presented a first assessment of English in Croatia in the non-educational setting of tourism. In Sections 3.1 and 3.2, a qualitative analysis of oral English use by tourism workers in Croatia has been presented based on a data set of 10 audio-recorded interviews. It has been found that these data include morphological and syntactic features that are commonly found in ELF contexts. On a morphological level, it has been shown that all speakers drop the third-person singular present tense verbal inflection -s. The other features of ELF use mentioned by Seidlhofer (2004), however, i.e., overuse of semantically generic verbs, overexplicitness, and unconventional forms of tag questions, have been found considerably less commonly (cf. Section 3.1). These lower numbers of occurrences could be caused by language-internal and external factors: the less frequent use of structures such as tag questions offers fewer opportunities to (mis-)form them and the overall quite high proficiency level of the speakers, their frequent use of the language, and the fact that they have learned English as an additional language in formal educational settings for years is likely to be reflected in a relatively extensive lexicon.

Although not all syntactic features listed by Seidlhofer (2004) have been found, those that do occur, do so quite often. The vast majority of speakers in this dataset use articles in English unconventionally, i.e., omit them when traditionally required and/or use them when they are not, and confuse the relative pronouns *who* and *which*. Less commonly, the speakers use *that*-clauses to replace infinitive-constructions which might be due to the more complex structure or, again, the speakers' high level of proficiency (cf. Section 3.2). While the occurrence of the presented syntactic features of ELF, i.e., confusing the relative pronouns, unconventional use of definite and indefinite articles, and replacing infinitive constructions with *that*-clauses, has been expected, a closer look might suggest that they might not be generic features of ELF but (also) results of L1 influence. For example, the fact that articles are not part of the Croatian language – definiteness is partly expressed through nominal inflection (cf. Heinz & Kuße 2015) – might explain why users in the current dataset omit them. Furthermore, the Croatian relative pronoun *koji* has broader reference than the English pronouns *who* and *which* and can be used to refer to animate and inanimate antecedents. The unconventional use of *who* and *which* that has been found (cf. Section 3.2) might, therefore, result from the speakers' first language, Croatian, influencing their use of English.

Due to their high level of proficiency in English as well as the often existing competencies in other additional languages, Croatians can access and utilize their linguistic resources in unconventional, flexible, and constantly changing ways. This creativity is a central aspect of ELF interactions, causing scholars to refrain from understanding these non-standard instances of language use as errors (cf., e.g., Jenkins 2006b; Seidlhofer & Widdowson 2009). It has been argued that it would be of little relevance whether or not these creative ways of using English were to stabilize or not, as ELF communities are often constantly changing and highly transient (e.g., Brunner, Diemer & Schmidt 2018). However, looking further into the impact of the Croatian language on L1-Croatian speakers' use of ELF would be interesting: in the dataset at hand, for example, speakers have used quantifiers instead of articles, SOV sentence structures, and unconventional prepositions (cf. Sections 3.1 & 3.2). While these features could be explained by L1 transfer mechanisms and potentially be aspects of learner English, they could also be more generic and reoccurring, reveal parallels between individual speakers, and represent potential first indices of stabilization. Further research is needed to clarify this issue.

5. Conclusion

Although not all features that Seidlhofer (2004) lists are present in the dataset at hand, the presence of most of them seems to corroborate the assumption that tourism in Croatia is an ELF context. Furthermore, the dataset has revealed features that are not generally associated with ELF contexts, i.e., linguistic characteristics realized by ELF users across L1-speaker groups, but might have been transferred specifically from Croatian. Further, larger-scale studies need to be conducted to fully assess how English is used by Croats in international contexts and to corroborate which of the found features might be transfer features or even features of a more generic realization of English, such as Euro-English (cf. Jenkins, Modiano & Seidlhofer 2001).

English in Croatia might be more than ELF use and the perfect framework to contextualize might not have been found yet. However, the study at hand has shown that English is one of the — if not *the* — most important foreign languages in Croatia and an unavoidable constituent of its multilingual ecology.

References

Baker, Will. 2015. *Culture and Identity through English as a Lingua Franca: Rethinking Concepts and Goals in Intercultural Communication*. Berlin: De Gruyter Mouton.

Brunner, Marie-Louise; Stefan Diemer & Selina Schmidt. 2018. "It's always different when you look something from the inside" — Linguistic innovation in a corpus of ELF Skype conversations. In Sandra C. Deshors, Sandra Götz, & Samantha Laporte (eds.), *Rethinking Linguistic Creativity in Non-native Englishes*, pp. 193–220. Amsterdam: John Benjamins.

Bugarski, Ranko. 2004. Language and boundaries in the Yugoslav context. In Brigitta Busch & Helen Kelly-Holmes (eds.), *Language Discourse and Borders in the Yugoslav Successor States*, pp. 21–37. Bristol: Multilingual Matters.

Bugarski, Ranko. 2012. Language, identity and borders in the former Serbo-Croatian area. *Journal of Multilingual and Multicultural Development* 33(3): 219–235.

Bunčić, Daniel. 2008. Die (Re-)Nationalisierung der serbokroatischen Standards. In Sebastian Kempgen, Karl Gutschmidt, Ulrike Jekutsch & Ludger Udolph (eds.), *Deutsche Beiträge zum 14. Internationalen Slavistenkongress, Ohrid 2008*, pp. 89–102. München: Sagner.

Cogo, Alessia & Martin Dewey. 2012. *Analysing English as a Lingua Franca: A Corpus-based Investigation*. London: Continuum.

Croatian Bureau of Statistics. 2022a. *Annual Gross Domestic Product — Annual Calculation*. https://podaci.dzs.hr/media/c51dcmbr/bruto-domaci-proizvod-godisnji.xls (14 June 2023).

Croatian Bureau of Statistics. 2022b. *1700 Tourism, 2021*. https://podaci.dzs.hr/media/gwcghawn/si-1700_turizam-u-2021.pdf (14 June 2023).

Croatian Bureau of Statistics. 2023. *Census of Population, Households and Dwellings in 2021 — Population of Republic of Croatia*. https://podaci.dzs.hr/media/3hue4q5v/popis_2021-stanovnistvo_rh.xlsx (14 June 2023).

Dewey, Martin. 2007. English as a lingua franca and globalization: An interconnected perspective. *International Journal of Applied Linguistics* 17(3): 332–354.

Drljača Margić, Branka & Irena Vodopija-Krstanović. 2018. Language development for English-medium instruction: Teachers' perceptions, reflections and learning. *Journal of English for Academic Purposes* 35: 31–41.

Drljača Margić, Branke & Irena Vodopija-Krstanović. 2020. The benefits, challenges and prospects of EMI in Croatia: An integrated perspective. In Slobodanka Dimova & Joyce Kling (eds.), *Integrating Content and Language in Multilingual Universities. Educational Linguistics*, pp. 75–96. Springer, Cham.

Eckert, Penelope. 2006. Communities of practice. In Keith Brown (ed.), *Encyclopedia of Language and Linguistics*, 2nd edn, pp. 683–685. Amsterdam: Elsevier.

Education First. 2022. *EF English Proficiency Index — A Ranking of 111 Countries and Regions by English Skills*. https://www.ef.com/assetscdn/WIBIwq6RdJvcD9bc8RMd/cefcom-epi-site/reports/2022/ef-epi-2022-english.pdf (12 October 2024).

Ennis, Michael & Gina Petrie (eds.). 2019. *Teaching English for Tourism: Bridging Research and Praxis*. London: Routledge.

European Commission. 2022. *Croatia*. https://eurydice.eacea.ec.europa.eu/national-education-systems/croatia/population-demographic-situation-languages-and-religions (12 June 2023).

Gerritsen, Marinel & Catherine Nickerson. 2009. BELF: Business English as a lingua franca. In Francesca Bargiela-Chiappini (ed.), *The Handbook of Business Discourse*, pp. 180–192. Edinburgh: Edinburgh University Press.

Gröschel, Bernhard. 2009. *Das Serbokroatische zwischen Linguistik und Politik: Mit einer Bibliographie zum postjugoslavischen Sprachenstreit*. München: Lincom.

Heinz, Christof & Holger Kuße. 2015. *Slawischer Sprachvergleich für die Praxis*. Frankfurt: Peter Lang.

Hülmbauer, Cornelia. 2013. From within and without: The virtual and the plurilingual in ELF. *Journal of English as a Lingua Franca* 2(1): 47–73.

Hynninen, Nina. 2016. *Language Regulation in English as a Lingua Franca: Focus on Academic Spoken Discourse*. Berlin: De Gruyter Mouton.

Ivanović, Sanja V., Jakob Patekar & Nataša Košuta. 2019. Do study programs in Croatia prepare future Foreign language teachers to work with young learners? *Croatian Journal Educational / Hrvatski Casopis Za Odgoj I Obrazovanje* 21(1): 307–344.

Jenkins, Jennifer. 2000. *The Phonology of English as an International Language: New Models, New Norms, New Goals*. Oxford: Oxford University Press.

Jenkins, Jennifer. 2006a. Current perspectives on teaching World Englishes and English as a lingua franca. *TESOL Quarterly* 40(1): 157–181.

Jenkins, Jennifer. 2006b. Points of view and blind spots: ELF and SLA. *International Journal of Applied Linguistics* 16(2): 137–162.

Jenkins, Jennifer. 2007. *English as a Lingua Franca: Attitudes and Identity*. Oxford: Oxford University Press.

Jenkins, Jennifer, Marko Modiano & Barbara Seidlhofer. 2001. Euro-English. *English Today* 17: 13–19.

Kachru, Braj B. 1985. Standards, codification and sociolinguistic realism: The English language in the outer circle. In Randolph Quirk & H. G. Widdowson (eds.), *English in the World: Teaching and Learning the Language and Literatures*, pp. 11–30. Cambridge: Cambridge University Press for The British Council.

Kordić, Ljubica & Vesna Cigan. 2013. Teaching and learning foreign languages for legal purposes in Croatia. *Studies in Logic, Grammar and Rhetoric* 34(1): 59–74.

Kostic Bobanovic, Moira & Jasmina Grzinic. 2011. The importance of English language skills in the tourism sector: A comparative study of students/employees perceptions in Croatia. *Almatourism – Journal of Tourism, Culture and Territorial Development* 2(4): 10–23.

Labov, William. 1982. Building on empirical foundations. In Winfred Lehmann & Yakov Malkiel (eds.), *Perspectives on Historical Linguistics*, pp. 17–92. Amsterdam: John Benjamins.

Labov, William. 1984. Field methods of the project on linguistic change and variation. In John Baugh & Joel Sherzer (eds.), *Language in Use: Readings in Sociolinguistics*, pp. 28–54. Englewood Cliffs, NJ: Prentice-Hall.

Lampe, John R., Dijana Pleština, Liz David-Barrett & C. W. Bracewell. 2023. *Croatia. Encyclopedia Britannica*. https://www.britannica.com/place/Croatia (12 October 2024).

Lave, Jean & Etienne Wenger. 1991. *Situated Learning: Legitimate Peripheral Participation*. Cambridge: Cambridge University Press.

Maci, Stefania M. 2018. An introduction to English tourism discourse. *Sociolinguistica* 32(1): 25–42.

MacWhinney, Brian. 2000. *The CHILDES Project: Tools for Analyzing Talk*, 3rd edn. Mahwah, NJ: Lawrence Erlbaum Associates.

Margić, Branka D. & Dorjana Širola. 2014. 'Jamaican and Irish for fun, British to show off': Attitudes of Croatian university students of TEFL to English language varieties: How entrenched are students' attitudes to national varieties of English? *English Today* 30(3): 48–53.

Mason, Jennifer. 2002. Qualitative interviewing. In Jennifer Mason (ed.), *Qualitative researching*, 2nd edn, pp. 62–83. Thousand Oaks, CA: Sage.

Matijašević, Miljen. 2013. Functionalist approach to teaching legal translation. *Studies in Logic, Grammar and Rhetoric* 34(1): 113–127.

Mauranen, Anna. 2012. *Exploring ELF – Academic English Shaped by Non-native Speakers*. Cambridge: Cambridge University Press.

Medved Krajnović, Marta & Stela Letica. 2009. Učenje stranih jezika u Hrvatskoj: Politika, znanost i javnost [Foreign language learning in Croatia: Policy, science and the public]. In Jagoda Granić (ed.), *Jezičnapolitika i jezična Stvarnost* [*Language Policy and Language Reality*], pp. 598–607. Zagreb: Croatian Association of Applied Linguistics.

Meierkord, Cornelia. 2004. Syntactic variation in interactions across international Englishes. *English World-Wide* 25(1): 109–132.

Mihaljević Djigunović, Jelena. 2013. Multilingual attitudes and attitudes to multilingualism in Croatia. In David Singleton, Joshua Fishman, Larissa Aronin & Muiris Ó Laoire (eds.), *Current Multilingualism: A New Linguistic Dispensation*, pp. 163–186. Berlin: De Gruyter Mouton.

Mortensen, Janus. 2013. Notes on English used as a lingua franca as an object of study. *Journal of English as a Lingua Franca* 2(1): 25–46.

Murata, Kumiko. 2015. *Exploring ELF in Japanese Academic and Business Contexts: Conceptualization, Research and Pedagogic Implications*. London: Taylor and Francis.

Paris, Dubravka. 2017. Teaching business English at Rrif College of Financial Management in Zagreb, Republic of Croatia. *Journal of Accounting & Management* 7(2): 41–52.

Petričušić, Antonija. 2004. Constitutional law on the rights of national minorities in the Republic of Croatia. *European Yearbook of Minority Issues* 2: 607–629.

Pitzl, Marie-Luise. 2018. Transient international groups (TIGs): exploring the group and development dimension of ELF. *Journal of English as a Lingua Franca*, 7(1): 25–58.

Požgaj Hadži, Vesna. 2014. Language policy and linguistic reality in former Yugoslavia and its successor States. *Inter Faculty* 5: 49–91.

Seidlhofer, Barbara. 2004. Research perspectives on teaching English as a lingua franca. *Annual Review of Applied Linguistics* 24: 209–239.

Seidlhofer, Barbara. 2011. *Understanding English as a Lingua Franca.* Oxford: Oxford University Press.

Seidlhofer, Barbara & Henry Widdowson. 2009. Conformity and creativity in ELF and learner English. In Michaela Albl-Mikasa, Sabine Braun & Sylvia Kalina (eds.), *Dimensionen der Zweisprachenforschung – Dimensions of second language research: Festschrift für Kurt Kohn*, pp. 93–107. Tübingen: Narr.

Stainton, Hayley. 2019. *TEFL Tourism: Principles, Commodification & the Sustainability of Teaching English as a Foreign Language.* Wallingford: CABI Publishing.

Strang, Barbara M. H. 1970. *A History of English.* London: Methuen.

Vida-Mannl, Manuela. 2022. *The Value of the English Language in Global Mobility and Higher Education: An Investigation of Higher Education in Cyprus.* London: Bloomsbury.

Vida-Mannl, Manuela. 2024. "How can I get into the city center?" – Pragmatic strategies at use in international tourism interactions in Croatia. *Frontiers in Communication* 9: 1407295.

Vida-Mannl, Manuela. Forthc. Investigating English on social media for international tourism purposes. In Jakob R. E. Leimgruber, Sofia Rüdiger & Sven Leuckert (eds.), *World Englishes and Social Media: Platforms, Variation, and Meta-Discourse.* London: Bloomsbury.

Vilke, Mirjana. 2007. English in Croatia – A glimpse into past, present and future. *Metodika* 8(14): 17–24.

Widdowson, Henry G. 1997. EIL, ESL, EFL: Global issues and local interest. *World Englishes* 16(1): 135–146.

Wilson, Adam. 2018. Adapting English for the specific purpose of tourism: A study of communication strategies in face-to-face encounters in a French tourist office. *ASp* 73: 53–73.

Wilson, Adam. 2021. Getting down to business – Intercultural communication and the utilitarian discourse system in an urban tourist destination in France. In Bal Krishna Sharma & Shuang Gao (eds.), *Language and Intercultural Communication in Tourism: Critical Perspectives*, pp. 159–178. London: Routledge.

CHAPTER 17

Envoi

How diverse is multilingualism research?

Simone E. Pfenninger
University of Zurich

1. Introduction

According to Bylund et al. (2023:1) "[r]esearch on the human capacity for language needs to have multilingualism at its centre". In this envoi, I suggest that a thorough theory on multilingualism not only necessitates *a sufficient sample size* for subsequent theory validation but also an *inclusive sample*, serving as a robust basis for theory construction. However, while unbiased sampling by unbiased scholars in a variety of contexts is crucial for generalization, participant, context, and language selection often introduce biases in practice. In sociolinguistics, for instance, Piller, Zhang & Li (2022) have addressed numerous concerns regarding the challenges faced by non-native English-speaking scholars in encountering epistemic exclusion, the influence of a decontextualized categorization of 'global issues' on publication standards, and the tendency to perceive social issues in research primarily through the perspective of the Anglosphere.

I argue in this envoi that besides avoiding the continuing silencing of the local languages, which is one of the main goals of this volume, we also have to think about ways of avoiding the continuing silencing of researchers and contexts beyond the so-called WEIRD demographics (i.e., Western, Educated, Industrialized, Rich, Democratic; Henrich, Heine & Norenzayan 2010), as well as non-WEIRD participants beyond the so-called WEIRD demographics who do not get access to English as a global language of education, media, and cross-cultural communication, so as to investigate concepts, phenomena, or processes outside Western experience and provide a solid foundation for theory building in multilingualism research. By discussing English on a par with other local languages, this volume presents encouraging evidence that linguists are reaching beyond their standard model of studying undergraduate students and focusing on English in isolation.

https://doi.org/10.1075/hsld.9.17pfe
Available under the CC BY-NC-ND 4.0 license.
© 2025 John Benjamins Publishing Company

2. Relying on a diverse participant pool

It has been highlighted in the social sciences that individuals classified as WEIRD — White, Educated, Industrialized, Rich, and Democratic — do not constitute a suitable representative sample of the global population; rather, they are outliers in various aspects (Henrich, Heine & Norenzayan 2013). Notwithstanding, multilingualism researchers, (second) language acquisition scholars, sociolinguists, and World Englishes (WE) scholars have had a tendency to rely on samples that are drawn from populations that are so-called WEIRD samples.

In applied linguistics, for instance, concerns about the demographics of the samples used in our field have often been raised (e.g., Bigelow & Tarone 2004; Cox 2019; Kormos & Sáfár 2008; Mackey & Sachs 2012; Ortega 2005, 2019; Pot, Keijzer & de Bot 2018; Tarone & Bigelow 2005). Analyzing 17 meta-analyses collectively covering 863 studies and a range of topics that applied linguists are concerned with, Andringa & Godfroid (2020) found that 88 percent of all adult samples are university student samples. Similarly, Plonsky (2016) estimated that 67 percent of research samples in seond language (L2) research are university student samples. Similarly, the distribution of articles on child bilingualism is highly skewed towards English (Kidd & Garcia 2022) — and, as Ortega (2019) has pointed out, change has been remarkably slow.

This underrepresentation is evident in the focus on privileged multilinguals, a smaller group mainly found in a limited number of countries, who "learn new languages by choice, without any material or symbolic threat to their home languges — and often aided by ample support in in the midst of great praise" (Ortega 2019: 27) in a formal, instructional setting. This stands in contrast to minoritized multilinguals, that is, immigrant communities, individuals from highly multilingual nations, those who are illiterate in multiple languages, and those who acquire languages unintentionally or face resistance from speakers of the target language (Ortega 2019).

As pointed out throughout this volume, there are also many indications that certain groups are underrepresented in World Englishes research. For instance, Zheng and Siemund (see Chapter 8) conclude that exclusively sampling university/college students to investigate the multilingual texture of Shanghai could not fully reveal the intricate complexity of the linguistic landscape of this multilingual global city. While learner-varieties have been much studied at universities in Nigeria, Schreiber and Möller (see Chapter 12) argue that research on language attitudes of entrepreneurs is much needed so as to better understand the ways people from all social-economic backgrounds communicate, navigate language use, interact across social class and ethnic groups, and assign symbolic meaning to their language choices. Outside of media and educational contexts, the professional sphere offers yet another arena where linguistic adjustments and negotiations of language attitudes unfold, shaping personal conceptions of achievement and language beliefs. Specifically, Schreiber and Möller explore the linguistic predominance of English within particular urban contexts and its connection to social change, examining social factors through an urban ethnographic lens with a focus on in small and medium enterprises in Lagos. English persistently arises as a symbol denoting an individual's economic middle-class status, often overshadowing considerations of one's background or ethnicity. Importantly, notions of convenience and accessibility — studies with non-university learners present greater challenges in study design — are also addressed. It becomes obvious that getting access to suitable participants is among the biggest obstacles to overcome when venturing beyond the educational context.

Similarly, research on English in Taiwan has mostly focused on its role within the educational system or its function as an international language (Leimgruber & Rüdiger, see Chapter 14). In order to examine the form and structure of Taiwanese English generally, and discourse-pragmatic uses of *like* by Taiwanese speakers of English more specifically, the authors employed the *Taiwanese Spoken English TASE* corpus with 76,000 words contributed by 21 speakers of Taiwanese English (university students). Using corpus data enabled them to find that the use of *like* as a discourse marker, discourse particle, and quotative is quite prevalent, although "it is not the kind of use typically found in most textbook- and classroom-based teaching activities" (p. 331). Since the participants had very little contact with L2 English speakers, the authors hypothesize that the acquisition of such informal forms may be due to the consumption of pop-culture products and media, often from the US, their utilization on global social media platforms, and the possible entrenchment of these discourse markers through frequent use within the Taiwanese English-speaking community.

Also relying on corpus data — a translingual and multimodal corpus comprising images, tweets, and songs "composed and performed by the super-diverse population of Qatar" (p. 340) — Theodoropoulou (see Chapter 15) observed "While English varieties are employed referentially to highlight Sheikh Tamim's achievements and character, linguistic varieties such as Standard Arabic and Arabic dialects are used more personally, either to address him directly or to convey his thoughts through direct speech." The chapter thus proposes a fresh perspective on translanguaged ecologies by linking them to attitudes.

Relying on a limited participant pool poses several issues, primarily jeopardizing the internal and external validity of our findings. By studying a phenomenon in stereotypical populations, we risk skewing our understanding of the role and spread of English in the new millennium, limiting the generalizability of our results, and introducing implicit bias that can affect who enrolls in studies through self-selection. For pedagogy, this implies that teaching methods cannot be adequately guided, resulting in a suboptimal service to these groups of learners (Ortega 2005). Other possible consequences of sampling bias could be that behavior attested in particular groups is simply absent in other groups (e.g. illiterate speakers typically do no exhibit noticing where literate speakers do). What is more, we may underestimate the range of variation in language learners and language learning outcomes (e.g. correlations are hard to detect in the absence of variation). To give an example from SLA, the overwhelming presence of English in reading research has led to "distorted theorizing with regard to many issues — including phonological awareness, early reading instruction, the architecture of stage models of reading development, the definition and remediation of reading disability, and the role of lexical-semantic and supralexical information in word recognition" (Share 2008: 584). Importantly, in this volume, Fuchs, Wiltshire and Sarmah (see Chapter 13) also point to the issue of having research confined to sources written in English, since "sources written in local languages may also offer more insights into the [language] ecology" (p. 313) of a particular country.

Many chapters also address inquiries regarding the preservation of linguistic diversity, the promotion of multilingual development, and the management of language-learning requirements for migrants with limited or intermittent formal education. For example, discussing the strive to make "Cameroon's citizens become truly bilingual in the official languages" (p. 67), Stein (see Chapter 4) describes the imbalance in using the official languages English and French that is mirrored in an imbalance in the distribution of political power in East vs. West Cameroon: "Cameroonians identify with either French or English as 'their' language, leading to alienation and feelings of contempt for the 'other'" (p. 67). While English and French are heavily promoted and attitudes towards them become more positive, the introduction of early childhood education in indigenous languages seems to be generally opposed by most parents in Cameroon — although there is a growing interest in indigenous languages by a young generation seeking to express an African identity.

Taken together the chapters in this volume challenge hegemonic monolingual narratives. They remind us that we have to be mindful of "invisibilization" (Havinga & Langer 2015), i.e., to pay attention to what has been erased from the discursive record and why.

3. Making research applicable to various cultural contexts

The need for geographic diversity in multilingualism research has attracted even less attention than biased sampling. According to Baltes et al. (2006), 'development' — including language development — is influenced by contextual and sociocultural variables, since learners and speakers participate in language as much as they acquire/use it, i.e., they are coupled with their language environment. Or in Kramsch's (2002, n.p.) words: "How can we know the dancer from the dance?" According to Plonsky (2023), much of the published language acquisition research appears to be conducted within a small range of institutional settings. Collins and Muñoz (2016) inspected 97 primary studies on classroom-based "foreign language" learning published in the *Modern Language Journal* during the 21st century. They examined demographics and other characteristics. Nearly half (45%) of the studies were conducted in the United States, with Japan and Canada accounting for 10 percent and 5 percent of the studies, respectively. In multilingualism studies, contexts where receptive multilingualism is the norm, that is, when an individual speaks their own language but has receptive knowledge of their interlocutor's language (e.g. Singer 2018; Pakendorf, Dobrushina & Khanina 2021), are understudied.

In this volume, research on multilingualism primarily takes place in multilingual societies, thus venturing beyond microhistoric case studies. The fifteen contributions cover fourteen countries across three continents, including examinations of regions, countries, and linguistic settings that have rarely, if ever, been explored in this context before, such as Botswana, Kurdistan, Taiwan, Qatar, and Croatia. The majority of chapters utilize a language ecology approach, enabling the integration of a broader spectrum of factors affecting language structure and usage compared to system-oriented approaches. As Vida-Mannl, Buschfeld annd Grohmann (see Chapter 8) rightly point out, such an ecological approach to language description is less limited but aims at depicting the ecology of language, namely "interactions between any given language and its environment" (Haugen 1972: 325).

One of the main goals of this book is to capture the universality and variability of multilingualism phenomena across different individuals and contexts. The authors discuss a range of contexts for language learning known as folk or circumstantial bilingualism (Fishman 1977; Romaine 1998), also called grassroots multilingualism (Han 2013). This kind of multilingual learning is experienced by many people whose languages and/or communities have been minoritized and who must embark — without much choice and often with little support and much hostility — in the learning of a new majority or postcolonial language or in the (re-)learning of a minoritized (ancestral, regional, indigenous, community, heritage, or home) language. Often, the new language is learned mostly naturalistically rather than through organized instruction. In Shanghai, for instance, a large metropolitan city that neither constitutes a former British colony nor has massive transnational migration, students often develop English-centered bilingual language profiles, typically paired with the national lingua franca, and these profiles may be further enhanced by heritage languages or economically useful world languages (Zheng & Siemund, see Chapter 7). Zheng and Siemund analyze the interplay between individual plurilingualism and societal multilingualism among university students, finding that functional multilingualism seems to be the norm, typically with a Chinese Putonghua-English bilingual profile and limited multilingual combinations. English is used for academics, LOTEs for entertainment, and Sinitic dialects in private, with Chinese Putonghua symbolizing national unity and English representing globalization.

Lusekelo and Kießling (see Chapter 10) trace the "progressive translocation" of English as an ex-colonial and elitist (co-official) language in Tanzania from urban spaces such as Dar es Salaam, Dodoma, and Arusha to the remotest rural corners. They examine the visual representation of English — which competes with the national official language Swahili in addition to 120+ vernacular languages — at the rural Tanzanian grassroots level. English expressions are adopted, altered, and innovatively adjusted to suit local requirements and ambitions during their transfer as representatives of global culture. According to the authors, the presence of grassroots signage displayed by private entities on signboards and shop fronts in these rural areas offers a window into language attitudes by indicating a favorable disposition towards using English symbolically, despite a notable lack of English proficiency. Also focusing on less urban areas in Tanzania's semi-autonomous archipelago Zanzibar, notably tourist spaces on Unguja island, Mohr (see Chapter 11) stresses the importance of language practices being analyzed locally to assess language ecologies. English seems to be intricately linked with the many languages it interacts with, hence aptly termed a "multilingua franca". Mohr argues that the differences observed between Tanzanian and Zanzibari English, despite their nominal association within the same country, underscore the necessity of shifting away from analyzing English solely within the framework of nation-states.

The chapters in this volume also reflect a shift in research from focusing on language itself to concentrating on individuals and communities. For instance, the widespread use of English as a lingua franca has been suggested to be a consequence of — rather than an impediment to — linguistic diversity, for instance in the states of Northeast India, which often lack a single local majority language (Fuchs, Wiltshire & Sarmah, see Chapter 13). While English serves as a language of the elite in most parts of India, in the Northeast it has the potential to play a wider role for the general population. Fuchs et al.'s analysis based on the Government of India's 2011 Census reveal that at the state level, while at the local level, linguistic diversity is somewhat lower but still exceeds the rest of the country.

Finally, from a methodological perspective, "descriptive and qualitative work remains under the radar, but such work often foregrounds the contextual and situated nature of language learning and use over its generalizability" (Andringa & Godfroid 2020: 138). The studies presented in this volume represent a diverse array of methods, from ethnographic and discourse-pragmatic approaches, questionnaires, interviews, statistical analyses, to linguistic landscape studies, and corpus work. Relying on qualitative data (in addition to quantitative) data, Zheng and Siemund (see Chapter 7) are able to show *how* (rather than *if*) English has become integral to students' academic life in Shanghai; furthermore, they highlight the instrumental benefits and emotional values attached to Putonghua as a national language, as well as LOTEs being valued for their cultural diversity, and Sinitic dialects being seen as emotional conduits and identity markers. In order to investigate linguistic repertoires and language choices in Zanzibar, Mohr (see Chapter 11) collected ethnographic data (i.e., observations, questionnaires, and interviews). This allowed her to work out that despite the status of English as a "multilingua franca with a distinct Zanzibari character" (p. 252), Zanzibari English(es) are not a significant part of Zanzibaris' identities and there does not seem to be a "Zanzibari English" acknowledged in its own right. Finally, Fuchs, Wiltshire and Sarmah (see Chapter 13) suggest that follow-up questions can elicit further details about the contexts in which each of the speaker's languages are most commonly used: where, when, with whom, and about which topics.

4. Discussing English on a par with other (local) languages

As pointed out by Bylund et al. (2023), the languages spoken in the Global North display limited diversity from a typological viewpoint, as many of them come from a single linguistic branch (i.e. Indo-European, with an overrepresentation of English, see Majid & Levinson 2010; Nielsen et al. 2017; Blasi et al. 2022; Kidd & Garcia 2022). Bylund et al. (2023) examined over 2,000 articles published in specialized top-tier journals of SLA and multilingualism research from 2010 to 2020, recording the languages under study (183 unique languages), author affiliations, and the country in which the research was conducted, inter alia, "English was overwhelmingly the most common language" (Bylund et al. 2023: 1), as L1, L2, and L3, followed by Spanish and Mandarin Chinese. What is more, although English is widely regarded as one of, if not the most, commonly learned additional languages globally, there are numerous multilingual communities where English is not a primary additional language (Plonsky 2023).

As amply demonstrated in the fifteen chapters of this volume, people in various parts of the world frequently promote English and strong regional languages at the expense of their less powerful home languages. Various studies exemplify tension that is identified between official language policies and real-life local practices. In Botswana (Shah, see Chapter 3), for instance, English is the *de facto* official language in Botswana, predominantly used by the educated urban elite. Setswana, the *de facto* national language, is the most widely spoken first language and is also commonly learned as a second language. It is extensively used in daily life. Both languages occupy the top of Botswana's language hierarchy, dominating marginalized languages that are threatened by extinction due to a lack of recognition and support by the government. English is crucial for social and economic advancement, whereas Setswana represents national unity and social cohesion. Shah suggests that this power struggle could greatly influence the country's "language ecology", that is, the diversity in specific socio-political contexts where language use processes establish, mirror, and contest particular hierarchies and dominant structures, even if they are temporary (Haugen 1972). Zheng & Siemund (see Chapter 7) demonstrate that English serves as a gatekeeper in Shanghai, allowing other world languages to filter in. This suggests that languages are stratified in a local context, mirroring the global linguistic hierarchy, with English dominating and marginalizing other foreign, heritage, and home languages/dialects. In Chapter 8, Vida-Mannl, Buschfeld and Grohmann examine, for the first time, English within the intricate linguistic landscape of Cyprus, particularly in relation to the two primary local languages, the local varieties of Greek (Cypriot Greek) and Turkish (Cypriot Turkish), as well as Cypriot Arabic and Armenian as the languages of officially recognized minorities. The authors note that while the prevalence of English stems less from past colonization and more from the overarching impact of globalization and the significant role English plays in contemporary society, the status and prestige of Greek as the language representing the homeland in Southern Cyprus, particularly when contrasted with Cypriot Greek as a symbol of Cypriot identity, is heavily influenced by the perspectives of individual speakers. Relying on interviews with three academic experts, policy makers, as well as Kurdish students, Paul and Ibrahim (see Chapter 9) describe how English has gained significant importance in the Kurdistan Region of Iraq, serving as a vital language for business, education, and employment opportunities, with its necessity underscored by regional officials and the public. This shift has led to a proliferation of English-medium instruction schools, reflecting a belief among parents that investing in their children's English education is crucial for future success, despite potential cultural and identity ramifications, including the diminishing perceived value — perhaps even linguicide — of Kurdish, the region's majority mother tongue. This perception stems from the belief that proficiency in English paves the way for a brighter future for students. The remarkable extent of popularity and influence of English in Kurdistan is unusual considering the contrasting situation in the broader region, encompassing neighboring countries. However, it also brings attention to the social disparity apparent in the accessibility of English-medium instruction for various families. Who gets access to this "brighter future" (p. 191) that is afforded by better English skills?

Language practices may also not align with language policy. Focusing on the privileged role of English as part of the Philippine linguistic ecology alongside local languages in government communications, Lising (see Chapter 5) reports on the overwhelming use of English as a lingua franca in regional governments' communications to their local constituent despite an Executive Order mandating the use of Filipino in government communications, with little bilingual practice i.e. use of both English and Filipino. The author argues that this may enhance the perception of English by some as a now-local language and an integral part of language use in many domains.

Striving for more diversity in this realm is important for our understanding of multilingualism, as typological distance – both actual and perceived – can impact various phenomena including interlanguage morphology, cross-language activation, code-switching, decision-making, and neuroanatomical representation (Bylund et al. 2023). This is why scholars in World Englishes, SLA, and multilingualism research (e.g. Spinner 2011) advocate for the inclusion of diverse language samples to reduce dependence on English. In Chapter 1, Mesthrie argues for the existence of a third space, in which fluent bilinguals in English and Xhosa keep both languages active in their speech via certain kinds of code-switching and the rules of Xhosa and English show mutual influences not found in monolingual varieties of either code. That way, Mesthrie suggests, World Englishes research can be enhanced by examining the interactions between new (or relatively new) local varieties of English and the local languages with which they coexist. Similar calls have been made in other linguistic domains (e.g., Slobin 2014; Norcliffe, Harris & Jaeger 2015; Pye 2021; Christiansen, Kallens & Trecca 2022) and within the broader cognitive sciences (Evans & Levinson 2009; Majid & Levinson 2010; Barrett 2020; Blasi et al. 2022).

Several papers in this volume demonstrate how L2 learning in a monolingual target-language environment is fundamentally different from L2 learning of a lingua franca in a highly multilingual environment. In Chapter 6, for instance, Pillai and Zainuddin analyze the effect of top-down policies, as an ecological factor, on the language profiles of students from different ethnic and economic groups, language backgrounds, and medium of instruction streams at a public university in Malaysia. Over the years, while language and education policies have prioritized Malay as the national and official language, English language education has remained significant due to Malaysia's colonial legacy and evolving national and global priorities and opportunities. Over time, a local contact variety of English has developed in Malaysia and is now used as a lingua franca among people of different ethnic and language backgrounds, carrying a distinctly Malaysian identity. Many Malaysian speakers switch between colloquial and standard varieties of English depending on the context, although there remain tensions between the use of these different varieties. As Pillai and Zainuddin rightly point out, in contrast to monolingual instructional settings, the native-speaker benchmark is irrelevant in the presence of different Englishes in the language ecology of Malaysia.

In sum, the fifteen chapters in this volume provide ample evidence that a comprehensive theory for multilingualism needs to be able to account for language use and learning that take place in a variety of settings and contexts, and with learners of many different backgrounds. The various studies demonstrate that multilingualism requires examination across its entire range of diversity in the spirit of social justice in the study of language (Ortega 2019).

References

Andringa, Sible & Aline Godfroid. 2020. Sampling bias and the problem of generalizability in applied linguistics. *Annual Review of Applied Linguistics* 40: 134–142.

Baltes, Paul B., Ulman Lindenberger & Ursula M. Staudinger. (2006). Life span theory in developmental psychology. In Richard M. Lerner & William Damon (eds.), *Handbook of Child Psychology: Theoretical Models of Human Development*, 6th edn, pp. 569–664. Hoboken, NJ: John Wiley & Sons.

Barrett, H. Clark. 2020. Towards a cognitive science of the human: Cross-cultural approaches and their urgency. *Trends in Cognitive Sciences* 24(8): 620–638.

Bigelow, Martha & Elaine Tarone. 2004. The role of literacy level in second language acquisition: Doesn't who we study determine what we know? *TESOL Quarterly* 38(4): 689–700.

Blasi, Damián E., Joseph Henrich, Evangelia Adamou, David Kemmerer & Asifa Majid. 2022. Over-reliance on English hinders cognitive science. *Trends in Cognitive Sciences* 26(12): 1153–1170.

Bylund, Emanuel, Zainab Khafif & Robyn Berghoff. 2023. Linguistic and geographic diversity in research on second language acquisition and multilingualism: An analysis of selected journals. *Applied Linguistics* 45(2): 308–329.

Christiansen, Morten H., Pablo Contreras Kallens & Fabio Trecca. 2022. Toward a comparative approach to language acquisition. *Current Directions in Psychological Science* 31(2): 131–138.

Collins, Laura & Carmen Muñoz. 2016. The foreign language classroom: Current perspectives and future considerations. *Modern Language Journal* 100: 133–147.

Cox, Jessica G. 2019. Multilingualism in older age: A research agenda from the cognitive perspective. *Language Teaching* 52(3): 360–373.

Evans, Nicholas & Stephen C. Levinson. 2009. The myth of language universals: Language diversity and its importance for cognitive science. *Behavioral and Brain Sciences* 32(5): 429–448.

Fishman, Joshua A. (ed.). 1977. *Bilingual Education: Current Perspectives*. Arlington, VA: Center for Applied Linguistics.

Han, Huamei. 2013. Individual grassroots multilingualism in Africa Town in Guangzhou: The role of states in globalization. *International Multilingual Research Journal* 7: 83–97.

Haugen, Einar I. 1972. The ecology of language. In Anwar S. Dil (ed.), *The Ecology of Language: Essays by Einar Haugen*. Stanford, CA: Stanford University Press.

Havinga, Anna & Nils Langer (eds.). 2015. *Invisible Languages in the Nineteenth Century* (Historical Sociolinguistics 2). Bern: Peter Lang.

Henrich, Joseph, Steven J. Heine & Ara Norenzayan. 2010. The weirdest people in the world? *Behavioral and Brain Sciences* 33(2–3): 61–83.

Henrich, Joseph, Steven J. Heine & Ara Norenzayan. 2013. The weirdest people in the world? In Stephen M. Downes & Edouard Machery (eds.), *Arguing about Human Nature: Contemporary Debates*, pp. 198–216. London: Routledge.

Kidd, Evan & Rowena Garcia. 2022. How diverse is child language acquisition research? *First Language*, 42(6): 703–735.

Kormos, Judit & Anna Sáfár. 2008. Phonological short-term memory, working memory and foreign language performance in intensive language learning. *Bilingualism: Language and Cognition* 11(2): 261–271.

Kramsch, Claire (ed.). 2002. *Language Acquisition and Language Socialization: Ecological Perspectives*. London: Continuum.

Mackey, Alison & Rebecca Sachs. 2012. Older learners in SLA research: A first look at working memory, feedback, and L2 development. *Language Learning* 62(3): 704–740.

Majid, Asifa & Stephen C. Levinson. 2010. WEIRD languages mislead us, too. *Behavioral and Brain Sciences* 33(2/3): 103.

Nielsen, Mark, Daniel Haun, Joscha Kärtner & Cristine H. Legare. 2017. The persistent sampling bias in developmental psychology: A call to action. *Journal of Experimental Child Psychology* 162: 31–38.

Norcliffe, Elisabeth, Alice C. Harris & T. Florian Jaeger. 2015. Cross-linguistic psycholinguistics and its critical role in theory development: Early beginnings and recent advances. Special issue of *Language, Cognition and Neuroscience* 30(9): 1009–1032.

Ortega, Lourdes. 2005. For what and for whom is our research? The ethical as transformative lens in instructed SLA. *Modern Language Journal* 89: 427–443.

Ortega, Lourdes. 2019. SLA and the study of equitable multilingualism. *The Modern Language Journal*, 103(S1): 23–38.

Pakendorf, Brigitte, Nina Dobrushina & Olesya Khanina. 2021. A typology of small-scale multilingualism. *International Journal of Bilingualism* 25(4): 835–859.

Piller, Ingrid, Jie Zhang & Jia Li. 2022. Peripheral multilingual scholars confronting epistemic exclusion in global academic knowledge production: A positive case study. *Multilingua* 41(6): 639–662.

Plonsky, Luke. 2016. The N crowd: Sampling practices, internal validity, and generalizability in L2 research. Presentation at University College London.

Plonsky, Luke. 2023. Sampling and generalizability in Lx research: A second-order synthesis. *Languages* 8: 75.

Pot, Anna, Merel Keijzer & Kees de Bot. 2018. The language barrier in migrant aging. *International Journal of Bilingual Education and Bilingualism* 23(9): 1139–1157.

Pye, Clifton. 2021. Documenting the acquisition of indigenous languages. *Journal of Child Language* 48(3): 454–479.

Romaine, Suzanne. 1998. Early bilingual development: Fromelite to folk. In Guus Extra & Ludo Verhoeven (eds.), *Bilingualism and migration*, pp. 61–73. Berlin: Mouton de Gruyter.

Share, David L. 2008. On the Anglocentricities of current reading research and practice: The perils of overreliance on an "outlier" orthography. *Psychological Bulletin* 134(4): 584–615.

Singer, Ruth. 2018. A small speech community with many small languages: The role of receptive multilingualism in supporting linguistic diversity at Warruwi community (Australia). *Language & Communication* 62: 102–118.

Slobin, Dan Isaac. 2014. Before the beginning: The development of tools of the trade. *Journal of Child Language* 41(S1): 1–17.

Spinner, Patti. 2011. Review article: Second language acquisition of Bantu languages: A (mostly) untapped research opportunity. *Second Language Research* 27(3): 418–430.

Tarone, Elaine & Martha Bigelow. 2005. Impact of literacy on oral language processing: Implications for second language acquisition research. *Annual Review of Applied Linguistics* 25: 77–97.

Language index

A
Acholi 212
Afrikaans 25, 29–30, 42, 45, 47–48
Albanian 368
Arabic 13, 107, 121, 123, 125–126, 128–129, 131–132, 147–149, 152, 167, 178, 191–192, 194–201, 204, 209, 214, 241–242, 335–336, 341–342, 345–347, 349, 352, 354, 356–358, 360, 386, 391
    Arabic fuṣḥá see Modern Standard Arabic
    Cypriot 167, 178, 391
    Modern Standard 121, 335, 345, 349, 352, 354, 356–358, 360, 386
    Palestinian 345
    Qatari 356
Armenian 167, 178, 391
Assamese 291, 295–297, 307–309

B
Badini 196
Bamileke 69, 72, 84
Banjar 132, 135
Basaa 69, 84
Basque 239, 242
Bemba 212–213
Bengali 295–296, 307
Bicolano 95, 104–107
Bisaya 94–95, 111
Boholano 95
Bosnian 366–367, 372
Botswana Sign Language 42
Bulu 69, 72
Burunge 211, 214

C
Cameroon (Pidgin) French 72, 75, 78, 84
Camfranglais 16, 18, 69, 71–72, 75–76, 78–80, 82–83
Cantonese 117, 131–132, 135, 151
Capizeno 95
Cebuano 94–95, 101, 102, 104, 107, 111
Chavacano 95
Chewa 212
Chinese 15, 116–117, 120–124, 128–129, 131–132, 134–135, 137–138, 143, 146, 148–153, 156, 158–161, 214, 223, 226, 318–319, 322–323, 327–328, 389–390
Chishona 45, 47–48
Croatian 364–368, 372, 374–379
Cuyunon 95
Czech 242, 365, 367

D
Danish 149
Datooga 211, 215–216
Duala 69, 84
Dutch 239, 242

E
Ewondo 69, 84

F
Fang 69
Filipino 13, 16, 91, 95–97, 100–111, 392
Fipa 220
French 18, 64–73, 75–76, 78–79, 81–84, 125–126, 128, 131, 148–150, 152, 160, 199, 212, 221, 239, 241, 243, 345, 365, 368, 387
Fulfulde 69, 84

G
Gan 151
Gawwada 57
German 82, 125–126, 131, 148–150, 199, 239, 241–242, 248, 345, 365, 367–368, 373–374, 377–378
    Swiss 242
Gorwaa 211, 214
Greek 17, 166–173, 175–178, 180–184, 391

Cypriot 166–171, 177–178, 181–184, 391
Cypriot Standard 177, 181, 184
(Standard) Modern 167, 170, 177–178, 180–182, 184
Gujarati 42
G|ui 44–45, 47, 56, 58
G‖ana 44–45, 47, 56, 58

H
Hadza 215
Hakka 151, 317–321
Hausa 69, 259, 270
Hebrew 149, 239, 242
Hiligaynon 95
Hindi 24, 214, 242, 291, 295–297, 307–309, 311, 336, 345
Hokkien 117, 131–132, 135, 138, 317–320, 322
Hungarian 367

I
Ibaloi 95
Iban 116, 120, 125
Ibanag 95
Igbo 259, 270–271, 282
Ikalanga 40, 42–43, 45, 47, 58
Ilocano 95
Iraqw 211, 214–215
Iraya 95
Isanzu 214–215
Italian 126, 131, 241–242, 365, 367–368, 372, 374, 378

J
Jamaican Creole 21
Japanese 125–126, 128, 131, 148–150, 152, 160, 239, 242, 319
Jin 151

K
Kadazan 116
Kadazandusun 120, 125, 132, 135
Kankanaey 95
Kanuri 69

Kapampangan 95
Karay-a 95
Khoekhoegowab 44
Khwe 42, 44–45, 47, 57
Kinyakyusa 242
Kinyambo 242
Kinyarwanda 212
Kiswahili 42, 148, 209–210, 212–223, 225–227, 231–234, 236, 239–249, 251–252, 389
Kiunguja 233
Korean 125, 131, 149–150, 152, 160
Kurbetcha 167
Kurdish 13, 167, 191–192, 195–204, 391
Kwadi 43

L
Latin 71, 242, 366
Lozi 212
Luganda 212, 232
Luo 211

M
Maasai 211, 215
Macedonian 366
Maguindanao 95
Malay 13, 116–125, 127–138, 146, 392
    Baba 118, 120
    Chitty 120
    Kedah 131
    Kelantan 120, 131
    Sabah 120, 132
    Sarawak 120, 131
Malayalam 336, 341
Mambwe 213
Mandarin 117, 120, 122–123, 125–129, 131–134, 137–138, 146, 149, 151, 153, 317–323, 328, 390 *see also* Putonghua
Maranao 95, 110
Masbate 95
Melaka Chitty 118 *see also* Chitty Malay
Melaka Portuguese 118, 120
Min 151
Modern Hebrew 149
Modern Standard Arabic *see* Arabic
Montenegrin 366–367

Mungaka 69

N
Nagamese 295, 307, 313
Nakagawa 56
Namwanga 213
Naro 42, 44–45, 47, 56–58
Nepali 295, 307
Nigerian Creole 21
Nilamba 214–215
Nyanja 212–213
Nyaturu 214
N|uu 44

O
Otjiherero 43, 45, 47–48

P
Pangasinan 95
Papiá Cristang 120
Persian 167, 180, 201, 214, 345
Portuguese 68, 149, 263
Putonghua 15, 149–153, 156–161, 389–390 *see also* Mandarin

R
Romani 387
Romanian 167
Romblomanon 95
Romblon 94–95
Runyankore 212
Russian 131, 148–150, 167–168, 178, 183, 239, 241–242, 367

S
Sandawe 211, 215
Sanna 167
Sebirwa 40, 43, 45, 47
Semai 116, 120, 125
Serbian 366–367, 372
Sesotho 55
Setswana 13, 17, 40–58, 391
Setswapong 43, 45, 47
Shanghainese 150, 159
SheBolaongwe 57
Shekgalagadi 40, 42–43, 45, 47, 53, 55–58
SheShaga 57
Shiyeyi 40, 42, 45, 47, 58
Shua 42, 44–45, 47, 55
Shuakwe 55

Sindebele 45, 47–48
Slovak 148
Slovenian 366, 368
Sorani 196
Spanish 32, 82, 96, 126, 131, 148–150, 152, 167, 241–242, 263, 368, 374, 378, 390
Sukuma 214–215
Surigaonon 95
Swahili *see* Kiswahili
Swahinglish 212
Swedish 149, 152, 242

T
Taa 42, 44–45, 47, 56
Tagalog 94–95, 111, 239, 242, 336
Tamil 117, 120–123, 126, 128–129, 131, 137–138, 146, 296
Tausug 95
Temuan 117
Terengganu 131
Thimbukushu 42, 45, 47
Toka-Leya 213
Tonga 212
Tshwa 42, 44–45, 47
Ts'amay 57
Ts'ixa 42, 44–45, 47, 57
Tumbuka 212–213
Turkish 17, 148, 166, 168–172, 175, 178–184, 201–203, 242, 345, 391
    Cypriot 166, 171, 179–184, 391
    Standard 179–181, 183, 184

U
Urdu 180, 336, 341, 345–346

W
Wandala 69
Waray 95
Wu 151, 153

X
Xhosa 13, 20–21, 25–34, 392
Xiang 151

Y
Yoruba 259, 262–263, 270–271, 280, 282
Yue *see* Cantonese

Z
Zulu 20, 25, 27, 33

!Xun 42, 44–45, 47
'Ongota 57

ǀXaise 55
ǁAni 42, 44–45, 47, 57
ǂ'Amkoe 42, 44–45, 47, 56

Subject index

A
acrolect 1, 2, 259–260, 263
additional language 17, 42, 131, 152, 167, 178, 241, 313, 317, 320, 365, 368–370, 378–379, 390
advertisement 71, 78, 177, 196, 213–214, 216–217, 220–221, 322, 351
affect 335, 340–341, 345–346, 350, 359
affinity score 266, 278, 280–282
African American Vernacular English *see* English(es)
agency 12, 335, 359
alphabetization 71
alpha diversity 291, 298, 302, 309
  see also gamma diversity
American English *see* English(es)
Analysis of Variance (ANOVA) 152, 278, 281, 283–284
Anatolia 170, 192–193
Anglophone Crisis 67–68, 83–84
Anglophone problem *see* Anglophone Crisis
ANOVA *see* Analysis of Variance
AntConc 323
appraisal 15, 335, 338–341, 352
appropriation 16, 214, 226
articles 211, 375–376, 378–379
  definite 371, 375–376, 378
  indefinite 371, 375–378, 379
Arusha 214, 226, 235, 389
Asian Englishes *see* English(es)
attitudes 68, 70, 146, 197, 208, 282, 312, 335, 359–360
  language 6, 15, 52, 55–56, 64, 68, 79–84, 91–92, 119, 144, 146, 149–150, 177, 179–181, 210, 226, 232, 234–236, 250–253, 258, 260–261, 264, 266–267, 278, 281–282, 284–286, 288, 322, 368–369, 372, 385–387, 389

speaker 4–5, 13, 17, 157, 159–160, 162, 168, 175, 177, 182, 251, 266–267, 284–285, 319

B
Bantu languages 17, 25–26, 29, 40, 42–43, 45, 47, 54, 56–58, 209, 211–212, 233
basilect 78, 263
bilectalism 167–168, 170–171, 174, 178, 181–182, 184
bilingual 20–22, 24, 27–28, 43, 82, 124, 134, 170–172, 202, 213, 220, 225, 339, 392
  conversation 34
  education 67, 96, 111–112, 122
  education policy 96, 111–112 *see also* education
  mode 17, 23, 25, 32–33
  profile 143, 161, 163, 389
  users 372
bilingualism 17, 65–68, 146–147, 181–182, 312, 320, 322, 385, 388
  individual 119, 144, 147
blockade 335–338, 340–345, 347–348, 350–354, 357–359
borrowing 16, 20, 22, 27–29, 33, 203, 223
Botswana English *see* English(es)
British colony 161, 172, 262, 292, 389
British English *see* English(es)
British India 292–293, 296

C
Cameroon English *see* English(es)
Cameroon Pidgin English *see* English(es)
capital 145
  communicative 263, 286
  economic 96

  linguistic 323
  social 264
  symbolic 162
catchment areas 215, 302, 304
census 44, 48–49, 69, 96, 119, 146, 177, 180, 261, 292, 295, 297–300, 304, 307, 320, 367, 390
  data 15, 93, 97, 291, 298, 300, 307, 310–313
China 3, 14, 117, 120, 133, 143, 145, 148–149, 151, 157, 160–161, 226, 294, 318–319, 321
class identity *see* identity
code-mixing 6, 20, 212, 214, 264, 339
code-switching 6, 16, 20–25, 31, 33–34, 50, 105, 150, 176, 203, 264, 339, 341, 392
colloquial 32, 79, 120, 125, 132, 136–137, 245, 248, 331, 393
colonialism 21, 176, 178
colonization 118, 178, 391
commodification 16, 245–246, 248
  of language 232, 234–235, 249, 252
communities
  African 46
  bilingual 134
  creole 263
  Cypriot 170–172, 181, 183–184
  diaspora 43
  ELF 379
  expatriate 180
  hunter-gatherer 44, 57–58
  immigrant 385
  linguistic 58, 304
  multilingual 390
  of practice 286, 369–370
  speech 2–3, 5, 160, 169
contact-induced variation 263

corpus 15, 32, 51, 77, 259, 341, 390
  GloWbE 33
  ICE 17, 259
  multimodal 335, 340, 386
  SPOKE 323, 325–330
  TASE 317, 323, 325–330, 386
  translingual 336, 387
correlations 15, 30, 261, 268,
  281–282, 284, 305, 322, 360, 387
cosmopolitan 176, 217, 226–227
COVID-19 42, 93, 98–100,
  107–108, 372–373
cram schools 321–322
creole 21, 76–77, 263, 285, 295,
  307, 313

D
Dar es Salaam 210, 213, 217–218,
  221, 226, 250, 389
decolonization 80, 172, 292
dialect 22, 52, 97, 112, 146,
  149–150, 158–159, 162, 196, 312,
  339, 366
  bidialectal 181
  Chinese 15, 148
  Cypriot 166–167, 169–170,
    177, 180–181, 184
  in India 310, 312
  levelling 264
  of Arabic 335, 341, 345, 356,
    360, 386
  of Malay 131
  Sinitic 149, 151–156,
    159–162, 389–390
discourse 31, 324
  analysis 351, 359
  marker 32, 250, 324,
    327–328, 330–331, 386
  particle 324, 327–328,
    330–331, 386
discourse-pragmatic *like*
  317–318, 322–323, 325, 328, 386
  see also quotative *like*
diversity index 15, 169, 298–299,
  309–310
domain 71–72, 92–93, 97, 137,
  258, 260, 281
  official 42, 70, 177, 231–232
  of use 13, 50, 55, 64, 112, 156,
    166, 168–169, 174, 176, 180,
    209, 225, 250, 312–313, 392

private 4, 15, 72, 161, 176,
  183
professional 133, 201,
  264–265
public 4, 40–42, 58, 73, 146,
  156, 175, 180, 182–183, 191,
  197, 208, 252
social 133, 155, 200
dominance patterns 258–259,
  285
Dominant Language
  Constellations 5–6, 17, 144,
  147, 161, 262–263
dominant vernaculars *see*
  vernacular
donor language 22, 209
Dubai 143–144, 147–150, 161, 163
Dynamic Model 1, 21, 74

E
East Asia 148, 291–292, 322–323,
  331
ecological
  approach 117–118, 174, 182,
    388
  factor 116, 392
  perspective 144–145
  system 118, 144
ecology 13, 15–16, 118, 145, 212,
  263, 291, 298, 302, 309, 359
  language 3–7, 40–41, 43, 49,
    92, 98, 109, 116–119, 130,
    137–138, 144–147, 149,
    161–162, 169, 173–175, 179,
    184, 192, 196, 211, 231–232,
    241–242, 258–259, 313, 335,
    387–389, 391, 393
  linguistic 12, 17–18, 64, 79,
    91, 118–119, 144, 156, 162,
    166–169, 175, 178, 181–182,
    184, 190, 200–201, 225,
    259–264, 291–292, 294,
    297–299, 309–313, 318,
    364, 392
  macro 208–209, 214
  micro 214–215, 259
  multilingual 1–6, 18, 22, 64,
    68–69, 76, 78–79, 84,
    91–94, 96–97, 109, 111–112,
    137, 145, 169, 180, 231–232,
    236, 241, 252–253, 317, 365,
    368, 377, 380

translanguaged 335, 360,
  386
economy 41, 234, 259–261, 291,
  337, 347, 351, 368, 378
  global 73, 319
education
  policies 50, 65, 96, 111–119,
    126, 138, 145, 392
  system 70–71, 80, 82,
    121–122, 124, 128–129, 137,
    172, 200, 209, 263, 305,
    317–322, 386
EFL *see* English as a foreign
  language
ELF *see* English as a lingua
  franca
elite 1, 40, 42–43, 51, 58, 305, 391
EMI *see* English-medium
  instruction
emotion 15, 74, 157, 159–161, 340,
  390
emotional stance 335, 341, 359
endonormative stabilization *see*
  stabilization
English as a foreign language
  183, 251, 253, 369
English as a global language 160,
  162–163, 259, 369, 371, 384
English as a lingua franca 250,
  253, 291, 331, 364, 370–372,
  374–376, 378–380
  multilingua franca 231, 243,
    252, 389–390
English as a Second Language
  183
English(es)
  African American
    Vernacular 21, 354, 356,
    358–359
  American 73, 263–264,
    266–267, 272, 275, 278,
    280–282, 285–286, 324,
    330, 354
  Asian 2, 322, 331
  Botswana 51–52, 58
  British 51–52, 73–75, 77,
    180, 262, 263–264,
    266–267, 272, 275, 278,
    280–282, 285–286
  Cameroon 66, 73–75, 77, 84

Cameroon Pidgin   16, 18, 64, 69, 71–73, 71, 73, 75–78, 80–81, 84
contact variety of   125, 393
Expanding Circle   331
grassroots   3, 208, 235–236, 253, 389
Gulf   147
Hindi   24
Hong Kong   24
in education   91
Irish   22
Korean   317, 323–325, 330–331
Malaysian   122, 132
Namibian   24, 51
Nigerian Pidgin   259, 263–264, 266–267, 270–272, 275, 278, 280–282, 284–288
Nigerian Standard   259–260, 262–264, 266–267, 270–272, 274–275, 278, 280–282, 284–288
Outer Circle   74, 234, 331
Philippine   2, 92
Singapore   22, 24, 122, 146
Singlish   24, 119, 146, 161
South African   16, 51
Swahinglish   212
Taiwanese   317–318, 322–324, 330–331, 386
Tamil   24
Tanzanian   210–211, 217, 219, 234, 252–253
Zanzibari   232, 250, 252–253, 389–390
English for Specific Purposes   369
English-medium
 education   129, 320
 instruction   64, 122, 191, 202–203, 391–392 *see also* medium of instruction
 school   43, 50, 82, 122, 125, 198, 203–204
entrepreneurial orientation   258, 261, 264–265, 267, 274–276, 281
entrepreneurial success   258, 260, 264

ESL *see* English as a Second Language
ESP *see* English for Specific Purposes
ethnic   6, 74, 118–119, 123, 125, 145, 176, 182, 184, 192, 260–262, 281, 284–285, 337
 community language   210, 212, 214
 group   41, 116–117, 130–131, 138, 146, 166–167, 265–266, 269, 285–287, 311, 348, 366–367, 385, 392
 identity   33, 43, 79, 120, 127, 134–135, 137, 266, 311–312
 inter-ethnic   53, 72
 minority   194, 262, 367
ethnography   112, 258
exonormative stabilization *see* stabilization
Expanding Circle Englishes *see* English(es)

F
Facebook   14, 16, 91, 93–94, 97–107, 109–111
first language *see* language
foreign language   143, 148–150, 152, 154–155, 161–162, 168, 190, 197, 234, 240–241, 243, 365, 368, 370, 388
functional
 category   324–327
 language   197
 multilingualism   152, 389
 range   317, 324
 roles   6, 12, 233, 258
 value *see* value

G
gamma diversity   291, 298, 300, 302, 309 *see also* alpha diversity
Global English *see* English as a global language
globalization   5, 21–22, 64, 121, 123, 148, 161, 176, 198, 208–210, 231–234, 262, 320, 389, 391
government communications   16, 91, 93, 95, 97–98, 105, 109–112, 392

grassroots Englishes *see* English(es)
greeting   16, 99, 101–103, 231–232, 235–236, 243–250, 252
Gulf English *see* English(es)

H
hashtag   101, 104, 340–341, 345–346, 353
heritage language *see* language
hero   341–342, 351–354, 356–360
Hindi English *see* English(es)
Hinglish *see* Hindi English
Hong Kong English *see* English(es)
hospitality   238, 378
Human Development Index   299–300, 305
H variety   177, 184
hybrid language practices   339

I
iconic expressions   245
identity
 African   32, 72, 387
 class   258, 266, 286
 creation   21, 318
 cultural   33, 134–135, 391
 ethnic   33, 79, 120, 127, 134, 137, 202, 204, 266, 285, 311
 local   96
 marker   161, 183, 390
 national   53, 119, 121–122, 125, 136, 158, 171, 177, 180, 182–183, 319, 358, 393
 personal   151, 158–159
 preferred   269
 projection   21
 religious   269
 social   260, 266, 286
 sociolinguistic   32, 68, 80–83, 145–146, 177, 202, 251, 285, 322
 speaker   5
ideology   4, 28, 67, 112, 144–145, 158, 260, 264, 286, 318, 331
indigenous language *see* language
infinitive constructions   371, 375–376, 378
inscription   213, 218, 222–225, 227
interference   74, 263

interlanguaging 264, 392
internationalization 15, 124, 138, 144, 147, 158, 210
interpersonal 339
interview
　ethnographic 236, 390
　qualitative 15, 200, 323, 372
　semi-structured 14, 143, 150, 372
　sociolinguistic 14, 371–378
　telephone 268, 287
Irish English *see* English(es)
isogloss 259

J
Japanization 319

K
Kachruvian circles 234, 370
Kamtok *see* Cameroon Pidgin English
koiné 170, 179, 285
Konglish *see* Hong Kong English
Korea 331 *see also* South Korea
Korean English *see* English(es)

L
L1 *see* language, first
L1 transfer 379
L2 *see* language, second
L3 *see* language, third
language
　dominance 271, 274–275, 278, 280–282, 284–285, 287–288
　endangerment 55, 57
　first 43, 50, 54–55, 58, 69, 120, 167, 211–213, 260, 263, 271, 278, 294, 298–300, 302, 304–309, 311, 319, 323, 328, 367–370, 372, 374–375, 379, 390–391
　heritage 17, 57, 127, 132–135, 137, 162, 167, 262, 389
　hierarchy 41, 58, 391
　indigenous 12–13, 18, 41–42, 69–72, 78, 80, 84, 116, 118, 120, 125, 132, 134–135, 137, 318, 388
　majority 25, 178, 259, 292, 389

minority 15, 42, 57, 64, 71, 79, 137, 183, 213, 233, 367
mixing 127, 133–134
national 13, 41–42, 46, 49, 53, 55–56, 58, 64–65, 70–71, 75, 78, 90, 96–97, 109–110, 112, 118–119, 121–122, 124–125, 147, 149, 151, 157, 160–162, 168, 201, 212–213, 225–226, 233, 311, 318–319, 321–322, 368, 390–392
official 16, 41–42, 49, 65–68, 78, 80–81, 83–84, 116–117, 120–121, 147, 156, 166, 175, 178, 182–183, 197, 199, 209, 212, 215, 216, 225, 296, 336, 347, 364, 366–367, 387, 389, 391–392
planning 203, 322
policy 16–17, 49–50, 65–66, 68, 70, 84, 93, 95–98, 109–112, 125–126, 145–146, 158, 172, 191, 201, 209, 213, 216, 233–234, 296, 305, 318–319, 321, 391–392
practice 2, 6, 93, 97–98, 101, 105–107, 109, 110–112, 144, 146, 150, 232, 235–236, 240–241, 250, 252, 339, 389, 392
proficiency 4–5, 130, 137, 150, 154, 172
profile 93, 117–119, 123, 126, 131, 134–135, 137–138, 144, 147, 149–150, 152–153, 161–162, 389, 392
regional, 7, 13, 84, 97, 111–112, 391
repertoire 6–7, 13, 17, 55–57, 130, 144, 150, 152–153, 172, 236, 260
replacement 57
second 43, 50, 96, 111, 122, 168, 200, 251, 253, 278, 281, 284, 296, 299, 306–308, 311, 385, 390, 392
shift 17, 22, 42, 44, 56–57, 302, 312, 318–320
subsidiary 298–299, 311

third 43, 125, 202, 274, 278, 296, 299, 305–308, 311–312, 390
variety 5, 69, 79, 84, 122, 134, 150, 157, 159, 168, 253, 339
working 146–147, 197, 233–234
Language Learning Score 279–281, 283
languages other than English 105, 143, 148, 150, 155, 157, 160–161, 389–390
leadership 336, 341–342, 348, 351–352, 357–358
liberalization 124, 137, 209–210
Likert scale 150, 239
lingua franca 16, 48–49, 69, 76, 110–112, 158, 175, 209, 319–320, 336, 368, 378 *see also* English as a lingua franca
　global 167, 183–184
　intranational 232
　local 56, 125, 305, 307–309
　national 53, 72, 292, 389
linguialities 170, 181
linguistic
　conservatism 126
　diversity 15, 94, 112, 169, 259–261, 286, 292, 296, 298–305, 307–309, 311–312, 339, 367, 387, 389–390
　ecosystem 145
　landscape 15, 69–70, 162, 169, 181–182, 196, 202, 210–214, 223, 225–226, 241, 245, 385, 390–391
　repertoire 4–6, 17, 125, 134, 138, 147, 179, 202, 240–243, 262, 264–268, 311–313, 339, 365, 372, 390
　resource 6, 15, 145, 339, 379
Living Standard Score 265, 276–277, 281
loanword 26–27, 29, 209, 212, 223, 225, 227
local diversity *see* alpha diversity
Local Government Areas 260–263, 269, 284, 287
localization 16, 130, 226

LOTE *see* languages other than English

M
majority language *see* language
Malaysian English *see* English(es)
Manyara region 214–215
media
    English language 369, 385
    mass 51, 77, 320
    new 21, 51, 58, 210
    print 50, 176
    social 21, 24, 93, 98, 109, 127, 132–133, 150, 212, 331, 336–338, 341, 352, 365, 386
medium of instruction 42, 50, 57, 96, 111–112, 122–124, 127–129, 137–138, 175, 204, 210, 233, 368, 392 *see also* English medium instruction
migration 14, 17, 118, 145, 147, 161, 184, 195, 260, 262, 293–295, 389
minority group 194, 367
minority language *see* language
mobility turn 21
mother tongue 96, 146, 191, 199, 202, 239–241, 243, 248, 271, 298–299, 310–311, 391
    education 70
    status 78, 84
Mother-tongue Based Multilingual Education 96
multidialectal 143, 145, 148
multilingual
    global cities 144–145, 147, 149–150, 161–162, 385
    turn 21
multilingualism
    individual 145–147, 161
    post-colonial African 25
    societal 144–148, 183, 389
multivariate studies 276

N
Namibian English *see* English(es)
national language *see* language
national language policy 49, 96 *see also* language policy

native English speakers 251
neoliberalism 210
Nigerian Pidgin English *see* English(es)
Nigerian Standard English *see* English(es)
Nilotic languages 211, 215
non-parametric test 278, 281
normalized frequency 325–326
noun class 26, 28, 43, 212, 214

O
official language *see* language
orthographic 221, 223, 227, 239, 372
Outer Circle Englishes *see* English(es)

P
participant observation 231, 232, 236
Philippine English *see* English(es)
Pidgin English *see* Cameroon Pidgin English, Nigerian Pidgin English
pidginization 16, 73, 231, 232, 245–246, 252
Plain Language Bill 97
plurilingualism 148, 259, 389
popular culture 160, 201, 214, 248, 328, 386
portrait 337, 342–351
postcolonial varieties of English 259, 297
power 65, 112, 162, 173, 194, 203, 319, 391
    colonial 46, 92, 169, 171, 193, 365
    dynamics 21
    economic 168, 225
    explanatory 4, 174
    language power scale 17, 40–41, 58
    political 67, 387
    social 17
prestige 1, 15, 21, 28, 51, 56, 75, 84, 162, 167, 169, 183, 208, 210, 212, 259, 318, 346, 391
    covert 18, 77, 81
    overt 18, 77

pseudo-monolingual 318

Q
questionnaire 14, 82, 126, 143, 150–151, 231, 232, 236, 239, 240, 243, 261, 264–266, 268, 280–281, 287–288, 367, 373, 390
    ethnographic 371
quotative *like* 324–331, 386 *see also* discourse-pragmatic *like*

R
regiolect 297
regional differentiation 297
regional language *see* language
relative pronoun 371, 375–376, 378–379
Republic of Cyprus 166
Republic of Northern Cyprus 167
resemiotization 335, 338, 343, 345, 348–351, 360
Rift Valley 208, 211, 214
rural areas 48, 57, 69, 127, 180, 214, 217–218, 220, 226–227, 233, 302, 389

S
sampling bias 387
second language *see* language
self-assessment 240, 265
signage 15, 183, 211–214, 216–217, 222, 225–227
    bilingual 213, 223, 348
    bottom-up 211, 213–214, 216, 226
    monolingual 176
    multilingual 212
    top-down 216
Siliguri corridor 293
Simpson's D 291, 298–300, 302, 309–310
Singapore 31, 118–119, 121, 143, 144, 146–150, 161, 163, 321
Singapore English *see* English(es)
Singlish *see* English(es)
slang 245, 339
small and medium enterprises 258, 263–264, 286, 388

social
    class 4, 258, 260, 265, 277, 281–283, 285–286, 337, 385
    construction of language 91
    milieu 77, 259–260
    personae 236, 247, 249–250, 339
socioeconomic status 265, 276
solidarity 24, 40, 146, 162, 259–260, 266, 336–337, 342, 347–348, 350–351
songs 15, 335, 338, 340–342, 354, 356–360, 386
sophrosyne 352, 354, 359
South African English *see* English(es)
Southern Cushitic languages 211
South Korea 317, 323, 330
space
    enclosed 237, 246–247, 249, 252
    multilingual 243, 253
    open 231, 247, 249
Speak Good English Movement 119
Spoken Korean English corpus 323–330
stabilization 288, 379
    endonormative 259
    exonormative 84, 137, 251, 253, 282
style 5, 29–30, 34, 74, 360
stylects 208, 212, 226
subsidiary language *see* language
substrate 211, 217, 223
superdiversity 14

Swahilization 209, 233
Swahinglish *see* English(es)
symbolic value *see* value
syntax 31, 52, 223, 227, 297

T
Taiwanese English *see* English(es)
Tamil English *see* English(es)
Tanzanian English *see* English(es)
Tanzanian languages 209, 211
third language *see* language
top-down policy 111, 321, 345, 392 *see also* language policy
tourist destination 51, 53, 235, 249, 294, 348
translanguaging 3, 14, 17, 21–22, 33, 125, 134, 335, 338–341, 351–352, 359–360
translocation 16, 208, 210, 214, 217–218, 220, 226–227, 389
transnational
    attraction 21, 75
    migration 14, 145, 148, 161, 289
triglossia 208–209
trilingualism 13, 181, 298, 312
tweet 15, 335, 338, 340–342, 352–353, 359, 386
Twitter 341–342, 346, 352 *see also* tweet

U
Unguja island 231–232, 236–237, 390

university students 14, 50, 110, 119, 127, 143–144, 146, 149–152, 154, 161, 385–386, 389
urbanization 71, 259–262

V
value 4, 13, 17, 68, 70, 73, 77, 80, 92, 122, 143, 157–162, 168, 177, 191, 234–235, 241, 245, 279–280, 285–286, 340, 353, 356, 390–391
    functional 259
    symbolic 159, 260
variation 4, 15, 27–28, 78, 84, 158, 166, 169, 174, 182, 211, 259, 285, 300, 305, 311, 331, 387 *see also* contact-induced variation
variety *see* language variety
vernacular 21, 84, 96, 125, 177, 181, 208–209, 285, 317–318, 322, 354, 356, 358–359, 389
    dominant 95
    local 180, 184, 319
vernacularization 359
vertical medium of communication 209

W
WEIRD 3, 384–385
working language *see* language

Y
Yugoslavia 364, 366–368

Z
Zanzibari English *see* English(es)